Acknowledgements

To my Brother - I could not ask for a better brother, thank you mate! You have more patience than I do, and putting up with me for over 50 years!

To my Sister-in-law: Thank you for all the help, and encouragement in writing, and early edits of the book, without you, this book would not have been written.

My two Nieces: I am so proud of you.

To all my friends: I am really lucky to have such great mates, who make life worth living.

To Lee (the editor): Thank you so much for all the hard work, and encouragement.

To Victoria (Legal advisor): Thank you for great advice, and kind words.

To Asher (Artist): I love your artwork, thank you so much for all your hard work, and help making this all happen.

To Marcia (Publisher): Thank you for all your hard work.

Finally, to all the Men, and Women of the Police, past and present, who work extremely hard, with precious little thanks, who risk their lives every day, without fear or favour, to try and keep the rest of us safe. Thankyou!

Chapter 1
HENDON

It was 8 a.m. outside Hendon police training centre (aka 'the Peel Centre') on a sunny Monday.

I checked the letter for the twentieth time that morning, confirming it was 9 a.m., main gate, in the Green cohort.

I knew I was an hour early, but "It's better to be an hour early than a minute late," as my dad used to say. A sudden pang of sadness pricked me. He'd have told me I was mad to go into the police, but he'd have been so proud at the same time.

God I miss you, Dad; I still feel it even after twelve years.

Why was I putting myself through that? Why? Must be mad! What had I done so far in my life that would indicate that I was in any way sane?

I was 33, a qualified secondary school science teacher with three years of experience under my belt. I had a life, a steady career.

So, why go into the police? It wasn't just that I'd failed three times to get in, and I don't like failing. I think it was an itch I needed to scratch. My grandad and great-grandad were both police officers. I was raised around other police officers, on tales from my mom about how she grew up living above a police station in Sunderland.

My grandad was a chief superintendent who was awarded the King's Police Medal (highest award you can win as a police officer).

All the way through my childhood, it was something I knew I had to do.

So finally, finally, I was there. *God, please, please don't let me screw this up. I beg you!*

It was a lovely sunny day (unusual enough for England), with just a breath of wind blowing the impatient white clouds across the clear blue sky.

As I was waiting to get the courage to go to the front gate, I heard a woman's voice behind me. "This place used to be a WW2 RAF base."

I turned around and saw a young lady (25-ish), 5'6", slim, pretty and with an infectious grin, standing with a wheeled suitcase that was clearly carrying everything but the kitchen sink (similar to my own). As I looked, the wind did its best to pull her straight brown hair from the tight bun holding it in place. How do women get their hair that tight? But, let's face it, women are an enigma to us blokes.

As I looked on, she turned and waved at a young man driving off in a car. She looked back at me, clearly sizing me up in a similar way to what I'd just done.

She stuck out her hand and said: "Paige Shore. Most people call me Shorey. I take it you're on the Green cohort? Should we go and book in, or are we just going to eye each other up for a little longer?" All said with a serious face, until the end when she grinned.

I thought about lying, but thought better of it; this lady was not one for bullshit, which suits me. I looked her straight in the eyes and replied: "Sounds like a plan. I'm Richard Armstrong, Richard if you prefer. That your boyfriend dropping you off, since you caught me eyeing you up?"

To my surprise she giggled and replied: "Don't worry, I did it too, but yes, he's Brian, my fiancé. I'm going to call you Richard."

At that point she walked up to me and playfully shoved me forward, "Let's go."

Once we'd presented our letters at the gate, we were directed to the canteen: "Past the big statue, up the stairs and into the long building just before the tower block. Oh yeah, and don't run, or walk on the grass!"

As we walked past the huge bronze statue of Sir Robert Peel, I looked to my right to see a large swimming pool, and an impressive field with football pitches and running tracks set out. The buildings, although well maintained, clearly dated from the seventies to more recent times, with a real mixture.

The large, functional canteen with long serving counters along the right wall and a white lino floor had rows of tables and chairs set out.

It was interspersed with young men and women, all in their M&S suits not dissimilar to my own, all nervously trying to make polite conversation.

As we watched, more recruits (willing victims) were arriving. I had a chance to chat with Paige. "Where are you from, Shorey?"

"Wembley. What about you?"

"Brentwood, Essex."

"Oh no, an Essex boy. You're not a boy racer, are you?"

"Errrr, well, I do drive an XR3i and have a motorcycle."

Paige started giggling, "Please tell me it has a go-faster stripe down the side."

"Yeah, well it does have a pink and grey stripe on it, and a big whale tale, as well as a huge stereo. Look, I know it's a stereotype, but I was desperate for a car, and my mate from the football club didn't tell me it was an XR3i."

"What, you didn't see it before you bought it?"

"Well I did, but I was a bit drunk and it was dark and parked against a wall."

"Oh Richard, that's just made my day!" She started laughing.

At this point the doors banged open and in walked two large guys, laughing and joking.

The first was a tall, round-faced, stocky man of about 30 years. The other was a fair bit taller, with a strong jawline, well built, with a wide smile.

I exchanged looks with the first guy. He walked over and sat down heavily, saying: "Hi, I'm John, this (pointing at the tall guy) is Pete. Don't mind if we join you but you seem like you're having a good laugh, unlike the rest of the boring lot in here." He looked dismissively around, gaining a few disapproving stares in return.

As we were exchanging pleasantries, the door opened again and in walked a young man (25 years), slim, handsome, with black, slightly too long hair and deep, dark, intense eyes.

Paige pipes up: "Wow! He's gorgeous!"

I looked at John and Pete and cheerily replied: "Oh, and what are we? Fucking gargoyles?" Which elicited a big laugh. The gorgeous young man stopped, looked over at us, walked over, saying: "Do you mind if I join you? By the way, why were you laughing?"

I replied: "Paige said you were gorgeous and I asked her what the rest of us were, fucking gargoyles?"

Paige once again started giggling, and blushed, as did the newcomer.

John said: "Stop it, Richard; you're embarrassing the poor lad. I'm John, this is Pete, Richard and Paige. What's your name, mate?"

"I'm Paul. I was a bit nervous, but you lot are a right bunch of nutters. I feel at home already." Once again, a round of laughter.

The door went again, and I looked up and noticed the other small, scattered groups of recruits were all looking at us, somewhat aghast.

The new arrival was a short Mediterranean youth with a well-cropped tash and slightly too long, windswept black hair. He took one look around the room and made a beeline for us.

Sitting down next to me, he said: "Hi, I'm Karim. It's an Algerian name."

Another big laugh from the slowly growing gang of reprobates.

At two minutes to 9 a.m. the door opened and a uniformed police officer walked in. He had an intense, hard look about him. The room went silent and he said: "Right, when you're quite ready, silently follow me to the lecture room where you'll receive your introductory lecture."

Turning smartly on his heels, he left the room. We shared a look, struggled to collect our belongings and tried to follow him as quickly as we could.

A short walk later, we filed into a large, tiered, semicircular lecture hall, with dimmed lighting. Struggling to find seats and organise our bags, there was a bit of chatting.

A few minutes later, a short, and clearly very senior officer walked in and stood impatiently at the lectern. He stood stock-still and glared until we were silent, starting with a loud, clear and hard-edged voice. "Right, when you recruits have shown me the courtesy of shutting up I'll begin ... My name is Chief Superintendent Galbraith. I am the senior officer at Hendon. You are here to meet the standards I set. Some of you will not meet those standards and you will leave. I don't care if none of you reach those standards and you're all kicked out. My job is to provide the boroughs with competent officers who won't get their colleagues killed. I'll be honest with you: I have rarely seen such a miserable excuse for an intake. I'll be surprised if half of you make it.

"Here are the rules: follow all the instructions you are given immediately; you will address members of staff as staff, sergeant, sir or ma'am, nothing else; you will be polite; you'll do your best at all times; you'll not fraternise with the opposite sex. There is a men's accommodation block and a women's accommodation block, so if we find a man in the women's block, he will be removed from the course. If a woman is found in the men's block, she will be removed from the course. You will be monitored the whole time you are at Hendon. If you say anything we don't like, you will be removed. If when you go home and say or do anything we hear about, you will be removed. There will be ABSOLUTELY NO RACISM AT THIS ESTABLISHMENT! Remember, you're being watched at all times, and we already have an eye on one or two of you. I'll now hand you over to Inspector Turner, who will put you in classes."

At which point he turned on his heel and walked out of the room. I could feel my stomach tighten and looked at Paige; her face was set and determined. I could feel the chilling effect this had on the other 150-plus recruits.

A tall, angular man of about 40 walked stiffly (almost comically) to the lectern, his light brown hair swept back, giving him a harsh appearance.

He took the lectern and waited longer than was necessary for absolute silence, then started: "My name is Inspector Turner, Sir to you, and it is my unenviable job to turn you bunch of wasters into useful members of the Metropolitan Police service."

Pause ...

"I will call out a class, followed by a list of names. Upon hearing your name, you will WAIT until I finish with that class. At which point you will SILENTLY collect your miserable belongings and make your way as quickly as you can out the left door, where you'll meet the poor, unfortunate members of staff who will do their best to turn you into vaguely competent probationers."

Taking a breath, he consulted a sheaf of papers, and reading out a number of classes he said: "Right, H Class ..." and proceeded to read out my name and all the members of our little gang in the canteen, along with names I didn't recognise.

We got up at the end and made our way outside, where four uniformed officers awaited us. There was a friendly man, aged about 35, Sergeant Johnson, and a short, slim woman aged about 40, Sergeant Brownstone. There was also a short, stocky Scot aged about 45, PC McNish, and a tall, smiling Asian lady, PC Patel.

Sergeant Johnson spoke first and introduced the other members of the training team. He said: "Well, if no one else says so, welcome to Hendon. I guess you're all a bit nervous. Don't worry; we're here to help you pass out and become brilliant police officers. I'm sure you'll have 101 questions; there'll be time for that later. Right now we need to sort out your accommodation and let you know what you need to do next."

He paused, smiled and gave us room numbers and keys. Men and women separated in the two tower blocks. My room was on floor seventeen (the top floor). After doing this, he walked us to our classroom, saying: "Make sure you remember this room. It'll be your classroom for the eighteen weeks you're here. First test, go to your rooms, store your stuff and be back at the classroom 10:30 hours sharp. What are you waiting for? Off you go. Oh and don't run or walk on the grass. Oh, and before I forget, remember to bring the white notes you were sent; I really hope you've studied them."

We did as we were asked, and when I arrived at my room, I found it was small but tidy, with attached toilet and shower. This accommodation was similar to the university halls. Looking out the window, I had a view of the sports field to the right, and to the left the Tube line we'd be using to return home for the weekend. In the centre of the tower block there were communal areas to iron our clothes. Sitting for a moment on the bed to collect my thoughts, I took in the room I hoped to be spending the next eighteen weeks in. It was a simple, functional room, white walls and ceiling, with a large smoke detector centrally mounted, a simple bed, a desk and chair, a built-in wardrobe and a small bedside table with an ancient lamp. It was clean and tidy, if a little worn. Underneath the window was large metal hook, about 3 inches in diameter. What the hell was that for?

Looking back out the window, I had the sudden urge to cry. I was so scared of failing. I couldn't imagine the feeling of getting so close to my goal and failing at this last hurdle, again.

I was pulled out of my thoughts by a loud knock at the door, and without me saying anything the door opened and a tall, slim man aged about 25 walked in. He said, in a strong Essex accent: "Hello mate, I'm Terry. We're both in H class. I've got the room two along from you. Are you ready? I was going to head over to the classroom. You know what they say: better to be an hour early than a minute late."

He smiled. I got off the bed, glad to have been dragged out of my dark thoughts, and reminded myself to lock the door from then on.

I said: "Hi Terry. Yeah, I'm ready to go, just trying to get my head around all this. That bloke in the lecture hall was a bit of an arsehole, but our staff seem nice enough. I'm Richard, by the way."

Terry grinned, and said: "Yeah, I know who you are; you're one of those loud ones in the canteen. Talk about drawing attention to yourself. Don't worry, it's cool. I think we all need a bit of spirit to get through this. By the way, best keep your voice down if you're going to call the guy who runs this place an arsehole."

Remembering to pick up my white notes, I quickly followed Terry.

We made our way down in the lift, picking up about half a dozen other recruits, exchanging nervous looks until we stopped at the twelfth floor, when John and Pete got in the lift.

John looked at me and said: "Bloody hell, it stinks in here. Did you fart in here, Armstrong?"

I replied, "No mate, it was Terry here. It was a silent one; he thought no one would notice."

John, Pete and Terry burst out laughing and, nervously, the others did too.

Terry looked at me saying: "Oh, I see that's how it's going to be. Game on!" Grinning all the while.

We made our way in a growing gaggle across to the classroom. Upon arrival at 10:00 hours, no one was around. I walked over and knocked on the door. No reply. I opened the door. The room was empty of people.

I turned round and asked the rest of the class: "Should we go in?"

John replied: "No point in standing around like prize plums; in you go mate."

We filed in to find a desk and chair at the front with an all-too-familiar whiteboard. Facing it were twenty chairs with attached flip-up tables arranged in four rows of five. We found a seat each. I was sat at the front on the right, one row from the door. We started to chat. Paige was sat on my immediate left, Terry to my right. We lost track of time and were just enjoying getting to know the people we were going to spend a lot of time with.

The door opened and in walked our four members of staff. The chat stopped. Pete, who was talking with his back to the door, quickly turned and loudly said: "Oh shit!" We all turned to look.

Sergeant Brownstone stepped forward and said: "The usual address when members of staff enter the room is 'Good morning, Sergeant,' not 'Oh shit!' But it's your first day, Mr Beck, (someone had been doing their homework on us) so I'll let you off. This time."

He replied, in a clear voice, "Sorry Sergeant!"

She allowed herself a slight hint of a smile and replied: "Well, at least you listened to something this morning. Also, it is customary to stand when we walk into the room, and I am one for custom."

She straightened up, squared her shoulders. "Mr Armstrong, who told you, you could enter the classroom? The other classes were waiting, silently lined up outside for their staff to arrive?"

It was clearly a test, sussing out the recruits on the first day, seeing who'd stand their ground and who'd back down or flap.

I didn't miss a beat and, in my best teacher voice, replied: "Sergeant, we had no instructions as to what to do. The door wasn't locked, and I took the decision it would save time to get into the room and get ready. As well, we would be able to talk and get to know each other without disturbing other people in the corridor. If there's blame for overstepping the mark, it's mine. If I did overstep the mark, I apologise, Sergeant."

This was delivered in a clear, yet polite tone. I inwardly took a deep breath. *You've opened your big mouth again; where will it lead?*

With relief, I saw Sergeant Johnson and PC Patel trying to hide grins.

Sergeant Brownstone looked me in the eye and said: "Oh yes, you're the teacher. I suppose I shouldn't be surprised you'd just walk into a classroom without so much as a by-your-leave. Initiative is to be commended, but be careful not to overstep the mark. You're not the teacher in this classroom. Over to you, Sergeant Johnson."

Sergeant Johnson came forward and sat on the corner of the desk (very, very teacher style, I was impressed) and, using his hands to emphasise (all which is a way to soften what he was going to say, this man knew is stuff), said: "Before we start, I'm Sergeant Johnson. I've been in the Met ten years. I was based at Camden. I worked on relief for eight years and the last two here. Now I've introduced myself, I'd like you to stand up and introduce yourself. Not your life story, just what you did before coming here, where you're from, why you joined up, OK?"

Silence.

"Good. Right, Paige, off you go."

Paige stood up, and spoke clearly and loudly: "I'm Paige. Paige Shore from Wimbledon, but I live in Wembley with my fiancé. I did my degree in financial management in Nottingham, and I was working for a finance company in the City. Honestly, I was bored out of my mind. I wanted to do something more exciting."

She sat down. Sergeant Johnson said: "Interesting. You said more exciting. Any other reason? Helping people, maybe?"

Paige replied, "Oh yeah, of course, that too."

A ripple of laughter around the room. The sergeant grinned saying, "Yes, I suppose that's just for the interview?"

Looking at me, he said: "Richard, your turn now."

I stood up, and spoke to the class, as I was well used to doing, and with more confidence than I felt. "Good morning. I'm Richard Armstrong. I live in Essex. I taught science in secondary school. I got my pilot's licence a few years ago and travelled around America. I joined the police because I'd wanted to be a policeman ... Oops, sorry, 'police officer', since I was a boy. It's a family thing. Also, can I be honest, Sergeant?"

I looked at Sergeant Johnson. He smiled, nodded and said: "You're past the interview stage, so you can be honest."

Everyone laughed at that. I continued, "I'd like to drive police cars with blue lights and sirens, and catch villains."

This did get a good laugh, including from the staff. When it quietened down, Paige piped up: "Well, he is from Essex, what do you expect!" More laughter.

Sergeant Johnson said, with a wry smile, "It's refreshing to have a bit of honesty. In the Met, you'll have plenty of opportunity to nick villains!"

Sergeant Johnson went around the room with similar results. John had been a self-employed builder from Norwich, Pete had worked at a supermarket in Hertfordshire, Terry had trained to be a professional cricketer at Essex but hadn't made the first team. He too was from Brentwood. There were various other occupations: photographer; mechanic; student; HGV driver; bus driver; a couple from the armed services, etc. A real eclectic bunch.

At the conclusion of the introductions, Sergeant Johnson said: "Right, this is what's going to happen: you'll be here for the next eighteen weeks, sixteen of which will be exam weeks. What's that mean? Well, starting from this week, we'll work through a set of notes, and we'll help you learn them. So, starting this Friday morning, you'll do a test. It's multiple choice, and the pass mark is 70 per cent. You must pass fifteen out of the sixteen tests to pass out. If you don't, you'll be asked to leave. On top of this, there'll be three physicals, all of which you must pass, and four scenarios you must pass as well. On top of all of that, your conduct on and off work time must be exemplary. There are so many ways to fail. Oh yes, you'll also have to learn to march, and keep your uniform up to the required standards. There's class parade every morning, so ironed shirts, tidy hair and polished shoes. Any questions so far?"

A slight pause. I had 101 questions but didn't want to interrupt. I think everyone was a bit stunned at the bluntness of the reality before us; this was really going to be a test of stamina. John piped up at this point: "When do we get our uniforms, Sarge?"

He replied, "At the end of the third week, when we've weeded out a few of the, err, unsuitable candidates. No point wasting a good uniform on a bad candidate."

Pete replied: "Well that's you out in three weeks, mate!" A round of laughter (easing the tension).

The sergeant waited until the laughter died down and said: "You're a lively lot. That's good. Most classes are so quiet and scared at this point. A word of caution, though: some members of staff won't appreciate that, and John and I don't mind being called 'Sarge' when other members of staff aren't around, but some will bite your head off, so be wary."

He waited for that to sink in, then continued: "No more questions? Right. Today is a bit different; we're going to start on the white notes you were sent and we'll work through them. After your meal tonight, at 20:00 hours, you'll need to be back here ready to go. We have a little exercise for you."

He got up and walked halfway to the door, as we settled ourselves down with the notes we'd been sent on theft. He said, as he, Sergeant Brownstone, PC McNish were walking out: "I'll leave you in the hands of Staff Wood. See you tonight."

PC Patel waited until the other members of staff left and sat on the edge of the desk and smiled: "Hi, I'm PC Patel. Staff Patel to you when anyone else is around, Yasmin when we're alone in the classroom."

Pausing for a moment, looking around the room, she said in a softer tone: "Richard, how long were you a teacher?"

"Three years, Staff. Err, sorry, Yasmin."

She smiled: "Don't worry, it's a lot to get used to so quickly. This is the first lesson I've ever taught. You'll have to let me know how I've done at the end. You see, you are my only intake. I'm going to have a baby at the start of October. I hope I'm able to be at your passing-out parade."

Paige piped up: "That's lovely Yasmin. You must be so excited."

Yasmin smiled and said: "Yes I am. I wanted to keep working, but away from the front line, and this post came up, so I took it. Anyway, has anyone not read the notes?"

Silence ...

"OK, good, how did you get on with it?"

Pausing, looking around the room: "OK, put your notes on the desk so you can't see them. Right, what are the five aspects of theft? We call them the five fingers of theft. It's a bit of an in joke, because you steal things with your hands!"

She held up her hands with fingers spread.

Paul put up his hand, Yasmin pointed at him and he stood up and said, "The five fingers of theft are: dishonestly taking property belonging to someone else, meaning to keep it, sell it, hide it or destroy it."

He sat down. We looked at him with a new level of respect.

Yasmin said: "That's good, Paul. It's all correct, but we need to use the specific words from the act of parliament. But well done, you've clearly studied it, we just need to learn the right words."

Paul replied: "Thank you, Yasmin. I'll do my best, but I do find it hard to remember the exact words sometimes."

Yasmin nodded at this and said: "You will have to work on that. To answer the questions correctly, they do rely on specific words."

We carried on with the lesson, until the lunch break, when we were told to go back to the canteen and to be back punctually at the time specified.

As we were walking to the canteen, we noticed a large number of uniformed police officers with blue lanyards, marching along one of the paths going around the sports field. There were two uniformed members of staff shouting at them loudly and aggressively, both of whom had strong Scottish accents.

I wondered aloud: "Who are they?"

From behind me, a voice with a strong Scottish accent said: "They're the bastard ex-guard drill sergeants teaching Blue Course how to march, as they're passing out in a few weeks, the lucky sods! I'm Angus, by the way. You're the teacher, Richard, right?"

"Yeah, that's right. Angus ... you're ex-army, aren't you?"

Angus exclaimed, rather too loudly, "Army? Fuck off. 40th Royal Marines Commando, mate!"

"Sorry mate! No insult intended, but how do you know they're ex-guard regiment?"

Angus replied, "D'nee worry yeer heed aboot it, man, it's the way they march and the order of drill they're using. The stuck-up fucking bastards, marching aroond like ya got a stick up yeer arse. I tell ya that never won any bastard a fucking battle." Pause. "Eh, you said your family's from the north. Are your relatives Scots?"

Thinking for a moment, I replied: "Yes, there are relatives a few generations back who are Scots; the other side of the family are all Burns, and Finlays."

Angus seemed satisfied and said: "Ah, well, we'll have ta have a glass or two of a fine malt before we leave here."

We carried on walking to the canteen.

The rest of the day was spent going through the different aspects of the theft act, running through different scenarios. It wasn't particularly difficult, but it did use very specific language, and there was a lot to get through and remember. At the conclusion of the lesson, Yasmin asked me to stay. After the others had left, she said: "So, how did I do? I did say it was my first lesson. Please be honest; I need to know how to improve."

I paused for a moment, giving myself time to organise my thoughts, and said, "Really, really good. You were clear, you knew the material and you made a good connection with the students."

Yasmin smiled, and let out a short breath. "Thank you," she said. "Any things I can improve on? I want to do a PGCE at some point and go into teaching in schools."

I was a little taken aback by this: I was being asked by an instructor to critique their teaching of me. Also, why did she want to teach? She was a police officer? Oh well, she asked me the question, and the teacher instinct of wanting to answer took priority over my inquisitive nature.

I said: "Teaching for me is fairly simple: first establish the rules of the game. Rule one: you're in charge. Not too much of a problem here. Rule two: know the material you're teaching. There's no quicker way of losing the trust of a class than when they ask a question, you don't know and try to fudge the answer. Rule three: be kind and approachable. Establish that playing your game is fun and safe, i.e. you're not going to make them feel stupid. Last rule: make sure the material you give them is appropriate, because you can deliver a perfect lesson, but if it's over the heads of the students, they won't learn anything."

Yasmin waited a moment, clearly thinking about what I'd said.

"Thank you, that was very clear and well thought out. You are a good teacher," she smiled.

I replied: "Thank you, Yasmin, that's really appreciated. I just hope I can be a good police officer. I tried three times to get in the police. I'm really scared I'll fail and let everyone down."

Yasmin looked at me straight in the eyes and said: "Honestly, I think it'll be hard for you. You're older, more confident and that will rub some people up the wrong way. I get the feeling you're a sensitive person like me, and that makes it doubly hard. But you will be able to reach people through your sensitivity that others won't. And, between you and me, the job isn't what it used to be, and I fear the way it's going. All I'll say is, be really careful what you say, and watch your back.

"Anyway, I've probably said too much. If I need any teaching advice, I know where to come. Also, if you need to talk, ask any of us. Gary Johnson is a sweetie. Amanda Brownstone has a frosty outer shell, but she's really lovely and very supportive. John McNish may come across as a bit of an old sweat, but he'll listen and he gives great advice. Even if you don't want to hear it. Anyway, best you get off to the canteen before all the less dreadful food is gone."

I thanked her, and walked off, lost in my thoughts. What did she mean? I felt she was trying to warn me about something. I wasn't entirely sure what it was though. Watch your back? What did that mean?

At the end of the corridor, Paige and Paul were waiting for me. They both looked at me before Paul said, with mock sincerity: "Well, are you still on the course, or did you get kicked off on the first day?"

I grinned: "No, I haven't been fired yet. She just wanted some teaching advice."

Paige said: "What? Really? On your first day the trainers are asking you for tips on teaching? Did she say anything else?"

Remembering what Yasmin had said (unusually for me), I was careful with my words. I replied: "No, it was mainly about what it was like being a teacher."

At this, their curiosity was temporarily sated, so we made our way outside, and as we walked along the path to the canteen, I said quietly: "One thing she did say," (waiting until I had their attention), "she said watch what you say. I'll leave it at that. Oh, and she said the food was shit!"

Yasmin was spot on with the food. It was badly cooked, low quality and bland. I think it was a rite of passage, as to whether you could stomach eighteen weeks of that swill. What I didn't know was that was the high point for food quality during my entire time in the Met, with one exception.

After lunch, we made our way to the classroom, went in and sat down. At two minutes to 8 p.m., in walked Sergeant Johnson. We all stood up and, a little too loudly, bellowed: "Sergeant!"

He looked at us and, rolling his eyes, said: "You are going to piss off so many people! Oh well, at least you remembered what to do."

He was carrying a medium-sized cardboard box with a clipboard resting on top. Putting the box down on the desk, he said: "For tonight's exercise we want you to work in pairs. You'll be given a radio and a torch, both of which you'll have to sign for and return in one piece, or they'll dock it from your pay."

He then called out the pairs and we duly signed for the equipment. Once we'd settled down, he said: "Right, did anyone read the form you just signed? It said you've had enough of the canteen food and you're off home tomorrow."

He paused and, after a moment of surprise, we started to laugh. He cut us short and, in a rare moment of intensity, he said: "Be careful to read whatever you sign, before signing it! I'm 100 per cent serious. It can cost you your job if you sign the wrong thing. You're police officers now, not fucking clueless civvies!"

He eyed us with a steely glare, which stunned us all into silence.

He continued: "Your objective tonight is to quietly follow me over to the multi-storey car park and go where you're directed. Now, look at your radio. On it are two letters and two numbers. Those are your call signs.

When they want to contact you, they'll use that call sign. You'll hear for example: 'Papa Charlie 2 2'. That's PC22. Who's got that?"

A hand went up at the back of the room.

"You reply: 'Go ahead', then you will listen to what they want you to do, and acknowledge that you've heard by saying: 'Received Papa Charlie 22'. Remember, this isn't a fun walkie talkie to take the piss out of your mates with. It's a test, and the senior officers will be monitoring it. So, if you want to be leaving tomorrow morning, mess around. Any questions? Right, good, let's get going."

I was paired with Gary, a short man, a little older than me who had been a professional pet photographer and who reminded me of an accountant with his slightly fussy manner. Our call sign was Papa Charlie 24.

It was dark by that stage of the evening, and although it had been a long day, we were buoyed with excitement at being able to play policemen with some toys.

We lined up in our pairs outside the car park. We were unusually quiet. Sergeant Johnson said: "Right, make your way inside, and start looking around. You've been told there's been a series of thefts from cars. Go and see if you can identify any cars that have been broken into, and listen to your radios."

As we waited our turn to go in, Gary and I exchanged glances. I had the radio, he had the torch (on account of my experience talking on radios as a security guard as a young man). I could feel my grip tighten on the walkie talkie-style radio. It was old and had chips and scratches on its rough, textured surface, and the "PC24" was crudely written on it in what looked like Tippex. Welcome to the Met; everything with extra cheapness.

I remembered my security training, and deliberately calmed down my breathing and tried to focus on my surroundings. We were still in the suits we'd worn all day, and I began to notice how grubby I felt.

We were one of the last pairs to enter the car park. The poor lighting and multiple levels made any sound echo. It was hard to pinpoint where it had come from as we made our way around, almost subconsciously crouching, straining our hearing for anything that would give us a hint.

It was Gary who spotted something first. "Here, Richard, I think I see some damage to that light-coloured Beemer over on the right, tucked up near that door over there."

As soon as we started moving, we began to hear screams and yells and running feet. There were plenty of expletives. The radio lit up with shouts of "help", "what the fuuuuck!", "run", "get off".

A clear woman's voice cut in over these frantic calls: "Correct radio procedure, please."

Then a reply came, calm and measured with a less noticeable Scottish accent (I recognised as Angus): "Papa Charlie, Papa Charlie 21."

"Go ahead, Papa Charlie 21."

"Papa Charlie, there appears to be an unknown number of armed masked men ...". Message cut off.

I looked at Gary; the colour had drained from his face. We made our way to the BMW he had indicated. He went around the far side of the car, near the door, and said triumphantly: "I told you, there's damage he ..."

At this point a man in dark clothing, and a balaclava, wielding a black baseball bat burst through the doors shouting. I heard a noise behind me. Too late: I felt a firm blow to my right kidney area. I was roughly turned around and I looked into the face of a man of about my height (6 ft ¼ in, never forget that ¼ inch) staring back at me through a black balaclava. He said, in a strong clear voice: "You're dead mate. Go back to the entrance."

He wasn't nasty about it. I could tell his accent was from east London, but I didn't recognise him. Gary was visibly more shaken than I was, although he did his best to hide it. For me, this wasn't my first rodeo, so to speak. When I was in my early twenties, I'd worked for a security company, doing what they called cash-in-transit, and I'd been held up at gunpoint a couple of times. But still, it wasn't the way I'd thought my first day in the police would have gone.

The night air was cool as we waited for all the other pairs to make their way out of the car park. I could feel my premium M&S all-cotton white shirt stick to my back (all-cotton shirts, and all wool suits, you can't go wrong!) and I shivered involuntarily.

When everyone was back outside and the radios and torches had been returned and signed for, Sergeant Johnson addressed us.

"Right, if you were really working on the streets, you'd all be dead! Just think, do I want to do this job? Think about it tonight and you can leave in the morning, no shame. 'The Job' isn't for everyone. For the rest of you, learn. You aren't police officers: you are training to be police officers. At this stage you know NOTHING. DO YOU HEAR ME? NOTHING! You are currently a liability. But if you work hard and listen, you can make it. Now go back to your rooms and I'll see you in the morning, nice and sharp tomorrow. Dismissed!"

On the way back, all the banter had gone; the bravado was knocked out of us. Reality was beginning to set in. The rules of life had just changed. I wondered if I had what it took?

The next morning, at least one person had left, although I'm not sure from which class. But that was one down, first blood, so to speak.

First day of parade was going to be Wednesday, so on the Tuesday we were walked through it. We'd assemble, in our classes A to L, left to right, just along from Sir Robert Peel's statue. Two ranks of ten, straight lines, backs straight, looking forward, arms straight down by our sides feeling for the seams of our trousers between forefinger and thumb. I had been repeatedly shouted at as an ATC cadet when I was a teen.

Honestly, I was glad of their teaching at this juncture. The ex-servicemen and women were encouraged to assist us after initial instruction by the staff. The staff walked off, and enjoyed the comedic and faintly ridiculous sight we clearly were. I tell you, when you are a part of twenty utterly clueless, uncoordinated ex-civilians trying to master the art of standing still in two lines, and going from at-ease to attention, it is chaos at the start. All I could see in my mind was *Dad's Army* with Captain Mainwaring, Jonesy, Pike and the crew. The ex-service types varied in levels of patience. Surprisingly, Angus was a very good instructor. He had an acid sense of humour, but when he did point out what you were doing wrong, you always got the impression he wanted to work with you, not against you.

After a shambolic half an hour, it started to look like we might not make a total dog's dinner of it the next day.

The rest of the first week went by at lightning pace, until Friday morning and the dreaded first test loomed. Honestly, I was reasonably confident I knew the material. However, I guess the difference was between practising walking on a high wire 10 ft off the ground and 100 ft off the ground. Same wire, different outcome, if you fall off.

There were four possible answers to each question. At least one, if not two, of the answers could be discarded, but the remaining two or three were usually very similar. That was where it got tricky and, unlike in regular school teaching, there were questions to trick the unwary. So, honestly, these tests were never a foregone conclusion and required concentration.

As we sat silently at our desks, and the test papers were handed out, I tried to use the hard-learnt technique of mentally distancing myself from the outcomes of the test score, and focusing purely on the words on the page, i.e. the wire, not the fall.

All too soon, PC McNish said: "Time's up, you lot! Put your pens down, and remain silent and still as I collect your papers."

No one moved, which was unusual enough for A class, or "Animal House" as we were already being called, due to our boisterousness.

Once PC McNish had all the papers on the desk at the front, he said: "Not so cocky now, are we, hey?" He had a slightly smug look on his face, which quickly changed into a smile. "Off you go and get yourselves some coffee. Be back at 10:30 hours for your results, and do'nee worri, can cannee change the results noow."

We sat in the canteen, trying to hide our nerves, because no matter how hard you studied, you never truly knew how well you got on until the results were out. There was the usual dissecting questions and debating the answers, one moment buoyed by a perceived shared correct answer, then nervous when the answer you gave was outside of the norm. Each of us was thinking of the ramifications of a failure at the first hurdle, only to have the possibility of ignominious failure and expulsion from the course looming over us with just one exam mistake. The thought of hearing your friends and loved ones saying: "Don't worry, it just wasn't meant to be."

With those words ringing loud in my head, I looked for the hundredth time at my watch, then at the clock on the wall hoping and dreading in equal measure that the time of worry would be over. Eventually the time came, and we walked back to the classroom and sat down. The door opened and Sergeant Johnson's smiling face popped in around the doorframe, and quickly said: "You all passed!" Instant relief, not just for ourselves, but for our friends. It is surprising how quickly you forge the bonds of friendship when you're all struggling together.

There were a lot of exhalations of breath, and John said what we were all thinking: "Thank fuck for that! Oh, sorry Sergeant!"

That broke the tension and we all laughed; the tension I didn't know I had in my shoulders and neck released.

The sergeant smiled, waited until we were all quiet and said: "I'm not one for swearing in a classroom normally, John, but just this once I'll let it slide."

He sat on his now customary desk corner and, reading from the piece of paper he was holding, addressed the class: "I'll read out the scores. Remember I'll only do this for those who've passed."

He went down the list. Most people were safely in the 80s. Then it came to the last few names: "Richard 100%, Paige 100%, Terry 97%, Paul 76%, John 94%, Pete 94%. Well done, Richard, it looks like the teacher's going to have a bit of competition. Keep it up, Paige, see if you can beat him!"

Paige and I high-fived, much to the others' amusement. I turned around and exchanged smiles with my friends. When I came to Paul, I could see that he had scored the lowest, and although he was trying to hide it, he had a pensive look.

The sergeant, sensing (as good teachers do) the concern for Paul, looked over to him and said: "Don't worry Paul; a pass is a pass, and it was your first exam for how many years?"

Paul looked up, tilting his head to one side, as if trying to remember, "Err, nine years, Sergeant."

The sergeant replied, "Well then, just think Richard here has been studying and teaching virtually all of that time!"

He looked at me for backup. Supportive teacher mode engaged: "That's true. I've either been doing or setting tests since 1990. I have no excuses for doing badly in exams. It just takes a little bit of time to blow away the cobwebs. You'll get better and better at these tests as the course goes on. Trust me, I'm a teacher, and teachers are never wrong!" I said, with a slight grin as I finished the sentence.

There was much laughter, and Paul seemed to perk up at bit. I shared a quick look with the sergeant; I could see he approved. I determined at that point we were all going to pass that course if it bloody killed me! I didn't know it, but that was going to be my toughest teaching assignment yet.

The notes for the next week were handed out and we were reminded to study them over the weekend. We were further warned that our behaviour was being closely monitored, and that we would be removed from the course if they didn't like what they heard.

There was a buzz as we all filed out of the classrooms, and had the freedom of the weekend, albeit with clear instructions to learn the notes, and to do nothing that would bring discredit on the Met.

As we were packing our bags with our washing to take home for the weekend, we started hearing stories from the other classes of people failing the first test, of having meltdowns, being taken out of the class and given final warnings not to fail another one. Strangely, though, this was not universal. Some of the recruits were told not to worry that they'd failed, that they'd be all right. Odd, but I didn't think any more about it; these stories likely were exaggerations or only partially true. I was certain the system was fair. Why would it not be? Didn't they want the best candidates to get through?

I was awoken from my thoughts as Terry burst in through the door ... again (why had I not locked the door, again?) "Here, get a move on or we'll miss the Tube and train connection to Brentwood."

I could see he had his backpack and was ready to go. I looked down at my own backpack. What did I need? Socks. Did I pack all of them? Nothing worse than finding an odd sock when you got home. Shirts. Did I pack all of them? I counted quickly. Five, that's OK. "Right, I'm ready mate."

Terry replied: "No you're not: don't forget your notes; they're there on the table. Muppet!"

I silently cursed my own stupidity, God, that would have been a disaster. The following week's pile of notes was twice that of the first week. 'Assault' was the following week. We'd have precious little free time that weekend if we were to do the notes justice.

I picked up my notes and, all too carefully for the liking of Terry (who looked on with an impatient scowl), put them flat in a folder and stored them securely in my bag. Eventually we were out of the gates and jogging along to catch the Tube. Terry moved with surprising grace for a man of 6 ft 5. I had trained hard for the course, with twelve weeks of weights and cardiovascular. I was in the best shape of my life, 6 ft ¼ in (never forget the ¼ inch), body fat percentage in single figures, and 11 st 4 lbs. I could bench press 120 kg and leg press 250 kg. I was, for an amateur, pretty fit. But I looked at the ease with which he moved and realised the gulf that existed between us.

I asked, "What was it like being a professional cricketer?"

He said, without turning, "I only played with the first team a couple of times in practice matches. It's a different level, and utterly ruthless. There's no room for being nice, mate; it's dog eat dog. Your only goal is to get into the first team and stay there."

I took this in and replied: "What do you think of the physical tests they're going to get us to do?"

Terry replied matter-of-factly: "Piece of piss mate. We'll have no trouble. Although there will be people who do struggle, 'cos they're lazy sods who've never trained in their lives."

I almost lost pace for a moment, a bit surprised. "What, you really think there are people that stupid who have done no training for this? The bleep test is only level eight and a half. My gran could pass that, and she's been dead for ten years."

Terry snorted at that, and said, "Trust me, some of those muppets will struggle. I'm guessing you can get to level twelve on the bleep. As I said, it's a joke. They lowered it recently; it's almost an insult now."

I grinned, and replied: "You're a pretty good judge. I ducked out just before level thirteen. I didn't think I could make fourteen, and I hate the number thirteen."

Terry slowed the pace as we passed over the uneven pavement of a couple of driveways. He looked at me for a moment and said, "What you, a sciency type, superstitious? Really? Didn't think you'd fall for that old nonsense, mate."

I had to duck under a couple of low-hanging branches that Terry had adroitly manoeuvred and left to swing back at me. I caught my breath and replied: "Look, not all the things I've seen can be explained in a purely rational way. Besides, I've had two car crashes, and both were on Friday the 13th. Do you know the statistical probability of that happening? It's astronomically small. I really, really hate Friday the 13th, and the number thirteen, all right?"

We had come to a busy road we needed to cross, so had to stop to wait for a gap in the traffic, and, raising his voice to be heard, Terry turned to look at me, saying: "You're serious, aren't you? Well, you do surprise me.

"I guess we all have our things. Don't tell anybody, but I hate birds. No I don't mean the two-legged ones; don't worry, I ain't gay. Not that there's anything wrong with that sort of thing ... you're not gay, are you? No, the way you and Paige flirt, I know you're not. And before you say anything, yes, I know you're both just having a laugh. But I mean the feathered little bastards. There, over there, those fucking pigeons. My dad calls them flying rats. Horrible, nasty, flappy things, with beaks and claws and disease. They shit all over your car. I hate 'em."

I was somewhat surprised to hear that this great, big, tall man would be scared of a simple bird. I guess we're all scared of something, and his fear was avian. I said, scanning for a gap in the traffic: "We're all scared of something." Indicating we should cross, and rushing over, I added: "I won't say anything about birds, if you don't mention the number between twelve and fourteen."

We were within sight of the Tube station, and resumed our jog. Terry said: "What do you call it? Twelve plus one, or fourteen minus one? Ha-ha."

With fake annoyance, I replied "Is that how it's going to be?"

He said: "You started it with that lift fart gag!"

We both started to laugh, as much as you can while wearing a backpack and jogging for the Tube.

The journey home was uneventful, except for the fact it seemed like every other person on the Tube was a recruit from Hendon.

The weekend was full of study and endlessly telling the same story over and over again to family and friends.

Before I knew it, we were back in the classroom, waiting for Monday's lesson, chatting to each other like old friends who hadn't seen each other for years.

The week went by in a flash, and once again we found ourselves sitting in the canteen, awaiting our test results, a little more relaxed. We'd been there almost two weeks; we were old hands at it.

When the results were announced, we'd all passed again, with broadly similar results. I had dipped down to 94 per cent, and Paige 97 per cent. Oh, she was so smug about that, I couldn't let that one stand. Paul managed 76 per cent again. He didn't seem too upset; a pass, as they say, is a pass.

As we were being given out our notes for the following week, we were told that we'd better make sure we had our PT kit (clean, plain – no logos etc. – dark T-shirts, and plain shorts or tracksuit pants and trainers), as week three would involve a fitness assessment (one of the three we had to pass). It involved sit-ups, press-ups, a bleep test and run.

The mood in our class was pretty buoyant. We'd once again heard of some failing the tests and final warnings, and one of the recruits had failed both tests, and was still on the course. That was clearly a mistake.

Again, the weekend shot by, and we went through the now-routine procedures of the last couple of weeks. The PT assessment was on the Wednesday, and if we passed the written test on Friday, we'd get our uniform. It would be another step towards becoming police officers.

Wednesday morning came around, and we all filed into a huge gymnasium, 150-plus of us.

The people running this were not our usual staff; they were civilian fitness assessors, mostly ex-army types, with a nice line in ritual humiliation and a sideline in sadism. The type of person who would routinely say: "No pain, no gain!" "Go hard, or go home." "Pain is just weakness leaving the body," and who weren't satisfied until at least someone had thrown up. I had spent some of my degree studying the effects of exercise on the human body. We had been to army training sessions, and I knew this type of instructor all too well. I resolved to keep a low profile, and do what was necessary to pass.

Once the usual warm-up was over, and the leading knucklehead (oops, sorry, instructor) had given his obligatory "who's in charge? I am!" speech, we were split into groups of two classes (approximately forty) and we did the bleep test. This was watched over by the aforementioned knuckleheads. The other classes watched on as we all lined up on the starting line, and we were given the usual instructions: we should start off slowly and build up, walking, jogging and eventually running between the two lines 20 metres apart. There were two bleeps, and you had to start running from one line on the first bleep, and arrive at the second line by the second bleep. The time between the bleeps got shorter.

They called out what level you'd achieved. Level eight and a half was required to pass. As I already mentioned, I could do level twelve. Really fit people could get to level fourteen, and professional athletes up to level twenty. So, level eight was within the reach of anyone who was reasonably healthy and had done even a little bit of training.

We lined up, with Paige to my right. On the far side of her was Terry, and Victoria (one of the Animal House, she was a quiet Scottish woman in her mid to late twenties) was on my left. I turned slightly, making eye contact with Paige and Terry; game on, folks. I looked at Victoria, and she did not look happy at all. I said quietly to her: "Don't worry, just keep pace with me and you'll be fine. It's not too difficult." She gave a weak smile, and returned her worried gaze forward.

The beep sounded and we were off. I walked, knowing to pace myself, slowing the build-up of lactic acid (technically it's called OBLA – Onset of Blood Lactate Accumulation). It's when you feel your arms and legs burning; that's the lactic acid. A sudden burst of activity will cause this to happen more quickly, so a slow and steady build-up delays this.

I could see from the start Camilla was going to struggle. She didn't seem to want to do anything but walk.

Level one passed, level two passed, level three everyone was still there, level four and I could hear Camilla starting to breath more heavily – worrying. Level five and she was beginning to struggle, level six and a I could hear a few deep breaths, and Victoria was really suffering. I looked across and she was almost done. She was late for the bleep and received a warning, next time she'd be out.

I risked being shouted at, and said loudly (trying to get the rest of the class to encourage her): "Come on, Camilla, you can do this, a couple more levels to go." This was echoed by the onlooking classes, although I did notice the head instructor give me a hard stare.

Level seven – Camilla had dropped out, bent over, breathing heavily. Damn! Damn! Damn! Nothing I could do for her. Focus on the battle for bragging rights with Paige and Terry. So, relax, breath steadily, concentrate.

Level eight – a couple more dropped out from B class.

Level nine – good everyone, but Lucy in H class had passed. A lot of people dropped out of the test, leaving two guys from B class, Pete, John, Terry, Richard Edwards, Paige and me. Time to sort the wheat from the chaff.

Level ten – John dropped out, and Paige did one more bleep than John, Pete one more than Paige, and one of the B class also dropped out.

At this point, I could hear the other classes starting to cheer on their favourites. I could even hear my name ... surprisingly?

Level eleven – Richard, Terry, the guy from B class (Edward, I later found out), we were all in this. I was not going to lose!

I could feel the slow build-up of tension in my muscles and joints. I fought hard to keep my breathing slow and regular. There was no rest between arriving and departing the line. I could feel the beads of sweat running down my back.

Level twelve – the other Richard dropped out, as did Edward, although I didn't notice at the time. It was me and Terry. I could feel his gaze for a moment as we turned. He knew the game: neither of us were going to back down from this.

Level twelve plus one – passed. This was new territory for me. The pain was building in my legs and I was struggling to control my breathing. I MUST NOT LOSE. PAIN IS JUST WEAKNESS LEAVING THE BODY!

Level fourteen – we were sprinting at this point. I could vaguely make out the figure of the instructor standing at the far line watching us intently. I could hear Terry's breathing getting ragged. Good. I had him.

Level fifteen – just, passed the line and felt myself stop and try to turn, but I was done. Nothing left. The instructor was in front of me saying, "That's it, lad. Breathe, breathe. That wasn't the worst bleep test I've seen."

As I struggled for breath, I risked a look up at him, "Did I beat him?" He grinned and stepped aside, and I could see Terry bent over, struggling for breath. Dead heat. Damn, damn, damn! I must win!

We had time to recover as we watched the other classes doing their bleep tests. There were plenty of congratulations from the other recruits. I couldn't bring myself to look at Terry for a few minutes.

Then I remembered Camilla, and felt a pang of guilt; I'd been so wrapped up in my own battle, I'd totally forgotten about her. I walked around until I found her and Paige talking. Camilla had smudged make-up and had clearly been crying.

"Camilla, are you all right?" As soon as I said it, I thought of a hundred better things to say. God, I am an insensitive idiot!

She looked up at me with big, watery eyes, and said: "I failed, but the staff said I can retake as many times as I need to." She was trying to do her best to smile.

I said: "OK, that's good. Don't worry, we'll help you. You will pass this! You won't let this beat you, will you? You know we'll all have our challenges before this course is over." I moved over and gave her arm a little squeeze.

She smiled and put her hand on my arm, and replied: "Thank you, you're really kind, I think I'll take you up on that. Oh, by the way, how did you manage level fifteen? You and Terry, who was a professional cricketer, dead-heated. That's mad!"

I tried to keep it matter-of-fact by saying: "I train every day, and I love running. Besides, I couldn't let him win, he'd be insufferable. But thanks."

When Camilla had walked off to chat to some of the other ladies on the course, Paige pulled me to one side and said: "I can't believe she failed that. You know what she said when I asked if she had trained for this? She said, 'Oh yeah, I do Pilates once a week.' The stupid bitch! I asked her why she hadn't done any CV. She said it made her make-up run and she felt unattractive! The fucking vacuous tart! She's the sort of bimbo who gives the rest of us girls a bad name!"

I was a little taken aback by this and, after a moment to collect my thoughts, I said: "I thought the staff said you couldn't fail this, but she said she could retake this as many times as she needed. What's all that about?"

Paige glared at me for a moment, and stepped in close, taking my arm and almost whispering in my ear, "That's the worst of it; they only do that for the women. The men are only allowed one failure, women can fail as many times as they like, and will get one-to-one tuition to get through.

Can you fucking believe it! It's the most sexist bullshit I've ever heard! Like women can't pass the level eight bleep without 'special help'. I thought the standards were the same. The fucking villains won't care if you're male or female. This is so fucking insulting!"

I looked at her and could see her just about keeping her fury under wraps. I said: "That's so, so out of line. I can't believe they'd do that! You don't need help to reach level eight!"

I looked round and noticed everyone was getting ready for the next activity. I said: "Right, best get back to the others. Take your frustrations out in the exercises, show them that Shorey don't need no special treatment."

Her face was like thunder, but she nodded, and we rejoined our class for the next exercises.

The rest of the morning was made up of the other, almost ludicrously simple physical tests.

The rest of the week went as the two previous ones had. The test went well. No one in our class failed; we all got in the mid-eighties or low nineties. Paige and I tied on 94 per cent again. Paul got his now obligatory 76 per cent. He took it with a stoic resignation. This time Karim dipped to 70 per cent – just a pass. Upon hearing, he blew out a long breath and sat back in his chair.

Once again, we heard stories of members of other classes failing. Some were asked to leave. Others, mysteriously, were still on the course.

As Sergeant Johnson was handing out the notes for the following week, he said: "Well, next week you'll get your uniforms, as long as your measurements haven't radically changed." He said this with a friendly smile.

Pete turned to John and said: "Well, I'm still here. You lost that bet!" Much to our amusement.

The sergeant added, as a final thought, "Oh, one last thing (real Columbo style). If you've done any crimes you weren't caught for, now is the time to leave. The Met gets your dabs next week. Ha-ha!" He grinned.

White notes in hand, we made our weary way home, excited we'd be getting our uniforms and start looking like real police. Even if we didn't feel like it, yet.

Chapter 2
PASSING OUT

Monday morning rolled around again, following another weekend slogging through the notes. Some progress though, as the Blue intake were going to pass out that week, so the following week there'd be spaces in the car park, allowing us to park our cars. No more slogging back and forth on public transport.

Uniforms, car parking privileges, soon we'd be learning how to use our toys (cuffs and sticks – truncheons), and the first of the video-taped practical role plays. We were moving up in the world. As Angus said, RHIP (Rank Has Its Privileges).

As we sat in the classroom catching up on our weekends, I took a quick last look at the notes for the week, on statements and note-taking. I wondered if that week would be the week where one of us dropped the ball and we lost someone. I knew most of the other classes had lost at least one recruit. I looked around the room; who was it going to be? Paul, Karim, John, Gary, Terry, Pete? Ask not for the whom the bell tolls, it tolls for thee. Was I worried for my friends, or about myself?

PC McNish opened the door and walked in. I stood up and Terry gave the usual greeting: "Morning Staff!" We all echoed this.

PC McNish gave us an old-fashioned look and said: "You are learning! Right, it's time for the Met to waste its money and give you a uniform, but before that, fingerprint time. Leave your stuff here, and follow me. And keep your traps shut so you don't make me look bad!"

At this he turned and walked out of the room at a good pace. We shared grins and Paige winked at me, and off we went to find out whose fingerprints were in the system. *I haven't done anything, have I?* You start doubting yourself.

We made our way to the main building, and lined up outside the fingerprint-taking room. This was also going to be used as a teaching opportunity to show us how to take dabs. We were called into one of the two small rooms in small groups and were shown how to take fingerprints, using our classmates as guinea pigs.

Our instructor was an old man (50-ish), with grey hair. He was in reasonable shape, about 5'10", slim. His epaulettes were well-worn, even if the metal letters were all shiny. We were beginning to notice these things. His name was PC Jackson. I hadn't seen him before.

When we'd quietened down, he said: "'Ello folks. I'm PC Jackson, but please call me John. I hate all this formality; I'm no better than you. I've been Job (slang for the police) since the seventies. I'm not far off retirement. Between you and me, I can't fucking wait. It ain't the same, and I don't envy you lot. Anyway, basics of fingerprinting haven't changed, so first, legibly fill in the top of the Phoenix papers. Oh yeah, that's we call these things (holding up the A4 fingerprint sheet that we'd all been handed as we walked in). Can you all do that now. You'll find pens on the tables. Oh yeah, and where it says sex, the top brass get their knickers in a twist if you put 'yes please'."

There was a round of laughter. *Good!* I thought. *This is going to be a laugh!*

He waited patiently until we'd filled in our name, race, sex, height, eye colour, hair colour, marks and scars. Eventually, when we'd completed them, PC Jackson said: "Right, get into a place where you can see. You (pointing at Terry), you're the first victim."

He held out his hand, and Terry handed him his Phoenix form. In front of him was a 12-inch-long, flat block of bronze attached to the edge of the table. Next to it were a couple of what looked like tubes of black paint, and a pack of hand wipes, and a small, ink-covered roller.

John took the paint (actually fingerprint ink), and very carefully drew a line of it along the left half of the bronze block, leaving the right side clear and, with a practised motion, spread it out over the surface, using the roller until it was evenly applied in a thin layer, leaving the right side clear. He made it look easy, but I had a feeling it wasn't.

At this he said: "What's your name, mate?"

"Terry, Staff ... I mean John."

John said: "Right, place your right hand, face up." Terry did as he was asked. "Close your fist, leaving your thumb out, and carefully roll your thumb in the ink from nail to nail so you get a nice, even layer on it."

Terry did it, holding up his now inked thumb up to the rest of us triumphantly.

John said: "Give me your hand, and let it relax." Terry reluctantly complied. Gently taking Terry's hand, John took hold of the base of the thumb and carefully rolled it once from right to left on the paper, leaving one clear impression. It looked easy but, trust me, until you practise it a couple of hundred times, it isn't. It's a bit of an art and, the better the fingerprint impression, the more likely it'll be matched or eliminated.

John did this for all of us in a very short time. The ink had a certain smell to it, hard to describe, a bit like the smell you find in the art department at school. As he was completing the fingerprints and checking our forms, he regaled us with a story, in policing known as "swinging the old blue lamp" and a tradition as old as policing. He said: "I had to ask the German police for a set of dabs from this stiff they had on ice, 'cos we suspected he was involved in a bit o' naughtiness we were investigating. You know, turning breathing people into not-breathing people, that kind of naughty." He waited for the obligatory chuckles and continued: "Well, the next day a box turned up, only to find two severed hands in it. The bleedin' Krauts ... Oops, am I allowed to call 'em that?

He looked around, no one said anything, so he continued. "They'd not just taken dabs, they cut the stiff's bleedin' hands off so we could do 'em!"

When sufficient exclamations of shock were forthcoming, he continued: "Just shows you the difference between countries, don't it! Well, that's enough from me. Off you go to the stores to collect your kit. Honestly, at this stage of your careers, it'll be a stick for the petty-minded staff to beat you with. Don't 'show out' (police slang for standing out from the crowd)."

I didn't realise just how true those words were. John directed us to the stores, and as a parting shot, said: "I wonder how many of you'll get an invitation from CID to have a little chat when these dabs go live on the system?"

Once we'd collected our uniforms from the ladies in stores (we'd sent in our measurements weeks before), they proceeded to check the fitting. Most of us were fine, apart from a couple of small adjustments. I was really surprised just how much kit we were given: shirts, helmet (they take some getting used to wearing, trust me), uniform cap, jumper, epaulettes (but no numbers, those were for later), red lanyards, two ties, belt, light raincoat, heavy raincoat, two pairs of light trousers, full dress uniform (heavy formal tunic, two pairs of heavy trousers, white gloves, and a whistle on a chain with a police box key. I never found out if it'd fit the TARDIS, but apparently there was still at least one police box left in London – in Chelsea, I think?).

We waddled back to our rooms, piled up with our uniforms. Paige said to Camilla, "Trousers or skirt?" Camilla did her best to answer in a girlie voice: "I'm a girl, so I wear a skirt!"

Much to our amusement, Paige replied cheerily: "Trousers for me all the way; skirts are just too impractical. I think even the thickest bloke should be able to work out I'm female!"

Again, too much amusement. I was now trying to balance all this stuff, and laugh, and walk.

The rest of the day was spent with form-filling. We were advised to complete a will (a sobering thought, compounded when we were told, if we were killed on duty, our nearest and dearest would receive £1,000,000 if we were wearing our Metvest (body armour); if not, they'd receive only half of that).

The Police Federation rep came down and explained they weren't a union, so we couldn't go on strike. They were just there to allow us to have a representative ("friend" is the word they used) who was another police officer if we had a disciplinary hearing. Another sobering thought, especially when he said most police officers had at least one during their service. They had a raffle, and were there to advise on pensions and organise social events. Even at that early stage of our careers we'd heard rumours of the 999 parties, which involved police, doctors, nurses and firefighters. Strangely, the ladies did seem to perk up when they heard that firemen would be there.

It was stressed to us the date we joined, was important for, in twenty-five years or age 55 (if you were still serving) or 60 if you'd left, you'd receive your pension. That's a big deal. We didn't realise it at the time, but it's a really big deal.

The next day we were to have our first uniformed parade. So, I set out to iron my shirts and, to my surprise, Karim and a number of other recruits had never had to iron their own shirts. Quite honestly, they were clueless. I donned my teaching hat once again and walked them through it. Angus (who was on the same floor) came around and helped us get a good shine on our shoes. He said we should buy Doc Martens with toecaps, and that there was a way of getting them to a mirror-like shine. So, between the two of us, we made sure everyone was ready for the first uniform inspection.

On the way down in the lift the following morning, at the first stop the lift made, I instinctively said, "Oh fuck!" when the doors opened and half a dozen uniformed recruits got in, much to everyone's amusement. Not least because a couple of those who were outside had the same reaction. It'd take some getting used to, seeing friends all in uniforms.

As we saw each other in uniform for the first time, all we could do was laugh and mock each other. Bad move! The staff waiting for us were not amused. Who were the loudest class? H class (aka Animal House) ... again.

Over the remaining weeks at Hendon, and during our probation period (two years), all of us were shouted at at least once for minor uniform infractions. John had, indeed, been right.

Since the bleep test the week before, a number of us had taken turns attempting to get Victoria into shape to pass. This involved early morning jogs (in her case, mostly walks) around the running track. It was going to take some doing!

On the Wednesday, we started practising writing statements – MG11s, as they're known (it stands for Manual of Guidance form 11, and there are more than twenty different types of form you might have to use, and each one has to be completed in a certain way). This means that if you are a victim or witness in an incident, the police have to write down your account of what happened. It's a real art and a discipline, and there are so many rules you must follow, as they are what's read out in court. A bad statement can lose a case.

These rules were explained and we looked at different examples. Then Yasmin (who was our teacher that day) gave us all MG11s to fill in and told us to look out the window into the car park below. At that point we saw a woman walking to a car, fumbling in her bag for the keys, while a masked man ran up, they had a struggle and he took the bag and ran off.

Yasmin then turned and said: "Write a statement of what you saw."

Wow, it was suddenly a little more real. We then went through the statements and feedback was given. The mid-morning coffee break was called, and Paige was asked to stay. Not unusual; we often chatted with staff to clarify things.

We filed back in, comfortably sated with coffee and biscuits. This time Paige had arrived early and sat nearest the door. We were set a task of correcting a poorly written MG11. Suddenly, the door burst open, and two men in masks ran in, the first with a handgun (a cheap version of Colt model 1911 – I knew my guns) in his left hand, and the second with a sawn-off shotgun (double barrelled, side by side) held at the hip. Both were shouting, "Stay where you are. Don't fuckin' move!"

The first man reached out and grabbed Paige by the hair (unusually it was loose, unlike her normal, bomb-proof bun) with his right hand. She screamed and grabbed the hand holding her hair with both of her hands and was dragged screaming out of the room.

Instinctively, I made to stand up to help her, but before I could rise out of my seat, I was looking down the barrels of the sawn-off, with the owner shouting: "Don't fucking move or your head comes off!"

I had a nasty feeling of déjà vu from my days in the security firm, when I'd had a somewhat similar experience. I could see him look past me and, while still keeping the barrels of the shotgun hovering about a foot from my face, saying: "Sit the fuck down you two fucking heroes or this pig gets it!"

I could hear Angus and Paul sit back down.

Honestly, none of us really had much time to think. The men, having grabbed Paige, backed out of the room, and the door slammed shut.

As soon as they left, there was a moment of silence. Yasmin, who had remained calm and motionless in the teacher's chair, said in the same tone she'd used earlier: "Now write a statement of what you saw. You'll find a new MG11 under the one you were correcting."

There were a few expletives, and exhalations of breath. Yasmin stayed stock-still, expressionless.

Terry said: "Yasmin, is Paige all right?"

It was followed by a few noises of agreement. Yasmin calmly but firmly said: "Write your statement, please recruits – I won't answer any questions."

Even though I know adrenaline reduces your fine motor skills, it didn't stop my hands from shaking as I desperately tried to remember the correct order of the required parts of the statement. I looked down after I had finished, though my handwriting looked like the death throes of an ink-soaked spider crawling across the page. It was dreadful. This was clearly a test to see how we reacted to real conflict, and gave us an appreciation of what the victims and witnesses might be feeling. It sounds harsh, but I think it's necessary.

After we'd all completed our statements, we heard a knock at the door and in walked Paige nonchalantly, as if nothing had happened, and she received a round of applause and plenty of checks on her welfare. I noticed her bomb-proof bun was back in perfect form (how do women do that?).

At the end of the lesson, as we were walking out, Paige squeezed my arm, and said quietly: "Thank you, that was very brave! The staff instructor from D class said that's very unusual for someone to try and take them on."

I shrugged, a bit embarrassed. It had in no way been a conscious action, but purely instinctive. Bravery and courage come from conscious actions, not instincts. I felt myself welling up. It was a reaction to a burst of adrenaline. It moves emotions closer to the surface. So, I said gruffly: "No worries mate. It was just instinct. And it wasn't just me."

I had to get a grip of myself. It's unprofessional to cry in uniform!

Paige replied: "Thank you anyway!"

The rest of the week went without any further dramas, until the test on Friday. It was one of the tougher ones, with a couple of really dodgy trick questions. I saw them coming and worked hard to focus on them, finishing just as the timer pinged.

I could see worried faces as we walked out. Paul, Camilla, Pete and Karim looked particularly nervous. Not to be put off, John said: "Well, that was a fucking sneaky little bastard of a test. I could be taking an early bath after that one!"

That broke the tension and we sat in the canteen, our usual raucous selves, with a few notably quiet, though.

Sergeant Brownstone came in, calm and impassive as usual, and said: "Could Karim, Victoria and Pete go outside now please. The rest of you, please stay in your seats."

This was devastating. No one had been asked to step outside at that stage before. I could feel a tightness in my stomach. The three of them filed past, with the rest of us looking sympathetically on. When they'd left, Sergeant Brownstone said: "Everyone in this room has passed. Your friends did not. Don't worry, they won't be failing the course at this stage."

I could feel my hands shaking. I clasped them together to hide it. *I have to be strong*, I thought. *I'm the teacher. They'll need a calm voice of encouragement.* But honestly, I just wanted to cry; these were my friends. I know it sounds crazy, but they were my brothers and sister. I loved them.

The sergeant continued: "Scores are as follows: Paul 76 per cent, Paige 89 per cent, Terry 89 per cent, John 73 per cent." The rest were in the eighties. Then, "Richard, well done: 100%." I almost fell off my chair. There was a chorus of "well dones". It made me feel really guilty, like I was rubbing my friends' noses in it by doing so well. I didn't have to wait long for a humbling lesson.

I wanted to talk to my friends who'd failed, to offer them any sympathy I could and to find out what their situation was. But they weren't very talkative, and with the Friday rush to get on the Tube home, I didn't get a chance. So, it wasn't until the Monday that I could speak with them.

Monday rolled around and we were looking forward to the first videoed role play scenarios in the new video suite. This one, the first of four, had a grading system of one to four, with one being the best, two being good, three being acceptable (but borderline – only two of those were acceptable), and four being unacceptable (only one of those was allowed). So not much margin for error. Getting a good starting grade set you up for the other three.

That evening, I had a knock at the door. It was Karim. He looked dreadful, with all his usual bravado gone, shoulders hunched, face downturned. He came in and sat on the chair at the writing desk, not saying a word.

I said: "Karim mate, what's up?"

For a moment he tensed, then slowly relaxed, as if someone had walked over his grave. He slowly replied: "I can't fail this course."

I tried to empathise: "I know mate. I'm petrified of failing too!"

He looked up quickly and said in a harsh tone: "No, you don't get it. I can't fucking fail! They told me I'm the only Algerian in the Met, and they'll do anything to get me through. They won't let me fail."

Puzzled, I couldn't quite comprehend what he was getting at. So, I pushed further: "You mean they'll help you pass tests, personal tuition? That's good, isn't it? That means they want to help you."

At this stage, I hadn't caught on to what he was saying. This time he was angry. He balled his fists, and I could see he was on the brink of crying.

He raised his voice and said: "You don't fucking get it. I can fail every single fucking test, every single fucking practical, everything, and still pass out. This is not to help me, Karim, but because I'm Algerian! They don't look at me as Karim; they see me as a fuckin' ethnic, as a token. As a fucking flag to say, 'Look, we're not racists!' Oh they said it in a nice way, building bonds, be a voice for your community. Increasing diversity in the Met, a role-fuckin'-model for disenfranchised youth. If they see a face like yours in a uniform, they're more likely to join! You'll be the first of many. Mate!

"I hate this patronising shit so much! I've had it! THIS IS WHAT RACISM LOOKS AND FEELS LIKE! They don't think I can pass all the tests 'cos they think I'm some thick fuckin' ethnic! I'm going to tell that cunt in charge tomorrow just how far up his arse he can stick this fucking job! And I wanted this job so much, so much! I wanted to make my mom proud, to show her just what I can do. Actually making something of myself. I've been a disappointment to her all the way through my life. Just once, just FUCKING ONCE I WANTED TO ACTUALLY ACHIEVE SOMETHING WORTHWHILE.

"She moved here when I was little, from Algeria 'cos my worthless piece of shit dad was beating the crap out of her. It weren't easy growing up in Hackney. All the gangs, no one expected us to do anything other than rob and sell H. I was always getting into trouble. One day we were driving round like idiots, and my mate who was driving the car in front of me tried a stupid overtake on a lorry. He was going too fast, and lost it. He ploughed straight into that lorry. I'd known him all my life. He was the closest thing to a brother I'd ever had. I saw him die. I tried to help him. I tried and tried to get him to breathe. I kept calling his name. I was so stupid. He was in bits. His face was gone. Just blood and brains and skin. There was nothing I could do.

"Covered in his blood and brains, I just sat on the side of the road and cried. I was 16, and I just wanted to have died with him! I just wanted to die; there was nothing left. Then a policeman sat down next to me and put an arm around my shoulders and he talked to me. Not like I was a piece of shit, but like a father talks to a son. He calmed me down, not judging, not shouting, just gentle and kind, and honest.

"For the first time in my life, a policeman had cared about me. He drove me home to my mom, he kept in touch throughout the court case and inquest. Always there to support me, and listen.

"He was PC Cliff Montgomery. He helped me. He didn't see my skin colour; he just cared. I decided that I wanted to be a policeman. I could finally see a way out of my life. I could do something worthwhile. He gave me hope, and belief. I could be something better, to do some good, regardless of who the people were. Not race, sex, anything. Just helping. And now ... NOW they're taking that away from me. Not letting me achieve it, not the same as you or anyone else.

"I don't want special treatment! I just expect to be judged the same as you! These cunts are as racist as the skinheads who used to call me a Paki. Why? Why? 'Cos they think I can't make it without their help. Otherwise, why would they lower the standards? They expect less of me than you! How fucking racist is that? I'd rather be called a Paki than be thought of as less able than you because of the colour of my skin! They think they're helping, the self-righteous fucking idiots! I hate them for that! I hate them!"

He stopped, and bowed his head. I could see tears running down his cheeks, but he was too proud to acknowledge them.

I was stunned. I couldn't believe what I'd heard. I felt hollow inside, sick to the core. I believed in the same standards for everyone, so everyone knew that we'd all met those same standards. It was a shared respect. Positive discrimination? There's NOTHING positive about discrimination!

This wasn't about treating people equally. This wasn't it. The standards were based on your race, your sex. Different standards. Part of me wanted to quit as well. Why would I want to be part of that bullshit! I wanted to feel the satisfaction of telling the pompous arsehole of a superintendent where to stick his job. I started to feel an anger building. How dare they treat Karim like this. Make him feel his achievements were fake, that he hadn't earned his place as a policeman. A fake, a phoney. They weren't going to do that to my friend.

He wanted to help everyone. He wanted to be a part of an organisation that didn't care what people looked like, not judging them based on skin colour or sex, or sexuality. Content of character, not colour of skin.

Right, I thought, *it starts here*. Karim needs my help. *If it's us rank and file against the dickheads in charge, bring it on!* I looked at Karim, put my hand on his arm, and he looked up. I kept my voice low, but clear. I made eye contact and said: "Only thing you can do mate is show these worthless motherfuckers that you're Karim. You don't need their racist charity. You're good enough to pass out on merit, on your talent and hard work! Show them, show your mom, show PC Montgomery and, most importantly, show yourself that you're worth something. I know you can – I have faith in you. Every correct answer, every passed test, every passed physical and practical is a 'fuck you' to those cunts in charge!"

He looked at me for a long moment, nodded his head and said: "You're right. If I quit now, it'll prove them right, that I couldn't make it on my own merit, that I aren't worth anything! I won't do that. I'm going to pass every fucking exam, every test. I'm going to show them I don't need special treatment. You remind me of Cliff Montgomery. You'll be a really good policeman, and dad."

I could feel a lump in my throat, and wondered how much I needed to prove, and how much I missed my dad.

Karim got up and, with a grim determination, walked out without another word. I hoped that he'd stay the course. I got off my bed and sat down at the desk to continue my studies, with a lot to think about. Did I really want to be part of this organisation? Is this what Yasmin had been trying to tell me. I'd pass out, do my probation and get confirmed as a substantive PC, to prove I could do it. Then I'd decide whether to stay on.

Over the next couple of days, word spread in H class of what had been said to Karim. We were all rightly angry. No one thought it was right that there were different standards in play.

The rest of the week shot by, filled with going over the notes, various role plays both inside and out, where we practised how to speak to people as a police officer. We took turns playing victims, suspects, witnesses, with differing levels of believability based on our acting abilities. Apparently, I can play a pretty passable drunk. I leave you to draw your own conclusions. Thursday's assessed role play came around. This was held in a long, tall building with five rooms on either side on the ground floor. Above it in the centre was a viewing gallery, from which you could look down through a glass ceiling into the various rooms.

We'd individually be given a brief, and be sent into the rooms, while being watched by our classmates, and on video link by the instructors. Honestly, it felt false. You couldn't react naturally; you weren't truly immersed in the scenario and were trying desperately to remember the law. What do they want to see? Because the briefings were deliberately vague and misleading, it was easy to misread a situation and ignore the bloody obvious.

Well, that was my excuse as I walked out of there with a barely acceptable three. This wasn't helped by the fact everyone else in the class had got twos. Paige and Paul had got ones. It turned out Paul had found his niche; he was so good at dealing with people. It came naturally to him, we could all see it – students, staff, everyone. He had that rare gift of being very hard to dislike. He was, by far, the best police officer in our class. The academic stuff was where he struggled which, ironically enough, was only really relevant at Hendon.

For me, it wasn't a total disaster, but it did put pressure on the rest of my practicals. I was crushed. I could see the others looking on with pity.

I started to realise what Paul was going through every week. How could he do it, walk that tightrope, see the pitying looks and the words of 'encouragement'?

The following day, during the test, I could feel my mind wandering back to the role play, playing it over and over in my mind, all the negative thoughts of how stupid I was, that I was fooling myself I was good enough.

That led to me scoring my lowest score yet: 80 per cent. Still OK, but it did get a few looks. Karim knocked it out the park with a 97 per cent. At this, he turned in the direction of the Chief Superintendent's office, stuck two fingers up and said under his breath, "Fuck you." PC McNish saw this and scowled. At the end of the class, he asked Karim to stay.

When we caught up with Karim later, we asked him about it. He said he'd been honest, and told McNish everything. At this, McNish had clapped him on his shoulder and said: "You're learning, son, but be careful where you do it next time!" This brought forth another round of laughter, and a different opinion of McNish. Maybe it wasn't just us against the management; we had allies.

We could now park in Hendon, so I took the opportunity to drive my Essex boy-racer car up. When I'd picked up the parking pass from the gate guard, I was acutely aware of the disapproving looks it was getting as I drove it through Hendon. Not sure which bit it was – the lowered suspension, the pink and grey go-faster stripes down the side, the huge whale-tail on the boot, or the extra loud exhaust. I did feel like I'd brought a lamb into a wolves' den. I was waiting to be stopped and the car to be taken off and crushed.

When my friends saw the car, the merciless ribbing went into overdrive. Paige was beside herself, giggling like a schoolgirl. The only ones who didn't rip the piss out of me were Paul and Richard E. Paul asked me a whole load of technical spec questions about it, and Richard E asked if I wanted to sell it.

Paige was doubled over laughing at this possibility, that someone would want to buy such a monstrosity. Although I was used to this response, this was a new level of piss-taking. In between her bouts of giggling, Paige managed to ask where the sun strip was with "Wayne and Tracy"? Ha bloody ha! She then pointed out that there had been a large decal along the side. She eventually worked it out from the marks in the paint. She said, between fits of laughter: "Why did it say, 'Deaf by Decibels' along the side?"

Huge laughter.

Rather defensively I replied: "It used to be a demonstrator car for a car stereo installers called Decibels."

Once again, huge laughs. I was beginning to think it was a mistake. This was compounded when the training staff (I wonder who tipped them off ... Paige!) started making wisecracks about Essex boys and their XR3is. You can really go off someone, Paige!

The next few weeks ground on by, with the weekly tests, physicals and practicals. I continued with scores in the eighties, but my confidence had been knocked. I passed all the physicals, but picked up another three in the role play, and then a two. It came down to the last role play. A two would be an automatic pass. I didn't want to know what a three meant.

During this time, I had to report to the infirmary for sick parade. The dodgy food had finally caught up with me, with very unpleasant results. It's times like those you find out how petty bureaucracy works. There were forms to fill out, a return from sickness interview. The hardest part was not shouting at the inspector when he indicated that sickness was frowned upon, and that if I missed any more days, I might have to be back-classed (nightmare – leaving all my friends and joining the newest intake and having to go through it all again), all for being ill through the dodgy food they had provided. It wasn't just me – there were a number of us who were incapacitated from the dodgy food, and all of us went through the same BS.

God, I hated the rigid, unthinking following of rules, when they're clearly absurd. I hated it so, so much!

Camilla (with much training and encouragement) finally passed the bleep test – barely though, meeting the minimum required level and stopping.

At this stage we started what was euphemistically called "officer safety training". Giving a bunch of recruits a metal baton, a pair of rigid handcuffs and CS spray and telling to practise on each other doesn't involve officers being safe!

We received our ASPs (two-and-a-half-feet long, extendable metal truncheons), technically called a 'friction lock baton'. You extended them by swinging them, and the two sections extended out from the handle. You caused them to retract back into the 7.5-inch handle by reversing your grip so that the extended part faced downward and giving them a good, hard thump on the ground. This caused them to fully retract. That was usually fine until you were in a seventeen-floor tower block with a bunch of overly excitable young men practising extending and retracting the said ASPs (feel free to make up your own jokes), which involved them loudly closing the ASPs on the floor endlessly, especially when you were trying to sleep.

As I have already mentioned, the men and women were segregated in different tower blocks, with security sitting in the lobby at a desk checking the sex of those people who entered or left. This was only a slight impediment to the course of true love (or lust), because there was a shared basement where there were washing machines. So all one had to do was take the lift to the basement, walk to the other lift and go up to the desired floor for your illicit rendezvous. I am told it was a regular occurrence.

However, one particularly hot night, I was awoken by the sounds of such an, errr, romantic encounter. It was coming (so to speak) from outside. I peered out into the gloom and looked down to where the wheelie bins were stored (classy), and I could just make out (ha-ha) a couple in the shadows. Upon completion (?) of this activity, there was a ragged round of applause from the block. This was followed by some laughing from the couple, and I swear the bloke took a bow. Who said romance is dead!

During one of these weeks, we were ordered to attend a briefing in the lecture hall. This wasn't that unusual, as we'd regularly all be called in for one of the (far too many) senior (never call them superior, as merely the fact they have attained a higher rank does not make them right or better, as my grandad used to say) officers to shout and berate us all for the minor infringements of a few. One could speculate as to their motives, but that would be rather petty.

The usual berating began (the chief superintendent this time – it must be something bad), but this time he said: "The Macpherson Report into the murder of Stephen Lawrence has been published. It will say that the Met is institutionally racist. It'll say that we failed that young man and his family because we treated him differently because of his race. That we didn't investigate it thoroughly due to our racism. We will publicly admit we, as a force, are institutionally racist. Changes will and are being made to combat this. So, when you go home, admit to your family you're racist. You need to admit this before you can fight it.

"So, what does that mean for you? We as an organisation are racist. I am racist, you are racist. I'm not just talking about the systems and organisation. It means you as individuals are ALL RACIST. We have already implemented special training starting next week to show you your racism. You'll be given a folder of terms that are considered offensive, and their acceptable alternatives. We will not tolerate racism in the Met. If you hear anyone saying anything racist, it is your duty to report it. If you do not, you too could and will be kicked out. I've already done that to a number of the people on your course, and I am proud to have done it. Remember, YOU ARE A RACIST!"

This (even by their standards) was harsh. To be flat out called a racist was shocking. No one had ever seriously called me – a Labour-voting, liberal teacher – a racist. It left me stunned.

After the lecture, as we were walking away from the hall, Karim walked up to me, and when he was certain we wouldn't be overheard, said: "Well, mate, what do you think of that?"

I replied: "I can't believe it. How am I going to tell my mom that in a few months I've been turned into a racist!"

He laughed a humourless laugh and said: "You think you've got trouble; I've got to translate that into Algerian and tell my mother I hate myself!"

I replied with an equally humourless laugh. I guess we were all in it together. Everyone outside the police would view us as racist and hate us. Our own 'senior (mis)management' had branded us all racists. I had seen absolutely no evidence my colleagues were racist. In fact, quite the opposite. We all just got on, and it was the most accepting environment I'd ever worked, in which you were judged by what you did and said, not what you were. So why had the management said this? The only conclusion I could come to was fear. They were afraid of being seen as racists, and they were prepared to sacrifice us, the rank and file, to draw attention away from themselves. They'd made no defence of the rest of us who were good, decent, hard-working police officers. Cowards! So, if it was us versus the world, so be it!

Honestly, I'd been really impressed with the way Karim had gone after his task of passing everything. He was working like a Trojan. "You can't control what life throws at you, only how react," as my mom was want to say.

The training continued. The exam grades were pretty much in line with what we'd already had. As promised, the next week brought our racial awareness training. We had training on how different communities might see things.

It's not called 'stop and search' in the police. The technical term is: "detaining for the purposes of search under sec.1 of PACE (Police and Criminal Evidence) Act 1984." It also talked about the things you could do that might cause offence. Finally, we came to the talk from a community leader.

We were told he would go in and the staff would leave the room, and nothing said was going to leave the room. Yeah, right! We'd already heard rumours of people being forced to leave because of one ill-considered word or comment. At that stage, with much invested in our police careers, no one was going to chance it.

Our training staff left, and the community leader walked in. He was a tall Black gentleman in his mid-forties, who sat down and proceeded to explain to us that he couldn't be racist, because he was Black. That we could be racist, because we were white. That racism wasn't discrimination or prejudice based on race; it was prejudice plus privilege. We were privileged because we were white and we were oppressing Black and Asian people. Basically, we were evil because of our race. And regardless of what we said or did, we'd always be evil.

At this point, no one wanted to say a word; it could literally be the end of your policing career, and the Met could jump up and down saying they were doing something about racism by sacking 'racist' officers.

At the end of his lecture, he asked for questions. Silence (unusual as that was for the Animal House). He wasn't impressed and left, but we'd survived. No one dared say anything where they could be overheard. Suffice to say none of us were in the slightest bit racist, and we did not agree with a word of what he had said, or his ideology.

There was no time to dwell on these negative thoughts. The juggernaut that is Hendon just kept on rolling. Tests, assessments, role plays.

The next few weeks shot by, until we were within sight of the finish line, with four weeks to go. A new intake had just arrived, and we were being drilled regularly by our new nemesis: the drill sergeants. Unless you've had to endure drill sergeants, it's hard to fully explain the fear and dread you feel when you're about to start a series of marching manoeuvres, with the clear knowledge that if you get it even slightly wrong, you'll be publicly humiliated, berated and shamed, then required to do the same thing again. The thing is, it's not just you involved, because there might be up to a hundred others relying on you. If you get it wrong, they look like idiots as well. There's absolutely nowhere to hide on a drill square.

There was a series of outside trainers who came in to teach us first aid and give a lecture on what a bomb looks like (that was a one-hour lecture, I kid you not). A lady came to speak to us about domestic violence. It was a closed session, just the class and her. We didn't sit in our usual classroom; it was a quiet, more comfortable and private room.

The lady was in her forties, with light-coloured hair, and she was very quietly spoken. She started off telling us about how she'd fallen in love with a guy. He seemed really kind. They got married, and had a daughter. At this point, things went wrong. He became abusive: shouting, berating and belittling her, then physically hitting her. Each time, it got a little worse. Then, after, he'd apologise and promise it wouldn't happen again. She was torn, still in love with him, and wanting their daughter to grow up in a cohesive family.

Things got worse and worse: hospital visits, trying to hide the injuries, lying to her family, friends, the hospital staff. Eventually, she called the police. The response wasn't great, and she continued to be treated worse and worse. Serious injuries, hospital stays. Then he tried to kill her, and she thought of her daughter growing up without a mother. That's what made her cut ties, but he followed her. Eventually he was arrested and gaoled. But it took years.

Honestly, I had never heard such a horrible story. It broke my heart. I wasn't alone; there were plenty of tears. We were all struck by her courage, and had huge sympathy for this poor lady.

When it was time for questions, Victoria asked what help there was for women in terms of shelters. The lady said there were quite a few set up for women, but none set up for men, and that men made up (at that time) about one third of victims. This was a shock, not only to me, but we were stunned. Women attacking men? But if that was the case, why were there none set up to help men?

She could see our surprised reactions, and she said the lady who set up the first shelters for women had done so off her own bat, and had plenty of help and assistance from men, who were horrified at the plights of these women. This came to the attention of some of the biggest feminist organisations. They started to provide financial support, on the proviso that men would not be involved, as they were thought to be untrustworthy, and might scare the women there. That hadn't been the case, but the shelters needed their money.

When there were five or six women's shelters set up, the lady who set up the first one decided to set up one for men. At this, all the feminist organisations said they refused to support it (fair enough, feminists support women, right?), and they went further. They said if she did set up one for men, they'd withdraw all their funding to the women's ones as well. They didn't want men to be seen as victims, so they'd prefer to see the women's shelters close than a man's one open. They went further still, and wrestled control of the women's shelters away from her and stopped her from entering or having any contact with the shelters she'd set up. They hounded her so badly that she moved abroad.

My jaw hit the floor. I was a lefty, Labour-voting liberal teacher, who considered himself a feminist. I wasn't the only one. We all left that lecture with our eyes fully opened to just how manipulated our views had been. We were being force-fed a diet of harsh realities; it was a lot to take in.

The following was the last role play, and I scraped in with a two. Right down to the wire. We started making plans for our passing-out parade on Friday.

On the Monday of the fourteenth week, we were all sitting rather nonchalantly waiting for our morning lecture. At that point, we were all pretty confident we'd make it. Some by the skin of our teeth (Paul had consistently got low seventies all the way through, but had aced it in all the other aspects of the course) but, as a class, we'd done it! We should have taken the advice of Hans Solo to Luke Skywalker: "Don't get cocky kid; we aren't there yet."

In walked Yasmin. She was by this stage visibly pregnant, and not wearing uniform (she said they didn't make a uniform for pregnancy). We all stood up and said the now routine, "Morning Staff!" She smiled (without her usual beaming grin), and said: "Please sit down. Before we start today's lesson, the stations you've been assigned to have come through, as well as your numbers."

There was a sharp intake of breath, and whispers, and we started looking around, wondering who we'd be working with. Until then it hadn't seemed real, that it would all end. The people we'd struggled with, cried with, encouraged, rooted for, argued with and competed against would soon be gone. And we'd have more tests, more training and a whole new family to try to find our places in.

So, with excitement tinged with sadness, we waited. I just wanted one person I knew. Please!

Yasmin said: "Right, Richard Armstrong 272PT, that's Earlham. That's in the East End. And Terry you're 273PT, also at Earlham."

Relief! At least I knew someone, and apparently there were ten more from our course split up between the two police stations. Paige was off to Paddington, Pete and John to Park street, Karim to (surprise, surprise) Hackney (the largest Algerian community in London).

By the end, we'd all got our postings. Most weren't too disappointed. We could put our metal letters and numbers which identified us on our epaulettes. It was becoming all too real. This was going to be my new identity. I ceased being Richard Armstrong, the police recruit, and became PC 272PT. It's a number I'll remember for the rest of my life.

We were all a little too excited to fully concentrate on our studies, and Yasmin had to work harder than was fair to get us through it. Just three more exams to go.

At the end of the morning session (traffic tickets – I hate traffic, give me villains to nick), Yasmin asked Paige and me to stay behind.

As our friends were all leaving, buoyed trying to find others with whom they were going to share a station (new bonds made, old ones weakening), Yasmin asked me to close the door. This wasn't too unusual. I did so and waited. Yasmin looked at us for a minute, as if debating whether to say something or not. Eventually, she took a deep breath and said: "They want to fail Paul!"

I was lost for words. I looked at Paige and we both said: "Why?"

I continued: "He's the best police officer amongst us, and has passed all the exams. His practical scores are brilliant."

Yasmin, I could see, was barely keeping it together, and a tear rolled down her face. I stopped and gave her a moment, as she clearly cared about all of us. She said quietly: "I know he hasn't failed any exams, but his average grades are low. If he doesn't get decent grades in the remaining three exams, he's out."

Paige piped up: "But Yasmin, plenty of people have failed three or four exams, and don't have the grades in the practicals Paul has. Why would they do this? It's just not fair! I don't understand?"

Yasmin waited a moment and said: "Think about which people have failed those exams. Do you not notice a pattern?" I looked at Paige, and was really confused. Surely there was one standard, one set of rules, the same for everyone? Surely Karim was a one-off?

Yasmin continued: "It's because he's a male and white. They have enough white men in the police. They don't care about him. They'll only help women or Black or Asian people."

I sat back in my seat, stunned. There it was, straight out. Paige was beginning to get angry, not at Yasmin, but at the system. She resisted the urge to snap. It was Yasmin; it wasn't her fault.

Paige finally said: "But you can help him, can't you? I know other staff have tutored recruits to help them. Why can't you do it for Paul?"

Yasmin looked down for a moment, and said: "We've been ordered to not say anything, any of us. When Gary (Sergeant Johnson) and Amanda (Sergeant Brownstone) heard, they went to the course inspector, then over his head to the superintendent. They fought, and argued, and had a shouting match. They were both disciplined for it. We were ordered not to help him. ORDERED not to help him. They didn't care about him because of his sex and race. They just don't care."

I was so grateful and impressed with our sergeants; they really did care about us, and were prepared to go into bat for us.

I said: "Why are you telling us then, if you've been ordered not to? Won't you get into trouble?"

Yasmin gave a wan smile and said quietly: "You really think they'd discipline me? I'd take them to the cleaners! Just let them try!"

I wondered if she was referring to the fact that she that was female, Asian or pregnant?

A steely grin danced across her features. She looked at Paige then settled her gaze on me. "We want you two to do what we can't. You need to get Paul into the eighties for the last exams, preferably at least one in the nineties! You're our ace in the hole, our last chance. We've fought as hard as we can without being sacked. As it is, I think Gary will be moved on from Hendon fairly soon."

Teacher mode initiated. "Right! Challenge accepted," I said. "Looks like me and the Gigglebox (Paige's nickname; she did like to giggle a lot) here have our work cut out. No disrespect to Paul. I'm up for the challenge. What about you, Shorey?"

Paige looked slightly offended and said: "There's no way in hell I'm letting them chuck Paul off this course. If he goes, so do I! It's not coming to that. We're going to get him through this, if we have to drag him kicking and screaming."

I had a thought: "Agreed! Does Paul know yet?"

Yasmin looked at me and said: "Gary will tell him when he gets back after lunch. By the way, you'd better go now, or you'll miss out on all the lovely food."

As we walked to the canteen, Paige and I were planning our tutoring strategy. We'd meet in my room with Paul at 7 p.m., straight after the evening meal, and we'd work to 11 p.m. He was in for a shock to the system.

Paul came back after his talk with Gary, trying hard not to show his shock. It must have been devastating to get so close, and having the possibility of having it snatched at the last minute. When I spoke to him, he was a bit reluctant to come to my room. But I sat him down and laid it on the line to him, how much the staff were risking. And that Paige would kill him if he didn't at least try. I then said we'd both quit if they chucked him off the course. That did it.

The three of us met up in my room, with Paige having to do the cloak-and-dagger trick of using the lift to the basement. I think she quite liked the excitement of it.

When we got started, it was hard work. Not being nasty to Paul, but the way Paige and I worked was entirely different from the way he did. It took a lot of false starts, and Paul walking away in frustration, but he was determined, and so were Paige and I. The first night was the worst. We got precisely nowhere. I think he was more confused by the end. But the Tuesday night, we made a bit of progress. And slowly, then quickly, we got him into the mindset to think at a different level. It was without doubt the hardest I've ever worked in terms of teaching. By the end of the week, Paige and I were knackered. But when the results came out, Paul had got 84 per cent, the best score he'd achieved by far. It was good, but we needed better.

We hadn't told the others, but they were getting suspicious. John made a crack: "You know, I've seen a bloke have a woman in his room, I've seen him have a man in his room. But I have to take my hat off to you, Richard; you've had a man and a woman in your room every night for a week. Fair play mate, good effort!"

A huge laugh went up, and we had to let the rest of the class into the secret, on strict instructions not to share with anyone, because of the dire consequences for staff if it got out.

The next week was the second to last week, and it was a tough exam. But Paul was so determined, he got 90 per cent. Outstanding mate! He was working so hard. But was it enough?

The last test week rolled around, and the following week was the interview training week, when we'd be doing lots of drill practice. We'd sent out our invitations for the parade to our friends and family. I just hoped Paul would be with us.

We were nominally on a rotation for fire picket duty. This meant, in the event of a fire drill, those on the rota would have to get the boards with the class names on and organise our classes so that the names could be checked off. During that week, it was A class's turn. But no one had ever been called on to do it.

At 3 a.m., the loudest fire alarms I have ever heard sounded. I am a heavy sleeper normally, but I was out of bed in a flash, pulling on my clothes, and then I found just how long it takes to run down seventeen floors, because the lift was off line during a fire alarm. As I was hurtling down the stairs, I saw that metal hook, under the window; it was there to allow the fire brigade to attach a ladder or rope to get down. Funny what you think about as you're running down stairs in the middle of the night.

We made it downstairs, if a little out of breath, and lined up at our posts, to see a number of fire engines pull in. It was only the men's block that had the fire alarm, but the women had been awoken by all the noise. The fire engines lined up very close to the women's block.

I'm a pretty broad-minded and easy-going person, but, my God, I was shocked at what the women were doing, leaning out the windows, catcalling the burly firemen. You'd have thought it was a Chippendales show. Here are a few of the more printable ones: "There's a fire up here. I need a big, strong fireman with a big hose to put it out." "I want to slide down your greasy pole." "Here, darling, that's a big axe. There's something up here that need's splitting." "I might need two of you boys to put out the fire in my room." "Oh, please, I hope your ladder is long enough to reach my window. There's some damsels in distress in here who need rescuing." "Phwoar, he's hunky. Oye, big boy, you could give me fireman's lift any day." "I think your helmet needs me to shine it for you. I'm really good at spit and polish!"

The firemen seemed to be taking this in their stride. The senior management, not so much. I swear their only contribution was to go around and shout at the people who were actually doing the job (no change there!).

It turned out one of the new intake had been showing off to his mates how to light a hair spray with a lighter, right under a smoke detector. What a MUPPET. He was asked to leave in the morning.

If we thought we'd had a bollocking before, oh boy, did we get one the next morning. Everyone got it: the boys, for setting it off, the girls for the catcalling. He threatened to sack us all and cancel the passing-out parade. But it was an idle threat (I could be really catty and say "a bit like him," but I shan't).

Finally, the last exam came around. I have never been so nervous about an exam, not on my degree finals, teaching, nothing. I wanted Paul to pass so, so much. I was shaking.

After what seemed like an age, the results were in, and Sergeant Brownstone made us wait, with the slightest hint of a smile. She waited to give his result until last. "Paul ... Excellent result: 100 per cent. Well done! We are so proud of you, Paul!"

We were cheering, really cheering. We went over to Paul and gave him a group hug. He was so embarrassed. Paige and I high-fived. Honestly, I was so, so happy he'd done it. It took Sergeant Johnson's arrival to quieten us.

He nodded to Sergeant Brownstone, and she went out through the door, and closed it after her. He then waved everyone forward and, in hushed tones, said: "Paul, that's brilliant, really brilliant, you can be proud of yourself. We're all proud of you. It's not over yet, though."

There was a sudden hush. No, no, they weren't going to get rid of him with these scores. They couldn't. Sergeant Johnson, said: "Look, it'll still go to a board of management and trainers, but you've given us the ammunition to fight your corner. I can't guarantee anything, but it's Amanda, oops, I mean Sergeant Brownstone, who's been picked to speak on your behalf. I'm not allowed because of last time. Trust me, she's a real fighter; there's no one in the Met who'd battle harder for you. She's brilliant! Now get your stuff together, Paul. I'll walk you over there now. The rest of you wait here, and read up on the notes for the PACE interview course next week. Please behave!"

We all wished Paul good luck. I honestly think he was overwhelmed by it. By nature, he was a bit quiet, and almost shy at times. This outpouring of support really touched him.

Despite our best efforts, we really couldn't concentrate. We'd agreed that if they failed Paul, we'd all resign in protest!

An hour went by, nothing! Two hours, and the door opened, and in walked Paul, face downturned, shoulders hunched forward, followed by

Sergeant Johnson, who also looked crestfallen. How could they have done this? Why had they whipped the rug from under Paul's feet? He'd done everything they'd asked him to.

Then, with a huge grin, Paul said: "I'm passing out with you. We started as a team; we'll end as a team." We started cheering, then the chant was started, I'm not sure by whom: "Paul! Paul! Paul! Paul!"

He grinned and performed a mock bow.

The rest of the day was filled with congratulations and thanks to the staff. The relief was tangible. But it wasn't quite over yet, as the staff pointed out to us.

But that weekend, we went home buoyed. We'd done it! We'd ALL PASSED.

The last week shot by. We were very busy with the PACE interview training. This was less intense, with no tests, just feedback and advice on how to improve. This wasn't conducted by our own staff. They were new. The female officer who was running our course made us realise just how fortunate we'd been with our staff. She was arrogant, rude and mean-spirited, picking on anyone who annoyed her, and flirting with the guys she fancied.

We were drilling for the parade two hours a day. Trust me, that's not fun. The number of times we messed up, and were shouted at, made us all cranky by the end of the week.

Our staff were busy completing all their paperwork for the course (I pitied them, I knew what that was like). Yasmin was having time off for scans, but promised to be back for our parade. Jokingly, she wondered if anyone had given birth at a passing-out parade before.

We'd all chipped in and Camilla and Paige went out to buy cards and presents for our staff.

The day before our passing-out parade, we all went over to where our training staff were working and made a presentation to them. Cards, flowers, chocolates, bottles of booze. A huge card for Yasmin and an even larger teddy bear, with baby clothes for the little one.

There were many tears, and hugs and thank yous. Paul turned up with a VHS tape, and we scrambled to find a working player. There was a big scrum to watch it.

When everyone had settled down, we pressed play. It started with him doing silly stunts on his motorcycle around the old perimeter road (well away from prying eyes). He then rode up to the camera, jumped off, ran over, took his helmet off and delivered a truly moving speech. He said that he'd grown up on a rough housing estate in south London, his dad had left when he and his brother were little, his brother had got into drugs, had died of an overdose, and if he could stop even one person from doing that, he'd feel like a success. He added that he had dyslexia, and no one had ever stood up for him like that and helped him. There were more tears. He explained that he found it easier to say what he really felt, rather than writing it down. There were more tears and hugs. It was emotional, folks.

Just one more day. However, that evening, we all adjourned to the bar for one more drink. Just one, because marching on a hot day in front of your nearest and dearest is not the time to have a hangover.

I sought out a quiet corner. It had been such a busy day, and I was trying to get my head straight for the next day. There was a lot riding on this and I didn't want to let anyone down. I began thinking of my family, my little brother. Why had I not invited him? We were very limited on the number of guests, but I knew I'd regret not inviting him.

Staring off into the middle distance (my dad used to say, sometimes I sit and think, and sometimes I just sit), I was just sitting. Letting my mind wander. The chair scraped on the floor next to me, and I snapped back. It was Karim, drink in hand. He looked at me, saying: "Nervous about tomorrow? I know I am. I really want to make my mom proud."

I held up my glass, saying: "Mate, you already have, the way you've pulled things around, passing every test, every practical. You put me to shame. You earned it! You can be proud man. I salute you."

We clinked glasses. He said, in a more serious tone: "Thank you. That talk you gave me, and all the help. I would have quit without it."

I shook my head and replied: "We are a team. We all helped each other. I wouldn't have made it without you guys either."

He nodded, and said: "True, but thanks brother. I'd better go and say goodbye to the others. I won't forget what you did for me."

At that we shook hands and he walked off.

I started thinking about the people who wouldn't be there the next day: my dad, my brother who lived on the other side of the world. Was I doing the right thing? Hendon was one thing, a controlled environment with rules (even if those in charge changed them for political reasons), but the streets were a different thing entirely. I'd be starting from scratch again. The new boy who knew nothing. Another eighteen months of probation, with more hoops to jump through than a performing seal.

The chair next to me scraped on the floor again. I looked over, and it was Angus. His face was its usual unreadable self. He held two empty glasses in his hand. He set the glasses down on the table in front of me, and did a quick look around to see if we were being watched and, when he was satisfied we weren't, he produced a small bottle of malt whisky from inside his jacket, from which he quickly poured two decent shots of whisky. Not too much, but just enough to get a taste, and a slight buzz.

He grinned, and said: "I told you we'd share a wee dram before we left. This is the good stuff, not the over-priced English muck they serve here!"

He picked up his glass, and we clinked glasses, and I said: "Good luck to us both. I think we're going to need it."

He nodded and took a good mouthful. I'm not a huge whisky drinker, but I had to give it him – whatever this was, it was smooth, and I savoured it. I felt a slight buzz fill my head. There was a gentle tang as it slid down my throat, and it had a smoky bite to it. For a moment, I was back on Lindisfarne (The Holy Island) as a kid, with the small log fires burning, keeping the cottages warm. The sky was dark and brooding, with thunderheads rumbling in some distant overture. I relaxed, for what seemed like the first time in months.

I looked up at Angus, and he too was lost in his memories. Then he snapped out of it, and we drained our glasses without a word. Sometimes they aren't necessary. I think we were both of a similar mindset. He looked at me and said: "Well, we did it! Between you me, and Paige, we got all these youngsters (looking at Paul and Karim, who were laughing the loudest, and telling stories) through. It's up to them now."

I nodded. I looked at him and started to speak. He stopped me, and said: "You don't need to say it, mate. I think we both know that what comes next is the real test. You're not the worst Englishman I've met."

He got up, patted me on the shoulder, and said: "Take care mate, and watch your back."

I nodded, and replied: "You too. Remember to duck."

He grinned, and then walked off. I'd miss that guy. For all his tough military ways, he was a genuinely grounded and decent man who had a deep sense of honour and unselfish civil duty. I then went back to my own thoughts, as the buzz slowly faded.

Once again, I heard the stool next to me scrape on the floor. I looked up at Paige. I smiled; there was a symmetry: we started together, we finished together.

"Going all moody on me, Richard? That's not like you." A big grin spread across her face.

I replied: "No, just thinking, thinking about the end of something, the start of something else. About what we've got to do tomorrow, hoping I'm not the one to screw it up. Excited about going on relief, but I'll really miss everyone. Even you, Gigglebox! Especially you, Paige!" I looked down, and let out a deep sigh. "I'm scared mate. I'm scared!"

Paige punched me in the arm, hard!

"Ouch! What's that for?"

She moved closer and said: "Listen here, Richard, don't be such a wuss! You will make new friends and move on. But what we went through together, all of us, how we all got through, against the odds, against the bloody stupid management – no one can take that away from us. We achieved something. Be proud!"

I sat and thought about what she'd said. She was right.

Paige waited a moment and said: "On a lighter note, who've you got coming tomorrow? I've got Brian, my mom and dad."

I took a mouthful of my diet coke (clear head for tomorrow) and replied: "My mom. You'll like her. My dad's sister to represent him, and Victoria and Julia."

Paige said: "That's good. Who are Victoria and Julia? Your sisters?"

I took a deep breath; this was going to get complicated: "Victoria's a ... friend I met during my teacher training, and Julia's a copper from West London who encouraged me to join."

I knew Paige would pick up on it. She looked at me with a hard stare.

"There's more to this, Richard. I won't let it go. Share!"

I knew I couldn't keep things from her. She wasn't going let up. "I met Victoria whilst training to be a teacher, and fell in love with her the first moment I saw her. I've never felt anything like it before or since. I waited a year until I was sure. We met up to start our second year. We both said we had something to tell each other. She made me go first (that's a decision I think about every day): I told her I loved her, she told me she was a lesbian."

There it was, out in the open. Not something I share with many people. Paige shook her head and said: "Oh Richard, that explains it. Julia's Victoria's girlfriend, and you're still in love with her, aren't you!?"

I nodded, and looked down. For once, I didn't have a comeback. She'd nailed it.

Paige said: "You'll spend the rest of your life mooning over her, won't you? You'll miss out on all the great women who are interested in you and could make you happy. I felt something from the start; I could flirt with you because you were safe. You weren't ever going to make a move on me, because you're already in love. I just couldn't quite put my finger on it. Damn, you're a stubborn fool. She'll eventually need to move on and ditch you. It'll break your heart all over again. And you'll spend the rest of your life alone. There's nothing I, or anyone else, can do to help, is there?"

Bloody hell, I knew she was right on all counts. How could she know that? But she was right, and I knew it. I just nodded.

She said: "You're a bloody silly, romantic fool, and I don't know whether to scream at you, or cry for you. Here's everyone else struggling on the surface, and there you are dying on the inside." She then hugged me. She said quietly, so no one else could hear: "Thank you, Richard. Life's going to get really tough for you. Promise me you won't give up! Promise me!"

I said: "I promise, Paige."

We both gently broke the hug, and I said, as Paige made a move to walk away: "After tomorrow, do you think we'll see each other again?"

She smiled and winked, saying: "Count on it!"

The next day, I woke up, nice and early. It was going to be a long day. I looked out the window; it was a beautiful day, with blue skies and white clouds, reminding me of that first day, when it all started.

Right, back to the task in hand. I got the shoebox out and cleaned my shoes for the hundredth time. There's a real art to get the mirror-like shine. Thanks Angus! I went over my uniform making sure everything was perfect. I walked through in my head the marching sequence, then packed away anything I didn't need. We'd do the parade, see our families, take our oath. Our families would leave, and we'd have a party and leave Saturday morning, reporting on Monday to our new stations.

Before we did anything, we sat with our class and instructors for the passing-out picture you'll likely see on the wall of every Met Police officer, past or present, arranged in three rows, instructors at the front, tall people at the back. As we were all preparing, Yasmin walked up, rocking a lightweight pink outfit (a rebel to the last, I loved that lady). We spent time chatting to her. I shook her hand, and thanked her. She gave me a beautiful smile told me to go and enjoy my special day.

We got prepared. A few last-minute words of encouragement, plenty of deep breaths. We were off: left, right, left, right. It had to be precise and focused, but you had to relax just enough not to look too stiff-limbed. That was called being a "teddy bear" or "wooden top" (by the ever-so-polite drill staff).

Getting into a rhythm, first the mounted branch would walk around and into the parade square where our loved ones were, and all the great and the good. The marching band were next. We were keeping time behind them. The beat was great for keeping time to. It all just clicked into place. All those hours of frustrating practice. It was hot in our tall hats and tunics. I could feel the wind rushing past my face. We were close in together. It requires great trust to move at such a fast pace, an arm's length away from each other. One mistake and everyone can trip up.

Then I looked on in horror as our inspector (who had not taken part in any of the rehearsals) took the lead. It was embarrassing. He was a big, tall teddy bear, arms and legs as stiff as boards. I could just make out a number of groans. After all our hard work, this muppet was going to look bad in front of our families.

Finally, we made it into the parade square, with one entire side made up of seats for our friends and family. One full lap, marching at a pace that allowed no room for error.

Back to line up, facing our families. Then the trickiest part: as a line we, on a command, moved forward and stopped dead in the middle of the square in perfect lines. This is a lot harder than it looks.

They then handed over the colours. The guest of honour gave a speech. We weren't really listening, but were trying spot our families in the crowd.

Eventually it was over. We turned, made one final lap of the square, marching past our families. Then we were out of the square to the escape into the safety of the access road. The halt was called, and we were dismissed to go and meet our families and take them to the hall for our oath ceremony. Then a buffet, then we were done.

The parade had gone off without a hitch. Flawless. There were lots of hugs and high fives. Now to see our families. I so wish my dad and brother could have been there. It's one of the biggest regrets that they couldn't. I will always regret it.

I went to find my mom, aunt and Victoria and Julia. I quickly found them. My mom was so taken aback with me in uniform. Honestly, it was the proudest day of my life. I knew, for absolute certain, she was proud of me, with her son carrying on the family tradition. To see her son wear the same uniform as her dad was special. My aunt was so proud; her uncle had been a deputy chief constable. I told you it was in the family.

Victoria was there, smiling and happy. Honestly, if I could pick one day to be my last, it was that day. As we were waiting to go into the hall to take our oath of service, my mom handed me a silver police whistle. I looked at it, and it was old.

She said quietly: "Richard (she always called me that), it's your great-grandad's and it's over a hundred years old. He passed it on to your grandad, and he carried it throughout his career. They would have wanted you to carry it too. Remember to always stay true to the oath you'll take. I'm so proud of you son."

She squeezed my arm and smiled. I could feel a lump in my throat. I couldn't cry, not in front of my friends.

We filed in, sat down and then one of the senior officers I hadn't seen much got up and explained that it was the first one of these he'd done. He then referenced the similar scene in the film *Police Academy* (without being explicit, but everyone knew what he meant) where hiding in the lectern was a prostitute who gave the senior officer a blow job. Who do you think laughed loudest out of the hundreds of family and friends? My mom! My quiet, well-spoken, Methodist mom. The woman who never swore, was never rude. It was my mom. All my friends noticed, much to their amusement.

Then the oath, and we stood up and recited it:

"I Richard Robert Armstrong, as a Constable of the Metropolitan Police Service solemnly and sincerely declare and affirm that I will well and truly serve our Sovereign Lady the Queen in the Office of Constable, without favour or affection, malice or ill will; and that I will, to the best of my power cause the peace to be kept and preserved, and prevent all offences against the persons and properties of Her Majesty's subjects and that while I continue to hold said office, I will, to the best of my skill and knowledge discharge all duties thereof faithfully according to law."

I said this, and meant every single word of it!

I was thinking what Sir Robert Peel had said, that we policed by the consent of the people, that the more force you use, the less authority you have. That police only do full-time what the rest of us should be doing all the time. That the people are the police. I was going to try my absolute best to uphold those ideals.

As a final "fuck you" to the senior staff who had tried to get rid of Paul, we voted him the most improved student in our class. So, the man who had tried the hardest to get rid of him, because of race and sex, had to call out his name, then look on as the Chief Constable of Northumbria (a really nice lady) presented him with an award. I think we all enjoyed that!

After this, we went outside and had plenty of photo opportunities. Pictures around the Sir Robert Peel statue were obligatory. My mom snapped a beautiful picture in front of the statue when Victoria attempted to jam my helmet hard onto my head, to make my ears stick out. I still have a large copy on display in my house. It proved to be a bitter-sweet reminder of that day. But it was such a lovely day. I don't think I've ever been happier.

Karim came over and told my mom how much I'd helped him. Paige came over and said hi. Paul made a point of letting my mom know that I'd helped him.

The day shot by, and we were soon saying goodbye to our guests.

We went back to our rooms and carefully packed away our tunics and polished shoes (we'd only really need these for court appearances, and ceremonial duties). Into our regular uniforms. Then it was down to the canteen for our last (lovely) meal. Then to the bar. Suffice to say, we had an unforgettable night, which included the odd glass or two. Plenty of ribbing, especially the fact my mother had laughed loudest at the crudest joke. Plenty of "the apple doesn't fall far from the tree". I shan't break too many confidences, but I do remember we had a conga line which may or may not have included our staff wearing the opposite sex's uniform hats, starting at the top floor of the men's block and making its way down several floors, getting longer and longer. What a way to say goodbye.

I woke up the next morning, not in the mood for breakfast. We had said our goodbyes the night before, and didn't see anyone as we left.

I got a lift back to Brentwood from Terry's parents. No one wanted to drive that day. His parents were really kind, and we had a good chat about starting together at Earlham on the Monday. We'd share Terry's car up there to carry our all our kit. I was in the middle of finalising buying a house, and getting the first new car I'd ever owned, having sold the XR3i to Richard E (what a mug).

I felt it was the end of a chapter of my life. Time to start a new one.

Chapter 3
BURKE

It was 08:15 hours and I was standing outside Earlham Police Station. I checked my letter for the hundredth time that morning: 09:00 hours, Earlham Police Station, report to the front office and ask for the street duties course run by Sergeant (uniform sergeants are referred to as PS) Burke.

I looked at the police station which would be my second home. It was an old building, red brick and concrete, and it looked like it dated back to the 1950s. It fronted out onto a main road, with a set of chipped concrete steps leading up to the wooden main door, with the dark blue paint faded and peeling. The building had seen better days. It was a metaphor for this area of London. To the right was a barrier-controlled entrance to the back yard.

Terry dropped me off with our suitcases and uniform bags at the front, while he went in search for a parking space, giving me an opportunity to take in our surroundings.

It was the East End of London and, during my days as a student, I lived about five miles to the east of there, so I had some knowledge of the general area.

The roads are narrow and crowded, and there's a mish-mash of old and new buildings, all piled on top of one another. There is a general air of neglect, the roads are dirty and pot-holed, and there's graffiti and vandalism everywhere you look. People walk quickly and avoid eye contact.

The background buzz of traffic is regularly punctuated by the sounds of police and ambulance sirens. I guess PS Johnson wasn't wrong; there'd be plenty of opportunity to nick villains.

I wonder what my grandad would have made of the place?

I heard a man's voice from behind me: "This area used to be the heart of the East End, you know."

I turned to see an average-height man (5'10") in his late twenties standing behind me, with a wheeled suitcase and uniform bag over his shoulder. I recognised him from Hendon. There was a swagger in his movement, bordering on arrogance. He turned and waved to an older man as he pulled away in a large silver Audi.

I said: "Hi, it's Edward, right?"

I tried to offer my hand, while juggling the two uniform bags I was holding. Edward ignored it and said: "Why are you waiting outside? You're blocking the pavement, and giving a bad first impression of the police station."

We'd been told to arrive in civvies, but to have all our other uniform and kit with us. Mildly annoyed that he had appointed himself in charge, I said with a sharper edge to my voice than I had intended: "I'm waiting for Terry. He'll be along in a minute. He's parking the car. Sir!"

He ignored my sarcasm and, as he made his way up the steps into the police station, without turning around, said: "You're still blocking the pavement!"

I was beginning to dislike this guy. Who the hell did he think he was? Arrogant, entitled sod!

A couple of minutes later, Terry jogged up, and said: "I had to park the car bleeding miles away! I hope some thieving git doesn't steal it!"

As I handed him his kit, he asked: "Have you seen any of the others yet?"

I replied: "Yeah, unfortunately, that arrogant bastard Edward from B class. He thinks he's God's gift! Still hasn't forgiven me for beating him in the bleep test."

Terry frowned, saying: "Mate there's twelve of us, and we'll be working together for the next ten weeks. Best to try to get on with him, even if he's an arsehole. Just think, there's only a one in five chance he'll be on your relief. Just try to avoid him for the next three months."

I groaned inwardly, as I hefted my kit and we made our way up the stairs into the nick. I'd never thought Edward might be on my relief. But Terry had just tempted fate! God, please no!

Our eyes adjusted from the bright sunlight outside to a slightly run-down and poorly lit front office. It was tiny, just about enough space for half a dozen people. There was a high counter facing you as you walked in, with a wall on the right with a noticeboard, and metal bench to the left, and at the far end was a security door.

A deep, gravelly voice greeted us with a heavy east London accent: "'Ello boys. You're the new puppies out for their first walking, ain't ya!" Before we could speak, he continued: "I'm supposed to check your briefs (slang for warrant card – police ID), but sod it, if I can't spot a probby (probationary police officer) by now I should a' bleedin' retired!"

He chuckled at his own joke. My eyes had now adjusted, and could see a round-faced man in his late fifties, with a greying moustache, big glasses and a bald head. He continued: "I'm Alf, by the way. What's your names, boys, so I can tick 'em off da list?"

Terry replied: "Thanks Alf. I'm Anthony Ward PT273, and this is Richard Armstrong PT272. Are you sure you don't need to check our warrant cards? We've only just got 'em!"

Alf laughed: "What, you mean your free train passes (at that time you'd get free train and Tube travel if you showed your warrant card)? Let's be honest, lads, you don't know your arse from your elbows yet and that's all they're good for."

Grinning all the while, he was clearly enjoying the reversal of roles. Usually, police officers look down their noses at civilian station officers. But it was good-natured. I think.

He continued: "Right boys, best you get along to the back canteen where Burke is waiting for you. Just go straight along the corridor, through the back door, across the yard, in through the door. The code is the obvious one if you're English."

I replied: "1066, Alf. I'm glad to see you have a picture of Her Majesty on the wall!"

He smiled even wider, saying "That does my old heart good to hear that some of you youngsters are royalists."

I replied: "I took my oath of service to Her Majesty, not to some politician, Alf."

He laughed and opened the security door. As we struggled through, he came over and helped us with our bags.

As quietly as Alf could manage, he said to me: "Watch your back with Burke; he's a nasty piece of work if you get on the wrong side of him."

As we made our way along the corridor, I heard talking from my right. I turned and saw an open door into an ancient control room, with four people in there with headsets on. The desks were old, the seats were worn, and the computer screens they were using were a mixture of a couple of modern colour monitors, but most were old, green-screen monitors.

I was shocked; I hadn't seen green-screen monitors for years. Ah, the Met and its extra cheapness.

We continued down the long, narrow corridor, which was poorly lit. It had white(ish) lino floors, cheap wooden panelling up to waist height, and ancient, peeling wallpaper with a number of wooden noticeboards along it. The door on the left opened up into a large, clean canteen with chairs and tables set out. We carried on, as we'd been directed, to the old wooden doors at the end. Terry held the door open for me as we both struggled through with our bags. He said, "This place is a dump. When did the Met last pay to clean or decorate it?"

I thought for a moment, and replied: "1066! That's the real reason for the door code."

I looked around the yard. Directly opposite us were a few stairs up into an even more dilapidated building, with crumbling, red brick, dirty windows encased in rotting wooden window frames. To our left was a one-vehicle-wide dead end with a security door to the left. To our right was a decent-sized yard with an open garage, another equally aged building, all surrounded by a twelve-feet-high red brick wall. Sitting alone in the middle of the yard was a forlorn, battered Fiesta panda car. The police sign on its bonnet was faded, and the stripe down the side was peeling off. The Met and its extra cheapness again!

I entered the code "1066" into the well-worn mechanical keypad on the door, having to attempt this a number of times. Finally we could continue through and along an equally sad-looking corridor, which eventually led into a large, L-shaped room with very old canteen with a service hatch and tables and chairs. At the other end, directly in front of us, was an enclosed, conference-style room, which was encased floor to ceiling in glass.

There was a long, dark, wooden table surrounded by padded, high-backed chairs. This was in stark contrast to the rest of the building. The effect was somewhat spoiled by a bucket sitting on the centre of this table, catching drips from a defective air conditioning unit on the ceiling above. The Met and its extra cheapness.

Seated in that room were ten people. A tall (6'3"), thin-faced man of about 35 years wearing the uniform of a sergeant looked over at us and, with a scowl, waved us over. As we were making our way, he walked to the door, stuck his head out and said: "Put your kit and jackets over there (indicating a pile of bags and kit stacked against the wall). Hurry up and get in here. You're late; we're waiting for you."

As we were putting our kit where we were told, I sneaked a look at my watch. It showed 08:35 hours. We weren't late. What was he on about?

Terry and I filed in and sat down at the two empty seats near the door. No sooner had we sat down when the sergeant said: "Don't sit there. There's more of you late arrivers to come. Don't be selfish. Come and sit over here (indicating the far side of the table, next to him). Hurry up, you're keeping everyone waiting."

We got up and struggled to push our way past the already occupied seats. I noticed Edward deliberately pushed his chair back into my path, and grinned at me as he did. I wonder if he'd said anything to PS Burke, who was clearly a candidate for sergeant of the year!

We managed to get to the seats indicated and sat down. Before I got the chance to get my bearings, the sergeant said: "Right, you're finally ready. Have you got your letters, and your warrant cards? I need to check them. Quickly now!"

I had to stand up to get my warrant card from my back pocket. With a sinking feeling, I remembered that my letter was in my jacket that I'd piled up outside. Oh great! I turned around, started to walk back past the chairs to collect my letter. The sergeant loudly said: "Stop! Where are you going?"

I turned slightly and said calmly, "Sorry Sergeant, I left my letter in my jacket, which is out there (pointing to the pile of kit outside)."

He said: "You really don't think, do you? You knew you needed that letter. Everyone else had the brains to bring it in here. Off you go and get it. We'll just sit and wait for you again!"

Annoyance was beginning to turn to anger. This was clearly a bully, but I couldn't react, and he knew it. In my teaching career I'd come across bullies; I hated them, and the way they tried to humiliate and dominate.

I retrieved my letter, and retook my seat. All the while, Edward smirked at my discomfort. I really didn't like the guy. I began to understand he felt the same way, but why? What had I ever done to him?

The sergeant made a point of waiting until I was seated until he said, "Letter and warrant card." I handed them over without a word. He checked them, and handed them back. I took them silently. He looked at me and said: "You are expected to be polite, 272. A 'please' and 'thank you, Sergeant' are expected."

I thought for a split second, that the sergeant (who still was yet to introduce himself) needed to be informed of his idiot status, but thought about how long and hard I'd studied at Hendon to get there. I was not going to let this petty authoritarian stop me. If putting up with this dickhead for ten weeks was necessary, so be it.

I said without expression: "Thank you, Sergeant." He visibly twitched at my lack of contrition, and was no doubt about to berate me further, when the door to the main canteen opened. He looked around and saw the remainder of the twelve street duties class make their way in.

The sergeant walked to the door. Opening it, he called out: "Put your kit over there with the other stuff, then come in and find a seat."

When everyone had found a seat (all the seats at the conference table were filled) and settled down, he said: "I'm Sergeant Burke. I'm in charge of this street duties course. Your other members of staff (looking at the four officers I didn't recognise from Hendon) are: PC Groves (a man of about 5'10", short dark brown hair, slim build, who was about my age); PC Hargreaves (a woman, 5'7", late twenties, average build, long, dyed-blonde hair held in a ponytail); PC Douglas (a man, 5'10", stocky build, late forties with salt and pepper hair); and PC Wilson (a man, 6'2", muscular build, late twenties, with slightly too long blond hair). This is a ten-week course to integrate you into the reliefs here and at Park Street. Now make a note of this. I'll tell you the relief and station you've been assigned to, if you complete this course successfully (looking at me when he said "if") to my satisfaction."

I felt my stomach drop. Surely it wasn't just down to this idiot whether or not I'd put in all the hard work at Hendon for naught. I'd be counting the seconds with this guy!

He went through the list of names. When it came to Earlham "C" relief, it was PT272 and PT271 (Edward). I thought, *Oh, great! Can I restart today!?*

Once we'd all noted this down (I couldn't bear to look at the grinning Edward), Burke continued: "Right, here are your locker keys. Men on the second floor, women on the first. We'll use Earlham as a base. Now pick up your kit, get changed into your uniforms, long-sleeved shirts and jumpers. Make sure you put on your Metvests. Be back in here at 09:30 hours. Do try to be on time (looking at me)."

We got up, picked up our kit and struggled up to the second floor. This had, at one time, been an accommodation block, and was run-down. There was a central corridor with rooms off each side and toilets and showers at each end. In what had been the bedrooms were a row of lockers, crammed in. There was little space in these rooms, and it was a struggle to fit in and unload all our kit, store it and get changed.

For those who have never worn body armour, I'll explain. This is like a corset (err ... so I'm told), with protective panels to the front and rear, which go from belt height to the collar line. It's made of layers of Kevlar, and these ones have layers of segmented plastic sandwiched in between. At the sides there's Velcro and it's elasticated. They are snug-fitting, and can restrict movement of the torso. They are very warm during the summer, and you sweat in them – a lot. Very unpleasant. You have to wear a T-shirt underneath, and they come with thin cloth liners, which you can take off and wash.

So as not to alarm the public and make them think we're in any way a scary, paramilitary organisation, we had to wear this armour under our uniforms. Once on, the armour stayed on for the whole shift of eight-plus hours. The Met, with extra cheapness, had chosen unbelievably uncomfortable (over long periods) armour. When you sat down, the bottom of your armour hit your belt, forcing the armour up under your chin, and you had to move around until it sat properly. It was apt to aggravate any back pain, and was so tight it could restrict breathing. Women had the more uncomfortable version of the armour as, when they sweated, the material was trapped between the armour and the chest, sandpapering their nipples. Nice! The more they protruded, the worse the effect.

With the belt and equipment, heavy uniform, boots and hat, you were carrying around several kilos of extra weight.

I was on my own (thankfully) in the room where my locker was, which gave me enough space to get changed. Others were not so fortunate, and I could hear insults and complaints from the other rooms as the others bumped into each other.

I checked my watch: 09.15 hours. I collected what I thought I needed, and made my way quickly downstairs to the conference room. I was one of the first down, and waited with the others, who all seemed as nervous as I felt.

At 09:28 hours PS Burke arrived, gave us the once-over, wrinkling his brow at even the slightest thing that didn't meet his approval.

He said: "Right, you'll split up into four groups of three, with a trainer each and they'll show you around Earlham. We'll then meet up in the canteen, have a coffee and then we'll go over to Park Street and have a look around there. We'll issue you with your CS spray, have lunch in the canteen there and I'll hand out the notes you'll need for your next written tests in four weeks' time, and I'll give you a timetable of what you're going to be doing over the next few weeks."

PC Groves checked his notes and called out PC272, PC270 and PC269. We stepped forward and he smiled and said: "Come with me, and I'll show you around." I looked at the other two pups (we were being 'puppy-walked', hence we were the 'pups'). There was a slightly shorter man (5'8"), PC270, who was in his early forties, stocky build with short black hair with just a hint of grey, and a taller woman (5'8"), in her early thirties, slim build, thin face, with mousy, light brown hair. Both were quiet, but seemed friendly enough.

As we were being shown around, PC Groves stopped when we couldn't be overheard and said: "When we're alone, please call me Roger. I'm not one for standing on ceremony. Look, we're all wearing the same uniform, I've just done this for a while. We're all here to help you get used it all. Don't worry: work hard, listen and you'll be fine. All right?"

He looked around at us. I must have let out a breath of relief without thinking (well, at least one of the training team wasn't openly hostile but, hey, the day was still young), so Roger turned to me and said: "I don't know if you know each other. Let's find out who you are. You (pointing at me), please introduce yourself to the others."

I looked at the other two and said: "Morning. I'm Richard Armstrong. I used to be a teacher, and I'm going to Earlham on C relief."

Roger grinned and said: "Oh, you'll like them; they're crazy ones!" I thought, *great, from the Animal House to the Crazies! I'll be right at home.*

He turned to the female pup and indicated she should introduce herself. She smiled and said: "Hello, I'm Mary Burns. I'm from Edinburgh and I used to work in town planning. Oh, and I'm going to D relief at Park Street." This was all said with a gently Scottish accent.

Roger replied: "That's good. That's my relief. You'll like it. Inspector Miller is firm, but fair. A bit formal, and by the book. But she's fair with it."

Mary smiled at that, and I could see a moment of relief flash across her face.

Finally, he looked at the last 'pup'. As he spoke, it was clear he was from London (I couldn't decide where, though): "Hello, I'm Paul. Used to be a builder, houses and the like. I'm off to E relief at Newham."

Roger nodded and said: "That's a decent relief by reputation. Haven't had too much to do with them, though."

Paul nodded, apparently satisfied with the relief he'd been assigned.

Roger continued our tour, upstairs in the main building, which opened up into a long, open CID office with desks strewn with clutter, cabinets overflowing with evidence bags, forms and files, to say nothing of discarded body armour and stained coffee mugs. The only people present were a sour-faced woman in her mid-forties sitting at a much tidier desk, wearing a creased M&S suit with a skirt. She eyed us with a scowl the whole time and made no attempt to greet us.

The other one was a man in his mid-thirties, tall, well built, if a little stocky. He was dressed in jeans and a T-shirt with the ubiquitous black fleece (apparently mandatory for 'plain-clothes' work). He was typing with one hand, and occasionally taking bites from an apple in his other hand and looking at a set of statements. He looked up and, in between mouthfuls of apple, said in a strong London accent: "'Ello there Rog'. Who's this then? They've not let you loose on a bunch of pups have they?" He lent back in his chair to get a better look at us. There was clearly a friendly banter between the two of them.

Roger turned to us and said dryly: "This is Detective Sergeant (DS) Gadd. He was on my relief until he was demoted to the CID, on account of him being a lazy waste of space."

Gadd put his head back and laughed. Roger introduced us, telling him which relief we were on. DS Gadd laughed and was in danger of falling off the swivel office chair his generous frame was overwhelming.

He looked at me and said: "You're going to C relief? Gawd 'elp you son!" He laughed at his own joke, and we smiled politely. He sat up a little more in his chair and said: "Look, here in CID we aren't as stiff and starchy as you wooden tops (police slang for uniformed officers). I'm John, and if you need any advice, come up and talk to me. We're usually run off our feet, but I remember what it was like when I first started, and I'll do my best to help."

Roger said: "That's very charitable of you, John."

John replied: "I'll get my rewards in heaven, mate!"

Roger quipped: "What makes you think the CID go to heaven, mate? I would have thought where you're going is just a little bit warmer!" They both laughed at this, and we politely joined in. All the while the sour-faced woman continued to glare at us.

We moved on and Roger said as we walked: "John's a diamond, and he knows his stuff. Be careful of some of the others in there. You can rely on them ... mostly."

I exchanged slightly nervous looks with the other two pups (the idea there were police officers you couldn't rely on was unnerving).

We crossed the yard, and went past the abandoned panda. I piped up: "Roger, when do we get to drive a police car?"

He turned and grinned: "Oh yeah, you're from Essex, I should have known! (Was it a requirement in the Met to take the piss out of people from Essex?) Well, once you're through your probation at the end of two years, you'll get to do the basic test and drive one of these (indicating the panda), then it's down to how quickly you impress those in charge to let you apply for a response course. That's the one you want: blue lights and sirens," he said with a grin.

The other pups laughed. It's funny that he knew what I was thinking. I replied: "Thanks Roger, that's all I wanted to know. Two years, mmm!"

As he laughed, he turned and we made our way to the small red-brick building on the far side of the yard. We went into this slightly rickety old building. The stairs twisted around to a series of small offices, well away from the main building.

We stopped at one of these rooms. The door was closed. Roger knocked and received a "Come in!" It was in a slightly sing-song voice. We all squeezed into this small office that had a desk, chair, computer and piles of paperwork stacked on the shelves, on the floor, the window ledge. Seated at the desk was a short (5'4"), slim, almost gaunt, well-dressed man who wore black jeans and a black cotton shirt. His hair was dark brown and short, and he was aged about 40. He looked up from the computer, and sat bolt upright in the chair. He had a very correct English accent, and his voice was slightly high in pitch. But, honestly, I was jealous: his speaking voice was beautiful. He very carefully appraised the three of us pups in a matter of seconds.

Looking at Roger, he said: "Oh, I take it by the look of our three friends here, they are three of our new street duties. You're the first person to have the courtesy of bringing them to the DIU. That's Divisional Intelligence Unit (looking at us with a kindly smile). This is where all the CRIMINTS you put on go, and all the arrests and stops you make are sent to be analysed by this computer and (gently patting the PC). I assess all the information and send it out for the morning briefings, and for those fools at the top to ignore, if it suits them. Do you have any questions?"

I said: "Sorry to be thick, Sir ..."

At which point, he interrupted me: "Please call me Alan. I absolutely hate all the petty bureaucracy. Technically, yes, I am a sergeant. Formally, I'm DS Engals. But please carry on with your question, and don't be scared. I'm not royalty, you know."

With a slight smile (I liked this guy), I said: "CRIMINT is a criminal intelligence report we enter into a separate computer. What happens to it then?"

He looked at us for a minute, and could clearly see that none of us understood. He turned to his computer, logged off his current task and called up another screen. He beckoned us to go over, and we moved so we could see the screen. He pointed at the screen and said: "That's a CRIMINT. See if you can work it out."

I looked at the new screen. It had a series of boxes and titles and headings, with dates, times, including: "reporting officer", "informant", "reliability of informant". I said: "That's a CRIMINT database entry, that someone has uploaded."

He nodded, saying: "Good, someone who at least knows what a database is. What did you do before coming here?"

"I taught science at secondary school, for my sins."

Alan nodded and continued: "Ah, another teacher. You'll get on well with Graham Manning, your inspector on C relief. He used to be a maths teacher. He's a nice man. A bit of a bombast, but a good man all the same. You see, if you want information, come and see me. Oh yes, right, the task in hand. CRIMINT. Now, young lady, what's your name, and what did you used to do?" He smiled in a gentle way (not creepy, just kind).

"I'm Mary Burns. I used to work in a town planning office."

Alan cocked his head slightly as she was speaking: "Edinburgh? Am I correct?" She smiled and nodded.

He continued: "Beautiful part of the world. I would guess, a town planner would know their way around a computer?" Again she nodded (not much of a talker, our Mary).

Alan continued: "So once the information is entered, it gets entered into several databases. I check it, collate it, similar MOs (modus operandi), locations, descriptions, and compile a daily and weekly report, and a monthly prediction. Does that answer your question?"

I nodded and replied: "Yes, thank you. Does it allow the relief inspectors to proactively police the hot spots?"

I was showing off! Alan looked at me for a moment, and burst out laughing, and Roger joined in, leaving us three pups looking at each other. Serves me right for getting cocky.

Alan said: "I'm sorry, we shouldn't laugh. It was a logical question. There's usually about sixteen officers on each relief, which means eight vehicles, and there are, over the course of an eight-hour shift, hundreds of calls. They can barely cope, and sometimes they're totally overwhelmed. This is reactive policing. There's precious little time for proactive work.

Reality of the situation, I'm afraid. You do occasionally get the opportunity to plan proactive jobs, but not on a regular basis."

Wow, that was blunt! So, running from call to call was the order of the day.

Roger said: "Right, we'd better get back. PS Burke doesn't appreciate lateness."

Alan stopped, and looked at us, saying: "You are kidding me? Jack Burke running a street duties course!" He shook his head, looked down at the keyboard for a moment, and said: "If you want to talk about intelligence matters, you know where I am. My door is always open." He looked up at us with what looked like pity.

"Good luck with your street duties course." And, under his breath he said (as we walked out), "Cos you're going to need it."

As we crossed the yard on our way back to the canteen, Roger said: "Alan's a really good source of information, about anything that goes on in or around the station. Right, we'll make it just in time (checking his watch)."

The coffee and biscuits were standard fare; at least they hadn't managed to make a mess of that. Burke was his usual, charming self. We made our way onto a minibus, and began to feel the discomfort of getting up, moving and sitting down in Metvests.

The trip over to Park Street Police Station took us through narrow run-down back streets. There was a mix of terraced houses, aged council estates, with the occasional sad-looking tree lifting up the paving stones on an already uneven pavement. We had to weave through badly parked cars, bollards, speed bumps and the occasional burned-out wreck of a car.

"This sure ain't Kansas, Toto!" I heard in my head. This made me smile for a brief moment. At that point, Mary gently elbowed me in the ribs. I looked round, and she said: "That's the first time I've seen you smile today.

Don't worry, it won't be that bad. We'll get through this." I was a bit surprised, as Mary had barely said a word all day.

I said: "Thank you, I appreciate it. Honestly, the next few weeks are going to be tough for me." I looked forward to Burke and Edward. Mary's brow furrowed and she replied as quietly as she could in a noisy minibus: "Try not to let them get to you, and keep your head down. Don't annoy them."

I shrugged my shoulders (not that anyone could tell under my body armour). "I honestly don't think I'll get much choice in the matter, but thanks for your concern. I appreciate it. You're kind." She rolled her eyes in a playful way and once again elbowed me in the ribs.

Park Street nick was set back from a main road by a patch of green in a morass of ugly brick and concrete. Talking of ugly, the building itself was modern, the sort of thing so unremarkable and bland that it had to have been designed by a soulless computer, or accountant (same thing). No human could have made something so mediocre.

When we got in through the sliding security gate, we were met with a crowded car park. The building and surrounding wall were made of a cheap red brick. Upon entering the building, we found it had plain white, modern, functional corridors that all looked alike. As we moved around, it was clear it had not been built as a police station (as Earlham had), or the person who designed it had no clue as to how the police operated.

The custody area (where the people you nick are housed) had no exercise area, there was a small booking in area with two terminals for about sixteen cells, whereas Earlham had the same number of booking in stations for seven cells. As we walked around the rest of the building, it became clear how many of the offices did not have windows, just antiseptic white walls, with harsh, artificial light from overhead strip lights.

For all Earlham's faults, it wasn't without a certain character. It reflected the area it was in: made for a different time, worn-down and dilapidated, but still hanging on in there. It had a soul, not like this place, which sucked the energy from you. Suddenly, I was glad I was at Earlham. The atmosphere was totally different. Give me old and run-down over modern and soulless any day.

Once we'd had a guided tour of the nick, we adjourned to the canteen. This was on the top floor, with Velux windows on the slanted walls (part of the roof). It was by far the nicest room in the building. It had natural light streaming in, and was open and long. It gave the space that the rest of the rooms so clearly lacked. I looked out of the window, over the roofs of the houses and buildings, and the sounds of traffic drifted up. I looked down to see just how much of a poorly organised mess the car park was. It wasn't designed for anything like the number of vehicles it held, leading to, shall we say, creative parking solutions.

We all sat down at the tables, and Burke said: "This week, we'll spend time going over the basics you'll need on relief, that Hendon didn't go over. Radio procedures, booking in procedures, expectations in terms of paperwork. We'll also get you certified with officer safety training to allow you to work on the streets. That'll be my relief, as they're doing theirs this week, we can just tag on to it.

"Let me just make this clear (looking at me): don't think just because you passed out of Hendon you know anything. You don't! This is where you learn how to do it right! Forget what they taught you at the Peel Centre; I'm going to tell you how we expect you to do it on relief.

"Next week, we'll start out in twos or threes walking the streets on day shifts. That means, as of tomorrow, we start at 08:00 hours, (looking at me at me, again). Do you think you can manage to be on time, 272?"

I bit back a sarcastic remark (firstly, I wasn't late – I had been at least twenty minutes early, and I wasn't even close to being the last one there), waited just a moment longer than was polite, and replied, while looking past him: "Yes Sergeant."

Burke stiffened at this, clearly getting the message. He glared at me and said: "Remember, I'm the one who has the authority to pass you or fail you on this course, and that would mean you'd be chucked out of the police, 272! Just remember that."

I really couldn't understand this guy. Why had he decided to pick on me? From the moment I'd walked in, he was on constant attack mode. I just didn't get it. Trouble with me is, I will not back down from a bully, under any circumstances, ever! As a kid, we'd moved schools a lot, due to my dad's work, and being the new kid in every school means you're a target. I learnt quickly, as soon as you show weakness, the bullies are on you, and they won't let up.

He turned, and continued to the rest of the class: "Also this week, we'll go to Leighston, the firearms and helicopter base, to show you around."

Finally, something he'd said provided something to look forward to: firearms and helicopters. I'd done a lot of shooting as a boy and young man. Both my great-uncles had been in the army during the war, and Uncle Edward had been the Deputy Chief Constable for County Durham, and he'd been a gun nut. Every time (two to three times a year) we went to see them, we'd be taken out onto the large field (that he owned) behind his house, and we'd be tutored in the use of pistols and rifles. My parents weren't keen, but didn't want to be disrespectful. I'd also shot in the air cadets as a kid. Then, travelling around America (for six months) a few years before, I'd done a lot of shooting, including with some of the Laws I met out there. Having police family connections opens so many doors.

On top of that, I had a fixed-wing pilot's licence and several hundred flight hours logged. I didn't have a helicopter licence, but I had flown them as a student several times. So, Friday was going to be a day I'd enjoy (I hoped). But we still had to get there.

Burke continued: "We'll take you to the coroner, and watch a post-mortem. We'll get you doing traffic stops, and handing out FPNs (Fixed Penalty Notices – the Met had acronyms for everything), then you'll join my relief for earlies (06:00 hours to 14:00 hours), so that means, 272, you won't be getting your beauty sleep."

He laughed, and the others joined in, with differing amounts of enthusiasm. I think some were beginning to feel uncomfortable at using me as the butt of every joke. He continued: "Lates (14:00 hours to 22:00 hours) and nights (22:00 hours to 06:00 hours). Finally, you'll go out in pairs, without instructors. So, by the end of November, those of you who meet my standards (looking at me AGAIN!) will pass your street duties, and join your reliefs."

He waited for a moment, looking round. Continuing, he said: "Tomorrow, we'll go through correct radio procedure. We'll look at the custody procedures, so be at Earlham, full uniform, at 08:00 hours.

"Then, Wednesday, we'll do your officer training assessment. You'll need your PT kit for that. We can get you signed off, so you're legal for the streets next week."

We were then taken back to Earlham in the minibus. We were dismissed, and allowed to leave. As I walked on our way back to Terry's car, he said: "Mate, you really know how to make friends, don't you!"

I let out a deep breath and replied, when I was sure we were out of earshot of the others: "I honestly don't know what that guy's problem is. From the moment he saw me, he was on my case. What's his problem?"

Terry sucked in a breath and replied: "Yeah, I don't understand the whole late thing. We both arrived at the same time. We were early; lots of others came in after us. Yet he picks on you. Do you think Edward might have put out the bad word about you? Anyway, you didn't exactly try to make things easy. You should respect the rank, not the person. Otherwise he'll make your life hell, and maybe fail you."

I bit back my pent-up anger (it wasn't Terry I was pissed off with) and replied: "I know, it's just I hate bullies, and he's a bully. If you give in, he'll just get worse and worse."

Terry shrugged and said: "He isn't going to back down. He is a bully, but he has power over your career. Just think of how hard you worked to get here. You helped a lot of people at Hendon. I'm trying to help you now. Leave it, smile sweetly, just take the shit he's dishing out, and when you're on your relief, you won't see him again."

I thought about it for a moment. He was right in some ways. I replied: "Thanks mate, I appreciate what you're saying. I'll bite my tongue, for now, but there's only so far you can push someone."

Terry nodded, saying: "Fair enough mate, I think that's a good move. Try to keep your head down."

We made it back to the car without speaking again. The car was miraculously still there, and in one piece. Terry had found where to park and we'd both been issued parking permits. So, the next day, we'd be driving in separately. I'd also have to submit my application for change of address, after the offer I'd put in on a house had gone through. But, believe it or not, the police could still veto it, if they decided they didn't like where I was moving to!

As I was driving in for the first time (nice and early – if I was the first there, there's no way he could say I was late), even at 06:30 hours the traffic was busy. They often referred to the A12 into London as the "wacky races", after the cartoon of the same name. The Highway Code seemed to be merely advisory, and no one had read it anyway. Passing cars on both sides, tailgating, using the hard shoulder, never using their mirrors or indicators was all part of the adventure of driving along that road. Fun, fun, fun!

Arriving at just before 07:00 hours, I used the car park pass, and parked up. I had just received delivery of my first new car ever. It was the only thing I could afford: a Ford Ka. It was a small, two-door that was the bottom of the Ford range, but it was new, and it was mine. Honestly, the reason I chose it over a couple of other makes was because of the little oval clock on the dash. It was uber-cute! All said in a manly voice. I reminded myself when I bought it that I still liked football, women and beer, just to get the straight/gay balance right.

I went in, got changed into my uniform, and made my way to the conference room (more commonly called the "goldfish bowl", due to the fact its walls were glass).

I was determined to make a fresh start, and put the bad start behind me. I checked my watch: 07:15 hours, definitely not late. Good, I was the first to arrive. Quick panic – was I in the right place? Calming myself, I went through the instructions in my head. Yes, I was in the right place. A couple of minutes later, the instructors arrived in a group. I said: "Good morning, Sergeant, (looking at Burke), good morning (to the other three staff)." I smiled and stood up to show respect.

Roger and Peter (Wilson) acknowledged me. Burke said, without looking me in the face: "We need to get prepared, and you're in the way. Go and wait in the canteen, until you're called, like you were told to."

I got up, collected my stuff, and walked out to the canteen, bought a coffee, and sat somewhat disconsolately on my own. There were a couple of uniformed officers having breakfast and chatting. They looked up at me once and continued with their conversation. I thought, *this is going to be a tough time if I literally can't do anything right in this guy's eyes.*

A few minutes later, the others started to arrive. We sat and chatted until we were called in. On the conference table were twelve radios, and belt attachments. Next to them was a pile of receipt forms and, next to that, various custody forms.

Once we'd all taken our seats, Burke said: "These are your radios. You'll sign for them, and are responsible for them from then on. At the end of the shift, take out the battery pack, put it in a charger, and at the start of the next shift, collect a charged battery, and insert it, making sure you always have a fully charged battery at the start of the shift."

The radios were handed out, and we did the required paperwork. I took a moment longer than the others to sign the form, as I read what it said, like I'd been told by Sergeant Johnson. Burke looked over at me and said: "Come on, 272. For an EX-TEACHER, you do read slowly. Or are you dyslexic, what I call 'thick'?"

I bit back a comment, and signed the paperwork. A number of photocopied and stapled pages of A4 were handed round to us.

Burke said: "Look at the instructions in front of you. These are how you are to use the radio. Do not deviate from those instructions. When you do a name check, there's a right way of giving information, and a wrong way."

He then went through a long list of instructions on precisely how to word things over the radio. This was not what we'd been taught at Hendon, but I wasn't going to say anything (remembering Terry's words).

Burke then said: "Now you'll go out in groups to different parts of the station and we'll practise getting it right."

We split up into groups, and did as we were told. It quickly became clear that absolute precision, and adherence to the procedure Burke had set out, was going to be strictly enforced. He did seem to ask me a disproportionate number of times to call out name checks, waiting for me to get the order wrong, i.e. male, IC1 (Identification Codes refers to someone's race, IC1 – white, IC2 – Mediterranean, IC3 – Black, IC4 – Asian, IC5 – Arab), date of birth, height, marks and scars, any other information. Without this list written down to refer to, it's very hard to remember. Often I'd say IC1 male, instead of male IC1. This would earn me a rebuke. The slightest variation was unacceptable. I became more and more disheartened by this, to the point where I began to avoid using the radio.

I couldn't do what he wanted, was rudely criticised, couldn't answer back. I became more frustrated, angry and dispirited.

We then went back and started on the practice custody paperwork. As we filled it in, I saw my work was being passed by the other staff to Burke to be personally checked by him, whereas the others were not. At the conclusion of the exercise, he held up my work and said: "There are a number of errors in the way you're filling these forms out. I can hardly read this, 272. I'm shocked you were allowed to be a teacher with such poor handwriting. The standards must have fallen a lot even since I was at school. No wonder you got out of teaching. From what I've seen so far, they must have been glad to see you go. Kids don't need bad teachers like you. Look, look here, I can't read any of this. Maybe I should send you to back to school for them to teach you how to write."

I was stunned. I know what friendly banter is, but he was openly being personally rude. This was plain bullying.

Knowing that I couldn't respond, I just let my head drop. I could feel my shoulders droop. He wasn't done though: "272, when a superior rank speaks to you, it's expected for you to show respect and reply."

This was the moment, if I reacted, he'd be able to discipline me and gain evidence for my failing the course and being sacked. I wasn't going to give it to him; I was going to keep my powder dry, and hit back when I knew I'd be in the right and he couldn't respond with impunity. I looked up and past him, saying in a level, emotionless tone: "Yes Sergeant. I'm sorry Sergeant."

The moment seemed to hang for an age. I could see he wasn't entirely sure if I was being sincere (I wasn't), but he couldn't be sure.

He then carried on with the lesson. I went home, despondent, and thinking I'd really have achieved something if I could get through the course.

Paul had his test at Hendon, so had Karim, and this was mine. I wondered if I could get through this course nodding in the right places, keeping my mouth shut, ignoring this petty, vindictive dickhead, and doing so all without punching his lights out which, quite honestly, he so richly deserved.

The following day, we started the OST assessment. This was held in the basement of Park Street nick. There were no windows; it was just a converted storage room. There were mats and pads and sponge-coated plastic truncheons.

We had teamed up with E relief (Burke's relief) to do their six-monthly reassessment, so there were about thirty of us. Having gone through the usual warm-up routine of jogging around in an oval, swinging our arms and stretching, we went through the safety rules of how we were to conduct ourselves.

The assessment was run by E relief, not Burke and his team, so I had a chance not to be picked on, and might have a fair assessment.

In pairs, we practised the various handcuffing techniques. These are the most dangerous techniques to practise and we use genuine 'quick cuffs', as they are called. They are handcuffs with a solid metal section between them, and also known as 'compliance cuffs'. Once you get one cuff on, you gain a lever controlling the other person's wrist. It's easy to cause pain and damage to the other person, up to and including a broken wrist.

They are by far the most effective piece of kit the Met ever issued. So practising means putting them on each other. So once we'd practised, we were called up in pairs to allow us to demonstrate the four different ways you can put the cuffs on someone: back to back (where your hands are facing in the same direction – this is what you see on cop shows), and the stack (where your hands face in opposite directions, the most effective method). Both of these methods can be done to the front, and to the rear. These were called out by the trainers, and we'd have to demonstrate them on each other. Terry was my partner, and we both performed these techniques to their satisfaction. Pass section one.

The next was the CS spray assessment. This is a spray that's used as an incapacitant. It consists of tiny crystals that are stored in a small can under pressure. When these crystals mix with the moisture on your skin, they react and cause a burning sensation, and can temporarily blind you. They are pretty terrible to use. Why? The spray is very short range and it's affected by the wind, so outside when you spray it, it gets anyone nearby. A section of the population are not affected much by it. You can't use it in anywhere that has an air conditioning system, because it will recirculate the CS so everyone gets a low dose, which is not good in a hospital. It wasn't mandatory to carry it, and a number of people didn't. We still had to train with it. How did we do that? We had the training version which was filled with ... water. In other words, they gave a bunch of coppers water pistols. The results were predictable: once we'd finished our assessment, water fight! So everyone used as little of their water for the assessment as possible, permitting them to have more 'ammunition' for the water fight.

All you have to do is hold the spray next to your chest, put out your other arm, step backwards, saying: "Get back, get back, CS, CS!" Then, as the 'assailant' walked towards you, you sprayed them with water in the torso, moving it up to the face. Job done.

Honestly, Terry and I had a laugh doing it. Towards the end of this activity, we'd moved away from Burke and his crew to be among E relief (who were a good bunch). Then the water fight started. Five minutes of letting off steam. I did notice Burke looking for me in an attempt to spray me, but I kept well away from him.

We had a break for coffee, which meant going back to our street duties course. Not fun! Burke proceeded to explain that he and the others would hold a demonstration at the end of the assessment, repeatedly mentioning that he was a black belt in "Wing Chun" (a form of martial art), how good he was and how much we could learn from him.

We then had a break, came back and practised and demonstrated in our pairs the Home Office-approved (I'm not joking, they have specific rules about everything) take-downs. Terry and I duly demonstrated these. Pass! It was going well. I was feeling a little of my old confidence coming back.

The last part was the use of batons. We were issued with our foam-covered plastic batons. To be fair, they were more sturdy than they sound. Being hit with one still stung, but not much else.

We demonstrated the required techniques, arm and leg strikes. No head or joint strikes. All done correctly. As Terry and I walked past Burke, I noticed him raise his baton to the ready position (horizontally over the right shoulder) and swing it at the back of my head. I instinctively threw myself into a forward roll and he missed. E relief started to laugh at this. I continued on to where Terry was standing (he was trying to suppress a grin). I could feel Burke's glare at my back.

The assessment was completed and we had all passed (thank goodness, Burke couldn't fail me on that). Now the demonstration.

PC Hargreaves got dressed up in a padded protective suit with a face mask grill and picked up an orange rubber knife.

Burke then said: "Right, I'm a black belt in Wing Chun, and I'm expert in martial arts, so the advanced techniques I'm about to show you are not to be attempted by you. They are merely to show how an expert can take down someone carrying a knife. I'll show you some less advanced techniques for volunteers to try out (he looked at me when said "volunteer") afterwards."

I realised there was no way he'd let the opportunity pass to inflict pain or humiliation on me. Great!

He then demonstrated some very flashy strikes, kicks and moves to disarm the slow, lumbering Hargreaves in the padded suit. After he'd received sufficient rounds of polite applause for his display of skill, he then showed us a far simpler one, that involved hitting the rubber knife out of the hands of Hargreaves.

The first 'volunteer' up was Mary, and Hargreaves slowly moved around, making it easy for Mary to strike the knife out of her hand. This happened three times – Hargreaves moved forward slowly, keeping the knife low and away from her body, making it an easy target.

When this was finished, there was polite applause. Mary left the padded area.

Burke then said: "Right, it's your turn now, 272. Let's see what you can do (he said it with a slight smirk)." I could see Hargreaves move her stance; there was far more tension in her movements, more intent. This wasn't going to be the same as Mary's encounter.

I stepped up. I could feel the slight perspiration in the palm of my gripping hand. I consciously controlled my breathing, loosened my stance, making sure I was able to react.

As soon as I was on the matted area, Hargreaves came forward with real speed and aggression, keeping the knife close to her body so it was harder to strike out of her hand. She held the knife in a right-handed grip. I moved my weight to my left foot and slowly turned to my left. Then, at the last minute, she lunged forward and made a thrust with the knife. I waited until the last moment and spun on my left foot, causing her to miss. She had her back to me as I'd spun fully around. I struck down with the baton and knocked the knife from her hand. I could hear E relief laughing, and allowed myself a brief moment of satisfaction. I wasn't starting anything, but I'd be damned if I was going to be anyone's punching bag (literally or metaphorically). Hargreaves retrieved the knife, and turned to face me. I could see that she was angry at missing and being laughed at. *Not my fault mate,* I thought. *If you'd played the same game as you did with Mary, we'd be cool.*

She readied herself and moved far more aggressively towards me, attempting a slashing attack. She had telegraphed this, largely due to her having to wear the padded suit. I once again stepped neatly out of the way and knocked the knife from her hand. Once again, peals of laughter. I could hear Hargreaves breathing heavily, and she was getting red in the face. She wasn't enjoying this, and nor was Burke. He wasn't laughing, and was glaring at me. Was he really expecting me to stand there to be knocked about physically? Really? He'd pushed me into a corner and I was fighting back, with the thing that he hated most: humour! He and Hargreaves were making fools of themselves in front of their own team!

Last round, and Hargreaves glared at me intently. She was furious! *Good! That'll make her easier to read and defeat.* I flicked the baton from hand to hand, which got a round of laughter. It wound her up more. She threw herself at me, moving hard to my left to try to stop me spinning as I had done previously. This time I'd anticipated that and spun to my right. As she shoved past me, I nudged her, causing her to lose balance and fall flat on her face at Burke's feet. Huge laugh!

She got up and dropped the knife and went to grab me. I made a feint towards her, then danced back out of the way, causing her to overbalance and fall once again, this time to her knees. She was panting heavily, due to the weight and bulk of the suit. Once again, laughter.

I stepped forward and offered her my hand to help her up (a huge insult in the martial arts world). She snarled and I let her slap my hand away. The crowd stopped laughing. There was silence for a moment. I looked at Hargreaves and Burke with an impassive stare. They both knew who'd won that battle, but war was ongoing. At that point, E relief's OST team stepped in and stopped it. They could see something outside the normal training banter was happening.

I nodded in formal respect to Hargreaves, and quietly went to stand next to Terry who, although he had been laughing, rolled his eyes at me. He whispered: "Is that what you call keeping a fucking low profile?"

The session was concluded, and as E relief were leaving, a number of them slapped me on the back and said that was the funniest thing they'd ever seen. Mary came over and said quietly: "I guess some people don't have to brag about doing martial arts. You've made a target of yourself, but that was so funny."

I was a bit surprised. Mary didn't say much, but when she did, it counted.

The next day went quietly, going over radio procedure, and if I thought I'd been given a hard time before, it was multiplied. Although it was wearing, I had the firearms and helicopter tour the following day to look forward to.

Friday arrived, and we made our way to Leighston (which had been a World War II base) by minibus. The base consisted of a series of long, World War II, vintage wooden huts. To one side was a helicopter pad and a hangar. The whole sprawling base was surrounded by trees and barbed wire-topped fences. There was a security barrier and guard post at the entrance.

We were shown around the base and went into the main firearms office, which was one of the wooden huts. It was an open office with a number of tired, untidy wooden desks and swivel chairs. There were bits of paperwork and maps scattered about.

There was one small room at the far end and the door to it was open. We made our way in, and Burke started in his now usual fashion: "272, remember to keep your mouth shut. You are without doubt the most fucking useless excuse for a street duties recruit I've seen. You will not volunteer or participate in any of the activities. Do you understand?"

I heard a familiar voice: "'Ello Richard. What you doing 'ere?"

I turned to see Larry, a friend I'd been introduced to by a musician friend (Sean), and I'd helped out as a stagehand/ driver/lighting and general dogsbody on a number of charity shows. Larry was a tall (6'2") mountain of a man, with a big, bushy moustache, slightly too long blonde hair, and 46 years old (birthday party last month). He was dressed in dark blue overalls, with body armour over the top and a utility belt at his waist. Larry then noticed the rest of the street duties course, with Burke looking on aghast. Larry continued: "Oh, you're with the puppy tour? Why didn't you tell me?"

Before I could speak, Burke said: "He's with me. I'm Sergeant Burke. I'm the one who organised this with your senior instructor. I'd consider it a professional courtesy if you addressed your remarks to me before socialising with the recruits."

Larry didn't flinch. He said: "Sergeant Burke, may I have a word with you in my office for a minute?"

Larry indicated a room in the corner. Burke stiffly walked to the office. Larry followed and closed the door after he'd entered. The plaque on the door read: "Inspector Larry Chumbley, Chief Firearms Instructor."

I looked at Terry, and he was rolling his eyes. I could hear his voice in my head saying: "Keep your head down." I thought, *not my fault, Burke did this to himself.* Even the other street duties instructors were stony-faced.

A few minutes later, a sour-faced Burke emerged, followed by Larry, who was beaming. Burke walked over to our group and said in a flat tone: "We're lucky. Inspector Chumbley will personally show us around the firearms unit. So I'll hand you over to him."

Larry, still beaming broadly, said: "Right people, 'ere in the firearms unit, we don't 'old much with formality. I'm Larry (he turned and pointed at an even taller, blond-haired man in his mid-thirties) and that's Ollie. Sorry, there's only the two of us in here today; the others are out on jobs or training at the sim-munitions (these are a type of ammunition that is like a small, very precise paint round) range. So I'll be showing you around. Right, who are you? I know that reprobate over there (pointing at me and giving me a sly nod). The stories I could tell you 'bout him!"

There was some genuine laughter, which broke the tension. Larry then said: "'Ere, Ollie, can you go and prep range one for us, usual drill. But I'll need extra G17 mags – five should do. Thanks mate." Ollie nodded and made his way out. He had the other pups and instructors introduce themselves.

Larry showed us around, until we were shown into "Range one", which was one more of the ubiquitous wooden huts. Ollie was just setting out the last of the G17 mags and was fiddling with a computer terminal at the back of the room.

Larry waited until we'd all settled. He said: "This is one of the live fire video scenario rooms. Look over there (pointing at a huge screen that had projected on it a large, Met Police logo). That's where we project different scenarios that play out, and the officers we train have to react to it. Sometimes it requires the use of firearms, sometimes not (pointing up at a series of cameras on the ceiling facing us). Those are cameras and microphones that record what the officers do, so we can dissect how they performed. All very high tech."

He paused, looking around at us, then nodded to Ollie, who came forward with two large plastic boxes, similar to the ones in a science lab where goggles are kept for experiments. Sure enough, there were safety goggles and, in the other, ear defenders.

Larry said: "Take a set of each of those and come up to the front, so you can hear the safety briefing. Don't put on the safety kit yet."

We moved up to the firing line (a thick, bright yellow line across the room, with a table on the right with a pistol and magazines sitting on it) and stood quietly.

Larry said: "We all have a laugh and joke round here; taking the piss is mandatory. We all take the piss out of each other regardless of rank (that's the way it should be done – just saying), and you know the saying: 'If you can't take a joke you shouldn't have joined.' Well, this is where that stops. There's absolutely no messing about here."

He paused and carefully looked around, catching everyone's eye. Point made and taken, with nods of assent. He continued: "There are four rules of firearms. One: always assume a firearm is loaded. Two: never point it at anyone you don't want to shoot. Three: keep your finger off the trigger until you're ready to shoot. Four: remember what's behind your target. If you miss or the shot goes through the target, who are you going to hurt? Are we clear on that (nods of agreement)? Any questions?"

Silence.

Larry continued: "By the way, notice I use the word 'firearms', not guns! Guns are what the Royal Artillery or the boys in the wavy navy have. That (pointing at the pistol) is a firearm. Are we clear?"

Again, nods of agreement.

"Now I'm going to get to the bit you've been waiting for: your chance to fire the shooty shooty bang stick." We all (except for Burke, no surprise) laughed at that.

Larry went over to the table, picking up the pistol, carefully holding it to point down range (towards the screen). Continuing, he said: "Notice, I'm pointing the muzzle down range the whole time, and keeping my finger off the trigger. Anyone know what sort of pistol this is?"

I put my hand up. Larry nodded at me. I replied: "It's a Glock 17 (G17)!"

Larry smiled: "That's right. We use this firearm because it's simple to use, extremely reliable, doesn't have an external safety that police officers can forget to switch off in the heat of the moment. Oh, yeah, the Met got them on a cheap deal from Glock."

We all once again laughed at this. I had to give it to Larry; he did know how to work an audience. The Met and the extra cheapness again!

Larry then went through how to handle and fire the G17.

He then said: "Anyone fired a pistol before, and I'm not talking about an air pistol?"

More laughs. A couple of hands went up. I caught Larry's eye, and gave the slightest of nods. He took the hint, because I didn't put my hand up.

He continued: "Anyone not want to shoot the pistol? I understand perfectly if you don't. These are serious bits of kit, and I blame no police officer for not wanting to."

He waited. Shyly, a few hands went up. Larry nodded, saying: "That's brave and honest of you. I appreciate it. I know it can be difficult to go against the tide and say no. No one (looking at Burke) in the police has the right to criticise or sanction you for not wanting to deal with firearms."

I could see relief on the faces of those who had chosen not to participate.

Larry established a queue of those who did want to shoot, which included all the staff. Larry made sure I was at the back of the queue. We put on our eyes and ear protection.

Ollie, using the computer, projected a human-shaped target onto the screen, which was set about twenty feet away. The students and staff then proceeded to shoot with varying degrees of success at the target. Honestly, pistols are really hard to shoot accurately, especially under pressure. The barrel length is about four to five inches and the slightest movement of the barrel will have a huge impact twenty feet away.

Burke was just in front of me in the queue, and had been one of the hands that had gone up as having shot before. Larry said: "You've shot before?" looking at Burke.

He replied: "Yes Sir, I've had some training."

Larry smiled and said: "No need to be so formal. OK, good. If you're up for it, I'm going to let you get your eye in and shoot at this target. Then I'll run a scenario for you?"

Burke grinned and nodded: "Good. Right, let's get started."

Burke then shot the human-shaped target pretty well. Larry nodded approvingly and turned to Ollie, saying: "Mate, can you take Richard outside and come back and run scenario three."

Ollie grunted and showed me out the door. I was a bit confused. Ollie saw this and, putting his hand on my shoulder, said: "Don't worry, Richard, it's just so you don't see what Jack does. We're going to run the same scenario with both of you, and see who does best (his face was impassive, I couldn't be sure what he was thinking, but I think I knew). Just a bit of good, friendly competition. I'll come and get you in a minute."

Ollie went back in. The soundproofing (for such an old building) was really good, and even standing so close with my ear defenders on, I could barely hear anything that went on inside.

A couple of minutes later, Ollie stuck his head out and beckoned me.

Looking around the room, I could see once again I was in the limelight. Everyone was looking at me. Pressure!

I walked over to where Larry was standing. His face, for once, was unreadable (something I never thought I'd see). He stepped back and waved me forward to pick up and load the G17. It all felt pretty familiar. The G17 was not my favourite pistol; it had a block rough texture and an uncomfortable angle on the handgrip. I much preferred the CZ75, 1911 or Sig P226. But this would have to do. I got the nod from Larry to start and I methodically emptied a mag into the target, first single shots then, at the end, a couple of double taps. *Damn, the sights on Glocks are crap*, I thought. Couldn't the Met at least have splashed out a couple of quid on after-market ones.

I stopped, cleared the weapon, removed the mag, putting both on the table, and looked at Larry.

He nodded saying: "I've seen worse, mate. When was the last time you shot?"

I thought for a second: "About eight years ago."

Still nodding, Larry continued: "You up for it if we run a scenario?"

I was expecting this. I wanted the challenge. What was it going to be like? It wasn't going to go well if Burke felt slighted by it. *Sod it! This is something I love doing. I'm not responsible for how he feels. That's down to him. He's an adult. He should grow up! Dickhead!*

I nodded. Larry smiled and said: "Not like you to be this quiet, Richard."

Another laugh. *Fair enough*, I thought!

He continued: "We have a blank screen and then a countdown. You'll start with the weapon pointing down in a two-handed grip, finger off the trigger, as soon as the countdown gets to zero. The scenario will start, and you must be ready to react from the first moment. You may or may not need to shoot. React exactly as you would in real life. These rounds are live. The scenario will end if you discharge your firearm. Remember, safety at all times. Do you understand?"

I nodded, saying: "Yes, I'm ready."

Larry said: "Pick up your weapon and load it, then hold it in the two-handed grip, pointing down. Ollie, get ready."

I slid the magazine into the pistol grip, and thumbed the slide release (loading a round into the chamber) with my right thumb. *I'm ready.* I gave a slight nod.

Larry turned to Ollie, saying: "Roll it."

The countdown flashed on the screen: 5, 4, 3, 2, 1. The screen went blank, then the scenario began. A suburban street, terraced houses in the background about thirty yards away, a building to my left, a pavement ahead and a raised flowerbed to my right.

Front and centre took my attention. There was a heated argument between two men. The one to the left was a large, muscular man (6'3") in his thirties wearing a white T-shirt and jeans. He had his back to me. The guy on the right was smaller (5'9"), slim build, in his early twenties. He was wearing black jeans, a dark shirt and a black leather jacket. I could see his left hand, but his right was obscured by his body. The two men started to struggle, and the larger man said: "Fuck! He's got a gun! He's got a gun!" Did he mean me, or the smaller man? I couldn't see a firearm, so couldn't shoot. The smaller man was doing something with his right hand I couldn't see.

I shouted: "Stand still, armed police!" But I still kept the pistol pointing down; I'd still not seen a weapon.

The larger man shouted again: "He's got a gun!" I repeated my instructions: "Armed police, stand still!" I felt my adrenaline surge. There were beads of perspiration on my back and forehead. The smaller man broke away from the struggle and turned to his right, shielding me from seeing his right hand. Still, I'd seen no weapon. He took off running. Man, they throw everything at you in those scenarios. The smaller man half-turned towards me. At that point I saw he had what looked like a dark pistol in his right hand. I brought up the G17 to a firing position, still with my finger outside the trigger guard. I shouted: "Armed police, stand still!"

Just as I was about to fire I noticed, directly behind the running man, across the other side of the road, a woman pushing a pushchair. Shoot or no shoot ... No shoot. I can't risk the shot if I'm not certain. At this the man turned back and continued running. I lowered the pistol. The tape froze.

With shaking hands, working on autopilot, I removed the magazine, and locked the slide back, catching the ejected round. I put them back on the table. And breathe out. I felt a little weak at the knees. That was intense. How the hell did Larry, or Ollie for that matter, do that every day? That shoot or no shoot, the power to end life with the pressure of a finger?

There was silence, and I took a moment. I looked at Larry and said: "How the hell do you do that every day? I was petrified? Did I get it right?"

Larry looked at me straight in the eye and, with a serious look (most unlike him, he's never serious), replied quietly: "It never gets any easier, not ever!"

I suddenly got a chill down my spine. He'd had to do that for real, had to pull the trigger. How can you live with that? I guess that's why he does things to connect him with people (music shows). To try to reconnect. *I honestly don't think I could do this,* I thought.

Larry seemed to shed his serious tone and said: "Why didn't you shoot?"

"I didn't clearly see a firearm until he turned, and by then there was a mother and pushchair directly behind him. If I took the shot, I'd either hit him, or the woman. No safe shot. I couldn't be certain, with my level of skill."

Larry nodded: "You made the right call. If you'd shot him on the word of the other guy, you weren't justified. It wasn't until you saw a firearm that you were justified to shoot. By then it was too late due to potential collateral damage."

He patted me on the shoulder, saying: "It was the only legal and ethical thing you could do. You could have taken the shot, but get it a couple of inches out, and you're looking at a manslaughter charge. Good call. Some do take the shot, but even then they fail this. You aren't Wyatt Earp, and this isn't the Wild West. You're a professional police officer. You are there to protect the public, not take chances like that with their lives. Well done, mate, well done."

Turning to the rest of the class, he said: "We're done here, Sergeant. I'll take you to the canteen, if that's OK? Ollie, put away the kit please, mate."

I was still shaking as we made our way over to the canteen. Larry chatted to Mary and a couple of the other students.

When we arrived at the canteen, he said: "If you have a bite to eat here, the flyboys will be along shortly to take you over to have a look at their expensive toys. Well done on the range. I hope you all enjoyed it, and learnt something about what we do." He grinned, and we thanked him, and the others made their way into the canteen.

Larry stopped me, and indicated he wanted to talk. Burke didn't seem happy that I was waiting outside, but wasn't in a hurry to cross Larry again, so left us alone.

Larry took me a little distance from the canteen, well out of earshot. He looked at me directly, and that look made me wary. He meant business. He said: "Mate, well done on the range. Not many make the right decision on that scenario. That sergeant of yours is giving you a hard time, isn't he?"

Before I got a chance to answer, he carried on. "Occasionally, you'll meet people like him. I can't really talk much now. But understand if it gets really stupid down the line, call me and I'll help you. I'm sure once you get onto relief you'll do fine. Keep in touch, mate. I really mean it; I've got your back. For what it's worth. Best get back in there."

With that he slapped me on the back and jogged back to the office.

As I entered the canteen, I could feel an atmosphere. There were absolute daggers from Burke, and a few dark looks from some of the other trainers. I went over to the counter and bought some food and a drink, and went to join the other pups. They were friendly enough, except for Edward, who had quietened down a lot since the first day. Terry and Mary would talk to me, the others were a little wary, I think would be the best word to describe it.

About half an hour later, a man in a pristine flight overall walked in and spoke with Burke. Then we got the bad news: the choppers were out on calls and wouldn't be back, so we'd just get a quick tour of the base instead. The tour was brief and interesting, if you're technically minded. But, without their centrepieces, it was just a couple of buildings.

We returned to Earlham and were told to return on Monday morning at "08:00 hours sharp!" That was when we'd start the street part of street duties. Finally, we'd be on policing, upholding the thin blue line between chaos and order and all that fine stuff. Other than a few short remarks and a few dark looks, Burke left me alone. Finally!

The weekend was filled with getting ready, reading the notes for the upcoming day's divisional training session. That involved an exam, but was not done by the street duties staff (yippee!). I was dealing with solicitors, mortgage companies and estate agents regarding my first house. Exciting times. I'd also updated Julia regarding the street duties. When she heard about what was going on, she was unimpressed! She put me in touch with Nina, a sergeant, who said she'd help if things were getting worse. At least I had friends in the police.

Chapter 4
ON THE STREETS

The next week rolled around (starting the third week; it was going past quickly). Monday was spent getting ready, making sure I'd got all the paperwork. I found out I'd be working one-to-one with PC Wilson. I wasn't too concerned, because he seemed reasonably chilled, and hadn't given me a hard time.

Tuesday rolled around, and my first day out on the streets in uniform. I was excited and nervous in equal measure. All that time getting ready for something, working, struggling, to achieve a goal, and there it was. Sink or swim! I stopped myself playing the 'what if' game. I put my uniform on and was ready and waiting at 08:00 hours (we weren't due out until 09:00 hours). You can never be too keen. The training staff arrived and, again, turfed me out of the conference room. I waited in the canteen with the others. At just before 09:00 hours, the training staff walked in, and we were paired up (Burke had drafted in a few 'volunteers' from his relief who were in on rest days to take us out).

As I left, Burke smiled at me and said: "Good luck."

I almost stopped in my tracks, and replied: "Err, thank you Sergeant."

I then continued out onto the mean streets of Earlham. That first step out from the front entrance, down the steps, and there I was, a genuine policeman, doing policey things. I put my hand into my pocket and felt for my great-grandad's police whistle, which my mother had given to me. It had been carried by a member of my family for over 100 years while policing. I'd promised myself that I'd carry it every day to remind myself of the oath I'd taken at Hendon. I wasn't going to betray that, made to Her Majesty the Queen, and in front of people I loved.

Walking along, chatting to Peter (he'd asked me to call him that when we were working) Wilson, he started telling me about the different places in the surrounding area: hotspots, what to look out for. As we made our way through the back streets, I said: "Peter, what should I be looking out for?"

"Look, Richard, this isn't rocket science. Just look around and if you see something dodgy, deal with it. Talk to people as well, smile, nod, say 'Hi!' You're here to protect people, and most folks appreciate that. You don't have to go overboard, don't try to chat up everything with a skirt and a pulse. That's creepy! But saying 'Hello!' sets a good example. You never know, if you do chat to someone, it might be the first time a copper has ever talked to them. Most of this job is talking to people, the rest is boredom, paperwork. Oh, and a few moments of fear or excitement."

I looked up at him. Well, that sounded easy.

He continued: "Learn to look at every car, every person. Who are they? What are they doing? Why's that car parked there? Just get used to reading the situation. People get into all kinds of trouble by not reading the situation!"

A short while later, we'd made our way to the Kenton Road, which is single lane in each direction, with a clearly marked "Bus Lane" on the outsides. It is a main thoroughfare in and out of central London, and is busy most of the time. Therefore, queues start to form, and impatient drivers chance their arms and drive down the bus-only lane.

That is what we were there to police, so we made our way along the bus lane until we came to the first side road turning (easy to direct drivers out of the way of buses, to issue them with a ticket, £30 at the time).

I stood on the kerb, watching, and Peter stood around the corner in the side turning. So it was my job to spot and pull over the errant cars. I stood out clearly. I wasn't trying to hide and be sneaky. If they were ignorant enough to drive down the bus lane, and stupid enough when they could clearly see police watching them, they deserved a ticket.

It didn't take long for a crappy old black Ford Orion (variant of the escort) to drive at pace down the bus lane, past all the patient, law-abiding drivers waiting.

There we go. It was a softball start. It was an FPN (N), which meant it was a fine, but not points on their licence. I heard Sergeant Johnson's mantra, "See traffic, think crime," in my head. Contrary to popular belief, it really isn't that easy to make out the race of a driver most of the time. Honestly, I never cared, and I honestly don't think my colleagues did either. It was a car doing naughties, a pull and ticket. End of chat!

I stepped out into the bus lane, raising my left hand in the stop position, and with my right pointed directly at the car.

The car slowed down and put its indicator on and tried to force its way into the line of stationary cars. You sneaky so-and-so! Not so fast, mate!

I walked towards the car and pointed at the driver, indicating it should turn into the side turning where Peter was waiting. The driver reluctantly complied. As I turned to speak to the driver, the windows of the two cars directly in front of me opened, and I heard: "Well done, mate! Give 'em a bleeding ticket!"

From the other car I heard: "Pity there ain't more of you lot handing out tickets. Good work, mate!"

I raised my hand in acknowledgement, and said: "Thanks, we do our best."

There were a couple of drowned-out replies as the traffic lights changed and the cars moved off. *Well, that was unexpected. This job is easy! People cheering you for handing out tickets. Sweet!*

I walked over to the car which stopped next to Peter. He was letting me deal with it, which was good. See traffic, think crime. So the car wasn't in the best of condition, with dents, rust. I walked up to the driver's door. The window wound down, and it's a 40-something Asian man, dressed in a black shirt and jeans. I said, in a clear, friendly tone: "Hello Sir. Would you please switch off the engine and join me on the pavement. Thanks."

I then went and stood on the pavement, and patiently waited for him.

He joined me, saying: "Mate, I didn't see the bus lane. Sorry about that."

I smiled and nodded, "OK Sir. Is this your vehicle?"

The man nodded, "Yeah"

"Is it registered to you?"

"Yeah!"

I got ready for a name and vehicle check. *Here goes nothing.* "What's the registration number of the car?"

He gave me the details. I noted them down, then asked: "What's your name, date of birth and address?"

He mumbled them. I had to ask for clarification. Eventually, I got his details down. The reason I didn't do the vehicle check before asking his name was he might overhear the radio, and give me that name back.

I asked: "Have you got any ID on you? Driving licence, bank card, please Sir?"

He produced a bank card, which matched the name he gave me.

Then I got on the radio. Deep breath. Burke would no doubt be listening. *Here goes nothing*: "PT, 272."

"Go ahead, 272."

"Can I please have a vehicle check and name check for a stop in the Kenton Road."

Slight pause as the controller got the screen up.

"Go ahead with the vehicle check."

I clearly spelt out the registration number using the phonetic alphabet. So far so good.

It came back to the same name he'd given me, and an address just around the corner. Well, he was lying about not knowing the area, and therefore the bus lane. Ticket time!

I then gave the details for the name check: IC4 male, date of birth (DOB), height, clothing description. He came back as known, not wanted, no driving ban. All good so far.

The radio sparked into life: "272, correct radio procedure when you conduct a name check. Male then IC code, not the other way around. Like you were repeatedly told!"

It was Burke! Really, he corrected me over the radio so that everyone could hear, for that! I took a deep breath, and looked at Peter. He looked slightly embarrassed by that, I could tell. Not great for my confidence, either. Never mind. We do the job in spite of those in charge, not because of them.

I said: "Do you have a current MOT and insurance to drive this vehicle on this road at this time (textbook Hendon)?"

"Yeah, I have. They're at home."

It was my chance to call his bluff about not knowing about the bus lane, giving me the moral high ground about giving him a ticket.

"I thought you said you didn't know the area, so you didn't know about the bus lane? Then didn't notice the signs, or the white lines painted on the road, or the fact that the bus lane is painted red?"

He shuffled his feet and said: "I forgot, all right."

"I'm going to deal with you by way of a fixed penalty notice."

As I produced the paperwork, he said: "Oh, bleedin' hell mate, do you have to?"

Peter interjected: "Mate, it's only a fine, no points!"

As he looked at Peter, and I was starting to fill in the very long-winded FPN form, a car shot past in the bus lane. The man said: "'Ere, you didn't stop him; that's not fair, I'm going to complain!"

Great, a complaint on the first stop, on my first day, Burke will have a field day with that. This job sucks!

Peter drew himself up to his full height, putting his hands on his hips and said: "Sir, you're fully entitled to make a complaint, however, the only reason we couldn't catch that geezer was because we were dealing with you. We can't be in two places at once!"

The man shrugged, still looking pissed off, and decided to shut up at this point. I filled out the rest of the form that I could complete at the roadside and explained his options for paying or contesting it in court. Peter was walking around the car, as I was talking to the driver. Had I missed something?

I issued him with the ticket, and the driver drove off. Peter said: "Not bad. You didn't check the car's tyres. With a crappy old motor like that, always check them. They were OK. We'll fill the rest of the FPN when you're back at the nick. Could you have done section 1 on the car (section 1 of PACE regards searching people and cars)?"

I knew a test when I heard one. I replied: "No, there weren't the grounds." Peter nodded. Clearly, he concurred.

We made our way through the back streets, chatting to people, getting an idea of the layout of our patch, so to speak.

As I went in through the front of Earlham Police Station, and in front of station staff and police officers, Burke came over and loudly said: "Poor radio procedure on that name check, 272. I expect better. DO NOT LET IT HAPPEN AGAIN!"

A little taken aback, and knocked out of my positive mood at doing my first stop and ticket, I replied: "Sorry Sergeant."

He glared at me as I went through to the writing room. It was a grand name for a simple, poorly maintained room with a number of tables around the edge and various assorted chairs of all different types in a range of states of repair.

I settled down to fill in the evidence section, where we had to lay out what happened. This would be checked, and if necessary be read out in court, so it had to be right.

Trying to remember the order of things, Peter looked over my shoulder and said: "'Ere, you all right with that? I'm off to the canteen to get a coffee and a bite to eat. Do you want anything?"

I replied, somewhat preoccupied: "A coffee and some biscuits please, mate."

"Good move; even the canteen can't screw that up. How do you like your coffee?"

I grinned, despite myself: "Black, no sugar. Simple and bitter, like me."

He snorted in mild amusement at that and walked off to the canteen.

I settled down to think. OK: "Day, date, time, and place, I came, I saw, I conquered." That was the saying.

My hand was shaking. Why? I was nervous about getting this wrong and giving Burke more ammunition against me.

Once I'd finished, and Peter had his snack, he took the FPN and said: "Yeah, that's not great, but it covers the main points. Why's your handwriting so scruffy? You nervous?"

I nodded.

He said: "You shouldn't be. It's just a form."

I looked at him, hoping he'd pick up on what I was feeling. If he did, he didn't show it.

A short while later, I was called into the conference to see Burke. I went in and sat down, as asked. Burke and Hargreaves were stood on the other side of the desk from me, with my FPN in front of them. Burke waited until I was settled in my seat, and said: "What's that (pointing at the FPN)?"

I said: "I think it's the ..."

Burke shouted: "You think! Aren't you sure?" he shoved the FPN across the desk towards me. "Look at it! Check it! Is that yours?"

I could see this wasn't going to be a good exchange. *Keep calm, play the game, let him have his little show of dominance.* I picked it up and inspected it. Yes, it was mine. I put it down on the desk and looked at him, saying in a calm, measured tone: "Yes, Sergeant, it is the FPN I submitted earlier."

Burke said sarcastically: "Are you sure this time, 272?"

"Yes, I am Sergeant."

This time he barked: "Well, it isn't fucking good enough, you arrogant little ex-teacher! How did you ever become a teacher with writing skills as poor as that!"

I began to understand that the calmer I remained, the more it angered him. He wanted to see me react and crack up. So, absolutely calm it was, then!

I didn't say anything, and waited. He leant forward over the desk, snarling: "I asked you a fucking question! Answer it you cocksure little shit."

I waited a moment, and Hargreaves chimed in: "The sergeant asked you a question, you little fucker. Answer!"

I looked at Burke, and said: "I'm sorry you found my work wasn't up to your standards, Sergeant. Please could you tell me in which ways I could improve it."

Burke slammed the desk right in front of me. I could see it coming, and fought the urge to flinch.

He said: "Don't you be disrespectful to me, you cunt! I'll stick you on a minor disciplinary, which is recorded on your personnel file!"

I could see he was beginning to lose his rag. Despite myself, I was quite enjoying it.

I kept a blank expression and said: "I meant no disrespect, Sergeant. I apologise if you felt I was being disrespectful."

He looked at me and said in a low voice, with real satisfaction: "You've failed this exercise. I'll record it on your file. You're not fit to be a police officer! Get out!"

I got up and walked out. *Well,* I thought, *if he's going down that road, I'd better speak with Julia and see if she can help.*

That evening, I heard the phone go: "Hello Richard, Larry here. How are you doing, mate?"

Serendipity is a strange thing! "Hi Larry. Not too bad mate. I didn't expect to see you the other day. Thanks for showing us around."

He said: "Straight to the point. Is that sergeant giving you a hard time?"

I waited a moment to collect my thoughts. Larry took the hint, saying: "I knew he was. That's out of line. It's a tough job, and people can be pretty hard on you, but there's a line, and what I saw was over that line. Where are you now on the whole street duties thing?"

I took a deep breath and explained the whole thing, from start to finish, not leaving out anything.

He waited a moment and said slowly: "right, I don't want to get directly involved, unless I have to. Bad form to step on other people's toes. But if you need it, I'll write it up for you. But try to keep your head down, mate. You'll be fine when you get on relief, believe me."

Although I was pleased he was going to help me, I had a bad feeling about where it was going. I said: "Thanks Larry, I really appreciate it. I'll do my best. I just want to pass and get onto relief."

Larry replied: "I know mate, I know. By the way, good job in that scenario. You did better than that sergeant of yours. He thought he was a crack shot and fired at the suspect, missed and slotted (shot) the woman with the pram in the head!"

I was shocked: "Really? No wonder he wasn't happy!"

Larry chuckled, wished me well and hung up.

It was going from bad to worse. There clearly was something to be worried about. At least I had one source of help. Let's see if I could get two. I called Julia, and I explained the situation. She said she'd get Nina (a sergeant friend of hers from central London) to call me. Good as her word, Nina called back within an hour, and I set out the situation yet again. Nina said to keep a diary of every interaction I had, and to take and retain or keep copies of all the paperwork. She gave me her number and said that, although she couldn't get involved directly, if I needed help she'd do what she could. I thanked her, and said I'd take her advice, which I did. I noted down as much as I could about what had happened, and resolved to keep or copy any paperwork.

The following day (Wednesday), I once again worked with Peter. I issued a number of FPNs and really tried to do the best job I could filling them in. I'll be honest, I was nervous filling them in.

I was about to make my first arrest. Just at the end of our shift (about 16:30 hours), a call came on the radio that a man was collapsed outside the hospital in a small side street . Were there any units to deal? The late turn (14:00 hours to 22:00 hours, which was the busiest shift, normally) were stretched thin. I looked at Peter (we were just around the corner from there), and he nodded with a slight grin (he knew the type of call it was and suspected what we'd find). I replied: "PT, this is 272 and 203, we can take that call."

Slight pause, as they didn't recognise us as part of their relief. "PT272 and 203, let us know when you're on scene, PT."

We walked over to the entrance to the grounds of the hospital, which is an ancient church surrounded by a stone wall. The hospital was a highly visible landmark. Sure enough, seated against the wall of the chapel, was a man in his mid-fifties, with bedraggled black hair, wearing a faded black jacket and blue jeans. He absolutely stank of intoxicating liquor (the court term for booze) and urine. Peter put us on scene with the radio. I looked at Peter, he grinned, and said: "He's all yours. You know the drill."

First aid check. I walked over and took a deep breath so I wouldn't have to breathe when I was next to him, then knelt down next to him. I went through the procedure I'd learnt: don't assume he's drunk; he might be diabetic, or on drugs, or ill in some other way.

I tried talking to him, but he only groaned at me. I put on my rubber gloves, put my hand on his shoulder and tried to rouse him. He started to stir, looking at me with bleary eyes. His breath was like a brewery. I went through the series of questions I'd been taught, about various health conditions. To no avail. He was drunk! What to do about it? He couldn't just sit there. I had to find out if he was capable of getting home, or if he'd be a danger to himself?

I tried to get him to his feet. No dice! *Right,* I thought, *"drunk, and incapable"* (drunk and can't look after themselves, with no one to help them). Being drunk, no problem, but being so drunk you're likely to walk in front of a car, or start a fight, that's a different ball game.

I looked at Peter, and he said: "What do you think, Richard?"

I replied: "He's drunk and incapable. He needs to come in to a place of safety, and we can provide it for him at Earlham."

Peter nodded in agreement. He called on the radio: "PT ... 203."

"Go ahead 203."

"PT. Regarding our last call, can you check custody has room for one more, please?"

Slight pause: "203, yep there's room at the inn for one more. What's he coming in for?"

"Yeah PT, drunk and incapable, and you chalk this one up to 272."

I felt a moment of satisfaction. It was very fleeting; a drunk guy who reeked – oh joy! Peter put on his gloves and got the other side of him. On three we lifted him up to sit on the low wall, and he was swaying. At this point I noticed why he stank of urine. He'd emptied his bladder, and his jeans were soaked.

I said: "I'll have to search him."

Peter looked at me and replied: "Indeed you do, young pup."

I carefully went through his jacket pockets and then his back pockets. Crumpled notes, keys, and a battered wallet with a tenner and some change.

Then it was time for the worst bit: the front pockets. It's a deeply unpleasant feeling as you slide your hands into a tight pocket and feel the cold of the urine-soaked jeans knowing it's the thickness of a rubber glove from your hand. But this was the job, looking after drunks.

The van arrived. I cautioned, and arrested him: "You do not have to say anything, but it may harm your defence if you do not mention when questioned, something which you later rely on in court. Anything you do say may be given in evidence."

That was for Peter's benefit, not the drunk guy's. So what did that actually mean? I'd taken the liberty of another human being. From now until he was handed over to the custody sergeant, I was responsible for his well-being. Odd feeling. Did I really have that authority? In this case it was easy: there was a good chance, if we left him there, that harm may have come to him. Better to get him in Hotel Earlham for the night.

We carefully manoeuvred him into the cage in the van, making sure he couldn't fall over during the extremely short trip to the custody suite.

The van pulled up, the doors opened and Peter and I picked up the man, one on each side. The smell wasn't getting any better. As gently as we could, we struggled through the doors into the custody suite, and its brightly lit, white-walled room. The left wall, with a long, low, fixed bench against it, carried on straight until it met the far wall with the door through to the front office. The right wall ran along until it met the small fingerprint and photo room.

There was also a door leading to a tiny exercise yard, where prisoners could go to have a smoke. In the centre were two high custody desks set at ninety degrees to each other, forming half a square. The custody sergeant's desk was facing outwards, the one other towards us.

Behind and to the left of that was a corridor to a couple of interview rooms, and the cells. The floors throughout were tiled.

That day, there was only one custody sergeant: a tall, lean, Black man of about 40. He smiled as we staggered in.

He said, in a friendly voice: "Hello there. Who have you got for me today?"

He must be part of C relief, the people who hopefully will become my new family soon. Best behaviour, good first impression. "Hello Sergeant. I've got this gentleman ..."

At that point, the man straightened up and gave a gagging noise, indicating he'd vomit. Peter and I did our best to turn him to one side, but he deposited the contents of his stomach all over the floor, and up the side of the custody desk. *Great, thanks mate. There goes my chance at a good first impression.*

The sergeant looked over the desk: "Are you two all right?"

I looked down, to the vomit on my trousers and boots. Nice! Peter had escaped.

I said: "I caught a bit of it, but otherwise I'm OK, thank you Sergeant."

The sergeant smiled: "Right, 272, walk him around to cell three, take the usual precautions, as this gentleman doesn't look like he's in any condition to be booked in at the moment."

We did as we were asked. As we struggled down the passage to the cells, a pretty, slim, young, light-haired (tied back in a tight bun) 25-ish woman of about 5'5" smiled at us, and opened the cell door, saying in a cute, Welsh accent: "That's cell three. If you hold him there for a moment, I'll pop in and get the mattress on the floor for you (this was done for drunk prisoners to prevent them falling onto the floor and injuring themselves)."

She did this, and after she'd stepped out, we carefully placed him on the mattress, and turned him to lie in the recovery position.

We left the room, and the young woman closed the cell door with a resounding thud. Once you've heard that sound, you don't forget it. She left the sliding wicket open, allowing a clear view of the prisoner without opening the door, and turned to me, wrinkling her nose: "He got you, didn't he? You'll have to go and clean up. Down the corridor and to your right is the tap and drain set against the far wall. Don't worry about our friend in there. I'll do ten-minute observations on him."

Noticing my shoulder number for the first time, she said: "Oh, you're one of the two street duties who'll be joining us. That's good; I won't be the newest in service soon. That means you get all the shit jobs instead of me. Not that I mind, and I won't give you a hard time. I'm Mel, by the way. Who are you?"

I liked this lady. She seemed kind, relaxed, and she had a lovely, lyrical accent.

I replied: "Thanks Mel. I'm Richard Armstrong. Sorry I've given you a nasty mess to clean up in the custody."

She smiled, patiently, and replied: "Don't worry, it's all part of the glamorous job in the Met. I'd best go and get the bucket and mop."

Peter nodded and walked back into custody while Mel and I walked down the corridor. As I was washing off my boots and she was collecting the mop and bucket, I said: "Look, I should really clear up that mess; he is my prisoner."

Mel stopped and looked at me, saying: "Stop! Listen, I know in civvy life being chivalrous is virtuous, but in here, we all wear the same uniform, we do the same job and get the same pay. So please don't treat me any different to any of the blokes. That's something us ladies are very prickly about. We don't want any special treatment. OK!"

It wasn't said in a nasty way, just very bluntly. Damn, I liked this lady. This was someone I could respect. I nodded: "Fair enough. I'm really glad to hear that. Honestly, that's something I absolutely respect. Judged by the content of your character, not the content of your underwear!"

Mel looked at me for a moment and then burst out laughing. She put her hand on my arm: "You'll fit in just fine in C relief, my lover. This can be the worst job. The management treat you like shit, the public treat you like shit and you get all the shittiest jobs. The only people you can rely on are your mates, and everyone, I mean everyone, has to have a sense of humour. If you can't take a joke ..."

She paused, looking at me, and I completed the saying: "... You shouldn't have joined."

We both laughed and made our way back down the corridor to clean up vomit. Another day in paradise.

When we got back to the custody suite, Peter was chatting with the sergeant. They looked around at us. Mel said: "Sarge, this is Richard Armstrong. He's one of the two who'll be joining us soon." She turned to me and said: "This is Sergeant Darling. He's one of the nicest men you'll meet. You'll like him."

Sergeant Darling grinned, saying: "Yeah, Peter was just telling me that. Welcome Richard. I'm looking forward to having you on the team. It's your second day out and you've already brought in a prisoner. I like your enthusiasm. It sounds like you'll fit right in. You've already got Mel here laughing. That's a good sign."

He looked up a whiteboard opposite. He handed me a board marker (all too familiar) and said: "You can put up your first prisoner on the custody board."

The whiteboard had a grid of taped lines with cell number, arresting officer, offence, suspect's name, etc. along the top, and columns to be filled in underneath them. I carefully and neatly filled in the line for cell three. I looked at Sergeant Darling as I got to the suspect's name. He picked up the hint and said: "Just write 'Johnson'. He's one of our regulars. Neat writing, by the way. What did you do before joining the Met?"

I hesitantly replied: "I was a teacher, Sergeant."

He nodded, saying: "I thought it would be something like that. You'll get on well with the guv'nor; he used to be a teacher too."

We finished up, and went off to write up the notes of the arrest. *Right,* I thought, *first milestone: my first arrest!* I felt I had something to work towards. C relief sounded like they wanted me. They were welcoming, and at least two of their number I could get on with. A ray of hope. I just had to get through the next few weeks.

I carried on, for the next couple of weeks, volunteering for every call, ticket after ticket, arrest after arrest. We had a day in the coroner's court. We had to get dressed in our dress uniform. I went to my locker – it wasn't there! No! No! I had been working so hard and keeping my head down. I realised I'd left it at home. It had been sent to the dry cleaner after the passing-out parade, and I'd meant to bring it in. No! I'd just handed Burke another gold-plated opportunity to bully me. I closed the door of my locker and slapped it loudly with the palm of my hand. When I looked around, I saw Burke looking at me. Oh, that day wasn't going well. He shouted at me, swore and told me how stupid I was.

We went to the coroner's, and were given the opportunity of watching a post-mortem. We were told it wasn't mandatory. I decided (the only one) that I didn't want to attend. Burke made a big deal out of that too.

We were beginning to be sent out in pairs, without instructors now. We began to feel more confident, and walked around with a little more certainty to our step. We were getting the hang of this policing lark.

Terry and I were sent out on nine beat (rows of old-fashioned terraced houses, with a few trees). For Earlham, it was nice. There'd been a number of thefts from cars. We were to show a police presence, and hopefully reassure the residents and deter the thefts.

To cover more ground, Terry took one street, I took the next. I walked along a line of parked cars, and when I came to a particularly crappy old black Ford Escort, I noticed a man of about 20 sitting in the driver's seat. He looked up and smiled at me, I nodded back and continued on my way. I was showing the great British public the friendly face of the Met, reassuring them that their property was safe, and the Met were on top of it. I felt my confidence growing.

After walking around the agreed area for about ten minutes, and not seeing anything suspicious, I met up with Terry and we began to talk about where we'd go next. We were approached by a man in his mid-forties, wearing jeans and a T-shirt. He said: "'Ere, I thought you lot were supposed to be stopping crime. My car's just been broken into. Where were you when that happened?"

I replied: "Sorry to hear that, Sir. Can you show us where it is?"

He walked us back to a street that looked familiar, to a crappy old Ford Escort that looked familiar.

The man said: "This is my car. I only left it for an hour and some little bastard's nicked the bleedin' stereo!"

Oh God! I'd actually seen the guy nicking the stereo and even smiled at him. *Burke will kill me for this. I've got to make this right, but preferably without dropping myself in it.*

I took the report and we continued our patrol. I confessed my mistake to Terry. Oh boy did he laugh. I mean, it was obscene! I thought he was going to have a heart attack! When he had finished laughing, he said: "You could always talk to Alan in the intelligence unit. He'd help you, I'm sure. If not, you'll have to brave confessing to Burke. But he'll have a field day with that."

I knew he was right.

We made our way along to the Kenton Road, and the bus lanes again, then took it in turns to pull over cars that were illegally driving down them. It was Terry's turn, and he pulled over this silver Mercedes (nice!) with two tall, South American men, both in their thirties. They were wearing expensive suits (no M&S there) and shoes. They were both very friendly and cooperative. Terry did the name checks and said: "Where are you from, gentlemen?"

"We're from Colombia."

Terry grinned and raised an eyebrow and turned to look at me (as I said, we were having a laugh with these guys). Terry said: "Colombia, you say? Here, Richard, do we need to search this vehicle? Have we pulled over international drug smugglers?"

They laughed heartily at this, and said: "Oh yeah, we're just on the way back from City Airport to sell to our low-level dealers."

Once again we laughed. Terry gave them the ticket, and we walked back to the station.

As we were making our way to the DIU and Alan, Terry got a call on the radio, asking him to see Alan in the DIU. Spooky!

We walked in and Alan said: "Wow that was quick. Thanks for coming to see me so promptly. It's almost like you knew I needed to speak to you. That last stop you did on that car with two Colombians. I need you to walk me through it and then put a CRIMINT on it, after you've called the area drug squad."

Taken aback by this, Terry gave a description of them, the car and why we'd stopped them. Alan listened carefully, while making notes on his computer. At the end, he said: "Well, you just stopped two of the most prolific cocaine smugglers in the UK. They were almost certainly armed, and were carrying the drugs in the car. If you'd searched that car, they'd almost certainly have shot you."

He waited for that to sink in. *Bloody hell!* He continued: "Well done, gentlemen. We now have a car to go with the two aliases they gave. It didn't ping on the PNC, but it sent a message to the area drugs squad so as not to tip them off. They'll be sorting out a hard stop (armed police, weapons drawn, immediately removed and cuffed, giving them no chance to shoot police) on them. I'll put in a recommendation that they send that awful sergeant of yours a letter of thanks. That should help. Well done. Intelligence, you see, saves lives, and makes us more efficient."

Wow, just a simple bus lane stop, and we could have died, but we end up with an LOA (letter of appreciation). Just shows, any stop can lead to bigger things.

Alan looked at us, saying: "Well gents, was there anything else you wanted? If not, you've got a phone call to make."

I cleared my throat and said: "Well Sergeant, there was one more thing (Columbo style, my turn this time)."

He looked at me knowingly and said: "Sergeant? This sounds like you need me to get you out of a bit of a pickle. Go on, hit me with it."

I took a deep breath and told him the whole thing. He had the same reaction Terry had. Thanks guys. Seriously, thanks!

He leant forward in his chair, and called up a number of faces on the screen. He said: "Shout when you see one you recognise."

He then flicked through a few photos. I soon found the culprit.

Alan nodded approvingly, saying: "He's one of the most prolific thieves on this patch. It'll be good to get him for this. I'll tell you what, I'll put this on CRIMINT as an intelligence report. I'll contact CID, and we'll get a raid on his house approved. There's more than enough grounds to do that even without your input. This will mean that he'll get nicked, the property will be returned, and no doubt there'll be plenty of other bent gear around there too. So you'll be off the hook."

I breathed a deep sigh of relief. The bad guy gets nicked and I don't lose my job. I thought for a moment and asked: "Alan, why does he steal things?"

Alan stopped and, leaning back on his chair, said: "Heroin! He's an addict. It's rife around here. Cannabis and heroin. Virtually nothing else. Different boroughs have different drug problems."

I thought that was sad. So many lives destroyed by drugs. Why?

We thanked Alan, and left. Terry stopped ribbing me about the guy in the car, because of the Colombians. This was beginning to get all too real.

A couple of days later, a call came out for a "sudden death". I volunteered for it. PC Douglas said he'd walk me through it. As I was walking out to the panda car, I dropped one of the pieces of paperwork I was carrying. Douglas turned around and could see me picking it up. I was shaking just a little bit. He looked at me in utter disgust and said: "What, you're nervous?" I nodded. He turned his back and, opening the car door, said: "What a fucking waste of space you are!"

I had never seen a dead person before; I didn't know what to expect. I took a few deep breaths and thought: *I'm going to do this regardless of how scared I am, and regardless of what a dickhead this bloke is!*

As we were making our way there, I read the CAD (Computer Aided Dispatch – a system that records the calls we get, and allows them to be handed out to the officers, and updates made, regarding their outcome. The system was adapted from an airline check-in system – the Met and its extra cheapness!) It explained the nephew of the caller had just been staying at his house, and had been found dead in the morning. There was an attached PNC showing that the nephew (Adam Hardy, 22 years) had just been released from prison and had an extensive record of burglary, theft, robbery and heroin convictions.

Douglas said: "Adam is well known. It's a regular thing that when they come out of prison, they OD (overdose) on H (heroin), 'cos they try and take the same size of hit. But their bodies aren't used to it, and die."

He said it so matter-of-factly. It was someone's son, brother, nephew. But I thought, if it was a regular occurrence to deal with, you'd have to emotionally distance yourself from it, or you'd drive yourself mad.

We pulled up to a row of terraced houses in a back street just off the main Commercial Road into London. They probably dated from the fifties, but were reasonably well maintained. These were what you'd call two-up two-down, one-bedroom affairs. There were tiny gardens out the front. They were very similar to my grandparents' house in Newcastle.

We were let in by a tall, thin man in his mid-fifties, wearing a light, checked shirt (it was buttoned incorrectly, as if in a hurry) and brown cord trousers. His light brown hair was unkempt, and was thinning. His eyes were watery. I looked at him with pity and, waiting for Douglas to finish introducing us, said: "Where is Paul?"

He didn't say anything and just pointed to the living room. I took a deep breath and walked in. It was a small, square front parlour (as my gran would have called them), with a battered old sofa which had a pillow and blanket on it (clearly, where he had been intending to sleep), and a matching chair facing an ancient TV angled in the far corner. Curled up in the foetal position in front of the TV was a young man. It was difficult to determine his exact age. He had jeans and a dark T-shirt on.

It was quiet, except for the sound of distant traffic from the London Road. There was a stillness you sometimes find when around the recently deceased. There was no smell, other than the mustiness from the room;

the window had clearly not been opened for a while, probably due to the traffic noise.

I walked over to where the young man was lying. As I got closer, I could see that he was slightly grey in colour, and had a slight trickle of now-dried blood from his nose. Lying next to his open hand was a pipe, a folded piece of tinfoil with a black line running along it and a cheap Bic lighter.

Douglas got out an evidence bag and handed it to me, saying: "Put some gloves on, and put those bits in here. They're evidence we'll have to bag. Once you've done that, we'll roll him over to check for any evidence of foul play, knife wounds or the like. After that I'll call the coroner, and you can search him, collect anything he has on him, and record them. Make sure you have everything fully noted in your IRB (Incident Report Book)."

I did as I was told, and then we carefully and as respectfully as you can, turned him over. He was cold and stiff, not like handling anything else. Having to get that close to a body is unnerving. I was glad when we'd checked and there were no signs of foul play.

Douglas then put in the call to Control to connect him to the control room. While he was talking on the radio, he referred to the body as "apparently lifeless", with the logic being that until a doctor had declared death, he wasn't legally dead. We weren't doctors and couldn't say someone was dead.

As we waited for the doctor to arrive, I spoke to the uncle, and tried my best to comfort him. He talked about how he'd known Adam since he was born, how he'd grown up as a lovely lad, kind and polite. When he'd become a teenager, he became moody and quiet (nothing unusual about that in teenagers). Then they found he'd been stealing. Eventually it had come out he was addicted to heroin at the age of 15. Older kids at school had dared him to take it and then, when he was hooked, they used to supply him outside the school gates. This really struck home for me: when he became addicted to one of the nastiest drugs around, he was in year ten. My God! How could that happen? My friend's kids were that age. I could feel myself welling up inside, then I suddenly understood why Douglas had seemed so distant: he had to put up barriers. How could you deal with that on a daily basis if you didn't?

The uncle broke down as he described how he had phoned Adam's mom and dad. How guilty they felt, because they'd told Adam he couldn't stay with them after his prison release, because they didn't want him to use in their house. The doubts and what ifs they must have been going through. *If only he'd been in our house, we'd have stopped him.* The guilt the uncle felt for allowing it to happen under his roof. He said that Adam had promised him he'd not use under his roof. I believed him, over the years since. I've found out that people will lie and lie and lie about everything. Some have absolutely no shame; they'll lie with horrible consequences for others for the most petty of reasons. But this guy wasn't lying.

The process of declaring death, and for the undertakers to remove the body to the mortuary, took a couple of hours. It's a bit of a lottery, depending upon how busy they are.

It took me a while to get my head around how such a waste of a life could occur. I was honestly glad of the intensely complex paperwork I had to complete. I'd have to attend coroner's court in couple of weeks, which was another milestone for me. An ordeal for the family!

We had our day's visit to the divisional training unit, where we had an exam with a 70 per cent pass mark, and a day's further training, for which we had to study, and we'd been given notes to prepare. I had done my required study. This wasn't as easy as at Hendon, due to the fact we were working, and having to absorb a lot. I felt pretty confident that I would at least make 80 per cent, given how I'd performed previously.

The day before, we were on a late shift. It was pretty new for us, but it was a way to get used to the shifts our bodies would have to adapt to. I'd be home (with no problems) at somewhere around 11 p.m., and have to be at the training unit at 09:00 hours. That was entirely doable.

That shift out of all the shifts was the busy time. Earlham was a late-turn ground, as they used to say. There were fights, robberies, stabbings, people coming home to find they'd been burgled and the like.

This may come as a surprise to some, but villains tend not to want to get out of bed early in the morning, or in the morning at all. Therefore, it was after lunch that it tended to all kick off. We were going to be assisting with this madness (albeit in a support role, mopping up the simpler jobs, in theory), so we worked in groups of three (two pups to one walker, so to speak). There weren't enough vehicles, so we were sent to walk around certain areas, and help out if anything near us needed dealing with. We were somewhat cautious because, as yet, we really hadn't developed our sixth sense for danger that experienced police get. We therefore had suffered injuries. Most had been struck at least once. Mary had a trip to hospital due to the fact one young lady apparently didn't much take to the idea of being arrested and thought that, if only she bit Mary, she'd be allowed to leave. It was a forlorn hope.

These assaults came in a number of forms. On one occasion, I arrested a particularly charming 'lady' in her twenties. She'd caused a disturbance in a local shop. Apparently, drinking half a bottle of vodka and going shopping wasn't a good idea. Who'd have thought?

When I got her back to the nick, I naively thought, because of her size (5'3") and state of intoxication, she wasn't a threat. I took off her cuffs and started to talk to the custody sergeant, who suddenly shouted "Look out!" as the 'lady', now armed with a soiled tampon, lunged at my face with it. I managed to wrestle her to the floor, and reapply the cuffs. While I hadn't been paying attention, she'd reached down her tracksuit pants and pulled the tampon out.

You only need to learn that lesson once. Always keep an eye on your prisoner, no matter who they are.

We spent the late turn dealing with the minor calls nearby. The other pup nicked a drunk and incapable at around 21:00 hours and got a lift back to the nick to book them in, which left myself and Douglas out on the streets. We began walking back to the nick when I saw a car coming along the road with only one headlight. It was now about 21:30 hours (the shift finished at 22:00 hours, and I had the training unit at 09:00 hours the next morning). I looked at Douglas with a do-you-mind-if-I-give-this-car-a-pull look. He nodded assent, and I duly attempted to stop it. The car speeded up and failed to stop. I jumped out of the way. Wow, that was new! As I was jumping out the way, Douglas (I'll give him credit, he wasn't a bad copper) was already on the radio calling it in. Honestly, I was surprised rather than scared!

A few minutes later, we got a call, saying the car had been pulled over, and would we like to deal with the driver. It was a courtesy extended to an officer at whom the driver had driven at.

Douglas looked at me, and I nodded in agreement this time. A passing police car picked us up and we were deposited next to this slightly battered black Ford Sierra. The door was open, and two officers were talking to the driver (a tall, slim man of around 30, wearing a black shirt and jeans), who wasn't in handcuffs.

I walked over and one of the officers said: "Are you the pup who tried to stop this car?"

I nodded: "Yes, I'm 272. Thanks for pulling him over."

He moved me away from the driver, and said: "I'll give you the honour of nicking him. He has a lump of narbis resin (slang for cannabis) on the floor of the passenger footwell. He denies trying to run you over. It would be an easy arrest for the drugs. It'd be hard to prove the running over bit. Then you could do a bit of process (slang for traffic tickets) on the motor when you get back to the yard. We checked him and the car. Both come back clean. So, you up for the overtime?"

I looked at Douglas, and he nodded. The job would be a relatively quick one: a couple of tickets for the crappy car, and a caution for the cannabis, as he didn't have form. Two hours, tops. Back home by 01:00 hours, a decent six hours' sleep. Yeah, I could do that. Also, I felt the pressure of wanting to show willing and not give Burke more ammunition about lack of commitment.

So, I walked over, and as I was going through the arrest procedure, the man kept saying: "I didn't see you mate. Sorry, I didn't see you."

Yeah, right. Six-foot copper in full uniform on a well-lit road? But I wasn't likely to prove it, so I'd settle for a good arrest and some process.

We got him back to the nick at just before 22:00 hours, booked him in and started on the paperwork. This is no joke; there's loads of it. We worked really fast, and were ready to interview him at around 23:00 hours (you can't interrupt sleeping prisoners for interviews, but he was awake, and this was about as late as we could manage).

We went down to custody (by then, the rest of the street duties course had left). We booked the prisoner out for interview. This was a taped interview run under PACE guidelines, which meant you had a double tape recorder. One tape was sealed, and kept as backup, and the other one we'd listen back to when we transcribed the interview, and it would be used to make a copy for the defence.

We settled down, making sure the prisoner was comfortable (toilet, a drink of water, food, etc.) It wasn't just to play nice with the prisoner, but was also so that we couldn't be accused of bullying him by the defence, or give him an excuse to break up the interview if we asked him questions he needed to think about (short for concoct some cock-and-bull fairy tale). It's the way the training explains it, but the bottom line when interviewing someone. Get them to explain what happened, don't interrupt, don't hassle them or try to trick them. Once they've gone through their account, while you take notes, you ask them about inconsistencies, if there are any, and, if they're being honest, give an explanation. If they're lying, allow them, encourage them, to LIE BIG! Then, if they were lying, let them tell the whopping lie in court. The default setting for legal representatives who go to police interviews is, if there's strong evidence, their clients do a 'no-comment interview', so they don't have to remember a lie months later in court. That's the cynical view, anyway.

The interview is just a chance for the prisoner to explain what happened. You try never to assume guilt, unless you actually saw them commit the crime, but go in with an open mind.

We started the tape rolling and I say, for the tape, the day, date, time, state persons present, and do a slightly altered version of the caution. All we had to do was talk to him about the cannabis. He admitted the offence, and we'd ask the governor for a caution, which they usually agree to. He leaves, we file the paperwork, job done. Not that day, though!

He said: "Look officer, I lied about my name. I'm on a ban, and I might have a warrant out on me."

I could feel my shoulders drop. This was a whole different ball game. We wouldn't be finished for hours. He gave me these new details. We suspended the interview to check. I went to the control room, and they got a hit and printed the details for me. Boy, oh boy! He was a disqualified driver, was wanted by the Met and Essex, and Kent's drug squads, for a range of other offences as well. It was going to be a long night.

I went back to Douglas, and he rolled his eyes, saying: "Well mate, looks like you and I are going to have a long night. At least it's some overtime money to help you pay for that new house of yours." I nodded, and thought: *I can't let him deal with all of this. I need to stay and split the work*.

He looked at me, for a minute, saying: "You've got that training tomorrow, haven't you?"

I nodded: "Look, I don't think it's fair to leave you here to do it on your own."

He nodded: "No, it wouldn't be. You'll just have suck it up; it's all part of the job, mate. If you couldn't take a joke, you shouldn't have joined."

In a lower voice, he said: "And honestly, mate, this job is a joke at times."

He paused for a moment, then said: "That being said, I'd better run this by Sergeant Burke. Hold on here for a minute, I'll give him a call."

I did as I was asked. About ten minutes later he reappeared, and nodded, saying: "The good sergeant agreed to it. In fact, he insisted you stay and help me."

I thought, *well that's that then; no sleep for me tonight!*

We spent the next six hours phoning different departments in different police forces, sending emails, completing paperwork, recording the crimes on the CRIS (Criminal Reporting System), doing CRIMINT entries, checking the car, then waiting until the drugs squads came on day shift to take over responsibility for the prisoner.

I finished at 06:30 hours. Douglas went home. I had a shower, changed uniforms, had a bite of breakfast, collected my notes and made my way over to the training unit.

I was beginning to feel it by the time I got there. I had been up for twenty-four hours, without sleep, and having to concentrate. I was having trouble focusing.

I met up with the others in the canteen (more coffee). Terry said: "'Ere mate, you look like shit. How much sleep did you get last night? I know you got off late."

The others looked over at me. I said: "None! The bloke had given us false pars (short for particulars). He was wanted by three forces for drugs."

The others' jaws dropped. Mary said: "What, no sleep and you're expected to pass an exam!? Why didn't they send you home and let them deal with it?"

I said: "To be fair, I didn't say no. I just didn't want to give Burke any more ammo against me. He already hates me. I thought it was my duty to stay on."

Terry stepped in: "That's really unfair. They shouldn't have let you. That's really out of line. I doubt they'd have done that to anyone else but you. You've made twice the arrests I have, more tickets, you've been working your arse off."

There was a murmur of agreement around the table. I could feel a lump in my throat. Maybe it was the lack of sleep, but I felt on the edge of tears. I began to realise just how hard I'd been pushing myself, and how much pressure I was under with Burke looking over my shoulder the whole time.

I said in a thick voice: "Thanks, just thanks. I really appreciate the support. I've been trying so hard, and been under so much pressure. I guess I hadn't noticed."

Terry (unlike him to show emotion) patted me on the back: "Don't worry, mate!"

The two staff members from the training unit walked in. The first was a stocky man in his late forties, and there was also a woman aged about 25, of about 5'6". The most striking thing about her was her hair: it was dyed bright red. I hadn't seen any police officer with dyed hair. We're not talking about the vanity-hiding type. This was someone who wasn't following the rules. I liked her immediately.

The lady said: "Good morning, I'm Mel, and this (indicating the man) is Keith. We're the divisional training team who'll be working with you today. It's lovely to see you. How are we all doing?"

Well, I thought, *this is unusual, and welcome.* The two of them sat down next to us and chatted in a very informal manner. They seemed genuinely pleased to see us, and friendly, and for a while I forgot how tired I was. Then we adjourned to the classroom for the test. The caffeine in the coffee was beginning to wear off. The warmth of the room made me feel sleepy, and it was a real struggle. I did my best with the test, but I knew it would be touch and go.

The tests were taken in, and we sat in the classroom, awaiting the results (with a smaller class, the tests could be marked more quickly). The door opened, and Mel and Keith walked in. I could feel my heart rate rise. *Please let me scrape this.* Keith looked at me, and my heart sank. I knew that look. He said: "Richard, can I see you outside." I could feel a sickness in my stomach, and I felt light-headed. I could feel the sympathetic stares of my friends. It was my last test! I'd fail the last test; it was exactly what Burke wanted. I'd fail at the last hurdle! *This isn't happening. This isn't happening.* Yet I was walking out the room to hear I'd failed.

Keith looked at me with a measured gaze. He said: "Richard, you got 67 per cent. You've failed. That means we'll send you back to the street duties course, and your sergeant will decide what happens next. Please wait in the canteen as I get the paperwork done."

He turned and walked off.

I could feel my legs wobble for a moment. I leant against the wall for support, then walked to the canteen. I was drained. I'd tried so hard, and it came down to one question (3 per cent equates to one question). I'd failed the test, and who knows what else, by one mark.

I dumbly sat in the sunny canteen, staring out of the window, just watching the sunlight shining through the leaves of the trees which lined the road outside. I was done, with nothing left inside. I'd failed! I tried to think, to feel anything. I couldn't. It was all gone.

I didn't notice when Mel spoke to me. She came over and gently put her hand on my arm, and I sleepily turned to look at her, not registering what she was saying. She smiled and started again: "Richard, you were away with the fairies there. When was the last time you slept?"

I tried to calculate. After a minute, I managed: "I can't quite work it out. I got up at about 08:00 hours yesterday."

She looked at me with concern. "What, you've been up for twenty-seven hours!? Come with me to the office; I need Keith to hear this."

I got up and silently followed her. A short while later, I was sat in a small office, with the two trainers, after the others had been given an early lunch.

Both were clearly concerned. They sat me in a comfy chair, and sat on the corners of their desks.

Keith said: "Richard, I need to hear from you what happened, and why you haven't slept. We're not part of your street duties course. We're responsible for all the training on this division. So, don't worry, we're here to help and support you."

I leant forward in the chair, and told them the whole story, from the start of yesterday to then. When I'd finished, they sat up straight and looked at each other. Mel said: "Why didn't you say something before? We had to hear this from your friends. Terry and Mary let us know why you'd failed. It's no surprise you didn't pass with no sleep. We'll give you time to recover and at the end of the day you can take the spare test, and only if you feel up to it. I think there's more to this. C'mon, we're here to help. What's really going on? You've never failed a test before."

I took a deep breath, and it all came out: the bullying, the belittling, the desire to not fail and not let anyone down, how I was pushing myself as hard as I could not to be the butt of his ire. I couldn't hold it back. I cried and cried. It was like a weight had been lifted off my shoulders.

I'm sure most people have been sleep-deprived, and it brings emotions to the surface. I hung my head, and once I'd calmed down, I just sat, feeling ashamed of both failing and crying.

There was silence in the room for a long moment. Eventually I looked up and I could see Mel and Keith looking at me.

Keith said: "Richard, I am so sorry mate! That's not even close to being acceptable. That's not how training should operate. This isn't the seventies. That is totally unacceptable. You do occasionally come across officers like this."

He paused, and I looked at Mel. She said, thickly: "I knew this went on, but to hear it in person is a different thing. I think I can speak for Keith. We're on your side. There are ways and means to train people, and what's happened to you is not it. The question is, what do you want to do about it?"

I was still trying to process it. I'd gone from the lowest point, where I thought it was all over, where I thought I was totally alone, to where two people who had told me what was happening was wrong and were backing me up. I knew deep down that what Burke was doing was wrong. I knew as a teacher it was wrong. It was such a relief; I had a lifeline, a way out of it. I might, just might, still make it. My dream hadn't faded quite yet.

I thought, *what do I want?* The answer came straight away: to pass, plain and simple. To pass and carry on doing the job, and never to see Burke again. Even in the few weeks I'd done the job, I'd never felt anything like the satisfaction of anything else. Not teaching, nothing! To protect people's right to walk around without being robbed, without coming home to find their homes burgled. To be there for people when they most needed it. This is what I wanted to do more than anything else I'd ever done. I didn't like policing – I loved it!

I looked at both of them and said: "I just want to be given a chance to succeed. To be judged on my merits, so that I can look every other officer in the eye and know we were judged to the same standards. Just to pass. I don't want Burke ... errr, sorry, I mean Sergeant Burke, to get into any trouble. I just want to get through and join C relief. That's all."

Keith nodded and said: "If you're sure."

He looked at me for confirmation, I nodded, and he continued: "OK, we'll run an intensive revision session for you and you can do the test at the end, once you've had some lunch, and plenty of strong coffee."

I grinned and he continued: "Assuming you pass, I'll send a corrected form through to him letting him know you've passed, and this is not up for debate, by the way. I'll send a confidential letter on your behalf to personnel letting them know our concerns regarding your treatment on the street duties course. Before you say anything, it is our responsibility to make sure that you get a fair crack of the whip, and that no one else has to go through it. Are you OK with that?"

I said quietly: "Thank you so much. I don't know what to say."

Mel said: "I'll walk you down to the canteen for the lovely selection of food (sarcastically), and you've got some good friends. Without them, we'd never have known all this."

We made our way through to the canteen. The others, except for Edward, were waiting for me. Mel left and the others were asking what had happened, and I told them about being able to retake the test at the end of the day. They were relieved, and when we'd completed our (lovely) canteen lunch, we made our way back to the classroom and I managed to chat with Terry and Mary. I said: "Thank you so much! I was done when they told me I'd failed the training. I had no fight left. So thank you, I really mean it."

Terry said: "Look mate, the amount of help you gave Karim and Paul, someone had to look out for you. At least it keeps you in the fight."

Mary added: "I just didn't think it was fair you were being judged without them knowing all the facts. It just wasn't right."

Before I could get all emotional again (Terry didn't do emotional), he said: "This course won't pass itself. Let's get you through it, mate!"

We worked hard for the rest of the afternoon, and when everyone had finished the course, it was my chance to retake the test. The others were free to go. They wished me luck, and I took a copy of the test. I took a deep breath. I felt far more confident and, with enough caffeine in me to keep me awake for a week, I started. Trust me, the alternate paper was no cakewalk, but I stuck to my task and really focused. I blocked out the thoughts of the consequences of failure, focusing just on the words actually written: question, what's the actual answer, now look at the options, eliminate the obvious red herrings, what's left? I heard my own words coming back to me, from the advice I'd given to Paul. I was not going to fail this. Every answer had to be right!

Finally, I finished, and handed the answer paper to Keith. He checked it, then checked it again. Then he looked at me seriously, saying: "I think your friends who've been waiting outside need to see this."

I shan't write what I thought at that moment. We walked into the classroom, and everyone but Edward was there. They could have gone home an hour ago, but they'd waited to see my results. Damn! They were determined to see me cry, weren't they?

Keith waited until they were silent, and without a word held up the result – 100 per cent!

The relief was like a weight being lifted off my shoulders. My mates congratulated me. Keith waited until they were quiet and said: "Well done, Richard. You've been up for thirty-three hours and, against the odds, you got the best score in the class. You really deserve to pass today. Now go home, and get some sleep!"

Before I left he gave me the form with "100 per cent pass" on it.

Terry gave me a lift home, as he didn't think I was in any state to drive, then picked me up in the morning. I was really grateful. We did occasionally give each other lifts, but when you work shifts with uncertain finishing times, it's not always practical. The next morning, I was still tired, but at least I had passed it.

I was called in by Burke to the conference room, where he said: "You let me down. You failed. That's not acceptable, 272. That's another thing you've failed. The only thing you're good at, Armstrong, is failing. No one has said anything good about you. You're by far the worst street duties student I've ever had. You need to think long and hard about going back to something that you're not fucking useless at. If such a thing exists. Now get out, and try not to fuck up too badly today!"

I got up and left the room, once again up one day and down the next.

I carried on for the last few weeks of the street duties course. On the third to last week of the course (the next week we'd find out if we'd passed or failed), Burke, who lived a few miles away from Brentwood, in Shenfield, had asked if Terry would give him a lift home because his car was in for a service. Not thinking he had much choice, Terry agreed.

The next day, Terry took me to one side when he knew we wouldn't be seen or overheard, and said: "Richard, watch your back. Burke has been asking all the students and staff for information about you to fail you. He made me swear to not tell you. He asked me if I had any dirt on you for the board he's going to hold for you next week. I told him I had no reason to say anything bad about you. I'm telling you this because I think he's out of line. Whatever issues you two have had, he's really stepped over the line this time."

He waited to let this sink in, then continued: "I can't go on the record with this, as he made it very clear he'd make life very difficult for me if I did. It's only you he's failing."

As I was trying to take this in, we saw Mary approaching. I thanked him and he walked off.

Mary again looked around, making sure we wouldn't be observed, and told me the same thing. She said: "That's really out of order. I know you've had your differences, but that's absolutely unprofessional to let his own feelings cloud his judgement. You've worked harder than anyone. You have twelve arrests, and loads of process done. The nearest person to you is me, with seven arrests. I thought I should let you know. Get the federation involved. They'll help you."

I said: "Thanks Mary, I really appreciate your help. I know you're taking a risk telling me."

She smiled and walked away.

Well, it was finally there: he'd been plotting all along to get rid of me. OK, time for plan B. It was almost a relief to finally hear it. The uncertainty was the real killer. And, thanks to the courage and decency of my friends, I had a weekend to plan.

I phoned Larry. He said: "Mate, I'll send a confidential letter to the head of personnel at Earlham. It's all I can do. Let me know how it goes."

I phoned Nina (Julia's sergeant friend from central London) and explained what was happening. She didn't sound surprised. She told me to bring all the paperwork, and to meet up on Saturday, and we'd sort a plan.

I didn't let on what I knew for the rest of the week. Burke was actually quite friendly towards me.

On the Saturday lunchtime I met up with Nina. She was a tall, 5'8", slim Black woman in her thirties, with short-cropped hair. There was something about her. I wouldn't say she was classically beautiful, but what she did have was charisma. I didn't have the will not to like her; she was the kind of person people gravitated towards at parties. Not loud, just softly spoken with a razor-sharp wit. Honestly, you can often tell if someone is a police officer, because they have a certain something about them. I've often spotted and been spotted by other police officers. She absolutely didn't have that. She had resisted that. She was a someone to be contended with.

Once we'd settled down at a quiet little cafe just around the corner from the nick, I spread out the paperwork I had, and explained the whole sequence of events, warts and all. Nina made copious notes and, at the points where I hadn't been on my best behaviour, she wrinkled her nose just very slightly. Once I finished, I let it sink in and took a long draft of my fast-cooling coffee. I waited.

A minute or so later she put down her notes and levelled her gaze at me, saying: "Richard Armstrong, you're an idiot!"

Of all the things I was expecting, it wasn't that. Honestly, it hurt more than all the things Burke had said. This was delivered straight and from someone who had real authority.

When this had sunk in, she continued: "You could have reacted in a far more professional way on a number of occasions. You could and should have done your best to de-escalate this conflict between you two. These are things you need to work on, or they'll cause you trouble in the future. Normally, I wouldn't bother helping an officer who had behaved in such a way. But I've done some checking up with people I know at Earlham and, from what they tell me, you have the makings of a really top-notch officer."

She stopped, and it was her turn to take a drink of coffee. I'll give her credit, she was an excellent interviewer; her timing was impeccable. Just the right amount of carrot and stick. Who did she know at Earlham?

She continued: "Having said that, I don't think, in this case, it would have done you any good. What you did right was politely stand your ground, seek help, and tell the training staff. Their word will carry weight. I've spoken to a Fed rep I know at Earlham. He's agreed in principle to be your friend at the board. So we'll produce a plan, and I'll pass it on to him."

I let out a deep sigh, and could feel myself relax. I had help, and this lady was not messing around.

Nina continued: "I mentioned I was impressed with a couple of things you did. You're still a pup, and I've seen and heard enough to be certain you've learnt from this. However, for an experienced sergeant, running a street duties course, his behaviour is utterly unprofessional and quite honestly disgusting. He's not fit to be a sergeant, let alone help young and inexperienced street duties pups find their feet. I for one will not tolerate him blatantly bullying an albeit 'gobby probby' (a term for a mouthy probationary police officer with all the mouth, none of the service). There are ways of dealing with headstrong people like you, and this isn't it. I'll give you credit for sticking with it, though. Right, let's get a plan of attack sorted."

Which we did, for the next two hours. It was meticulous. I pitied any criminal whose path she crossed. Yikes!

The next week arrived, and I was full of conflicting emotions. It turned out the federation representative I'd have on my side was Alan (the DIU sergeant).

I waited until the call to the conference room came. Burke and Hargreaves were waiting for me (I kind of thought it would be those two). I went in, and sat down.

Burke started: "I'm sorry to inform you, but you've not reached the standards required of you during the street duties course, and there'll be a board held tomorrow (he really wasn't giving me much of a chance to prepare a defence, if I wasn't ready for it). It'll be myself and the head of personnel present. We'll then decide what happens next."

During the entire time, Hargreaves stood with a sneer on her face. Burke did his best to look concerned and caring (practising for the next day, no doubt). As much as I knew it was coming, to hear those words was a blow. I thought back to how Paul must have felt, and I was going to handle it with dignity. I looked for a moment at Hargreaves. She seemed to be taken aback by my calm look, and stopped the sneer. Then I looked at Burke and, so as not to give the game away, I said: "I'm upset to hear that, and it's come as such a shock. I'll need time to prepare for it, Sergeant."

He nodded and said: "You'll have until 10 a.m. tomorrow in the meeting room in the personnel office. Don't be late."

Nice parting shot, I thought, and despite what Nina had said, I couldn't resist one last dig. I said: "I'd like to say thank you for your help and support, despite what's happened." I looked at both of them when I said that. And, with a straight face, I turned and walked out, then said, when they were out of earshot: "But I won't, because you didn't."

I walked straight over to the DIU and knocked on the door. Alan called me in. He said: "Ah, you're Nina's friend. Small world, isn't it!"

He gave a little, knowing smile. I sat down and he opened a large brown folder, labelled internal mail (clearly from Nina – she was as good as her word). Alan read the contents quickly and drew in his breath a couple of times. He looked at me and put down the papers, saying: "Well, even I didn't expect that. My God, that man shouldn't be in charge of a street duties course. You are a fighter, aren't you?"

He raised an eyebrow at me in a very Roger Moore kind of way. We then went over the strategy for the meeting the next day. As I left, he could see my apprehension, and said: "Don't worry, young Richard, you should be fine. I think I'm going to enjoy this."

I thanked him and thought, *well, I think he'll be the only one there who does!*

I didn't get a good night's sleep that night. It didn't help that I was getting close to the moving date on my first house. The thought I'd be saddled with a mortgage and no money coming in didn't fill me with joy.

As requested, I arrived early, and Alan was waiting there for me, with a large brown folder under his arm. He grinned, and I worried.

The head of personnel arrived. She was a tall lady, 5'8", in her mid-fifties, and had an air of quiet professionalism. Then (ironically enough)

Burke was the last to arrive. He too had a folder. He gave Alan a surprised stare.

The head of personnel introduced herself as Penny, and asked us to sit down and get comfortable. The room was a conference-style, with six comfy swivel chairs. On the table was a pitcher of water and a number of glasses. The room had a large window looking out over the car park. The walls had a number of packed bookshelves.

We made ourselves comfortable, with Penny at the far end and Burke with his back to the window, and Alan and myself opposite. At Penny's bidding, we poured ourselves glasses of water, and when she was satisfied we were all comfortable and ready, she said: "Good morning. We're here to discuss the outcome of PC Armstrong's street duties course, and to decide where we go from here. May I call you Richard?"

She was well spoken, with just a hint of a London accent. "Richard is fine. Thank you for the courtesy."

She smiled. Continuing, she said: "Don't worry, Richard, nothing is a foregone conclusion. We are here to discuss solutions, not labour problems. I see you've brought a friend from the Police Federation along. For the sake of formality, can I ask your name?"

Alan looked at Penny and said, in his best, cut-glass BBC voice: "I'm Sergeant Alan Dire, of the Police Federation, acting as Richard's federation representative. In accordance with his rights, in the terms of employment. Oh, please, no need to be formal; please call me Alan."

He looked at Penny with a winning smile. I thought, *that's a smart little move, Alan – not insisting on being called by your rank puts pressure on Burke to follow suit, which he'll hate.*

Penny smiled, and turned to Burke and said: "For the sake of formality, please introduce yourself, and why you're here."

Burke stiffened and sat upright saying: "I'm Sergeant Burke, and over the last twelve weeks I've been running the street duties 272 here has been on."

Before he could go any further, Penny said: "Please Sergeant, could you not refer to PC Armstrong as a number. This is a formal meeting and it's just a little impolite."

She smiled at Burke, but you could tell she wasn't asking. He won't have liked that.

Burke glared at me for just a moment then continued: "I'm sorry, Penny (no apology to me, I noticed). He's failed every single test and assignment. His attitude is dreadful, he's always late and disrespectful. All the instructors and even other students have complained about him. He has no place in the police!"

Penny looked straight at Burke for a moment and then, turning to us, said: "Please Alan and Richard, would you step outside for a moment. I would like a word with Sergeant Burke."

We followed her request, and stood outside. The door was thick and, with the traffic noise, we couldn't hear what was said. Alan grinned and anticipated my question: "She'll be reminding the good sergeant of what she said at the start, about constructive comments, and also that she's in charge in there. She won't allow him to bully you in there! But it cuts both ways. Remember, no matter what, be respectful!" He emphasised this with a stern look.

A few minutes later, the door opened and we were ushered back in. Burke was trying to hide it, but he was not happy. I kept my face straight as I took my seat.

Burke then went through incident after incident to illustrate his points, which were:

1. Poor radio procedures

2. Poor timekeeping
3. Poor completion of FPNs
4. Lack of commitment
5. Lack of respect/rudeness
6. Desire to avoid conflict
7. Lack of self-control (hitting the locker door when I forgot my tunic)
8. Not attending the post-mortem
9. Failing the ATU training sessions

He then sat back and said: "That's why PC Armstrong isn't fit to be a police officer."

Penny gave Burke a hard look, probably about the blunt and self-satisfied way he said the last bit. She turned to me and said: "Richard, this is your opportunity to put forward your side of events."

Before I got a chance to say a word, Burke said: "But I've told you what he did. There's no 'his side'. I'm his superior officer – my word should be good enough!"

Penny turned to look at me again, and said: "Alan and Richard, would you please step outside again, I need another word with Sergeant Burke. Thank you."

Even though she was very polite, I could tell she wasn't very impressed.

Alan and I again got up and left. Outside, Alan grinned, saying: "He's not helping himself. This is clearly him trying to assert himself. He hasn't realised that although this is a disciplined service, the personnel department operate outside of that. Effectively, Penny is in charge of who is hired or fired, obviously with reference to the superintendent."

A few minutes later, we were invited in again.

Penny once again smiled and said to me: "Richard, don't worry, just tell me what's your account of the events of the last eleven weeks."

Here I go, all or nothing: "First I'd like to look at number 9, the ATU training sessions. I'd like to state for the record that I didn't fail it: I passed it."

Burke jumped in at that point: "No, 272, you're lying. You failed the test. Here's the failure notice from the ATU." At this, he placed the initial failure notification on the desk.

Penny was running out of patience at this point, saying: "I will remind you, Jack (ouch, no sergeant) of what we spoke of earlier. You'll refer to Richard by his name and not by his number, please. And allow him to finish what he's saying."

It was said in a polite tone, but delivered with steely conviction, and the fact she did it in front of me spoke volumes. Burke glared at me, but sat back in his chair, indicating I could continue.

I brought out the later notification saying I'd passed, and then the one I'd received the following day I'd received from him that I'd failed. The look of surprise on his face was worth waiting for.

I said: "Please notice that I received a letter from the ATU upon completion of the training saying I'd passed, but the following day Sergeant Burke told me that I'd failed and handed me this failure notice."

Burke said: "Yeah, but you failed the first test, didn't you? You needed a second test to pass. So much for you being a teacher."

Penny gave him a sharp look and more gently turned to me saying: "Richard, why did you fail the first test?"

She couldn't have set it up better if we'd arranged it in advance. I explained I'd been up for more than twenty-four hours, and working for the previous sixteen, without sleep.

Once again, Burke butted in, saying: "Yeah, but you chose to do it. I didn't force you!"

Penny looked at him and said: "I don't consider it in any way reasonable for a street duties recruit to be asked to work for sixteen hours and then take an important test. The fact he tried indicates his commitment."

Looking at me, she said: "Please continue, Richard."

I said: "When I failed the test by one question, I explained the situation to the staff. They were sympathetic, and allowed me to retake an alternate test. On this I got 100 per cent."

Penny ticked off point 9 from the list, and indicated I should continue.

I said: "Point 8, failing to attend a post-mortem. I believe that is voluntary, not a compulsory part of the course."

Burke piped up: "Yeah, but he said he'd be OK and then changed his mind when he got there. It reflected badly on the Met."

Penny said, in a measured tone: "It doesn't matter when he decided to attend. It's not a requirement of the course and, therefore, I'll strike point 8 off too. Richard, please continue."

I continued: "Point 7, lack of self-control, and striking the locker door." *Here goes nothing,* "Yes, I did strike the locker door (I could see Burke suppress a slight, self-satisfied grin), but I did it once and with the flat of my hand, which did not cause any damage to the door. It was out of pure frustration, because I realised I'd need my tunic, and it was at the dry cleaner's after the passing-out parade."

Alan interjected at this point, clearly sensing me needing a gentle nudge towards the key point: "Richard, why were you so frustrated at not having your tunic. Honestly, it's not the end of the world."

I took a deep breath: *here we go; when I say this I'll make an enemy of Burke* (not that I was on his Christmas card list anyway).

I continued: "Because I was being picked on unfairly. The criticism was of a personal nature, and was not constructive, merely punitive. I was repeatedly berated and belittled. I was not given constructive criticism allowing me to improve. And I didn't receive support to help me."

At this, Burke couldn't contain himself: "That's rubbish, utter rubbish! How dare you accuse me of being unprofessional. That's insubordination. I'm going to stick you on (a form of censure, that goes on your personnel file) for lying! You have no proof. Whose word are you going to take? A sergeant with ten years' service, or this (emphasising "this") recruit!"

Penny looked at her papers and selected three statements, putting them on the table. She then looked at Burke and said: "You may have a point, if I had no other evidence. I have here two statements from an inspector, and a PC, in different units, both of whom corroborate Richard's version of events. Would you like me to read them, Jack (once again with the lack of rank)?"

Burke actually sat back in his chair slightly. He looked stunned and puzzled. This wasn't part of his plan. He was thinking fast: if these statements were read out, they'd be minuted and might go on his personnel file. If they weren't, they'd stay in my personnel file. Damage limitation would be the logical thing to do but, as we all know, people often don't operate in a logical fashion. Burke collected himself and said: "I want to hear what's been said."

Penny started to read from one of the statements (it was Inspector Chumbley's). He stated that he'd been a police officer for twenty years, and that he understood what banter was. It was a way to bond with your team, and encourage people to work with each other and correct undesirable behaviour. It was not to be used as a tool for senior ranks to bully junior ranks. In his opinion, what he witnessed was the latter, and it had no place in the Met. Burke looked confused and angry at that point. I could see he'd started regretting asking these statements to be read out.

I almost felt sorry for him; from his narrow frame of reference, he didn't understand why people saw things differently.

The second statement was from Keith at the ATU. It said he was deeply concerned that a recruit would be permitted to push themselves so hard as to turn up to an assessed training session having worked for the preceding sixteen hours. He said that, in his opinion, this was not in any way professional. This, again, confused Burke.

When Penny had finished, Alan said: "Penny, may I ask a question?"

"Of course, Alan. What do you want to know?"

He said: "At the start of the course, PC Wood and PC Armstrong conducted a stop on a car, and through diligent police work collected intelligence regarding Colombian drug smugglers. This was passed on to the area drugs unit and arrests were made. I passed on two letters of appreciation to Sergeant Burke to be put on their personnel files. May I ask if they were both put on their files?"

Wow! I didn't know about that. Penny said: "I'm not permitted to divulge without PC Wood's permission any personal details from his file. However, I can check the street duties file Sergeant Burke has passed on to me, and record what I find."

She leafed through a couple of files. When she'd done, I could see just the merest hint of annoyance. She said: "Sergeant Burke, I can't find the letter of appreciation from the area drugs unit on Richard's file. I do have it on PC Wood's file." She left the statement hanging; no accusation or question.

Burke said thickly: "If it's not on Armstrong's file, it must be a clerical oversight."

Penny nodded and said: "Thank you for clearing that up, Sergeant. Given the evidence presented so far, I'm going to strike off points 4 (lack of commitment) and 5 (rudeness/lack of respect). Richard, would you like to address number 2, timekeeping."

I continued: "I make real efforts to be early. I have not been late for any of the lessons or parades at any point of my policing career. On my first day on street duties I was berated by Sergeant Burke for being late. In fact, I'd arrived at least thirty minutes early, and others who arrived after me were not berated. This can be checked on at the front desk record, as Alf recorded the times we arrived."

Penny looked at Burke and asked: "Do you have any comment, Sergeant?" He shook his head; no snappy comeback this time.

Penny said: "That's point 2 struck off. Would you like to address any of the remaining points, Richard?"

I said: "Thank you, Penny. Point 6, avoiding conflict. I'm honestly confused. Would the reverse be to seek out conflict? If so, how does that fit in with the model of modern policing? I would have thought to avoid conflict was a positive, to get the job done without conflict?"

Penny nodded, and Burke stepped in: "Don't twist my words, Armstrong. I meant you go for the easy jobs. You deliberately avoid situations which require you to get into direct conflict."

I replied: "With all due respect, Sergeant (which in his case wasn't much), I've arrested twelve people. The next highest is seven. That's almost double the number of arrests. Taking away someone's liberty is about as confrontational as it gets. On top of that I've completed thirty-four FPNs, that's fourteen more than the nearest other person on the course (I'm a science teacher – I love facts and figures). I honestly can't see how that's avoiding conflict."

Alan chimed in: "If I may make an observation, the fact that Richard is here, fighting his corner, is proof enough that he's not avoiding conflict."

I could see Burke grinding his teeth at this.

Penny said, looking at Burke: "Do you have any further comment, Sergeant?"

He replied: "In my professional (at this point you're flogging a dead horse, mate) opinion, Armstrong's avoiding conflict on the street. That's all I've got to say on this."

Penny replied: "I'll strike out point 6. Richard would you like to continue."

I then pulled out the plan Nina and I had worked on. It was the final 'fuck you' to Burke. He wasn't going to like this.

I said: "Penny, may I give you my proposal of a plan to move forward?"

I held up two copies. When Penny nodded, I handed one to her and politely slid the other to Burke. He took it slowly and they both began to read it. Giving them a minute to scan it, I continued: "I realise that the street duties course hasn't gone well. I think that there's uncertainty over my competency to move on to relief. I believe that this is in no small part down to a clash of personalities between myself and Sergeant Burke. Therefore, I propose that a third, independent party assesses me on the two points still outstanding, i.e. number 1 – radio procedures, and number 2 – filling out FPNs, that this assessment be two weeks in length, and to be reassessed with a further meeting at that time, to make a final decision. (Here was the kicker.) And that, to eliminate any effect of the clash of personalities, Sergeant Burke and the street duties team take no further part in my assessment."

I sat back and thought, *well, that's it*. I wanted to leave Burke a way to save face. "Clash of personalities" didn't really cover bullying, but it did give me a fighting chance with him, and a way to get his toxicity out of the picture.

Burke was not happy! He said: "I accept the extension of Armstrong's street duties, but I should be the one who runs it, otherwise it'll look bad on me. I should be the one to decide what happens to him. He needs to reach my standards; it's my street duties course. He doesn't get to dictate these things. It's my responsibility."

Penny took a moment to think. She slowly settled the papers on the table. Looking at me, she said: "I'd like a moment to talk with Sergeant Burke. And make my decision. Please wait outside. Thank you."

Alan and I did as we were asked. As we stood outside, waiting to hear the fate of my policing career, Alan nudged me and said: "Well done, you did really well. Whatever happens, you couldn't have done more."

I replied: "Thanks, Alan, you didn't have to go out on a limb like that for me. Working in a small nick like this, Burke or his friends will likely get their own back."

Alan looked at me sharply, saying: "It's Sergeant Burke, and this hasn't reflected well on either of you. But he was in a position of authority and he clearly abused it. He won't be running any more street duties courses. I can understand why you reacted, but you shouldn't have done so in the way you did. Learn from this!"

I was stung by his words, but doubly so, because I knew there was truth in what he said. But that self-reflection would have to wait for another day, because the door opened and we were ushered back in.

Burke had a blank look that I couldn't read. When we'd settled ourselves, Penny looked at me and said: "Richard, having heard and read all the information provided to me, I propose the following: I'll contact A relief's Inspector Miller – she's an exceptionally fair person – and ask her to suggest a sergeant who can mentor you for two weeks, and the three of us will meet up at the conclusion of that to see where we are. Your time on the street duties course is over. The pass or fail decision will be deferred until then. The mentoring will not have any formal assessment, but will be entirely based on whoever Inspector Miller puts forward, observations. What are your thoughts, Richard?"

Well, I thought, *it's a fresh start. Two weeks to prove I can do it with an independent judge, away from Burke and his bullying. I guess I'll find out if I can cut it, no excuses this time.*

I said, slowly and carefully: "Yes, thank you, Penny, I think that's the best way forward. I just want to prove myself, and hopefully take my place on C relief. I really want to serve the people of Earlham to the best of my abilities. (Looking at Burke) Sergeant (he looked at me with a measured stare – here I go, shit or bust), I'm sorry that there was disagreement between us, and that you think I'm not good enough. If you felt I was being disrespectful, I'm sorry. I make mistakes, but I want to learn and improve, to become the best police officer I can be. But I can't be someone I'm not."

He looked at me for a moment. I think he was genuinely surprised at what I'd said. He just nodded.

Penny looked at both of us, then said: "I'll go and speak with Inspector Miller, as her relief's on duty now. Richard, please go and wait in the front canteen and someone will be along shortly to let you know what's happening. Has anyone got anything they want to say?"

Silence! She continued: "This meeting is adjourned. Thank you everyone."

I walked out with Alan. Burke sat and collected his papers. I looked at Alan and said: "Thank you so much mate, you were brilliant! I owe you and the federation a huge debt of gratitude."

He smiled and replied: "Think nothing of it. Just go and prove my faith in you is justified. I told you Penny was good."

At that he walked off in the direction of his office. I was deep in thought as I walked out through the doors into the yard. Alan had been right: Penny was good and fair. It's easy to get caught up in one small aspect of the police and not realise just how many really good, decent people there are working in there. I was humbled by their support. I felt a lump in my throat. Then I felt someone walking next to me. My heart sank when I realised it was Burke. For God's sake, couldn't I ever get away from this guy?

He talked as we walked along. He had a different tone in his voice. This was a different side to him. He said: "Look, let's just talk, one-on-one for a minute (I slowed my pace). You and I didn't get along. But I was only trying to toughen you up. You're a soft teacher; this will destroy you. Trust me, I've seen it before. It wasn't personal, mate."

I could feel my ire building. I bit back the worst of my temper, but said: "Can I speak plainly, Sergeant?" I stopped and looked at him. He looked at me and said: "All right, no ranks, off the record, just you and me. What have you got on your mind."

I was so, so tempted to let rip, but the words of Nina and Alan came back to me, and I said: "Are you kidding? Not personal? Not personal! You tried to destroy the dream I've had for over twenty years. I tried four times to get in. This is all I've wanted since I was a little kid. Policing has been in my family for generations. I know I can do this. I know I can make a difference to people's lives. Of course it's FUCKING PERSONAL! (getting control of myself again). There's nothing more personal. Nothing!"

I turned and walked away, not looking back, striding to the canteen. He didn't follow me. God, it felt good to have said that. I know it was stupid, and would probably cost me going forward. But for my own sanity, I was glad I'd said it.

I sat in the canteen, drinking the instant coffee and out-of-date biscuits, staring off into the middle distance. The canteen was its usual hustle and bustle of police officers entering and leaving, of constant laughter. In the background was the sound of quieter, more earnest conversations, with the ever-pervasive sound of the traffic you could never quite escape in London.

I didn't notice when the chair opposite was pulled out and a woman's voice said: "Richard Armstrong, may I join you?"

I snapped out of my thoughts, and found I was looking into the face of an attractive woman in her late thirties, wearing the uniform of an inspector. She must have been about 5'3", slim build, shoulder-length red hair, which was allowed to flow freely down her neck (RHIP). I was struck by her charismatic presence. Some people have it, but I don't, and she most certainly did. Her poise and charm were at once disarming, but she had a steely determination. This lady could ask you something ever so politely, but with absolute assertion you didn't have any choice in the matter.

She said: "I didn't mean to startle you. I'm Inspector Miller. I believe Penny said I'd come and speak with you. It sounds like you've had a hard time. Don't worry, I'm here to assure you that's over. I'm going to pair you up with one of my most experienced PCs: Jack Marshall. He's the most supportive and honest officer I've ever met. If anyone can be objective and fair, it's him."

She smiled and moved in a little closer, continuing quietly: "I can't abide bullying. It's a pity you had to go through what you've been through. Please don't think that the whole of the police at Earlham and Park Street are like him (referring to Burke)."

I replied: "Thank you so much, Ma'am. All I want is a fair chance to prove myself and do my best to serve the people of this borough (cheesy but honest)."

She nodded and said: "That's exactly what I wanted to hear. Now how about you finish that coffee and come with me to meet Jack. He's in the parade room waiting for us."

I calmed down. Here was someone I could respect, who understood how to lead. Even after just a couple of minutes, I'd follow this lady through hell if she asked.

I drained my coffee mug, almost burning my mouth at the same time, ditching the remaining biscuits in the bin and putting the tray back. I followed her not to hell, but to the parade room (feel free to make your own jokes up), where she introduced me to a man in his early fifties with short grey hair, of medium build, about 5'10". He had a craggy, weathered face, with sharp, piercing brown eyes. He spoke with a mild London accent. His voice was gentle and low. When he did speak, he made strong eye contact.

We started to chat, and a radio call came in, and Inspector Miller excused herself. Jack and I talked about everything; it was like talking with someone I'd known for years. He had an easy, relaxed way about him. Inspector Miller had been right about this guy.

We agreed to meet up on Monday. We'd being doing days for the next two weeks.

The next two weeks shot by. Honestly, it was hard work. Jack was his normal, calm self. His way of working was to talk to people first, unless he had to go 'hands-on'. It was cool and professional. I felt right at home. I could relax and "stop playing at being a policeman, be yourself and let the uniform do the work."

Before I knew it, I was back in Penny's office with Jack and Alan. Penny was her usual, organised, professional self. We went through the pleasantries, and then she looked at Jack and asked, "Oh Jack, how did it go? What's your assessment of how Richard has got on?"

Honestly, I really didn't know what he'd say; he kept his cards so close to his chest, and was so relaxed. He'd commented on a few things I'd done. He'd made suggestions, and I'd done my best to follow them.

Jack said: "Richard did OK. Not outstanding, but not bad either. He was about where I'd expect him to be at this point in his service. Initially his self-confidence was low, but after what he's been through, that's not surprising. His weaknesses are his police sixth sense for potential dangers. That needs working on, but that's nothing unusual at this stage. His radio work is passable. Once I'd pointed out a few things to improve on his writing up of evidence he reached a good standard, above average I'd say.

"His strengths are: he's keen; hard-working; honest; he has a really nice way with people, particularly the vulnerable. You can see the teacher's instincts coming out. Oh, he doesn't have a high tolerance for authoritarians. His tolerance for BS isn't high, either. That may trip him up. But maybe it's not such a bad thing. Overall, my assessment is a solid, if not outstanding, pass, and with the hard work and commitment that he's shown so far, he has the potential to become a good officer, or even outstanding if he finds the right niche."

I took a long, deep breath at hearing someone say that after all the time I'd spent struggling. I could have wept. Finally, someone who believed in me. Finally! Thank you, thank you, thank you! I wanted to hug him so much. But remember, you're a policeman now – none of that!

Penny smiled and looked at me: "Well, that's high praise from such a respected police officer. Did you know Jack here has one of the highest number of commendations, and letters of appreciation from the public.

Copies are up on the noticeboards in the hall in the main building. Check them out. It's heart-warming to read how much they appreciate his work. Therefore, I'm happy to pass you on the street duties course, and you can start on C relief tomorrow. They're on late turn. So, be ready to parade at 13:30 hours in the parade room. That'll keep you busy. Well done. I know this hasn't been easy, but you got there in the end. Is there anything you'd like to say?"

I took a moment to collect the millions of thoughts rattling around in my brain. There was so much I wanted to say. I settled, and said: "Thank you Jack, that was ... honestly one of the nicest things anyone has ever said. I think you're a brilliant police officer. I've learnt so much. In return, if I may be a bit cheeky, I know you were talking about retiring soon. The teaching profession is crying out for someone with your talents. Seriously! (had I stepped over the mark?) Alan, thank you so much. I really appreciate your support. Finally, Penny, thank you so much! You've been scrupulously fair, even-handed and professional. I'm not perfect and I've made mistakes, but I thought you were fair. So, thank you!"

There were the usual pleasantries, and platitudes and paperwork (and I thought teaching had a lot of paperwork!). There I was, ready for the next chapter. I was so glad to have finally passed my street duties. Now, to start the next phase, being a probationer on relief. The first time I could call myself a proper copper, even if I was still a 'probby'.

Chapter 5

C RELIEF

"For the sake of the tape, I challenge that remark!"

As I walked down the shabby corridor, remembering to look at the tatty wall display with copies of the letters of appreciation pinned to it, I was going over the mental checklist of things I needed: six IRBs (Incident Report Books), although I'm only required to have three, brief (warrant card – I tap my back pocket; good, it's there), Metvest, long-sleeved shirt under my jumper (it's winter, therefore the rule is everyone on a relief must wear the same version of the uniform, i.e. all jumpers, all long sleeves, or all short sleeves), lightweight jacket, cap, three pairs of rubber gloves, ASP, cuffs, CS spray, three ARBs (Accident Report Books, for car crashes), three process books (for giving out more serious traffic tickets, FPNs, both endorsable and non-endorsable offences), small first aid kit, radio (did I swap the battery? I think I did).

With all these things running through my head, am I on time? Check watch: 13:25 hours? Only five minutes to get to the briefing room. Technically, it's a 14:00 hours start, but I was told to be there for the briefing (thank you, Alan) and assignments, and also to allow the hand over from one shift to the next.

I walked up to the parade room door, slowed to a stop, deep breath. *Am I really ready for this?* When you focus so much on the battle to get somewhere, you sometimes lose sight of whether you can, or even want to do something.

Too late now! Sink or swim. I wondered if it was like this for my grandad or even great-grandad. My view of life is that society changes, but the world and people, not so much! That's why the great plays, poems, books still resonate, because they speak to us as people, and we haven't changed. Lost in my thoughts, I once again failed to notice someone standing behind me.

I heard a voice: "Move aside in the name of the law!"

I turned around to see a muscular young man in his late twenties with a curly mop of dirty blond hair, a little shorter than me (about 5'9") with a hugely infectious grin, and sharp, 'smiling' blue eyes that have no doubt drawn in many a young lady (and probably a few blokes as well). To my horror, I noticed he had a short-sleeved shirt, no tie, no jumper, and a battered hat under his arm. Had I read the signs wrong, and I was the only one to turn up in the wrong uniform? Not a good start!

He said, with an Essex accent: "'Ello mate. You must be the new, dodgy 'gobby probby' we've been hearing about. You've been pissing off all the right people. I approve! Now in you go; they ain't going to bite! Well, on second thoughts, some of them might. My advice: just bite back. I am the law! (said in a dodgy Stallone accent – referencing the *Judge Dredd* film). Actually, it's Laurence Marshall, hence they call me 'The Law'. Everyone gets a nickname; it's a sign you're accepted. Just go with whatever they give you. Best get in there."

He gave me a gentle shove in the back. I thought I'd better do as he said, and pushed open the door into a small, windowless, shabby room with about thirty chairs set out in what roughly approximated as rows. At the front was a worn, old brown wooden desk with a dirty whiteboard on the wall behind it. The walls had originally been painted white, but hadn't been troubled by a paintbrush in a decade, by the looks of it. The floor was a white and blue squared lino that hadn't been cleaned in a while, with multiple scuff marks from chairs. Along the edge of the walls were clumps of dust and dirt.

There were half a dozen officers in the room, all chatting away, some loudly. They were scattered around, all with different versions of the uniform. No two were the same. They all seemed to have customised or adapted their kit to suit themselves. So much for the all-looking-the-same rule.

As I walked in, the conversation quietened down, and heads turned towards me. Suddenly I felt self-conscious, but didn't want to show it – rule one as a teacher: never show weakness. Classes of kids have a pack mentality and will go for anyone new who shows weakness. So, I stood up straight, shoulders back, chest out (as much as you can in a bullet-proof corset), chin up, and confidently walked over to one of the chairs near the door. Before I got there, 'The Law' said: "Say hi! This is that dodgy 'gobby probby' who pissed off that wanker, Burke!"

There was a barrage of greetings and approvals over pissing off Burke. I took a mock bow, which garnered a few laughs, and took my seat.

Seated, I had a chance to look at my new family. The closest was Mel, who smiled at me, and I noticed for the first time just how her eyes twinkled with mischief in the harsh strip light of the room. I lost myself looking into those eyes for a moment (not hard to do). Before I had a chance to take in the other officers in the room, the door opened, and everyone's attention was drawn to it.

I turned around and in walked a tall (6'2"), stocky man, with an impressive moustache. He reminded me of someone, but I couldn't put my finger on it. He wore a jumper, and a minimally equipped belt. He was in his early fifties, but still had thick black hair, even if there were a few flecks of grey appearing in it. He had a presence, not easy to pinpoint, but people naturally looked at him when he walked in a room or spoke. Behind him were four sergeants, and half a dozen other officers, who all filed in and found seats. I did a quick head count, something teachers are well practised at: sixteen officers, four sergeants and one inspector.

The inspector walked to the desk, and stood in front of it, with the easy air of a teacher. He'd been the head of maths in a school prior to joining the Met, and it showed, with his feet planted shoulder-width apart, hands on his hips staring impassively at the parade (class). He waited, with absolute certainty that it would happen, for silence, daring people to be the last one to stop talking. The room became silent very quickly. Impressive. As he began speaking, it came to me who he reminded me of: Captain Mainwaring from *Dad's Army*. Before I could stop myself, I let out a laugh, caught myself and turned it into a cough. Mainwaring (oops, sorry, the inspector) stopped, and looked at me. I fumbled around, until Mel handed me her water bottle, which I gratefully took a drink from. As I handed it back, I winked, and she gave me a shy look. Nice!

When I'd recovered, I noticed the room was silent and the inspector was looking at me. He continued, dryly: "Are you all right there, son? I've never had an officer die at the parade on their first day."

There was a good laugh at this, and even I found myself smiling. I nodded. Once again, he continued, "Before I go any further, I'd like to introduce our newest member, Richard Armstrong, also known as 272."

Before he could get any further, a message came through on the radio that everyone took notice of (it's one of the skills you acquire, learning to ignore all but the relevant radio messages). A beautiful woman's voice said: "Any units free to deal? We've got a stabbing on Jackson Street, near Albany Park (which runs along the south side of Albany Park – our border with Hackney)."

Before anyone said anything, three officers were out of their seats. I heard a deep Scottish voice behind me: "I'll take PT3 (the area car) with Phil and Gal, if that's all right, Guv'?"

The inspector nodded, and the three of them jogged out of the room (now there were twelve plus one officer, four sergeants, and one inspector).

The inspector said: "Nathan (a 6'2" Black sergeant, slim build with a bald head, in his early forties), do you want to take Chloe (a woman in her early forties, slim build with highlighted brown, shoulder-length hair) in PT21 to back them up. And Sean (Deacon), do you want to go through to custody to relieve D relief, who's down as gaolie (gaoler – the correct English, not American-English term for a jailer, which was a standing joke)."

One of the other two remaining sergeants said: "That's Greg, Guv'."

Sergeant Nathan (Darling) and Chloe walked out to back up the first three, leaving twelve officers, three sergeants and one inspector.

Sean was a slim, short (5'8") man, casually dressed in a short-sleeved shirt and no Metvest, with a leather belt with his ASP attached, and a pair of old-fashioned, chain-linked cuffs tucked over at the back of his belt. Greg (6'2") was a stocky, lantern-faced man, muscular in build, with very short blond hair (he reminded me of Lurch from the Addams family, because of his build and the way he moved). The pair of them walked out towards the custody suite. Now there were eleven officers, two sergeants and an inspector.

The inspector started again, looking at me: "I'm Inspector Manning (I almost laughed – too close to Mainwaring). Good to have you aboard, Richard. You'll find this is a friendly relief. We work hard and play hard."

The radio went once again: "Units free to deal, we've got a robbery outside Mile End Tube on the Commercial Road."

Manning looked at one of the other two sergeants (a 6'4", hugely muscular man, with very short blond hair), saying: "Rob, do you want to take Shell out in PT22 to deal with that, and Lins (a tall 5'8", skinny woman, in her mid-forties, with a permanent scowl, and shoulder-length, thick black hair), do you want to take 'The Law' out in PT23 to back them up."

It was an instruction, not a question. Shell was a slim, short 5'5" woman in her early thirties with long brown hair, tied in a ponytail. They quickly left. Then there were eight officers, one sergeant and one inspector (all before we'd finished briefing).

Just as Inspector Manning was about to start speaking, the radio spat out its newest request: "Any units to deal? We have a number of calls regarding a fight in Commercial Park. Fifty fighting with weapons."

Without being instructed, all the rest of the officers got up and started jogging out of the room. The inspector got on the radio saying: "PT, from PT1, you've got three units on the way straight from parade. They'll update you en route with vehicle and shoulder numbers."

Reply: "Thanks PT1."

Now present: one officer (me), one sergeant, and one inspector.

Inspector Manning looked around and said: "It looks like it's going to be another day in paradise. You picked a good shift to start on. Before World War III breaks out, this (pointing at the last remaining sergeant) is your reporting sergeant (line manager in corporate (BS) speak). I want you two to take out PT2 (a van), and I'm sure you'll find something to keep yourselves busy with."

I looked at the last remaining sergeant. He was about 40, with slightly unkempt blond hair, of stocky build and about 5'10". He gave me a weak smile, and started walking towards the door. I got up and followed him. He turned and talked to me, in a strong Essex accent, as we walked towards the yard.

"Hello Richard. Welcome to C relief. It's our busiest shift. Have you met the control staff yet?"

I shook my head and said: "Not yet, Sergeant. Thanks for the welcome."

He grinned, saying: "I see you haven't got a bag (I looked down and noticed he had a small sports bag with him). Most of us carry a bag of some kind for anything you might need on a long shift where we're not guaranteed to get a refs (refreshments break). Things like a drink, a couple of chocolate bars, some extra IRB, ARBs, FPNs, a Maglite (a brand of torch), spare gloves, extra bandages. Those sorts of things."

He walked into the canteen and waved me towards the counter, saying: "Best you get at least a bottle of water and a couple of chocky bars to keep you going."

I nodded thankfully and bought what he'd suggested. It was considerate of him to make sure I'd be taken care of. As we walked out towards the last remaining van, a Ford Transit, he said: "I'll stick our stuff in the wagon, and check it over. Do you want to go and check in the control room for anything they want us to do? It'll give you a chance to introduce yourself to the people you'll be talking to over the radio. They're really important to get to know; they are the ones who'll take care of you. They'll know by the tone of your voice that you need help. They're good people."

I handed him my stuff, and walked quickly back to the control room. It was entirely different from the all-too-stiff and starchy street duties, or Hendon. I could get used to it.

As I approached the control room, I could hear the calls going out (the incoming calls could only be heard through the headsets). I remembered to turn down my radio's volume, which could cause issues in the control room. I stopped at the threshold and, looking for permission, I took in the scene. Seated there were three people, two in the uniforms of PCs and with their backs to the door, and a woman with gorgeous, waist-length, free-flowing straight light brown hair. I waited a moment. No one had noticed.

I said, "Hello there, I'm Richard Armstrong, 272, the new guy from street duties. I'm with ... (I paused – I didn't know the sergeant's name! Damn) a sergeant in PT2."

Damn, that sounded weak. I wanted to make a good first impression!

The young woman with the gorgeous hair turned around. Bloody hell! She was stunning! I mean one of the most beautiful women I have ever seen. She was in her late twenties with delicate, elven features, slim build, about 5'8", and with gorgeous brown eyes with a wicked twinkle in them. I couldn't find the words. I just stood there transfixed by this absolute vision of beauty. Wow! She looked at me with a knowing smile; clearly for her this was not unusual. Then she spoke. It was so lovely. Gentle, sweet, a slight Scottish accent. How could anyone not fall in love with her!

Then I snapped out of it when I realised she was talking to me. She said, in a silky smooth voice: "Hello, sweetheart. I'm Suzanne, but everyone calls me Sooz. It's lovely to have you as part of the family. I'm sure you'll be part of the team in no time. I've been hearing good things about you from Mel. Oh yes, you're with Robbie Roberts. He's lovely."

The two uniformed officers turned around and waved, but seemed to be tied up with calls. Sooz said: "That's Paul, and that's Annie. They're a married couple. They don't get out much. There's a name we give people who don't get out the station much: Tiddles – the station cat, because it doesn't get out much."

At which she gave me a lovely smile. I grinned back, like a fool.

She looked at her green computer screen and said: "There's reports of a fight in Manchester Road, just outside the school. Do you want that?"

I dumbly nodded. She looked back at the screen and printed off a sheet on the archaic dot matrix printer. I went over and tore it off. Dot matrix – that was out of date ten years ago. Ah, the Met and its extra cheapness!

I smiled and said: "Errr, thank you Sooz. I'll, errr, go and get in the van."

She held up her hand for a moment (clearly hearing something on the radio), and said: "Robbie says, hold the call. D relief left the van running on vapours, so the first call will be to the petrol station. He's waiting for you."

With a quick wink she turned back to her screen. That was me dismissed. I collected my thoughts (damn, she was ... stunning!).

I walked out and jogged back to the yard. Honestly, my was head spinning! The moment I met Victoria, I'll never forget, because it was like a thunderbolt. Nothing will ever come close. But, damn, Sooz was gorgeous! Way out of my league!

I ran to the van, opened the door, and jumped in. I looked at Robbie. He started up the van and said: "Yes, I know she's gorgeous! Her nickname is Sexy Sooz! Half the Met are in love with her. But, and it's a big but, she's far more than just good-looking; she's one of the most lovely people you'll ever meet. Guys miss that. Look, I know no one is perfect, but she's my friend, so whatever you do, be cool. This relief is very protective towards each other, especially Suzi. Having said that, it's off to the garage on the A13. Bloody D relief always leave the vehicles with no fuel. But this time they've surpassed themselves. The fuel gauge is already on zero. It must be running on vapours. But it'll give us a chance to grab a sandwich at the same time."

I had a sudden thought, and asked Robbie: "Sarge, how do the Met buy fuel for the vehicles?"

He said, as we gingerly made our way onto the road, "Look in the glove box, and see."

I did as I was told, and found a small folder with a fuel credit card on a sleeve on the outside. Inside was a log, with dates and amounts of fuel and cost.

I said: "Wow, really? The Met have fuel credit cards? That's crazy."

Robbie grinned, saying "It's cheaper than having our own fuel pumps. That's why they did it."

Ah, the Met and its extra cheapness!

We made our way to the A13 and the closest petrol station. It was the slowest I'd ever been in a police vehicle. Robbie was on fuel economy mode. We did not want to be having to push a police van down the street. Firstly, with the security cage in the back, a Ford Transit isn't light, especially when you're wearing your bullet-proof corset. Secondly, talk about losing the trust of the British public – we'd be a laughing stock.

We had to drive along the A13, take the slip road, go around the roundabout, across the flyover, around the next roundabout and back onto the A13 towards Kenton. Nail-biting stuff when we could run out of fuel at any moment. We were relieved to finally pull into the petrol station.

I jumped out and went to fill her up, when a slim man in his forties, in jeans and a T-shirt, came running over to me. He was obviously in an excited state, saying, "Quick, quick, some bastard's just nicked me car!"

Probably left his keys in it, I thought. I replied: "OK Sir, can you describe the car? What's its registration number?"

He pointed down the A13 (which at that point was a very long, straight road, with a large bridge on it), saying "It's that car there, mate."

I could see a red Astra speeding along the A13 in the outside lane. Robbie, by this time, was listening to the conversation through the open window. He said: "Quick, jump in, we'll see if we can catch him, if you're up for a little excitement."

The bloke didn't need to be asked twice, replying, "Oh, yeah, let's get the little shit!"

I slid the middle door open, and he jumped in. I got in as Robbie gunned the engine and we were off. My first chase in a van that had no fuel, with a member of the public, which was against all the regulations. Welcome to C relief!

I turned to the driver, and after telling him to stick his seat belt on, and that his presence in the van wasn't exactly according to regulations, I got his details and the car reg no. I put the radio call out about the stolen vehicle, and started the commentary. I'd waited so long for it. It was broadcast on the main set. These cover either the whole of north London or the whole of south London. This is recorded and monitored by senior brass at New Scotland Yard (NSY – the Met and its acronyms), so it's a big deal. Half the Met can hear if you screw up.

So, here I go: "MP, MP PT2."

"PT2, go ahead MP."

"MP, we are currently following an LOS (lost or stolen) vehicle, heading west along the A13, just going over the Canning Town flyover. The LOS vehicle was reported direct and isn't on the PNC yet. It's a red Astra car, VRM (vehicle registration mark) G235VRH. The traffic is light, the road conditions are dry, the driver is PS43. Current speed is 70 mph, 7 0 mph. PT2."

"PT2, all recorded. Carry on with commentary, and advise if any of the conditions change, MP."

That meant they were assessing the risk to other motorists, and would call off the chase if it got too risky. Something we hated! We were there to catch villains who nick people's methods of getting to work, go shopping or picking up the kids – not let them get away.

As I continued the commentary, I had a lot to think about. Where were we? What was coming up next? What was the 'bandit' car doing? As well as being thrown around in a two-tonne van which had not been designed for this. Contrary to popular belief, police cars in general (with very few exceptions) are entirely stock, just with blue lights and sirens, a couple of radios and some decals fitted.

As we hurtled around a corner, the van spluttered. I looked at Robbie. He was concentrating. I could see a moment of annoyance at the sound. Not good! Police drivers are, in general, so cool when they are driving quickly. Not relaxed, but focused and not shouting or agitated.

Other vehicles were converging on us as we pursued. It's a bit of a game, anticipating where the car will go, because you don't want to go to where the pursuit is, you want to be where it's going, so you can 'head them off at the pass', so to speak.

Such was the case with this pursuit. Most pursuits (in the Met) last less than a few minutes. It's usually in busy, built-up areas, and they tend to bail out and run, or crash and run. This one was six minutes and counting. Damn the fuel situation! We weren't in economy mode at this point. I spared a quick look at our passenger, concerned for how he was feeling, in the back of a police van, hurtling around the streets. I needn't have worried: he had a grin from ear to ear!

He said: "You get paid to do this? Where the fuck do I sign up?"

I grinned back and gave him the thumbs-up.

Things were getting grim on the fuel situation. Every corner we went around, you could hear the engine splutter. We turned onto a residential street. Robbie said: "Prepare for a decamp (get out and leg it); this leads to a dead end."

Sure enough, we turned a corner, and there were concrete bollards across the road. This led into a housing estate. The car skidded to a halt, but too late, and with a sickening crash hit one of the bollards and came to a rest. The thief, a white guy in his early twenties, ran off in the direction of a block of flats. As he approached the corner of the first building, he risked a look back at us (bad move, pal). He turned back to see the rather meaty arm of Inspector Manning straight out in front of him, at chest height. He ran straight into it, which resulted in him ending up lying prone on the grass staring at the sky (I believe the term is 'clothes-lined'). It took him a moment to recover his senses.

When he did, the inspector, myself, Robbie and the car's owner were all looking down at him. His first words were: "I didn't do it. It wasn't me!" I barely suppressed a laugh, but Robbie and the inspector didn't. The car's owner was incensed by the fact this bloke had nicked his car, driven it like a loony, crashed it (without doubt, writing it off), ran off and, the final insult, lied about it!

He couldn't contain himself. "You lying, thieving little shit!" Pointing at the thief, and raising his voice, "How am I going to get to work tomorrow, you scrawny little fucker! Not like you've ever done a day's work in your life. Scrounging off the dole, stealing from decent, hard-working people. How am I supposed to pick up the kids from school? They'll have to walk home, past all the druggies, street robbers, dirty needles. It ain't safe for them; they're eight and ten? How I am I supposed to go and see my mom in Enfield? She's 83. She can't drive, she lives alone! I haven't got the money to buy a new car. I'll have to wait for the insurance money, which could be weeks, and it won't cover a replacement. Mate, for the love of God, think about what you're doing to other people. I could lose my job if I can't get in on time. How am I supposed to provide for my family? Think about it! THINK ABOUT IT! Then you have the brass neck to say you didn't do it when I saw you nick my car, watched you drive it like a loony, and then crash it! You're taking the FUCKING PISS PAL. I'VE HAD ENOUGH OF YOU. YOU'RE A SELFISH LITTLE SHIT!"

At that, he turned around and stormed off to check on his car.

I looked back down at our car thief, who seemed scared. He said: "You heard him, he swore at me. I want him arrested. He can't do that. I'm innocent, and he (pointing at the inspector) assaulted me."

I looked back at him, trying really hard to keep the disdain I felt for him off my face. The inspector looked at me, saying, "Do the honours, Richard. I'm off back to the nick. Good work you two (indicating Robbie and myself)."

At that he strode off, not sparing any time on the "innocent" car thief.

I helped the 'gentleman' up (with a strong grip on him), cuffed and cautioned him. Then we walked past the written-off car to the van, where he was searched (drugs and a blade – naughty boy). He was further arrested for those two. We spoke with the driver, and arranged for the car to be picked up. We then gave him lift back to the nick. Heaven knows how we managed it on no fuel. At which point it stopped. We had to get the spare fuel can from the sergeant's car to get enough fuel in it to get it to the petrol station.

Because we were so busy, Robbie helped me get everything sorted with the processing of my prisoner. We walked into custody and Sergeant Deacon looked up from his desk and said, "Hello Richard. Blimey, you're keen. What have you got for me today?"

I explained the circumstances (being deliberately vague about the whole having a civvy in the van during a chase bit) and the arrest for TWOC (taking without consent), the blade and drugs, which was cannabis, by the looks of it. Sergeant Deacon nodded, and looking at the prisoner, said, "What's your name, address and date of birth?"

The name replied, "It wasn't me. I've never seen that knife or cannabis. I don't know nothing, mate!"

The sergeant gave him a gentle smile, as if he was talking to an errant child, and said, "Sir, you'll get a chance in interview and in court to have your say. Right now, I need to know your name, address and date of birth."

"Look, I know my rights. I want a solicitor! I've never been arrested before. I'm innocent! It's a fit-up. By the way, what's for tea?"

With more patience than most, the good sergeant said, "We'll get to all of that in good time, Sir. But first I need your name, address, and date of birth, please?"

"I've got special needs. I demand to see a doctor. I need my medicine, or I'm going to die. You'll have murdered me. You're all racists, I heard it on the news!"

Totally unfazed, the sergeant continued, "Sir, I can't help you until I know what your name, address and date of birth are. Then I can book you in, arrange a doctor, social worker, and give you a chance to call a solicitor. So please, what is your name?"

"John Miller. Now can I have my tea! I want a vegetarian meal, with strong tea, two sugars, and lots of milk. Have you got any biscuits, not those horrible, stale ones? The chocolate digestives, I like them. I know my rights."

The sergeant was now beginning to get a little impatient. He said, "Your name isn't John Miller is it, Daniel Shard? Are you still living at the flat in

Wood Street? Do I really have to hunt through the custody records to find your date of birth?"

Daniel (aka "John") said, "You've got it wrong! I demand ..."

The sergeant said, "If you're not prepared to cooperate with custody procedure, you'll be put in a cell. I'll call the doctor, a social worker, a drugs worker, and anyone else I can think of. There you'll wait until these good officers are ready to interview you. Greg, could you escort our 'guest' to number two, please? Would you like to assist, Richard?"

I replied, "Of course, Sergeant."

Greg and I took hold of Daniel and gently guided him to the cell, where I took the cuffs off. Daniel then said to Greg, "Here, mate, you haven't got any fags on you, have you? I'm dying for a smoke, and when do I get that tea? Remember: strong, milky and TWO sugars. I'm de-hydrated."

Greg gave him a quick look and said as the cell door was closing. "I'll get you a drink of water, but no tea, fag break or food until you play nice with the sarge!"

With that the door slammed shut, and we made our way down the corridor. Greg said, "You're making a good impression. A good body like him on the first day, well done. I'm Greg. It's Richard, isn't it? Pleased to meet you. Work hard, fit in and take part in the banter and you'll do just fine!"

He slapped me on the back, harder than I was expecting, and I for once was glad of the bullet-proof corset. I looked across and replied, "Thanks mate. I just want to do the best job I can."

He nodded, and we walked into the custody suite, where the two sergeants were chatting. The custody sergeant said, "Here's the pars on that guy. Why don't you see Sooz, and do a name check. See how many times he's been nicked. Also see if he's wanted."

Pleased at having an excuse to see Sooz again, I walked through to the control centre. Busy as always, it took a moment for Sooz to turn around and say, "Hi hun, what can I do for you?"

I gave her the details, and she said, "OK, Daniel Shard. Mmm, he has been a busy boy! Three current warrants, twenty-seven previous convictions. I'll print you off the details of the warrants. Well done. You've got a good catch on your first day. Oh, Alf said that your victim was asking after you. He's in the front office interview room."

I thanked her, and met Robbie walking through. We both went to see our victim.

I said to Alf, "Hi mate. Good to see you again. How's our victim been?"

He replied, "Good to see you again, boy! He's been as good as gold. He likes you! Well done so far; you've made a good first impression."

We went through to the interview room, where our victim was sitting, I said, "Hello Sir. Are you all right?"

"Thank you so much, fellas. You did right by me. I know you get a whole load of shit from those fuckwits on the telly, but you're all right!"

I replied, "Thank you, I really appreciate that. I'm sorry we couldn't get your car back in one piece. We did our best. Now I need to take a statement from you. Do you want a cup of tea or something at the same time?"

He wanted a cup of coffee, and we got the statement, and all the other phone calls and paperwork done. Then, when we had a moment, we dropped him off at his home on the way to finally getting some fuel. By the time we'd finally got everything done, it was 20:00 hours. What a first day! But we weren't done quite yet ...

As I hit the last keystroke of the paperwork, the radio crackled into life. It was everyone's favourite civvy.

"Units to deal. A disturbance in the Waterman's Arms public house."

Robbie was already out of his seat as I logged off and hit the send. He was on the radio saying, "PT2, we'll take that Sooz."

"Thank you PT2. Be careful, hun." (where's your correct radio procedure now, Burke?)

We jogged out to the van, stuck on the 'woow woows' and 'nee nars', and went for a BLATT (blue lights and two tones). *Damn, I love this job.* As per usual, there was a range of reactions from motorists to a police vehicle approaching with its lights and sirens going. From being totally oblivious (singing along at full belt to Oasis), to no reaction (they just carry on and ignore you), to actively hostile (refusing to getting out of your way), to slamming on the brakes so hard they cause other vehicles to run into the back of them (which goes down as a POLAC – police accident). On that trip, there was plenty of the first one of these. A frustrating time, trying to make decent progress.

We eventually made it to the pub, and as we were pulling up outside, I got on the radio, to put us 'on scene' (recorded on the CAD). "PT, PT2 on scene."

"PT, received."

The reality is, when you're really busy, you keep the messages short, and only send them when you absolutely have to. Robbie keyed his mike and said, "Can you show 43 and 272 entering the Waterman's Arms. Thanks."

"Will do, PT."

This is a formal requirement if you enter a pub while on duty, to stop allegations of officers drinking on duty, which is a very serious disciplinary matter. The Met and its rules.

We jumped out and jogged up to the door, pausing just for a moment to collect ourselves. We looked at each other (I had my hand on my stick, just in case), mentally preparing ourselves, as you're never quite sure what you'll find. Often the radio call will be of World War III breaking out, and when you arrive, nothing! Other times, it's an innocuous call, and there's blood and guts everywhere. It's a bit of a lottery.

We swung the door open, and swiftly walked in, to find an old-fashioned pub, busy with customers, most of whom turned around to look at us, then quickly turned back to their drinks as if nothing had happened.

To our left was a long, old-fashioned wooden bar, with pumps to the front, optics to the rear, and a large, middle-aged landlord looking at us. To the centre and to the right were various bar stools, wooden tables and chairs, a jukebox blaring out some song or other, and a dartboard with people playing in the far corner. So far it looked like a false alarm. Maybe there was a troublesome customer who needed to be ejected?

I look at the landlord, and he nodded his head to my left. I looked over to where he indicated, and there was a man in his thirties, slumped in the corner, with a screwdriver sticking out of his left shoulder. I looked at Robbie, he nodded, and as I went to render first aid, he used the radio: "PT, this is PT2. Can we have the LAS (London Ambulance Service); we've got a male, conscious and breathing with a knife wound. Thank you."

"Received PT2. Do you need any other units?" (Notice Sooz did not use "Urgent" or "Assistance", because those are the code words for, "Oh shit! We need help, now!" So it's an unspoken rule that you avoid using them.)

Robbie replied, "Thanks PT. If another unit can be making its way, sooner rather than later, we'd appreciate it."

He went over to the landlord to check what had happened, and also to keep an eye out for any further trouble. It was odd that there was absolutely no reaction to this guy in the corner.

I approached the man, saying, "Hello ..."

He shouted at me when I got about two feet away, "Fuck off, you cunt. I want nothing to do with you! Fuck off!"

I raised my hands in a placative gesture. Maybe he was scared, drunk, or just hated police, but he still needed help. I said, "Look mate, I just want to help. What happened?"

He shouted back, "Are you fucking deaf, you cunt? I said I want nothing to do with you! Just leave me alone."

I knelt down to be on the same level, I hoped, reduce his perception of threat. I still had my hands up in a placative gesture. It was also in case he tried to attack me, when I could react more quickly, making sure I had enough room to jump back, if needed.

I tried a different tack, saying, "Mate, at least let me help you, and do a bit of first aid. You don't have to talk to me if you don't want to. Just let me help."

This time he was snarling, "Are you fucking deaf! I told you I want nothing from you, you cunts! Now fuck off!"

I then spent the next ten minutes trying to negotiate with this guy, to let me do first aid, to find who he was, to find out who had done this. He just kept repeating the same mantra! Robbie had no better luck with the landlord; he didn't know who the guy was, didn't know what had happened, didn't have security cameras. Then when the backup arrived, they attempted to speak to the customers, who all claimed to have been in the toilets (thirty customers, and two tiny, two-person toilets!).

The LAS arrived, and it took another five minutes of us negotiating to get him to let the ambulance crew even look at the shoulder wound. Then another struggle to get him to go to hospital, only after they explained to him they couldn't just pull the screwdriver out and superglue his wound up in the pub, that it would require a trip to hospital.

All the while, he refused to speak to us at all. CID turned up just as the guy was being put in the ambulance. It was Big John (I'd met in the CID on street duties) and a gorgeous, slim, young (early thirties) Black lady whose looks reminded me of Halle Berry.

John walked over and slapped me so hard on the back even the bullet-proof corset didn't shield me from the force. He said, "Hello mate. Glad you got onto relief. John told me what happened. That was out of order. Really out of order! So what have you got for us today?"

Rather taken aback by this, I replied, "Thanks John." I turned, nodded and smiled at the lady: "Hello. I'm Richard, 272 (she smiled back, and almost took my breath away). Right, this job. Well, we got a disturbance call, found no disturbance, just this guy (pointing at the guy in the ambulance) with the screwdriver in his shoulder. He's been totally uncooperative, refusing to give pars, wouldn't even let me do first aid, nothing!"

He nodded, and looked at the lady, who said, "Don't tell me, but none of the punters in the pub would speak to you?"

Slightly surprised by this, I dumbly nodded.

She continued, "Not that unusual. What about the landlord?"

I shook my head.

She said, "Now that's a little more surprising. They tend to not want their licence renewal, which we handle, to be in doubt if they don't cooperate. Something to bear in mind. Your skipper (slang for sergeant) needs to let the licensing officers know. Oh, by the way, I'm Patience."

I thought, *how ironic, doing the job we do!*

John walked to the ambulance and said, "Patience and I will try to speak to this guy. He may react differently to someone not in uniform. You never know, people are strange like that."

He looked at the paramedic, who nodded, and climbed into the back of the ambulance, saying, "Hello mate, how are you doing?"

The reply was instant: "Fuck off, you cunt. I know you're the filth. I ain't talking to you cunts, now fuck off!"

John smiled, and said, "Look mate, I can see you're upset, which is entirely understandable. We'll see you at the hospital."

The man turned his head away and remained silent. John shrugged, stepped out of the ambulance, and nodded at Patience. She took his place in the ambulance and said to the man, "Hello Sir, do you have anyone we can contact for you? Just let them know which hospital you're going to? You don't hav ..."

The man turned around and shouted, "FUCK OFF, YOU CUNT! HOW MANY TIMES DO I HAVE TO TELL YOU THICK BUNCH OF PIGS, I AIN'T GOING TO TELL YOU NOTHING. NOW FUCK OFF, YOU THICK, FAT, UGLY WHORE BITCH!"

She didn't stop smiling at him, and with the same gentle tone replied, "You can still speak to us at the hospital, or tomorrow. We're here to help."

She then got off the ambulance. Honestly, it never failed to impress me that, no matter how many times I saw police officers (male, female, Black, white) take real abuse, they were still polite and dealt with people with good humour. She walked back to us, shrugged her shoulders, saying, "Well, we tried. Don't think he'll talk to us anytime soon. Would you mind creating the skeleton CRIS, and we'll pick it. This almost certainly will be NFAd (no further action) due to lack of evidence. If he won't make a complaint, and there's no witnesses, there's nowhere to go with it."

As a side note, yes he did break the law regarding public order. We could have chosen to warn him about use of the words f**k and c**t (the only words considered swearing under the law). He could have been arrested for breach of the peace, or for Section 5 of the Public Order Act, but he was in pain, and on a stretcher, and in an ambulance. I don't think it would look good in court, and would almost certainly have been chucked out.

Honestly, it's just a regular part of your day. It's a rare day someone doesn't call you a c**t, or a racist. Those words lose their impact after you've been called them for the 100th time! Which is shocking enough on its own.

We eventually made it back to the nick, and completed the various reports and paperwork. I looked at my watch: it was 23:30 hours. Not bad for a late turn. We had another three to go, then a quick changeover (finishing at 22:00 hours and back in at 06:00 hours for early turn), then a couple of days off.

Apparently, there'd be plenty of overtime working shifts. It was almost the rule rather than the exception. I didn't mind; I did enjoy policing, and the extra money would come in handy with my new house.

As we walked down the corridor towards the exit (there were about half a dozen who'd all finished at roughly the same time), someone started humming the tune to *The Great Escape*. A dark sense of humour was necessary. We'd escaped alive to fight another day. Although deaths in service were rare, injuries were quite common, and most reliefs had at least two or three people off at any given time with work-related ailments.

I felt the satisfaction of a job well done as we made our way to the car park, where my new car was waiting. I then heard a Yorkshire accent from behind me: "Oh, bloody hell, who let a hairdresser park their car in here?"

I could feel a moment of dread run through me. *Not again. They're going to take the piss out of my car, again. Oh well, if that's the worst thing I have to put up with, it isn't that bad. They might forget, or move onto other things*. Oh what a fool I was!

I thought, *I'm going to own this. If this is where they're going with this, I can take a bit of banter.* (really?) I strode over to my Ka, putting my hand on the roof, and said loudly, "That's my car. It's the first new car I've ever bought, and it's honestly one of the only new cars I could afford. Why, do you like it?" I stood there, big grin, almost daring them to come back at me.

They burst out laughing, all of them. Maybe it was relief from the tensions of the day, but they fell about the place. I thought, *well, at least they can see I don't take myself too seriously.*

The same Yorkshire voice (which I could now see belonged to a man in his late forties, short, light brown hair, about 5'10", medium build with strong facial features) said, "Well, Vidal Sassoon, that wasn't difficult to give you a nickname. It's Vidal after the hairdresser, because of the car. Oh, sorry, hair stylist!"

Even more laughter. Well, I suppose it could have been worse (really, *Vidal*). At least it seemed like they were accepting me. I thought, *they'll probably forget it in a few weeks ...*

We got in our cars and drove home. Out of all the shifts, I preferred the late turns, because you could have a lie in. They were insanely busy, with plenty of good jobs, plenty of overtime. The traffic in and out wasn't too bad. So far, I thought, *I can live with this. I wonder what the rest of the shifts and relief are like?*

I got a good night's sleep and enjoyed a lazy morning, pottering around doing a few jobs around the place. I got partially dressed in my uniform (known as half-blues). It was a common way of going to and from work. We had to buy our own footwear, and had been advised to buy high-tech Magnums, a hybrid trainer and boot. They had thick, grippy soles, and laced up to mid-calf height. You could wear them all day, run in them if you had to, but they provided a decent amount of foot and ankle protection. Not exactly Jimmy Choos, but what can you do.

About 12:15, I set off for the forty-minute journey down the A13, to once again join the "Wacky Races".

I parked up in the far-too-small car park, said hi to Alf and Sooz on the way past, went to the canteen to brave their food for some lunch. It was about 13:00, an hour before the start of the shift. I collected my food and was taking a moment to collect my thoughts before what was likely to be a busy one. I heard the chair next to me scrape (I really must pay more attention to my surroundings), looked up, and it was Roger. He smiled and gave a quick look around, in a conspiratorial way.

He leant in a little closer, and lowered his voice, saying, "Look, I'm really sorry about what the sergeant did to you. A couple of us really thought it was out of order. I'm really glad you made it on relief. You didn't deserve what he did to you. No hard feelings?"

He extended his hand. Honestly, I was taken aback, and genuinely touched to hear him say that. I gladly shook his hand. "Thanks Roger, you didn't have to say that. I don't feel any animosity towards you at all. You were nothing but supportive and professional. In fact, there were only a couple of the street duties team who I really felt were out of line."

He nodded: "Thanks, that's good to hear. It put myself and one of the other street duties team in a difficult dilemma. I hope you understand."

I thought for a moment, trying to understand what it would have been like to try to operate as part of the street duties training team, and be loyal to them, but also feel loyalty and a sense of duty to the students. It couldn't have been easy. I just appreciated that he'd taken a risk and had the humility to apologise.

I said: "Do you mind if I say something?"

Roger took another look around to make sure we weren't being observed, and said: "Go ahead."

I replied, "I was really impressed by the way you police; kind and reasonable, when you can, but tough and decisive when you have to. You're also a really good police driver. Some of them are a bit too full-on. You are really calm, and measured, very professional. I learnt a lot from you on how to be a policeman. Thank you!"

He seemed a bit embarrassed, and for the first time I could see him genuinely taken aback. After a moment, he said: "Thanks mate, that's really appreciated. I'm going to give you some advice: first, don't try to be a policeman, just be professional, let the uniform do the work. You don't have to show them you're police, they can see that already. Just treat them as well as they'll let you. If you can, always leave them a way out. There's nothing more dangerous than someone with nothing to lose. Finally, remember if you arrest someone, it may be just another arrest, and not personal to you, but bloody personal to them. You're taking away their liberty."

I thought about that, and thanked him, and he disappeared out of the canteen. I hadn't expected that. The advice was something I'd have to think about.

I finished my lunch, went up to my locker, freshened up, and finished getting dressed in my uniform. I made my way down to the parade room for another round of madness.

I could hear the gang chatting away as I approached. It went quiet as I walked in (from my teaching days, that always set off alarm bells). I looked around the room, trying to figure out what stunt they'd pulled. It wasn't long until it became clear.

The big Yorkshireman from the other night said: "There's seat over here for you mate."

He indicated the seat in front of him (he was leaning nonchalantly against the far wall). I knew it was some sort of trap, but I'd let them have their fun. I confidently walked over to the seat indicated, and sat down. With this he walked away from the wall, revealing a large picture of Vidal Sassoon, scissors in hand. Nice! This was accompanied by plenty of laughter and comments. I just grinned and thought it was actually quite funny and clever. I was cool with that. At least they were accepting me.

Everyone who came in had a laugh, or a quick, witty comment, asking when I was free to do highlights etc. This continued until the inspector came in. He looked across at me, then the wall, saying "You haven't been given your nickname already, have you?" I nodded, and grinned. He said: "It's not something I think I should know."

He gave the Yorkshireman a long stare, and the man did his best to look innocent. Then the inspector said: "Jamie, why do I have a feeling this is your doing?"

Jamie replied, "I don't know, Sir. Maybe your suspicious nature."

The inspector harrumphed at this, and chuckled quietly. Then he stood upright and handed out the assignments. I was in PT21 with Andy Foxwell (I hadn't spoken to him yet). He was in his late forties, slim build, short black hair, about 6'. This time we managed to almost get to the end of briefing before the calls came in, and we dashed off left, right and centre.

I walked over to where Andy was waiting by the door, and he smiled a kindly smile. He came across as Mr Chilled. He stuck out his hand, and I shook it. "I'm Andy. Nice to meet you, Richard. I've a feeling this might be a little less manic than yesterday. But that might be wishful thinking. Oh, do you need anything before we go. If you do, we've taken over from C relief, so the car's probably running on fumes, so we'll have to stop at the petrol station."

I had taken the advice from yesterday and brought a small sports bag, and had my Maglite, more first aid supplies, some food and water. I was just about to thank him when the radio was calling us.

"Units to deal, forty-plus fighting with weapons, the High Street, outside the college, PT."

I didn't hesitate. I replied, "21." There were a number of units answering in the same way: "22", "20". Normally you'd say, "PT21, can you show us dealing." Or something similar. But when a number of units are likely to respond quickly, you have to just give the information control need, in the shortest time.

Andy looked at me, saying, "I guess that's our first call. I like your enthusiasm, and it's not far, so the fuel situation shouldn't be a problem."

This was said as we jogged out to the car, a MK3 Astra. They were absolutely stock, and had a 1.4L engine. They were reasonably light, so weren't too slow. They were all well-worn, and had a hard life. The trim inside was all battered and the front seats had tears and rips in them from the sharp items on police belts. They had myriad creaks and rattles. To say they looked tatty was an understatement. They were mechanically reasonably sound, but cosmetically! Well, let's just say, even the best second-hand car dealer would have had their work cut out to sell those at anything like the Parkers guide price.

We chucked our bags (including caps) on the back seat. I was beginning to understand that most people didn't wear their caps when in cars. You tended to forget them, lose them, or they fell off in struggles. I looked at the impressive array of switches for the various combinations of lights and sirens. Then I saw the radio. One of the buttons had fallen out, and had been jury-rigged to work with a piece of tinfoil and blue tack. Ah, the Met and its extra cheapness.

We made our way to the High Street, and Andy made sure our sirens were on a good distance from the call. This puzzled me a little, until Andy explained that we were so few in number (six), up against forty-plus, with weapons, so it was best to let them know a distance off, to give them ample time to disperse. The last thing you wanted was to be outnumbered more than six to one. Those aren't good odds. As we approached, we saw dozens of young men (a mixture of mostly Asian, with a few white, and Black youths all aged between 15 and 25) walking away. The fight was over, by the looks of it.

Then, as we approached the college, a white Ford Orion pulled away in front of us, and clearly on the boot were splatters of blood.

I said: "That's blood, isn't it?"

Andy nodded and put the blue lights and siren back on again when it failed to stop. He nodded saying, "Put it up as failing to stop, and get a vehicle check for us, will you Richard?"

I did as I was asked. It wasn't easy to do, as you had to use your personal radio for the vehicle check first, then get onto the main set radio to do the pursuit. I was slow at doing this, but Andy was patient with me, despite having to drive the car and coach me.

We followed the Orion. It wasn't driving particularly quickly, or breaking too many laws. I could see the car was full of young men. When we did manage to stop it, we would definitely be outnumbered, at least two to one. Not a good situation, but you just have to deal with things the best you can. On the radio, I could hear other units were on their way, but they were a distance off at that point.

We turned into a residential square, with housing blocks on all four sides. As we drove around the square with the sirens and lights on, we were attracting attention, and people were starting to come out onto the square. This didn't look good. Whatever happened, we'd be badly outnumbered.

The car went towards the exit on the other side of the square. It was a relatively narrow, enclosed archway leading out.

Andy said, "Prepare for a decamp." I relayed that via the radio and, sure enough, when the car was under the cover of the archway, it stopped and the four occupants jumped out.

We stopped right behind them, so the bandit car was blocking our only exit. When they'd opened their car doors, they touched the walls, essentially blocking us in. Their only way out was past us. Andy and I jumped out and started shouting at the four men from the bandit car to stay where they were, as they were advancing on us. Then, to compound things, I heard shouting behind us. I risked a quick look, and saw about twenty young men walking towards us, blocking us in.

Both groups were Asian and were shouting in a language I couldn't understand. They were angrily waving arms and pointing at each other. Their voices were raised.

At that point, I didn't know if they were angry at us, or each other. We really were caught in the middle, and outnumbered. I don't know if it was Andy or myself who first hit the emergency button on our radios, but both were hit. Now this silences every other police radio in the area, and whatever you say for the next five seconds is broadcast. We didn't have to say anything – the shouting said it all.

All the training about keeping a distance went out the window; we just didn't have the time. Neither of us had drawn our batons. Once again, there hadn't been time, and honestly it would have just made the situation worse. We had no chance. If these men meant to do us harm, they could.

They got closer and closer. The crowd inside the square was increasing in size, and was now about forty strong. The mood became more and more hostile. I felt pretty helpless at this point. *Just keep calm, and don't provoke anyone.* But what if the groups hated each other and the larger group was going to attack the smaller one? We couldn't just stand by. It seemed, unless we got help, and quickly, we'd have to fight either way. The larger group were now within touching distance. *Here we go,* I thought!

With all the shouting, which echoed in the enclosed archway, and the flashing police lights, it was very disorientating. Then I saw the lights of a number of police vehicles entering the other side of the square. The cavalry had arrived. Man, was I happy to see them.

That's the difference between the Met and the county police. In the Met you work in pairs, and you go to more dangerous calls. However, there's plenty of backup close by if you need it. In the counties, you go to less dangerous calls, but backup can be a long way off. At that moment I was so glad I was in the Met.

My colleagues all piled out and walked outwards us, shouting at the crowd in the square to move, which they reluctantly did, seemingly prepared to stand at a distance to shout. They quickly formed a cordon around the rear of our vehicle, and allowed us to go in and grab hold of the four from the bandit car. They didn't resist, other than to continue to shout back at the people in the square. Very quickly, more officers arrived, and we got the four in vans and we drove the bandit car, and the prisoners, back to the nick, just to get away and defuse the situation. All in all, pretty exciting, even if it was what they call 'a bottle test'.

Back in the yard, we opened the boot in front of our four prisoners, and it was filled with knives, machetes, baseball bats, and all manner of sharp and blunt instruments. A few of them had fresh blood on them. Suffice to say, Andy and I had a busy shift, processing our four prisoners, bagging and recording evidence, putting on CRIS reports, doing case papers, contacting the gang squad. They turned up, and seemed pleased we'd collected some good intelligence.

It turned out that this was part of a gang who had been causing trouble for a while, and we'd caught their weapons car. This car would drive round to where fights were being organised and let the participants collect weapons, have their fight, and then drop off the weapons again, so none of the young men involved would be caught with a weapon, on the way to or from the fight. They'd just been unlucky they'd done it so close to a police station, just after shift change. I was glad to see the back of that late turn. Talk about a baptism of fire! Honestly, I loved it. It was so much fun!

The next few days shot by in a blur, then we had a couple of days off, and the first day back would normally have been a day shift. This was to catch up on any unfinished paperwork and interviews. However, this time we'd be providing security for S Club 7 at the London Arena. We'd meet up at the station at about 17:00 hours, be briefed, and get off around 01:00 hours. This was something new. Over the years, I'd been to plenty of rock concerts: Bon Jovi, Motorhead, AC/DC, Metallica and the like. I'd even played a lot of gigs in various rock bands. Then, when I was at university, I'd done stewarding at the Pet Shop Boys and a few football matches, so I was familiar with concerts. But policing one was a different ball game. Also, the demographic of an S Club 7 audience, I suspected, might be different from that of, say, Iron Maiden.

We all met up in the back canteen, and as I walked past the conference room, I shuddered slightly at my recent bad memories of that place. This gathering had a totally different feeling about it. Relaxed was the name of the game that day. C relief made their way in dribs and drabs, found seats among the debris left by TSG (Territorial Support Group), also known by us as the "Knuckle-draggers". These were the riot squad. They were used in a support role by each division, at football matches, as support at marches, protests, riots, etc. They were also used as backup in times of crisis. Their reputation for tough, no-nonsense policing preceded them. Every unit has a reputation, and usually a nickname. The TSG were great if you were in trouble, but they were loud, obnoxious, and thick! Well, that's what their reputation was, anyway.

The reality was far more nuanced. They did train all the time: riot training, running about, keeping a high level of fitness. They were also trained in group surveillance, and invaluable in dealing with the most violent of offenders.

Having said that, wherever they went they left a mess. They'd constantly play practical jokes on other officers, and if they came down on an operation, they'd upset the local population, due to their more direct approach. Am I saying they were bad? Absolutely not. The fact I'm still here is down to them. They were tough, fearless police officers for the most part, who get a lot of unfair criticism, and precious little support from senior management, which is true of all units within the police.

It only took about ten minutes for us to throw away their old pizza boxes, and half-drunk coke cans. The banter was subdued. I think we were all a little tired; shift work is very wearing. Robbie came over and had a chat with me about the opportunities to see how other units worked, so we agreed I'd work on the next day shift with a 'Rat' (police slang for traffic police). This might seem like a derogatory term for that unit, but it is one they embraced, and if you look carefully, you might occasionally notice a small oval sticker with the face of a long, thin rat on it. That's what some of them put on their own cars.

So what's the reputation of the Rats? They were rule-conscious, finicky, petty-minded types, who it is said would lift aside the dead body in the boot to check the tread on the spare tyre. Although that's not wholly accurate, there are more than a few elements of truth in it. In general, they are regarded with suspicion by other police officers. They do have a tough job; they deal with a lot of the really nasty car accidents. Or, as they now insist on them being called, "Road Traffic Collisions." I told you they were petty.

Then, for my two-week attachment, I'd work with the CSU (Community Support Unit), who were the plain-clothes unit who dealt with domestic violence, racially motivated and homophobic crimes.

Robbie suggested this, as it was thought that I was good at dealing with vulnerable victims, and that might be an avenue I'd like to consider in the future. Not by me, if I'm honest – nicking villains and driving cars fast, that's what I wanted. I'm from Essex – what do you expect?

As we were chatting and waiting for our start time, in walked the inspector, with a couple of civvies, with visitor ID badges. We stopped chatting and looked over.

The inspector said, "Afternoon folks. We've got the TV news people in again. They want a couple of volunteers to film walking around for the background shots over news items to do with the police." He turned to look at the visitors, and said: "I can spare two officers for about thirty minutes. I'll need them back after that. Take your pick."

He then went off to make himself a cup of tea.

They were two middle-aged men, dressed casually. The more senior of the two looked slightly uncomfortably at us and said: "Would you and you like to come with me? It won't take long. All you have to do is walk back and forth outside the police station as we film you."

The two officers he picked (Mel, the youngest, prettiest woman, and Sergeant Darling, a Black man) got up and made their way reluctantly towards the door. When they'd left, there were a few groans and sighs of disapproval.

A large man, whom I hadn't been introduced to yet, turned around and said: "I fucking hate those bastards in the media: the BBC, Sky, Channel Four. They lie and smear us, never say anything good about us, and then they have the unmitigated gall to expect us to prance around for them like a bunch of prize tarts!"

There was a round of laughter and, as it died down, Roger called out, "For the sake of the tape, I challenge that remark." More laughter.

I looked at Robbie, and he could see I was confused. He looked over at the large man, and said, "That's Campbell. He's one of the area car drivers. He's been here for donkey's years. Watch him; he knows this job inside and outside."

Campbell reacted to his name, looking across at me saying, "Oh, you're the new gobby probby, Vidal." He laughed at his own joke, and the others joined in.

Alf walked in with a pile of newspapers. He said, "Afternoon folks. How you all doing today? Here's your papers. Who wants *The Times*?" A few hands went out, and the papers were handed out. Who wants the *Telegraph*?" Hands went up, and they were handed out. "The *Mail*?" Hands went up, and they were handed out. He continued through all the usual suspects.

I looked around, and the majority of people had a paper, and were perusing them. He held up one single, lonely paper. He said: "Anyone want The People's Communist Propaganda Paper, also known as *The Guardian*?" Everyone laughed, and he shrugged saying "Oh well, I tried."

I put my hand up, and said, "If no one else wants it, I'll take it, Alf."

Silence! I mean tumbleweeds. Campbell put on a pair of rubber gloves, took the paper from Alf, and walked over to me and dropped it on the table next to me. This got a good laugh, but I still had looks of shock from all present. *The Guardian*, really? I was enjoying it. I picked up the paper and enthusiastically read it. Honestly, I didn't usually read *The Guardian*, even though it was the staple of the staff room.

When no one was watching, I sneakily got notes out, that I had to study for the next training session, and read those instead. If wind-ups were the game, two can play.

A short while later, our two TV stars walked back in, to a few catcalls. They sarcastically took bows, and the banter was on. Campbell said: "Here, Mel, you want to be careful hanging around on street corners waiting for the film unit to say 'action'. The locals might think you're on the game."

Much laughter, and a couple of "For the sake of the tape, I challenge that remark." Mel looked at him, screwed up her eyes and made a face. This emboldened him, saying "I wonder how much you would charge."

And before anyone could react, Mel smoothly said: "I don't know Campbell. How much do your mother and sisters charge?"

The relief erupted at this with, again, a few "For the sake of the tape, I challenge that remark" thrown in.

I furrowed my brow, and naively looked at Robbie, for clarification. He nodded and said, "Campbell, would you like to explain to our new friend here why we say, 'I challenge that remark'?"

Campbell put his paper down and, with a huge grin, that slowly changed into a deadly serious scowl, said: "Well, my leftie teacher friend, let me explain to you what that communist bastard Blair, and our glorious senior management, have done. Earlier this year, two of our traffic colleagues were alone in a police car, which had a camera and mike set up to film the great British public. One of them made an off-colour remark, the other said nothing. The tape was, by chance, checked. A senior officer heard the off-colour remark. And what do you think happened?"

I thought for a moment, and replied: "The one making the comment would have been disciplined in some way, but no member of the public had heard it or complained. So maybe docked a few days' pay?"

A few dry laughs, and Campbell was slowly shaking his head, indicating that I had missed the mark. I tried again, "Maybe, the officer was sacked?"

Campbell looked at me and almost casually said: "About half right. Both were sacked."

I was confused. "Why both?"

He said: "The second officer was told he should have challenged that remark, even though they were alone." I suddenly thought of school and *1984*. Wow, real thought-control stuff.

Campbell wasn't done, and said: "It fits their purpose. They can say 'we're fighting racism, look how many racist police officers we're getting rid of'. Or, if they're looking for the next rank, they have to fulfil certain criteria, and you bet one of these criteria is showing you've done your bit to fight racism. They have to give examples of each one, so they'd see that as another box ticked and, in the process, destroy some poor, hard-working sod's life. Not that they care about any of us! We're just their tools to get them up the chain of command. Evil bastards!"

There were plenty of voices of agreement.

Wow! I knew the rank and file really did hate the management! I was beginning to see why. Then a thought occurred, and just before I began to speak, Campbell anticipated my question. He said: "You're going to ask, but why say it in here. Well, it's good practice to say it everywhere, however, we have seen maintenance people messing with the ceiling in here. They weren't the usual ones, and wouldn't talk to us, which is very unusual. You know there's an entire department in the Met dedicated to getting rid of us. They're the complaints department. We have a few other names for them." He finished grimly, and with plenty saying, "I challenge that remark."

I was having a hard time believing it. Surely they were just being paranoid? Campbell, bored with all the serious talk, wanted to have fun, and I was on the block for banter today (I noticed Edward was keeping his head down, and being ignored).

Campbell said: "I guess if we ask nicely, Vidal, we might be able to get an autograph from your favourite band tonight."

The relief, needing relief, warmed to this line in banter. I thought, *OK, let's play along*. I said: "Oh, really, do you think so? They really are my favourite band. I sold my tickets when I found out I'd be getting in for free."

This went down well, and Campbell took up the challenge, and continued, and continued.

Honestly, for the next three hours, it was have a pop at Richard. Now I do have a sense of humour, and I can take a joke at my expense but, really, three hours? Even my patience was wearing thin. By that time, we'd overseen the entrance of the band, and the fans. We were really just for external security, and traffic control.

We adjourned to the staff canteen area for some sad-looking excuses for sandwiches, cans of coke and some crisps. Ah, the combination of shit food, and the Met's extra cheapness. All rolled up into one, semi-edible bundle.

With the pre-recorded backing and vocal tracks playing full blast, we sat down to play cards and wait until the we were needed to supervise the crowds on exit. The fortunate ones were on patrol outside.

Honestly, if I hear 'Reach for the stars' once more, it'll be too much. We started playing cards. So being, as Campbell put it, the dodgy, gobby probby, lefty, *Guardian*-reading hairdresser, I'd be recording the scores.

I thought, after Campbell's last three hours of piss-taking, I'd see if he could take a joke. I went round the table, "Paul, P A U L, Andrew A N D R E W, Melody M E L O D Y, Robbie, R O B B I E." Came to Campbell, I said, "Tosser T O S S E R!"

Stunned silence, and then Campbell slapped the table, put his head back and laughed, slapping me on the shoulder. The rest of the team joined in. I could see a few of them were nervously looking at me, as if to say, "Wow, are you sure about that?"

Campbell dispelled that by saying, "You know, it's a while since a probby has had the balls to take the piss out of me. Richard (he used my name – a sign of respect, I thought), you're all right in my book. You can take it, and you dish it out. Fair play mate! I respect that!" Then he leant in close and, with his best evil villain look, said: "But don't try it too often."

Then he laughed, leaving me pretty sure he was joking, but not certain. This guy was good. I could get on with him.

The concert came to an end, and we made our way outside. Honestly, it was a nightmare. People were ignoring parking restrictions, blocking the road, blocking the parking for the coaches. Trying to argue with us, some of these parents were just downright rude, effing and blinding at us, complaining about how crowded the roads were and lack of parking. It came to a head when Mel and I were regulating the traffic leaving from the multi-storey car park, which led on to the main road where the coaches were. There was a long delay letting cars out onto the road because we were being given instructions to hold that traffic by the inspector who was watching on the cameras in the control room. Most of the motorists were understanding about it. They were not happy, but could see the amount of traffic, and parents with excited kids running about. We were just trying to get everyone out as quickly as we could, but without any run-over kids.

The queue was back into the car park. I then heard a car's engine being revved up, then the sounds of screeching tyres, then a large black BMW shot out from the up rank, and drove down the wrong side of the road, and pushed in front of the other motorists who were patiently waiting there.

Mel and I were standing at the hash markings, and this car stopped directly in front of us. The driver's window went down and this man in his fifties leant out, angrily shouting: "Get out of the way!"

At this point, that wasn't going to happen. I looked at Mel, and she indicated I could deal with this, while she stood her ground, not allowing the car to leave. The radio went, and it was the inspector. He said: "Richard, make that muppet wait until the last car has left. I would like a word with this gent!"

I acknowledged the call, and suppressed a grin. I walked over to the driver, and before I had a chance to say anything, he said: "I told you to get out of the way. It's ridiculous that we've been waiting this long. If you knew what you were doing, we'd all be out of here by now. You are so incompetent. I pay your wages. Why don't you let us all out? This road layout is stupid; the council don't know what they're doing. I'm going to make a complaint about you. I know about the police – my cousin is a special in Kent. I'll have your job for this, you incompetent fool. Don't just stand there, I told you to get out of the way!"

I was impressed; most stroppy adolescents run out of breath well before then. I smiled, and said, "Sir, I understand it's frustrating, but we're waiting for the coaches filled with children to pull out, which ..."

He interrupted, shouting, "I told you to get out of the way. Are you fucking deaf!"

I looked at the passenger seat, where a scared little girl of about 12 was sitting. I began to feel my anger growing. Blowing off steam at me is one thing, but to scare your own daughter is another.

I politely waited until he'd given me another barrage of insults, and tried to time it so that he wouldn't interrupt, as reasoning with this guy didn't seem to be working.

As soon as he'd finished, I leant in towards him and said quietly enough, so his daughter wouldn't hear: "You are waiting here until we choose to let you out, and if you get out of your car, I will arrest you for breach of the peace. If you swear at myself or my colleague again, I'll arrest you under Section 5 of the Public Order Act."

Before he could say anything, I walked back to where Mel was, and stood directly in front of his car. When we had our backs to him, so he couldn't see, Mel said quietly: "Sorted?"

"What do you think?" She rolled her eyes.

About twenty minutes later the coaches had left, and the traffic cleared enough for us to let the other drivers go. When they saw that we were holding up the guy who had driven past them on the up ramp, we got plenty of thumbs-up.

The driver was still fuming when the inspector arrived. The inspector had seen what this guy had done and, as he walked up, he asked for a process book (wow, I was impressed he was at the very least going to threaten this guy with a serious ticket). He nodded at me, and said: "Richard, I'll deal with this. There's a young woman who might need help, sitting on the wall down by the entrance. Mel and I will deal with Nigel Mansell here."

As I walked off, the driver tried the same trick with the inspector, who calmly started filling out the process book, and informed the driver he'd be receiving an invitation to the magistrates' court, where the footage would be shown of him driving the wrong way out of a public multi-storey car park when there were hundreds of small children running about, while he had a child in the car, then being abusive towards the officer who stopped him. I didn't hear the end of the conversation, but I did hear a couple of weeks later, when it went to court, the magistrate wasn't too impressed with his antics, and he received a hefty fine and points. I think the inspector really enjoyed that one!

Back outside the concert venue, I walked around to the entrance, and sure enough there was a tall, slim, beautiful young woman, sitting on the wall gingerly feeling her ankle.

I went over, saying "Hello there, Miss. Are you all right?"

She shyly smiled, and said in a charming Aussie accent, "Ah, thank you. I'm one of the dancers from the show, and I twisted my ankle in the second number, and had to dance on all the rest of the performance."

I said: "The show must go on. But, seriously, you must be in pain?"

She smiled, and coyly offered up her injured foot, saying, "You're trained in first aid. Would you have a look at it for me?"

One thing I knew about professional dancers was that they often work through injuries, and endure high levels of pain, and they know when they're injured. She didn't need me to tell her that it wasn't serious. She was flirting with me. Really, me? This was a pretty new experience. Normally women as good-looking as her won't even look twice at the likes of me. But, put on a uniform, and she's interested. Really!

She was really nice, but I am a professional, and I won't use my uniform to be sleazy, so I thought, *I'll be professional, and play it cool.*

I checked over her ankle (I have a degree in human physiology, and did extensive first aid training prior to becoming a teacher). From what I could tell, it was a sprain which would most likely swell up by morning. I said: "Look, I don't think this is anything more than a sprain. When do you have to dance next?"

"Two days' time is the next show. I really need to be able to dance then. It's my living."

I nodded, and said: "I'm sure you've got lots of anti-inflammatories, but the best one I've seen is an old-fashioned one: witch-hazel. You soak a clump of cotton wool in it, put it over the injury, and keep it in place with a firm, but not tight, crepe bandage."

She looked at me and said: "Really? That works? Where would I get that stuff at this time of the night?"

I had anticipated the question and was on the radio, asking Sooz to call me on a private channel (this was a way for a controller to have a private conversation, usually about a confidential matter). I explained the situation, and asked her where the nearest all-night chemist was. She found a couple, and I noted their addresses on a piece of Met notepaper and handed it to her. She thanked me and said her expensive taxi had arrived. I helped her up, and supported her (she was putting it on) to the car, explaining to the driver where the open chemist stores were. I then walked back to the rear passenger door to say goodbye.

She smiled, and was very appreciative, then said: "Look Richard, my name is Dawn. You've been so sweet, I'd really like to catch up with you next time I'm in London. I'll need someone to show me the sights. If you give me your number, I can call you. What do you say? I'd be fun."

Before I had a chance to say a word, the radio went, saying: "272, you're needed back at the bus, it's about to leave. Right now!"

I could see her disappointment. I was lost for words for a moment. First this beautiful woman had asked me out (this is a one-time event), and then even the chance had been snatched away. Honestly, I wasn't even sure whether she'd have called, or I would have gone. But to not have the opportunity was galling.

The radio went again. This time it was Sergeant Robertson saying: "272, get yourself back to the bus right away!"

I shrugged and said: "Thank you so much; you've made my year! I'm so sorry," as I turned and started jogging back to the van.

When I rounded the corner, they were all waiting for me. They'd been watching, and waiting for the worst time to call me back.

I looked at them and said: "You rotten bastards!"

This made them laugh even more, and as we walked back to the van, they slapped me on the back, and were pleased I'd taken it in good spirits.

When Mel asked who she was and I told her it was one of the dancers, they had even more of a laugh. *You evil sods!* I thought. These guys were professional piss-takers. I'd met my match.

I'd almost forgiven them by the time we got back to the nick. When they told Sooz, she was very sympathetic towards me, and told them they were very bad people. All with a wicked grin. This lot were a right handful, and no mistake.

It continued over the next few weeks, with crazy late turns running from call to call, basically just firefighting. Early turns were (in general) quieter, but you ended up tidying up after the night duty. The trouble with early turns was that you were always in danger of picking up a late job, meaning you staying on well after 14:00 hours. This might not sound bad, but if you'd been up since 04:30 hours, it can make you very tired. I wasn't keen on earlies for that reason.

But by far the shift I had most difficulty adjusting to was night duty. In the summer, you got up in the light, saw the sun go down, and worked all night, then went to bed just as the sun was coming up. My body didn't like that. I found it very hard to sleep during the day. In the winter, it was worse: you got up in the dark, and you went home in the dark. You never saw the sun. That was nasty!

Anyone who has worked nights will tell you that around 02:00–03:00 hours, your body slows down, and it's very hard to fight the urge to sleep. You have to force your way through it. That's really unpleasant, and has longer-term issues. We used to do seven nights on the spin, then a quick changeover to earlies. Those were killers. By the end of that shift pattern, you could feel your face sagging, and you knew your reactions and thinking had slowed down.

***

A few weeks later, at the start of a set of early turns, we got a disturbance call from the set of 'The Big Breakfast' show. Now, for those of you who aren't familiar with it, it was a live, morning TV show, which was light-hearted and involved humorous sketches, and was pretty good. It was filmed at the lock gateman's cottage on an industrial estate. This was from the time when cargo was unloaded at the docks, and transported via the canal to the cargo processing plants.

Now I was working with Andy, who was such a professional. Always so cool and calm, he was such a good example to us probationers.

It was early, 07:00 hours, and this was around the corner from the stables (where the mounted branch were stationed), and the horses were often exercised in the morning, away from the busy roads.

As we were making our way to the call, we got an update. It was a couple of people doing a publicity stunt, dressed as fruit, who had run on the set and interrupted the live broadcast.

I then heard one of the funniest things I'd ever heard. It was a pursuit from a mounted officer, who had come across these two publicity seekers as they were trespassing and interrupting the live broadcast, and chased them.

You have to imagine that talking on a radio as you're trotting on horseback requires you to break up what you're saying to match your motion. So, what you get is: "the suspects ... are turning right ... into ...", which is hilarious to hear. Both of us were trying not to laugh as we drove to intercept them. We pulled in at a T-junction to see a giant apple and banana being chased down the street by a policeman on horseback, who was giving a commentary in this broken fashion. We just stopped and laughed so hard, tears were rolling down our cheeks. What made it funnier was the fact the mounted officer wasn't impressed with our contribution and was, in between his broken commentary, berating us. Eventually, we pulled ourselves together enough to catch the criminal fruit impersonators.

We let them go, with a warning, once 'The Big Breakfast' crew told us they didn't want anything done about it.

That one had everyone in stitches at refs in the canteen. We were in a pretty good mood for the rest of the shift, but both hoping we didn't get an arrest last thing, so we could go home on time. But, fate being what it is, a call came about 13:00 hours. It was a shoplifter at Tesco. I knew everyone else was tied up, so I didn't even look at Andy, I just keyed the mike, and said: "PT, PT21, we'll take that one. I'll update when we're on scene."

The way it worked was, if you were free, you'd take the job, no matter how crappy it was or how inconvenient because, if you didn't, one of your mates would have to. We were all in it together, and we all pulled our weight. No complaints, or bitching about whose turn it was. If you got three shit jobs on the trot, so be it. Next week, it'd be someone else's turn.

We arrived, and I put us on scene. We walked in, and waiting at the service desk was the security guard. He said: "Ah, great, you were quick. Thanks. Good. She's in the security office. She's not violent or anything. Just gave up straight away."

I thought, and said: "How old is she?"

"She's an adult, 21 maybe."

A spark of hope. If she was an adult, and didn't have any previous convictions, maybe she'd be eligible for a caution (a two-hour process, as opposed to six hours, if it needed to go to court). He then dashed my hopes by saying: "It's not her first time here. She got caught and arrested by you lot last month." *Oh well, I suppose I can use the overtime*, I thought.

We walked over to the security office. The general rule was, I was the passenger (or pen), and Andy was the driver (or keys). This meant that I did the paperwork. The second reason I would be expected to take the lead was I had the least service (the amount of time you have in the police), so I would do all the dirty work. This wasn't just RHIP; it was a good way of learning. Andy had done this a hundred times, I hadn't, so I needed the experience. I would have been taken to one side and given a talking to if I didn't volunteer for every crappy job going. No one would tell you to do it, but you gained respect if you did.

So I walked into the office first, where I saw a young, slim, tall (5'8"), mixed-race woman of about 20–25. She was dressed in a worn T-shirt and jeans, with a heavy jacket on the desk next to her. She was average in looks (I'm not just being sexist, it is important later, so calm down), and it was clear she'd been crying. There was a female store security officer sitting watching her. As we walked in, she got up and walked out.

The male security officer walked over and picked up a bag of bottles of spirits, razors and batteries. They're a common thing stolen by drug users, as they're easy to sell, and small enough to hide.

I walked over and said to the woman, "Hello there, I'm PC Armstrong from Earlham Police Station. What's your name?" She looked up and, wiping a tear from her face, replied: "Roxanne Templeton."

She looked at me with big brown eyes and, despite myself, I felt a pang of pity. I thought, *she's stolen from a shop. Whether I feel sorry for her or not, I have to be fair and objective.*

I looked at the security guard, who held up the bag of stolen items. I looked back at Roxanne, and said: "You need to listen to the security guard, and then you'll have a chance to speak, OK?"

She nodded. I looked at the guard. He said: "At about 1 p.m. I was alerted by the camera operator that someone was taking items off the shelves, and putting them inside their jacket pockets. I went down to the aisle they indicated, and observed this young lady taking batteries, and instead of putting them in her basket, she'd put them in her inside pocket. Each time she did this she'd look around, as if to check to see if she was being watched. I was in plain clothes, so I don't think she noticed me. I then followed her past the tills, where she ditched the basket, and walked out making no attempt to pay for these items, the total cost of which was

£120.47. She then walked out of the store, where I stopped her. She cooperated, and I took her back to the security office, where my female colleague spoke to her. She admitted stealing the items, said she was sorry. So we called the police, and you arrived."

I nodded. It was a pretty good account. The quality of shop security evidence is, shall we say, variable, but this was definitely at the better end of the spectrum.

I thanked him and, turning to Roxanne, said: "Roxanne, you've heard what the security guard has said. What have you got to say?"

In between tears, she said: "I'm sorry, he's right. I did take that stuff."

She looked at the security guard and said: "I'm really sorry."

Even the security guard was a little taken aback. This wasn't the usual response. He said quietly: "Don't worry, you're not a bad person. You've just got to stop doing this. Let the police help you."

I thought that was a kind thing for him to say. The whole situation wasn't what normally happened, but I had a job to do. I arrested and cautioned her. I looked at Andy and, knowing what I was thinking, he said: "It's your arrest; it's your call."

I looked at Roxanne, and said gently, "I don't need to put handcuffs on you, do I?"

She shook her head quickly, saying: "No, I won't fight, or run off."

I nodded my head, and took my hand off the cuffs, saying: "I will have to hold you by the arm, but I will try not to make it too obvious. Now dry your face; we don't want people seeing you've been crying. They hate us enough already. I'd prefer not to be thought of as someone who makes young women cry."

Despite herself, she gave a wan smile, and the security guard handed her a tissue. She thanked him, and I took her to the car, as Andy collected the receipt (we don't seize the actual items stolen, just a receipt, as food items will go off if stored for a while), and the VHS security tape of the theft.

We then drove back to the station, and booked Roxanne in. Andy was going to stay on, and help me complete the case papers, as the case was going to court. As we booked her in (this was a rough procedure, where you have to put everything they have on them out on the desk for all to see, describe it, and it's bagged up), she was asked if she wanted to see the doctor (standard question), and she said she did, but didn't want to speak to a solicitor.

We collected the evidence, put on the CRIS, and I prepped for the interview. I planned what I needed to prove (known as "The Points To Prove"), and what questions I needed to ask, bagging up the receipt, getting the mobile VHS player ready to be played, if necessary.

Eventually, I was ready. The police saying was "failing to prepare is preparing to fail". I wasn't ready to fail this one.

We booked her out, and went to the interview. I did everything by the book. I took the lead in the interview. It was a full 'hands up', which is rare. Mostly people either say nothing, or lie through their teeth. Sometimes, it's similar to when a kid doesn't do their homework, and claims aliens stole it. Some of the fairy stories you hear would make Hans Christian Andersen proud!

This time was a rarity, with absolute honesty, and contrition. An interview is the person's opportunity to explain things, not for us to catch them out, or fit them up. You are trained to let people talk. At the end of the interview, I asked Roxanne why she had stolen (her word, not mine) the items from the shop.

She tearfully said: "I'm ashamed to tell you, but I'm addicted to heroin. I have been since I was 18. I'm so embarrassed."

I replied (throwing her a massive lifeline): "We do have independent drug workers who you can talk to, who can help, and maybe get you into a rehabilitation programme. Would you like me to arrange that now?"

This could be read out in court, and if she accepted, could give the magistrate more latitude in dealing with her. She nodded her head, and then said: "Please, if you can do that. But I was told by the doctor and the council when I asked for help that it was up to a year's wait."

I replied, "I'm not certain, but the last time I spoke with the drugs worker, because you've been arrested, they can get you in within weeks. Is that something you want me to do now?"

"Oh, yes please. I just want help. I hate this."

Honestly, I was so pleased to hear that. If we could help her to get free of the addiction, it would give her a chance to turn her life around.

We concluded the interview, and I put her back in the cell. Then I contacted the drug workers' direct police line, and made the referral. They said they'd send someone down asap. I let the custody sergeant know, and Andy and I had a much-needed coffee (I was beginning to flag a bit), and we got down to the job of doing the case papers. She would be charged by the sergeant as soon as he had a chance.

Case papers are a slog, but those weren't too bad, but they are long, tedious, and you have to be very precise. One even minor error, or oversight, means the case can be thrown out. This has consequences for the victims, and also for you, leading to possible disciplinary action being taken, so you have to really focus.

We got the call to attend custody, where the drug worker had just turned up, and the sergeant was ready to charge. We got Roxanne out of the cell, and she was charged. This basically meant the sergeant would explain that she would be referred to the courts, and she'd be notified where and when. Then we handed her over to the drug worker, and they went off into the interview room, where they could have a confidential talk. I had to wait around, as I was responsible for her while she was out of the cell.

Andy went back and did some more work on the case papers. About half an hour later, Roxanne came out of the interview room, looking the happiest I'd seen her.

As I walked her back to take her fingerprints and photograph, she said excitedly: "The drug worker said he'll put me forward for a residential drug rehab course in a couple of weeks, right after the court case. I'm so relieved. I can get treatment. Thank you so much. You have been so kind!"

She then stopped, turned, and I'll never forget the look she gave me. There was real hope in her face. I'd helped someone, who really needed help. If that wasn't what I was there for, I don't know what was.

She was bailed, her property was handed back, and I walked her out. She stopped at the front desk, and once again thanked me for my kindness. I was, honestly, humbled. I was only doing my job, but 'I' was doing 'The Job', not someone else. I felt proud. Sounds pompous, but I was making a difference. In teaching, yes, you can make a difference but, over time – it can take weeks, months, years. This was immediate, in your face, now, here, and it was intoxicating. I was, in the police paradigm, 'Job pissed'. Simply put, it means drunk on being a police officer. Not on a power trip, just trying to do good, and seeing it work, right there in front of you.

That moment passed, and I remembered Andy slogging away alone on the case papers. I went and helped him finish them off. He even told me I'd done a good job that day. It was one of those days you dream about at Hendon. Life was good!

Now don't think for one minute that time was all sweetness and roses. It was really hard, trying to get used to a totally new life, becoming a new person, having to adapt quickly to an ever-changing set of situations, feeling like you were always one or two steps behind everyone else, constantly getting things wrong, saying and doing the wrong thing. Everything you do is being watched and noted. And doing this while being constantly tired. It's not for the faint-hearted.

Chapter 6
ACCEPTANCE

Four weeks later, on the next 9–5 paperwork day, we all met up in the back canteen, and the usual banter started. The papers were handed out, and I took my copy of *The Guardian*. Everyone noticed, and I sat there bold as brass, enjoying their slight discomfort, while secretly reading my notes for the next training day.

In walked the now familiar TV news people, and we went through the whole rigmarole of asking (knowing full well) who they'd like to film. And, once again, politely Mel and the good sergeant got up and dutifully walked out for their starring roles, as background to a no doubt highly (and unfairly) critical report by so-called journalists.

At just before 10:00 hours, the Rat (traffic officer) walked in. I waved and he came over, and said: "PC Armstrong, 272, you fit?"

I picked up my bag: "Let's go."

Off we walked to his traffic car, to the usual catcalls about traffic officers measuring the size of font on car number plates etc. The car we were in was a Vauxhall Omega estate. He opened the boot (which was pretty full already – man did these Rats have a lot of toys), and put away my bag.

I went and sat in the passenger's seat. Now, *this* was a police car. It was spotless, and everything worked. It even had, get this, air conditioning, with two sets of controls, one for each side of the car. We were in a different reality. No more tin foil and Blu Tack switches.

I looked across at the traffic officer who was going to be showing me the ropes. He was an older man, in his forties, about 5'10", stocky build, with greying black hair.

I stuck out my hand, said: "Hi, please call me Richard. I'm here to learn. Just tell me what you want me to do, and I'll do my best to do it."

He looked across at me and shook my hand. He said: "Good to meet you, Richard. I'm Gary. Let's just establish a few ground rules. Don't touch any of the controls on the dashboard. If we get in a pursuit, you can use the main set. I'll do the first couple of stops, and you'll do cover. Then, once you get the idea, I'll let you take over. We have a different approach in traffic. Also, you'll need to get your cap from your bag. Unlike on relief, we always put them on."

I replied: "Oh, OK. I am here to learn, so I'd best go and get my cap then." I retrieved my cap, and we moved off.

That thing didn't rattle or squeak, and the car was smooth, as was Gary's driving. It was even better than Roger's.

"Gary, what are we doing first?"

"We'll go to base and park up, then I'll show you how to use the hand-held radar gun."

I grinned: more toys to play with.

He continued, "Have you used one of those before?"

"No, that sounds like fun. Are they easy to use?"

"They're not too bad. Main thing is remember how to save readings, and how to switch between settings, otherwise it's point and shoot."

Even better, I thought.

We arrived at the Earlham Road Traffic base, and Gary showed me how to operate it, away from prying eyes, so I didn't look like a fool in front of the public.

A short while later, and we'd paired up with another traffic unit, and they'd gone about half a mile down the road, to catch anyone who failed to stop for us. Then we were off. Gary did the first few, then let me take over. It was on the Kenton road, a 30 mph limit. There was a flyover, and a long stretch of straight road that people tended to speed on. There were regularly a number of serious accidents along that section of road. So, as far as I was concerned, it was fair game.

The traffic was unusually light, and I looked at Gary and asked how fast they had to be driving before I pulled them over? Gary held up four fingers, then five. Right, 45 mph or over gets a tug.

We stopped a number of cars, and either gave them warnings (45–50), or anything 50-plus got an FPN, and the eagle eye of a Rat running over their vehicle, which meant they often ended up with a number of other offences coming to light. I had done plenty of paperwork, and it was getting towards lunchtime, so Gary indicated we'd do one more stop then have a break.

I was standing with the radar gun pointing down the road and, for once, there was a break in the traffic, then I heard the sound of a car's engine being absolutely thrashed as it got nearer. I got the gun ready. Into view it came, a battered, old red Ford Fiesta, and I clocked it 97 mph, in a 30 mph limit. I checked it twice, with it still approaching as if the four horsemen of the apocalypse were on his tail. Gary took one look, and indicated for it to stop. As the driver tried to slow it down, Gary called the pickup car down the road, which eventually stopped it.

Gary looked at me and said quietly: "I'll deal with this one, Richard."

I handed him the gun, and followed dumbly behind him.

The driver was out of the car, and talking to the other traffic officers. The driver was a tall, skinny, sallow-faced youth who looked barely old enough to hold a licence. His tracksuit trousers were showing half his backside, and he was casually leaning on the roof of the car.

Gary walked up to him, turning the gun around so this guy could see the reading, and calmly and deliberately said: "Excuse me, young man, can you explain to me why you found it necessary to do 97 in a 30 limit?"

The youth leant back on the car's roof, and said casually: "Well the car wouldn't go any faster!"

Gary shot him a steely glare, and asked for his name, address and DOB, then for his driving documents. The lad gave his name, and an address a few streets away, then produced his pass certificate (this is what you get from the test examiner, before you get your licence).

Gary carefully unfolded this crumpled bit of paper, and checked it twice, and said: "You passed your test two weeks ago, and you're already more than tripling the speed limit?"

The lad just shrugged his shoulders. The car came back to a woman with the same surname, at the address he'd provided.

Gary said: "Is this your mother's car, by any chance?"

He replied: "Yeah, but she's cool with me driving it, and I've even got insurance, and everything. It's proper legit, mate."

I could see Gary bite back a comment, saying: "I'm going to complete the paperwork, and it'll be a court appearance, then I'll drive you back to your mom's and my colleague here will follow us in her car. And given she owns the car, we'll have a little chat."

The lad didn't seem happy, but at that point, he wasn't given a choice. The paperwork was all completed.

We drove round to his mom's and parked up, then all three of us walked up to the front door. Gary knocked, and a minute later a middle-aged lady with badly dyed-blonde hair, dressed in a tracksuit, came to the door.

She said: "'Ere, what are you pigs doing with my boy?"

Gary politely and calmly said: "Good afternoon. We pulled over your son, who was driving your car. He was driving at 97 mph in a 30 mph limit."

She went into overdrive, "Don't talk fucking shit; my car won't do 97!"

The son piped up, "Yeah it will mom!"

She shifted her view to her son, saying: "You fucking stupid little shit!" Landing a right hand on the top of his head, she grabbed him and shoved him inside, saying "Get in there, and don't think you've heard the last of this!"

Turning back to Gary, she said: "'Ere, if you see my son driving my car again, lock the little shit up and throw away the fucking key! He ain't allowed to drive it no more."

I handed her the keys, which she snatched and walked inside, slamming the door. We walked back to the car, and when we were safely inside, he said: "Welcome to traffic in the East End."

We both laughed. I was about to say something, but Gary be beat me to it: "Moderate chastisement of a child I think that right hand was called." I nodded (I wondered if I should say "I challenge that remark," but thought better of it).

We had our lunch at Elham Police Station's canteen, which was just across the road. Then, back out, while driving around, Gary let me spot, so I was the one directing us to pull over vehicles. Man was that fun. Very rarely on relief do you get to do any proactive police work. It was a welcome distraction.

There were a couple of stops that stood out. We pulled a silver Audi over, who was doing 50 in a 30 limit. As we were exiting the vehicle, he was already advancing on us, seemingly Mr Angry. He was in his forties, about 5'8", stocky, but well dressed.

He said: "I don't know why you've pulled me over. Why aren't you arresting burglars, and rapists? My house was burgled last week. Where were you, eh!? Eh! I know you were too busy giving upstanding, decent members of the community speeding tickets."

It was my turn to do the ticket, so I waited until he'd finished: "You've indicated you know we've pulled you over due to excess speed. We have you on the equipment onboard our car as doing 50 mph in a 30 mph area."

He exploded: "See, see, you got it wrong, you got it wrong (almost dancing with glee). I wasn't doing 50, I was doing 60, so YOU (pointing his finger at me), YOU GO IT WRONG! I wasn't doing 50, I was doing 60. So I win, I win, you lose!"

I pulled out a traffic process book and started to fill it in. Gary managed to calm him down enough to give us his details. Then I explained to the driver that he was getting a ticket for 60 mph.

He replied: (which is recorded for court) "Ha! You see, you admit it, you admit it, you got it wrong. It says 60 mph here. I win!"

We then explained he'd be contacted about a court date, and he went on his merry way, with a ticket for doing 30 mph over the limit instead of 20 mph over the limit. This is the difference between a fine and three points, and a fine and a possible driving ban. As he drove off, I looked at Gary, and he just shrugged.

Another young lad we pulled over for also doing 50 mph said: "Thank God for that. I was racing my mate earlier on, and we were really speeding then."

I said, "So what sort of car did he have?"

"A crappy old escort XR3i."

I winced at that, and said more out of cheek than anything, "Oh, what is his name?" He told me and gave me his mate's address and car registration number. We drove around until we found his mate, who was also driving like an idiot, and gave him a ticket too. Sometimes, some people are so, so stupid!

The end of the day came around really quickly, and I thanked Gary, and said I'd really enjoyed the day. He grinned and said: "Some of my colleagues give us a bad reputation, but most of us are reasonable. Oh, and don't say you enjoyed it too much."

I looked at him sideways for a minute, and he said: "Because, they'll give you stick for just saying you enjoyed working on traffic."

We laughed. Driving back home, I kept religiously to the speed limit. Maybe, just maybe, I was learning.

For the next few weeks I kept working tiring nights, long earlies and manic lates. There was arrest, after arrest, after arrest for drugs (heroin and cannabis), knives, robbery, burglary. I was working really hard. It was a struggle. I made plenty of mistakes, and tried to learn from them. I was probably slightly below average in terms of progress, and it didn't help that Edward just seemed to sail through everything. I was always being compared unfavourably with him.

One night duty, I was working with Lawrence (The Law). It was always fun working with him. We lived a couple of miles apart, along with another one of our team, Pete (no, not the one from training). He was a short, slim, ex-Royal Marine guy in his late thirties. He grew up in the East

End, and had a real 'rough diamond' quality about him. This particular night shift, we all agreed to share a car (The Law's motor, which was an estate). Nights weren't too bad for sharing a lift, because if we didn't get off at the same time, there was a good train service, and you were going against the tide of commuters, so you'd usually not have more than four or five people per carriage.

As we were driving in (it was winter, so already dark after 21:00 hours), we were having a bit of friendly banter, a nice social opportunity. Driving along the A13, as we passed the entrance to Tilbury Dock, we saw two new Toyota Land Cruisers pull onto the road directly ahead of us. The only illumination they had on were their flashing hazards lights. They had no number plates, and you could clearly see they were still covered in the white wax they used to prevent rust while at sea, along with their delivery stickers, for identification while in transit.

These had so clearly just been nicked; it didn't need Sherlock Holmes to work that one out. I was sitting in the back (I was a probby, so I always got last pick of everything). I had my mobile phone out, and was calling 999 before I needed to be told. I explained the situation, and I gave a running commentary of the progress of the cars. They continued down the A13, with the Met's cars getting closer and closer. Eventually, they pulled into the same petrol station my first pursuit had started in.

The police cars weren't far away, and we decided to jump out, ID ourselves, and stop the cars from moving off if we could. The Law and Pete were going to stop the front car, and I was going to stop the rear car from making off.

They were pulling up to the petrol pumps, one behind the other. We were going to have to use speed and decisive action to give us an advantage. At this stage we had no idea who was in the cars or how many people there'd be. Contrary to popular belief, the police cannot magically see the drivers when following behind them, especially unlit cars at night.

We took off our seat belts as we approached the pumps. I made my last update on the phone. As the bandit cars stopped, we pulled up behind them, and we all jumped out. As I approached the rear Land Cruiser, I was pleased to see the driver's window was down, and I could see an arm, and the keys were easily accessible in the ignition. I ran up, grabbed the driver's right arm with my left hand, and with my right snatched the keys out of the ignition, and shouted loudly at the very startled driver: "Police, don't move!" I repeated this, and looked at the driver. He was a very large Black guy in his mid-thirties. I could see that there was at least one more guy in the front passenger seat.

I could hear The Law and Pete doing the same thing to the driver in front. I then took stock of our situation: we were outnumbered by guys who were all bigger and stronger than me, and I was the biggest and strongest of the three police officers. We had no kit to help us. This could get interesting, really quickly!

By the time the occupants of the cars had come to their senses, behind me came the ever-so-welcome sight of blue flashing lights. I could feel the tension that had begun to build up in the man's arm relax. He had been preparing to fight me, but now realised the futility of the situation as three police vehicles arrived.

Pretty quickly, they were all cuffed, and a quick check with the port authorities confirmed the vehicles and transport keys had indeed been stolen. I think they were impressed, because they only just realised that they were gone.

Two Rats came over to the three of us and thanked us, asking if we wanted to nick them, which would have meant our relief would have been three short for most of the night duty. We explained the situation and declined. The Rats were pleased that they'd get a chance to get credit for the collar. However, we did have to write out quick statements, and give over all the information we had. This took some time, so we were about an hour late for our shift.

We arrived at the station pretty pleased with ourselves and got changed into our uniforms. As soon as we went down to the control room to get a job (Pete had been assigned gaoler duty), we had a message to go to see the superintendent in his office. I naively thought it was for a pat on the back, and the sympathetic looks I got didn't clue me up to the reality of the situation.

We knocked on the superintendent's door. I was impressed a senior officer was there after 17:00 hours, if I'm honest.

"Come in." We filed in, and for the next five minutes we were shouted at for being late, told that it was a dereliction of our duty and responsibility to our colleagues and the people of Earlham. He threatened us with disciplinary action if we "played hero" again. Then we were dismissed. I walked out, ears still ringing, with a new perspective on how out of touch the senior management were, and how little respect I had for them!

Then The Law and I were off to our first call. It was a sudden death – great! I looked at him. He didn't have to say a thing. He knew my question and said: "Look Richard, I don't know if you've cottoned on to this yet or not, but we do this job despite the senior management, not because of them. Don't worry, I know it's scary, but just do your job, regardless of whether you get a slap on the back or a kick up the arse. I've seen people get medals for screwing up right royally, and seen people being disciplined for being heroes. I honestly think it's down to the mood of the higher up on the day."

I struggled to get my head around this. "But what would he have done in that situation? Ignore it?"

Without taking his eyes off the road, he replied: "Yes."

I didn't expect that. "Really? A serving police officer would ignore a crime being committed right in front of them because it was inconvenient to them?"

He replied in a matter-of-fact way: "No one on our relief would. I can't think of anyone on the other reliefs who would, but senior management, they're a different matter. They think they're above everyone else. There's a reason they go into management. It's because they're cowardly, spineless sacks of shit who are prepared to trade the lives of brave police officers for the advancement of their careers."

I'd not heard people be that blunt before, and it did explain the superintendent's reaction.

Still not sure I understood, I pushed further. "Do you mean that he was judging our actions by his cowardly standards? He wouldn't have the courage to do the stop, so he couldn't understand why we would?"

The Law nodded, and said, as we were pulling up at the tower block (our call), "That's about the size of it. right, what was the number of the flat?" With this immediate situation to deal with, we stopped our conversation.

"23, mate. I'd reckon that is the second floor."

"You don't say. There's a place in CID for you, mate."

"Ha bloody ha. Lift or stairs?"

"You mean enclosed public toilet, or open public toilet? I'd go for open public toilet."

"The stairs it is then."

We made our way up the stairs, trying to breathe through our mouths to reduce the tang of urine, and other smells I didn't want to think about too much. There were plenty of spent needles, bits of tinfoil with burn marks on them and half-filled water bottles with tinfoil tops and straws stuck out. Nice!

On the second floor, we opened the fire door and went along the filthy corridor: 21, 22, 23.

"Here we go," I said.

I took a deep breath, and reached out to knock on the door, but it was opened from inside by a tall, well-built man in his thirties, who had clearly been crying.

He looked at me and said: "You took your time. Come in. He's here in the living room."

He turned, and walked down the narrow entranceway. I looked at The Law, and we carefully walked in. With all the heightened emotions at the time of a death, people can act in unpredictable ways. Sometimes there's grief, anger, rage, or a combination of all three, so it's best to be a little wary.

As I made my way down the narrow corridor, I noticed the carpet had originally been a deep red pattern, but was well-worn, the walls had been magnolia, but were now darker due to nicotine staining. The corridor turned right and widened, with a door to the bathroom directly ahead, and there was a trail of sick leading along the corridor to the right. As I passed, I looked in to see a couple of pots and pans which had clearly been used to catch vomit. To the right was a little kitchenette, and the large room directly ahead had an old, burgundy, three-seat sofa, a similar armchair and a glass coffee table. On the far side of the room were floor-to-ceiling windows and a glass door (with a the bottom panel broken – glass on the outside, indicating it had been broken from within) that led out onto a small balcony. There was an older couple hugging each other and weeping.

I followed their gaze, and as I moved around the armchair, I got a view of a large, naked man lying on his back near the coffee table.

The man who'd shown us in said: "There's John, my brother. He was a diabetic."

I moved closer, and then I saw his face. I stopped, stock-still, all my professional reserve gone for a minute. It was my brother; he was a diabetic, and I'd always feared he'd die alone due to diabetic coma. He was the same height, the same build, and for a moment I struggled to recognise that he wasn't lying there.

My worst nightmare, right there in front of me. My blood ran cold, and I froze. It's an image I still wake up to in a cold sweat, sometimes shouting out, twenty years later.

I quickly came to my senses, and respectfully knelt down to check him over. He had vomit around his mouth. I was no doctor, but he was dead, and it definitely looked like he'd died of asphyxiation due to inhaling vomit.

Then it struck me, as real as my vision had been when I saw this man, this was these poor people's reality. I went over to the man who'd let us in and talked to him gently and compassionately, remembering what I had felt like a few moments ago.

The brothers had been out the previous night, having a skinful, nothing unusual about that. He'd left his brother to go home, hadn't heard anything the rest of the day, and when they'd got no reply, had let themselves in with a spare key. He'd kicked the glass door panel out in sheer grief, then contacted their mom and dad. I really felt for the guy; he was living my worst nightmare. As The Law went outside to make the required radio calls, and I went over to the couple, it turned out it was his mom and her brother (dad being separated). I did my best to comfort them, and answer their questions.

I took all the relevant details, and explained that after they'd said goodbye, because of the circumstances, we'd have to close the flat until the doctor and coroner had arrived. They were understanding, and after saying goodbye, they left. Then The Law and I rolled the body over and checked for any signs of foul play, of which there none. We secured the scene. Inspector Manning arrived and asked The Law to go downstairs to wait for the doctor and undertakers, as they might have difficulty getting through the security doors, that only seem to stop the law-abiding, but do nothing to stop robbers and drug dealers.

Once we were alone, he asked me to explain the scene to him. This was a test, but I walked him through it the best I could. This seemed to satisfy him, and he said: "That's a reasonable interpretation of the scene. Good work, Richard. I know you're working hard. Keep it up. Oh, and officially I'll say you weren't correct stopping those two stolen Land Cruisers. Unofficially, good work. It does my heart good to see you and your mates taking the initiative and dealing with what you come across. Regardless of what was written about you before, I judge people on what I see and hear. So far, so good."

I honestly wasn't expecting that, and my head was reeling at the conflict of emotions and thoughts in that flat.

We heard the door being opened with the scratching sounds of a key, and turned to see an older man with puffy eyes walk in. He stopped and looked shocked at our presence.

Inspector Manning said: "I'm Inspector Manning. May I enquire who you are, Sir?"

The man tried to speak, cleared his throat, and in a hoarse voice said: "I'm his (pointing down to the living room) dad. My other son phoned me, and I came down as fast as I could."

At this he made to walk past us. The dad and the inspector were both similar in height and size. The inspector gently stopped the man, saying, "Hold on, Sir, please. We're waiting for the doctor to arrive. We're really not supposed to let anyone enter the room, until we've had the doctor tell us whether it was natural causes."

The man turned, looked at the inspector and said: "Look, I'm not being disrespectful, and I know you've got a job to do, but my son told me what had happened. With my ex-wife involved, she'll do anything she can to stop me attending the funeral. Please, this might be the only chance I get to say goodbye. Have some compassion. You must be a dad? You'd want to see your son too?"

If the inspector didn't feel anything at that, I did, but as a professional, I remained impassive. The inspector looked at him, and took away the hand that prevented the dad moving forward. He nodded, and the dad turned and said: "Thank you. You're a good man."

He walked in, and we stood, close enough to keep an eye on the situation, but without interfering. He spent about five minutes, knelt down, weeping and saying goodbye. I held back the tears, but only just. It was breaking my heart. He slowly got up, saying one more goodbye, and walked over to us. He shook both our hands: "I've hated police all my life, and I still do, but thank you!"

With that, he left. That was a clear breach of the rules, and we both knew it. I didn't say anything, because what we'd done was humane. The inspector addressed the elephant in the room, saying: "Technically, I should have stopped him, but it would have been inhumane of me, and it would have resulted in a fight, because he was going to say goodbye, and honestly I'd have done the same thing. If there's any comeback, I made the decision, not you. It's my responsibility. I'll record it on the CAD. What do you think?"

It took no time to reply. I said: "Sir, I'm with you all the way. You did the right thing. It was the decent thing to do."

He nodded, and patted me on the shoulder. At that, the radio went and the doctor had arrived.

We spent a good chunk of the rest of the shift dealing with that, and I went down as the reporting officer on that call, so I'd have to speak to the coroner, and do coroner's court. It was set for the following week, after I'd come off nights.

With the images of the flat burned into my memory, the statement I wrote out for the coroner was the most detailed I have ever written. Twenty years later, I can still remember it as if it were yesterday.

The set of nights dragged on. I found it difficult enough to sleep during the day, but with this nightmare fresh in my mind, I found it difficult to get a good night's sleep for many of those days.

Eventually, the coroner's court date arrived. I got dressed up in my tunic (not my Metvest, as it was very hard to wear that with the tunic), dusted off my glass-like shined shoes you only wear for court appearances, funerals or special occasions. I tucked my baton in the special inside trouser pocket and walked down to the court.

I arrived early, and went into the coroner's office, where the usual coroner (a Chinese gentleman) was absent, and the assistant coroner was. She was a tall, well-dressed lady in her late fifties with long, light-coloured hair. She was very precise in her speech, and sat bolt upright. She asked if I was new, as she hadn't seen me before. I said I was, and she very patiently talked me through the proceedings, and where I was supposed to be, when I was required to speak. Overall, she gave the best schooling in how to behave professionally and compassionately in a coroner's court. I owe her a debt of gratitude for her guidance.

The court started, and I stood up and gave my evidence, clearly explaining what had happened, and answering the coroner's questions. I looked over a couple of times at the family during the more sensitive parts of my evidence.

At the end, the assistant coroner looked over at the family and then me, saying: "I would like to thank and commend PC Armstrong for his excellent written and verbal evidence. When I was reading his account, it was almost like I was there on the scene. I can honestly say, in my twenty years of listening to police evidence in court, his is amongst the very best. Your professionalism shows great respect to the family present. Thank you, officer."

I wanted to stand up and scream. It's because I can't ever forget it; it's etched indelibly in my memory. I was really taken aback. This was high praise. I hadn't heard of anyone being commended in a coroner's court. Pity none of my sergeants or inspectors were there to record it. I wasn't going to crow about it. It was enough the family knew that I'd done the best job I could by their son. If it gave them any comfort at that time, I was proud of that. I didn't need a box ticked on my personnel file.

As I got up and walked out of the court, the family stopped me, and they all hugged me, and said how much they appreciated it. One told me that they hated the police, and that the man who had died was well known to us. I said: "Regardless of what someone did in the past, everyone deserves respect, and I try to deal with people with dignity. And thank you for your words. I am just so sorry about your son, brother, nephew. (I looked each one in turn as I said it)"

They gave me another hug, and I walked back to the nick. I meant everything I had said. In the end we all die, and it isn't for me to judge people, and treat them differently. My mom would have quoted the Bible at this point: "Let he who is without sin cast the first stone." Amen!

I just felt so sorry for the family, and resolved to call my brother at the first opportunity. It made me think about just how much he meant to me.

I made it back to the nick, carefully got changed, and got ready for another day in paradise.

A few weeks later, it was another 'paperwork day' and, again, our friends from Sky News appeared for more background police footage. They arrived just as I was getting comfortable waiting for the inspector to come to let us know the order of the day. I was pretending to read *The Guardian*, while catching up on the newest notes.

Robbie walked in escorting the regulars from the TV channel into the back canteen. He said: "We need two volunteers to do the background filming for TV. (Looking at the TV crew) Who would you like to do it?"

At this, Mel and Sergeant Nathan Darling gave each other a weary look and got up and started walking towards the door. The main TV news guy looked surprised, and said: "Eh, errm."

Mel and the good sergeant stopped, and looked at each other. Mel said, "OK, so you don't want us this time?"

The TV news guy said, defensively, "Well, actually, we do."

He turned and walked out quickly, followed by the second TV guy. When they were out of earshot, Sergeant Darling said, "I guess they just want the Black guy, and the hot chick."

Mel did an overly dramatic flustered look, putting her hand to her head as if she was about to faint, as if to say, "What, me? A hot chick? Oh, I am embarrassed."

He said, "And they call us racist!"

As Mel left, she added: "And sexist!"

This was met with roars of laughter. There were choruses of, "For the sake of the tape, I challenge that remark."

Honestly, it must be really insulting to be treated as a token. It's like, "Wheel out the ethnic minority, and the good-looking young woman," as if people are so shallow they need to be reminded at every turn not to be racist or sexist. Look, these media organisations often say that it's sexist to judge women purely on their looks, which is fair enough, but then, when given a choice, they'll go for the youngest, prettiest woman to put on TV. One standard for them, and another for everyone else!

Maybe, just maybe, it's the people who all wear the same uniform, work together, and take the same risks, where you're judged on what you do, who are the least racist and sexist. But I digress!

The inspector walked in, just at the tail end of the laughter. He grinned and said: "Settle down you lot. Robbie, are you still taking names of people who are forming the syndicate for the new National Lottery thing?"

A little cautious, he replied: "Yes, I am Guv, is there a problem?"

The guv'nor looked down over the top of the reading glasses he occasionally wore, and said: "I have a memo here from our lords and masters saying they're 'concerned' about the possibility that if one of these syndicates wins the top prize, we could lose an entire relief. They've sent out this memo, asking the inspectors to 'Take suitable action to stop this'. And I intend to do just that."

I'd just joined the syndicate, as had the majority of the relief. *He's not really going to ban it, is he?* That's clearly what the memo hinted at.

The inspector gave us all a stern look. He was building up tension. Robbie asked the obvious question: "So, Sir, do you want me to cancel it?"

The inspector, with his best solemn face, said in a deep voice, "No, Sergeant Robertson – I wish to join it. If you lot are retiring early to the

Caribbean, I don't want to be left behind. They can sort the mess out; that's what they're overpaid for."

This received a loud round of laughter. I thought, *good for him, showing us he's one of us, not tied slavishly to the many stupid edicts from those high up.*

When we'd settled down, he said: "Today, firstly, can I have a couple of volunteers to clear up this mess (there were the usual pizza boxes, still half-filled, discarded coke cans, etc.) left by our friends in the 'knuckle-draggers'. Oops, did I say that out loud? I meant the TSG."

There were a few "I challenge that remark."

When it settled down, he continued, "Do any outstanding paperwork. If anyone has a proactive operation they wish to conduct, let Sergeant (Sean) Collins know. He will then put out the call for volunteers to assist. Can I have a sergeant and PC to pop in at about 11:00 hours to give the E relief custody team a refs break. And another PC to give the station officer a break. That'd be much appreciated. Other than that, pair up, tall hats on, and off you go to make friends and influence people on those mean streets." He finished with a grin.

I looked around, and put up my hand, saying: "Sarg, I'll volunteer to give the gaoler a refs break at just before 11:00 hours, if that's OK?"

Sergeant Rob Smedley (a huge man) said, "Good on you for volunteering, son. I'll join you, and give the custody skipper a break."

I was pleased to have the encouragement. If you volunteer, it isn't always noticed, but if you don't, it most certainly is. Tip to any probationary PCs: volunteer for everything, no matter how tired you are, or how much you don't want to do it. No matter whether you think it's fair. Show your willingness to deal with the worst of things, and it will long-term gain you respect and, more vitally, experience!

I looked around, and saw Pete walking purposefully towards me (to be fair, he always did everything with purpose). As he got near he said to Sergeant Robertson, "Sarg, can you show me and 272 out walking around Futures Park. He's just volunteered for a bit of proactive policing. C'mon, Vidal."

A few catcalls came my way as I put my copy of *The Guardian* down and slipped my notes out of the centre without being noticed. I popped upstairs, dropped off my notes, and collected the kit I needed. It was just after 9 a.m., so I had just less than two hours to go around and find trouble. With Pete, that was an almost foregone conclusion.

To be fair, both of us had a reputation for being in the right (or wrong) place at the right (or wrong) time to find trouble.

Pete was impatiently (patience wasn't his forte) in the station office. As I approached he said: "Come on. I know it takes you longer than most to preen yourself, Vidal. Bleedin' hell mate, you take longer than my missus."

I retorted, "I'll tell her that at the next relief social."

He made a face and said under his breath, "Best not, mate; I'd be sleeping on the sofa for the next week."

I replied, "What, again!"

He snorted, and we walked out of the nick to a crisp, but bright, November morning. We occasionally shared a car in, and had become friends, so the constant banter had a little more bite than with the others. In truth his wife, Michelle, was a hairdresser, and did actually drive a Ford Ka. She was a lovely Essex girl, and kept him on a short leash. They were well matched. Honestly, it was kind of sweet.

Off we walked, along Austin Road, against the traffic. As we got to the lights at Kenton Road, and Burton Road, we had to stop for the fast traffic. Honestly, most of the time you have to ignore far more minor infractions than you deal with. Why? There's no point in giving someone a minor traffic ticket and ignoring the armed robbery around the corner.

As we were walking north along Burton Road, we came across a group of about half a dozen of the local lads, all aged between 16 and 20, wearing hoodies, with tracksuits and multi-coloured trainers.

There were a number of gangs, all based on localised geographical areas. They would have any race in them (70 per cent of the young people in the borough were Asian – mostly of Bangladeshi descent). It was tough for them. They often had a very traditional Muslim home life (some of their parents or grandparents had moved here years ago, and not learnt English), and then they had a second life with their friends. They had to try to balance those two clashing cultures, all in an environment of constant gang fights and rampant cannabis and heroin use.

Now the vast majority were decent, sensible kids, just trying to navigate around these competing cultures. But they had so many more opportunities and pressure to get involved in illegal activities. In my opinion, merely saying poor people = more likely to be a criminal is grossly unfair to the vast majority who, even though they have more pressure to break the rules, don't.

These lads were from one of the local estates, and weren't prominent in any gangs we knew about. As we approached, they slowed down to have a chat. Not looking for trouble, but with a mischievous manner. I could recognise that from my teaching days – they were looking for having a laugh, and either we supplied it or they would.

Pete said, "Good morning, boys. How are you doing?"

There were a few comments of "all right mate" and the tallest and oldest boy, aged about 19, stepped forward. He was an Asian lad, skinny build, in a dark blue tracksuit and new white Puma King trainers. He had a swagger, and walked with a put-on limp (it was an import from NY gang culture, meant to indicate you were tough because you'd been shot in the leg). He rolled his upper body as he talked, and rarely made eye contact. Their "Rep" (short for reputation) was everything, so he had to make a show of it.

He said: "Heh, geez. Who be dis noo po leess fella (indicating me)? I ain't never seen him before, init!"

Pete let me reply, "Yes I'm new (this was taking a risk). I like those Puma Kings. Are they new (looking down at his trainers)?"

There were a few comments from his mates: "Yeah, they're new; he only nicked 'em last week. Hahaha."

He waved his hands to shut up his mates, and said: "Yeah, day is noo, Mr noo po leesss man. You is got sharp eyes, init. What did you do before you was po leess?"

Pete chimed in (thanks mate), "You'd better mind yourself boys; he was a teacher."

Even more laughs and catcalls.

When it had calmed down, the leader said: "'Ere, what did you teeeach, Mr nooo po leess man, init?"

I thought, *oh well, better just be up front.* "I taught science at secondary school in Essex."

A few more catcalls, and one of the smaller, younger lads said, "'Ere, I loved science. I was wicked at phyyysics man, init." Much to the amusements of his mates.

I said: "That's good to hear. Come on, show off. What's the speed of sound?"

A few more choice comments, and the lad waited until it quietened down and said, "340 metres per second, init."

More oohs and arrrs, and ribbing.

I nodded my head, and said: "You are the bomb. Boom!"

His mates were laughing, and the lad struck a heroic pose, and soaked in the approval of his mates.

The leader (not wishing to be outdone) said, “Dey say on the BBC dat yoo is all racists, init?”

This time there was silence. Fair enough, the BBC had said that. It was a legitimate question.

I thought for a second, and said: “Why would I give up a nice cushy teaching job, and go through six months of really hard training, put on a silly uniform, making myself a target, and then risk my life protecting people who are mostly of a different race, if I was a racist?”

There were a few nods, and agreements. I wasn’t finished: “I went to an international school when I was a kid, where I was in the minority. I know what that’s like. I know it’s not the same as it is for you. I took an oath in front of my family saying I’d risk my life protecting everyone. I don’t care about what race people are, or whether they’re a man or woman, any of that. We’re all just people. I’m no better or worse than you are.”

There were a few agreeing comments. Pete was just standing watching, seeing how I was handling this.

The leader was about to say something when our budding physicist said: “I want to be po leess when has grown up, init.”

There were plenty of comments, some about his height. When they calmed down, I looked at him, and said: “If that’s what you want to do, go for it. It isn’t easy, believe me. But if you really want it, and you work hard, I think you’d make a good police officer. To have the courage to say that in front of your mates, knowing they’ll take the piss out of you, shows courage.”

There were plenty of jeers, and banter.

He said: "Thanks. What's your name, officer? When I apply, I'll say I spoke to you."

I took out the Met Police memo pad, and wrote down my name and shoulder number on it, then handed it to him. I said, "Please do. Here's all my details. If it's something you want, and you're prepared to work hard, go for it."

He looked surprised and said, "Thank you!"

The leader said, "Yeah, why should I want to be po leess?"

I replied, "First off, the uniform – it's a babe magnet." Lots of laughs, and even he grinned. I carried on, "You see this stick (pointing at the ASP)? We carry that to fight off the hordes of women who throw themselves at us."

This they really found funny, and even Pete grinned at that.

Pete indicated we needed to leave, but as a passing shot the leader said: "Ere, Mr po leess man, ain't you goin' to search us, init?"

I grinned: "Do you want us to?" Plenty of catcalls. I continued, "Do I need to? Do any of you have any bazookas, rocket launchers or weapons of mass destruction in your pockets?"

They roared with laughed at this, and one of the younger ones said to the leader, "You ain't got no weapons in your trousers."

The leader turned around and said, "That's not what your sister said last night!"

Oohs and arrs, and plenty of banter were forthcoming.

As I turned to leave, the leader said: "Heh, you is all right Mr po leess man."

I smiled and said, "Thank you, gentlemen. Don't do anything I wouldn't do."

We walked off, and when we'd got out of earshot Pete said: "You handled that well. I thought you'd got yourself in trouble a couple of times there. But you knew how to deal with them. Good work."

I wasn't used to Pete being complimentary. I replied: "Thanks mate. Dealing with cheeky kids, I can do. It's the management I struggle with."

We crossed the road to get to Futures Park. As we started to walk across, Pete looked like he was going to say something. Then we heard the sound of lots of gunfire, in a continuous, two-second burst. It sounded like it came from the tower blocks across the park.

Without hesitation, Pete drew his ASP, wracked it out, and placed it in the ready position over his right shoulder, and started running towards the sound of the gunfire, saying, "That's a submachine gun. Best we go and sort it out."

I shrugged, drew my ASP and followed. I guess that's what we were there for, putting ourselves between the public and the bad guys.

I keyed the mike on my radio and said: "PT, 272. Possible sounds of gunfire tower blocks north of Futures Park. We're going to investigate."

I'd waited until we were close to the tower blocks, so by the time they got back to us to tell us to hang back, we'd already be on scene.

As we rounded the front of the two tower blocks, the signal broke up (really, it did, honest guv'). We ran up to the door to the first block and rushed in. We went up and down the stairs, and found nothing. We went to the second block, and as we entered, I recognised the familiar smell of bleach. As we got to the landing on the first floor, it was even stronger, and there were a few splashes of blood and bullet divots in a line starting bottom right and moving up to top left, with a void in the middle.

With the extra elevation the first floor granted us, our radios could get a signal.

Pete spoke this time, and explained the situation. In short order, an ARV (armed response vehicle) arrived, along with a carrier of TSG. Between them they swept the scene, SOCO (scene of crime officer) arrived, and a number of spent shell casings were found in one of the large wheelie bins next to the tower block.

Apparently, none of the residents had seen or heard anything. As we were maintaining a cordon around the block of flats, the same group of lads we'd spoken to earlier walked over to find out what was going on.

The leader walked over to us and said: "Was up geez. We saw yous pulling out yours batons and running towards the shooting. Why you do that?"

Pete said in a matter-of-fact tone. "Because it's our job to put ourselves between you and the bad guys."

This took a moment to sink in, and the reply came from the lad who'd showed interest in the police. He looked at me and said: "PC Armstrong, you weren't joking about risking your lives for us, were you?"

"No, I wasn't! Any copper worth their salt would without hesitation do the same. No matter how dangerous. I wouldn't joke about that!"

For once they were being serious; they really listened. The leader looked at us and nodded as a sign of respect, and the rest of them silently walked off. I think our actions had spoken louder than our words. A couple of years later I found out the physics lad had joined the police, and had cited this incident as the reason.

A few hours after the gunshots, a known gang member booked into hospital in south London, with several gunshot wounds he wouldn't explain. It's not a crime to be shot so, other than ask him questions, there was nothing my colleagues could do. No one made any kind of complaint. Often, gang members won't speak to the police, regardless of the situation. They tend to sort things out themselves. Later, we found out that it had been a reactivated Ingram MAC-10 submachine gun. Pete had been right.

We had a few comments from the others, but although it was unusual, it wasn't unheard of.

A couple of weeks later, at the start of December, I was getting a lift in with The Law in his estate car on an early turn. We were chatting away. I'd learnt he was a guitarist. I was a bass player, and played in rock bands since I was a teenager, so we were discussing trying to get a band together as we were driving down the Kenton Road. We both spotted something that didn't look right: a man pushing a shopping trolley along with a large TV and VHS player in it at 5:30 a.m. in December. We didn't have to discuss this. The car was stopping, and I was getting out and 'briefing it' (identifying myself as a police officer, by showing my warrant card, or brief, as it's sometimes known).

I approached the guy (40-ish, black jeans, black jacket, black T-shirt, about 5'10", slim build, with long, salt and pepper hair). "Good morning, Sir. I'm PC Armstrong, from Earlham Police Station (I held up my warrant card). How are you doing today?"

He looked calmly at myself and The Law as he approached. He said: "Yeah, I'm all right. Are you stopping me?"

This is sometimes a tactic to brush the police off. I said: "We're just having a chat. May I ask why you're pushing a large TV and VHS recorder around in a shopping trolley at 5:30 in the morning, in the middle of winter?"

The Law walked around to the other side of the trolley, so it'd be difficult for the man to push past me, smiled and said: "It's a fair question my colleague just asked you."

The man said, "Look, I'm in a hurry. It's cold out here. Are you stopping me, or can I go?"

I could tell from his body language he wanted to flee.

I said: "Sir, we just want to find out what you're doing with all this at 5:30 in the morning, that's all."

I nodded very slightly to The Law, and while the man was talking to me, he phoned the control room. He walked off a couple of steps, and spoke quietly.

The man was still not wanting to speak to me much. I thought I needed to keep him talking, so I threw him a lifeline. "Sir, if you just tell me what you're doing, you'll be on your way."

He seemed to seize the hope, and said: "Look, I'm in the middle of moving, and I don't have a car, so I'm doing it bit by bit."

I nodded, and replied: "I know what it's like. I've just moved into a new house myself. I never realised I had so much stuff until I had to pack it up."

The man nodded and, feeling that he was making progress, continued. But I could just see The Law pointing at the TV, and I picked up the hint, and said: "That's a nice TV. You know, I need a new TV. Is this one any good? What's its make? Would you recommend it?"

I moved in closer, and said loudly (so The Law could hear): "It's a Toshiba TS1305, and a Panasonic Jc223 VHS player. Nice. I bet you get a really clear picture on a screen that size."

The Law finished his conversation, and walked over, nodding his head. I smoothly and quickly took hold of the man's arm and said: "I am arresting you on suspicion of burglary, of the TV and VHS player."

I then went through the caution with him. The Law had written the serial number down on a scrap of paper as I was holding the man. He checked them. They were a match for a burglary that was being reported just as The Law had been phoning in.

The police station was a couple of hundred yards away, so we put the TV and VHS player in the back of the estate car, after the man was searched, which yielded items used in burglary (screwdrivers, socks – a less suspicious form of hand covering (no joke), a face mask, etc.). I held on to him in the back seats, and we drove into Earlham at 05:45 hours having cleared up a burglary, recovered the property and nicked a burglar.

Once we'd booked him in and handed him over to the burglary squad, we popped to the control room. Sooz greeted us. Damn, how could that woman look that good at 6 a.m.! Was she some sort of vampire? She said, in her smoothest voice: "Good morning boys. My my, we have been busy little beavers, haven't we."

I grinned and said: "I aim to please, no matter what time of the day it is."

She winked and said: "Well, you were certainly a hit with that family. They were blown away that you'd recovered the property and caught the guy that quickly. They'll be on their way down to the nick in a couple of minutes to ID their property. You might want to meet them?"

I looked at The Law. He nodded, and I said: "OK. I'll go and get changed. Are we busy this morning?"

Sooz shook her head and said: "For once, it's quiet. Oh God, I've just tempted fate."

With that we went upstairs, got changed, and were just in time to meet the husband and wife, who turned up to ID their property. The burglary squad were tied up with processing the prisoner, so had asked us to take the statement from the homeowners. This was nice, because we had a chance to chat to the people whose property we'd recovered. Often in policing, you see bits of crimes, but rarely the whole thing. This was cool.

The couple walked into the station office, and we took them to the interview room where the TV and VHS player were. We did the formal

ID, using serial numbers and receipts. It was clearly theirs. Once we'd done their statements, we had a couple minutes to chat.

The wife said, "I still can't believe you were able to get our stuff back and catch the guy so quickly."

The husband added: "Thanks gentlemen (and shook our hands)."

The Law said, "Well, honestly, it was just a bit of good luck. We were driving into work, and we saw the guy pushing a shopping trolley with your property in it. We stopped and questioned him about it, as it looked very suspicious."

They started to laugh, and said: "You stopped him, before you got to work. That's amazing."

I said: "The funny part was, his excuse was he was moving, bit by bit, using a shopping trolley at 05:30 hours in the morning."

They were laughing so much, I could see tears rolling down the man's cheeks. We then explained the whole thing, and they were very appreciative.

The Law said: "Honestly, it's what we got into policing for, to nick villains and return property to decent, law-abiding people such as yourselves. In policing we come across the mad, the bad and the sad. I think you can work out which category this inept burglar falls into."

Once they'd stopped laughing, they thanked us again, and told us they'd have a good story to tell their friends.

We'd just got through helping the burglary squad by doing the initial CRIS report, the statements and handing it all over to them, when it was proven that Sooz had, indeed, tempted fate.

We got a call to do a welfare check. As we were driving to the address, I wrote down the details as Sooz relayed them to me. It was a man in his fifties who had no family except a brother who lived abroad. A couple of friends raised the alarm as they hadn't seen or heard from him in weeks.

I looked at The Law and, as they say in the best films, said: "I have a bad feeling about this."

Eventually, we arrived at the block of flats, and made our way up to the first floor, gained entry to the block and walked up to the flat's door. We exchanged looks. Even though we were relatively upbeat, there was an undercurrent of uncertainty.

I knocked loudly on the door (even today, my friends ask me not to do the 'police knock' when I visit them), we waited, and I knocked again. Still, no reply. I bent down to the letter box, took a deep breath and cautiously opened it. No flies, no smell (I inwardly relaxed, just a little). Then, there it was, just the merest hint of putrefaction. The Law caught my flinch when I smelt it. I leant down again to the letter box and called inside. No response. This wasn't looking or smelling promising.

I straightened up and looked at The Law, and he nodded. I called the station and informed them we were affecting entry. I took a half step back and kicked the door, where the lock was. Unlike on films and TV shows, only a fool shoulder charges the door. Doors are made of wood, and we are made of bone and flesh. If you use your shoulder to try to break a door, nine times out of ten it'll be your shoulder that gives way first. So you use your boot – your legs and feet are stronger. You use them at the point of the lock, so the door doesn't flex and absorb some of the force. If you practise, you can usually do a single-lock door in one really good kick. I wasn't practised, and this door had a chain on it, so it took several really good kicks to gain entry. This had been locked from the inside. Not a good sign.

The Law and I exchanged glances. He waited for me to enter first. Fair enough, I was the probby, but it still didn't mean I was looking forward to it. Still no smell. Surprising!

I walked in and down a narrow corridor with an ancient, threadbare, patterned carpet. The wallpaper was stained with tobacco. We passed a door on the right, and I pushed it gingerly open to reveal a tiny bathroom.

At little bit further and the corridor turned right, with the kitchen to the left. The kitchen was clear. I turned back to the living room. There it was, the once-smelt-never-forgotten aroma of death. I slowly walked into the living room, with a TV to my left and, to the right, a kitchen table piled with paperwork and, to the front, a battered old sofa with rugs scattered across it. There, lying on the rug directly in front of the sofa, was what had been an old man.

I turned to The Law, who was a couple of steps behind, and said, "He's in here!"

"Yeah, I just got a whiff."

I dug in my pocket, and pulled out the Vicks VapoRub. This is a tub of clear, sticky gel used to clear congestion. This may seem an odd thing to pull out at this time, but it had another feature. It had a very strong smell, rather like a football changing room. When smeared on your upper lip, right under your nose, it masked lots of strong smells. It didn't totally get rid of it, but did tone it down a bit. Most people in that situation breathe through their mouths, and the Vicks was just insurance, in case you forgot.

The Law was on the radio, calling it in. I walked around the man's remains. His skin had darkened, and was puffy, straining against the confines of his shirt. As the body decays after death, gases build up inside the abdominal cavity, and this can burst if you're not careful. That turns a deeply unpleasant experience into a nightmare.

I looked for signs of foul play (knife/gunshot wounds), but none were to be seen. Good. The Law came over, and we put on gloves and very carefully began to turn the body over to check for any signs of foul play.

As we did this, it released trapped gases, and the most utterly foul stench was emitted. Even breathing through my mouth, it was a struggle, and I had to give my abdominal muscles a workout, forcing myself not to retch. Every instinct in my body was screaming at me to run away. Believe me, those instincts are very, very strong, but I fought through them. Once we'd completed our examination, we had to collect any documents and bag any valuables, and log them into property, so the next of kin could collect them.

The smell had now been released, and it quickly permeated the flat and out onto the landing. As I looked through the paperwork on the table for anything relevant regarding the man's identity and next of kin to be notified, I started finding old pictures of what he looked like years ago. There's a certain poignancy at the end of a life, seeing happier times. I thought that, one day, someone would be doing that for me. I resolved to tidy up my house, make it easy for those whose job it would be, because everyone dies. You either die on your own (my fate, no doubt), or you die with someone. If you have a partner, either you'll have to deal with their death, or they'll have to deal with yours unless, by some quirk of fate, you both die together.

I'd watched my mother deal with my father's death. I looked back. *Is that maybe why I have always been so averse to having a partner?* Cowardice on my part, maybe. Are the good times enough to offset the pain of loss (either theirs or yours)? Maybe I couldn't bear the idea of inflicting the pain I saw my mom go through at my father's death on someone I loved?

It's all very complicated and confusing. I really didn't know how I felt, or why I did things sometimes. Maybe, I did things then tried to find rational reasons why after.

In the end, we all die. Life isn't about avoiding death: it's about what you did in life. For good or ill, that's it.

I snapped back out of my thoughts and did my job. The poor carpenter who'd been called to resecure the door was retching. I showed him the Vicks trick. He tried it and it helped. The old man's body was taken away. When we got back to the station, we had the tough job of informing the friends who'd tipped us off about his absence. Then we had to look through address and telephone books, and find family members to inform. This a heartbreaking job, so all you can do is focus on what needs to be done, and try to do it in the most humane way you can.

I got straight up to my locker, and changed my clothing, and had a shower to get rid of the residual, clinging smell. No matter how you wash, it still remains. What did Lady Macbeth say about the blood, and not being able to wash it off?

We spent the rest of the shift dealing with that call. That's the way it is in the police: the highs are higher than anything else, the lows lower. There's a reason it's called "The Job".

Christmas was approaching. We were due to work on Christmas Day, so we should have got New Year's Day off. Due to the shift system, you should in theory either get the morning or the evening off to spend with your family. Nothing is written down, but it's a convention that those without kids will take any overtime, allowing the parents to have the time off to see their kids. In the middle of December, when it was particularly cold, wet and miserable, we were on nights, and there was a crime scene (a rape) to keep secure. It was in a builder's yard, and we'd need to provide an officer to stay there, on their own until SOCO arrived to process the evidence. Edward and I were to do the job, because we were the newest in service (standard procedure). I'd take the first four hours, Edward would take the next four (he'd be in one of the cars, and we'd swap over).

As I was dropped off at the pitch-black, deserted builder's yard, it started raining. *Great,* I thought. I put myself on scene, via radio, and got ready for a long, boring, lonely night of getting wet. As the rain was soaking through my cap (the Met and its extra cheapness), and drips of water were starting to find their way down my back, I shivered, despite the multiple layers I had on.

Stepping from foot to foot, to keep the circulation going, I heard a noise over by the fence. I spun quickly around and fumbled to find my torch, under all the layers of clothing, eventually getting the beam on the source of the sound. It was a cat trying to find shelter under a stack of wooden crates. I cursed under my breath. Why did I feel like the unlucky fool who always got killed at the start of a horror film? Then I was annoyed at myself for being so melodramatic.

The time dragged on. One hour gone and the rain let up a bit, and there was the sound of distant sirens (now God, you are taking the piss!). Two hours down, and I was slowly drying out. Three hours, and the wind and rain started up again with a vengeance. Only another hour to go, and the rain was coming in at all angles. My trousers were soaked from the knees down and the water had found a way into my boots. I shivered involuntarily. *Not long to go now*, I thought.

I got a radio call from Edward saying: "272, PT22, we're on our way to relieve you," and for a moment I forget about how cold, wet and stiff I felt.

It had been a busy night, with radio call after call after call. The burglars and robbers were out Christmas shopping.

A couple of minutes later, I heard a police siren start up, and I heard Edward start the commentary on a vehicle pursuit and, as the siren became ever more distant, I knew my relief was not coming anytime soon. I could hear him, off enjoying himself, while I was still looking at another four hours on my own in the wet, windy dark.

My spirits sank, and then the radio went, and it was the 'private call' tone, so I fiddled with my radio with gloved fingers and eventually pushed the receive button. I heard Sooz's sweet voice in the dark, coming from the PSM speaker next to my ear. It was a private call, so only the two of us could hear. She said in a smoothing voice: "Hi hun. How are you doing, handsome?"

Despite myself, I couldn't help but grin, and replied: "Hi Sooz. Oh it's peachy here. The weather's so lovely, and the view's inspiring."

She chuckled: "Glad to hear you've not lost your sense of humour, sweetie."

Over the next ten or so minutes (in between calls), she just chatted to me. She realised how shit I must be feeling, and was doing her best to try to cheer me up. I said there was more to this lady than just good looks. She was really kind, and it was really hard not to like her. I don't mean fancy her, I mean like her.

Eventually, when the mad rush had died down, and it became clear that Edward was going to be tied up with a prisoner for the foreseeable future, the search for some way of relieving me was on, as I hadn't had any food or drink for about six hours. In the end, Sergeant Darling arrived in a panda. He jumped out, straight into a puddle, and squelched his way over to me, saying: "Richard, I'm sorry, but we can't spare anyone to relieve you. We're all tied up. Here's a sandwich, and a bottle of water. I've left Robbie in the custody on his own, and it's heaving, so I've got to get back."

Not what I wanted to hear, but I didn't blame anyone. It's just the way it is sometimes. I was just appreciative that Sooz, and the sergeant, had tried to help as much as they could.

I said: "No need to apologise, Sarge. I know it's been manic. I just appreciate you taking the time to give me a sandwich."

He smiled, and as he got back in the car he gave me the thumbs-up, and quickly drove off, splashing through the puddles.

D relief were slow to relieve me so, by the time I got back to the station, most of my relief were gone. I don't think I felt truly warm for a couple of days.

The next night, I was in the custody, as gaoler. I was working with Sergeant Darling. As I said, he was a really nice guy, very 'by the book', with a huge dose of humanity chucked in. As per usual, it was manic for the first few hours, with prisoners coming left, right and centre.

About the second prisoner in was a short (5'7"), young (18-ish), Mediterranean man who was swearing and cursing as The Law held on to him and tried to explain (with numerous interruptions from the youth) the circumstances of the arrest.

He said: "I arrested Tariq at 22:35 hours outside Honey's nightclub on the Kenton road."

Tariq interrupted: "You is lying, init. You ain't got no proof geez."

The Law patiently continued: "He had been detained by the door staff outside Honey's after being identified as trying to rob two of the female patrons at knifepoint."

Tariq interrupted again: "I didn't 'ave no blade. What is you chatting bout, geez? You is fittin' us up. I don't do no robbery, init."

The sergeant and the Law were studiously ignoring these interruptions. "I then arrested, and then searched him, finding he was in possession of this (holding up an evidence bag containing a clear plastic tube with a large kitchen knife inside) ..."

Tariq interrupted, "I ain't never seen that before. You is makin' it up fella. You is lying po leess man, init."

The Law continued: "I also found on him a quantity of black tar-like material I believe to be cannabis resin (holding up an evidence bag with a small block of a black substance in it)."

Tariq started to struggle fruitlessly against The Law, who was taller and far more muscular, shouting: "Get off, you fucking, pig. I is gonna fuck your mom up the arse, you pussy cunt."

Looking at the sergeant, he said: "Is he your boyfriend? You take him up the arse you batty boy, init."

Neither of the two officers reacted, despite the tirade of abuse. I stepped forward and, between the two us, we managed to search Tariq and put all his property on the custody desk. Due to his continued struggling and screaming of obscenities, the sergeant tried to give him a couple of warnings to calm down, so he could complete the custody procedure. He was having none of it. We were told to take him down to cell number two, until he'd calmed down.

We wrestled Tariq down, and put him in the cell, removed the cuffs, and just made it out before he rushed the door, which he started kicking. It was an inch-and-a-half-thick reinforced steel door set in a steel-framed, two-feet-thick concrete wall (good luck trying to kick that down). We shared a shrug as we walked down the corridor, hearing the continuous stream of vile abuse.

As we made it back to the custody area, the sergeant said: "Richard, can you do ten-minute obs on our friend down there, when he calms down? We will get him out to continue the booking in procedure. Laurence, Richard'll call you when we're ready to do that."

The Law nodded: "Thanks Sarge. I'll finish my notes in the canteen, and then the CRIS in the writing room."

With Tariq still shouting and screaming abuse, the door to the yard (through which prisoners were taken) opened and in walked Campbell, holding on to his prisoner, a large (6'2"), muscular Black man in his mid-thirties, wearing jeans and a black leather jacket.

As they approached the custody desk, the prisoner saw Sergeant Darling. At this point I was stood to his left, about six feet away from him. The prisoner looked directly at the sergeant, and before anyone else could speak, he said, "You fuckin race traitor! You're a coconut, bro. Why you lick the boots of the white man?"

This was the first time I'd heard this type of abuse directed at a police officer. I was taken aback. Sergeant Darling didn't move a muscle and, looking at Campbell, said: "Good evening, Campbell. Who have you got for me today?"

Campbell replied, "Good evening, Sergeant. I was called to a report of a domestic dispute. Upon arrival, this gentleman was identified by a female and two witnesses as the man who had struck her several times in the face, causing injuries that required her to attend hospital, namely a laceration above the left eye, and a broken nose. I arrested him at 22:40 on suspicion of assault causing ABH."

At this the prisoner tried to turn to look at Campbell and said, "Wah, man, why have to point out that it was a woman I hit, and is my partner? I ain't no batty boy (slang for male homosexual). Yah bumblaclot (slang for used sanitary towel)."

Campbell easily forced the man around, so he was facing the custody desk. All done without a word.

The sergeant said: "Right, thank you Campbell. I will note on the custody record the prisoner's admission that he struck the female victim.

Now Sir (looking at the prisoner), you've heard what's been said. Do you wish to say anything at this point?"

The prisoner said, "I admit I'd slapped that ho. Now you is doin' the white pigs' work, you uncle Tom. You porch n****r! You c**n! Ya is a disgrace to ya race, bro. You is a TRAITOR TO YA RACE! You should be ashamed man. How can you sleep at night, knowing you are killing your own, man?"

Once again, he continued on this rant as he was searched and his property safely sealed in an evidence bag. With help, we managed to get him to a cell, where he was left to calm down to a point where he could be properly booked in.

I went back into custody, and looked at Sergeant Darling. I thought, *my God, I wonder how much abuse this poor man has to take like this?*

I stopped at the side of the custody desk, and waited until I made eye contact with him: "Sergeant."

He smiled and nodded his head: "You're wondering how often that happens? Thankfully, not often. It ends up being like water off a duck's back. Could you do fifteen-minute checks on our friend? Let me know when he's calmed down."

I was genuinely struck by the sergeant's courage and strength of character, to just brush off those remarks. I honestly didn't know if I would have similar strength in his shoes.

Time to check on Tariq. He hadn't improved. I found myself walking up and down the corridor, checking in on the two angry guys, as well as a couple of others who were less rude. Eventually, after an hour or so, Tariq stopped screaming abuse at me every time I looked in on him. I said: "Hello Sir (try the nicey nicey approach). Would you like a cup of tea?"

He walked up to the wicket: "Don't want tea. I want COFFEE!"

Well, this was progress. For those of you saying we shouldn't pander to criminals, we do have to deal with them, and we are required to make sure they're fed and watered, regardless of our feelings towards them.

I said: "Do you want milk and sugar?"

"I don't drink milk. Black, two sugars, and make sure you stir it well. I don't want all the sugar stuck together at the bottom."

I thought, *what a charmer*, but nodded, closed the wicket and prepared the coffee he'd ordered from "Hotel Earlham". I returned, opened the wicket, and said: "Your coffee's on the custody counter. Legally, before we're allowed to let you have it, we need you to have a chat with the good sergeant through there. So c'mon."

He looked at me, uncertain for a moment (well, at least he'd not said no). I said: "It's just a bit of paperwork. I know it's silly, but those are the rules. I don't like them. But that's what it is."

I was trying for the anti-establishment angle, and it worked, partially. He replied: "OK, mate, but before I sleep I want a fag, so I need my stuff back."

I didn't smoke, but I'd been given good advice by Big John in CID that if you wanted prisoners to talk to you, sometimes pretending to have a fag with them would make them more amenable. I replied: "Marlboro OK? You can have one of mine, after you've been booked in. And it's at the discretion of the custody sergeant, so be nice, and I can help you."

I pulled out the battered pack of Marlboro I had in my top pocket. I could see I'd got him. He shrugged: "All right mate. Fair enough."

I opened the cell, and keeping a weather-eye on him, escorted him back to the custody desk, where he cooperated with the custody procedure. At the conclusion, I said: "Sarge, Tariq has asked if he can have a cigarette break, and since he's cooperated with us, do you mind if I supervise him in the yard for five minutes, while it's quiet?"

The sergeant looked seriously at Tariq for a minute, sizing him up. He replied: "Tariq, do you have any cigarettes in your belongings?"

Tariq shook his head. I said: "If it's OK with you, he can have one of mine, sergeant."

The sergeant nodded: "OK, but only for five minutes. If we get busy all of a sudden, we'll have to cut it short. OK?"

Tariq nodded.

I took Tariq out into the tiny, 20'-by-20' exercise yard, that had a wire mesh roof. I offered him a cigarette, which he took, and I lit it for him and lit my own, pretending to draw on it. It takes practice, but you can make it pretty convincing.

We started talking about anything: football, family, the weather. I let him direct the conversation. At the end, after I'd established a bit of a rapport, I looked at him in a more serious way and said: "Tariq, mate, I'm just talking one man to another; forget the uniform. Mate, you do know it's dangerous out there. If you continue shouting and being abusive to people, you're going to get hurt. Honestly, us police, we won't hurt you for saying bad things to us, but other people on the streets will hurt you. They might even kill you. I'm not trying to be the big man. But, mate, I don't want to see anything bad happen to you."

He shrugged: "Man, I'm tougher than anyone. I could take them all. I could take you, bro. I'm the best there's ever been."

I realised at that point I wouldn't get through but, as I was taking him back to his cell, he said quietly: "Thanks man, I know you're all right. Don't worry about me; I know how to look after myself."

As I slammed the door and walked away, I thought, *you might know how to look after yourself but, no matter how tough you are, there's always someone tougher.*

I went down, and tried the same trick with the Black gentleman who had been so abusive to the sergeant. This time he wanted a tea, which I duly got him. Eventually, after three separate visits, I thought he was calm enough to be booked in. For precaution's sake, due to the size difference between him and me, I made sure Campbell was present.

It was unnecessary; the man was surly and rude, but not abusive, and we got the custody procedure completed. After I had put him back in the cell, I asked if he needed anything before the sleep cycle started (a time designated for undisturbed sleep). He asked for a drink of water, which I got for him. He took it without a word, but I chanced my arm and said: "You know, the sergeant is one of the nicest men I know. He's really kind, and decent."

He looked at me for what seemed like an age and said, "I'm sure from your point of view he seems to be. But from my side, I see him as a traitor."

I shrugged. I couldn't change this guy's mind. It was already set. At least he'd been civil enough (just) to get the custody procedure done. I closed the wicket and walked back, somewhat saddened by the total intransigence of the man and the absolute certainty in his ideology.

I walked back and told Sergeant Darling about what the man said. He said: "Thanks for saying those things about me. Look, you can't win them all. Some people, Black and white, are just set in their ways. There's nothing you can do to change their minds. The hatred runs deep. Maybe he'll change, but most likely not."

Just as I was thinking we were done for the night at 02:00 hours, in came Mel, struggling with a tall (6'3") slim man, in his mid-forties, dressed in an expensive, crumpled, black pinstripe suit. He was singing loudly, but with no tune or discernible song. I moved to help, just as he pitched forward, throwing up, once again on my trousers and boots, and on the base of the custody desk. At that point, Craig came in behind them, and between the three of us we checked his pockets and manoeuvred him down to the last cell (no more room at the inn tonight). After we'd put the mat down on the floor, and put him in the recovery position, I went to close the door.

He looked up and said, in a slurred, upper class accent, "Where am I?"

Mel replied, "You've been arrested. You're in a cell until you've sobered up."

The man tried to focus, and said to me: "Officer, what's the charge?"

"No charge. It's a free service here at Hotel Earlham."

With that, I slammed the door. Mel said: "That was quick. You're funny. And you stink, again. Sorry about the puke."

I replied, trying to wash it off, then collect the mop and bucket, "It's my turn to clear up after your prisoner." I grinned, and went back to clear up more vomit. What a glamorous job.

Christmas came and went. In the morning (when we were on), it was very, very quiet. Apparently, after lunch, when people have a few drinks, is when the punch-ups start. Charming!

After a few police cars and officers had been decorated with a few bits of tinsel, to cheer everyone up, a directive had come down from our lords and masters saying this would not be tolerated, and must desist immediately. The inspector said he'd be busy doing paperwork in his office, not going out on the streets, or in custody. So, the following day, we were all wearing tinsel, and the cars had tinsel on the radio antennae, the rear-view mirrors, and the lights on top. Damn, I did like the fact we all held the senior management in such high regard!

In the new year, we were called on to provide aid to police at an FA cup match between West Ham and Birmingham City. I'd been to plenty of football matches (being a West Ham fan), but this was a new experience.

We all turned up at the nick on the morning of the match and changed into our uniforms, including our hi-vis jackets (mostly we hated the things; it felt like you were wrapped in tinfoil), and then the minibus arrived, and we were off to the base at a junior school near the ground where we could be fed and briefed.

There were plenty of chairs, but they were a bit on the small side. We had breakfast/lunch and then they asked who wanted to watch the match. A few of us put up our hands. Then who wanted to be inside or outside the ground. Apparently, they were different types of jobs. Inside the ground, we were the first response if it all kicked off during the match. Outside were there before and after the match, although the inside did escort the fans out at the end of the match.

There were more than 100 of us, and although Birmingham City and West Ham fans could be involved in trouble, there'd apparently not been any trouble with each other, so it was only a medium-risk game. After the food and briefing, we moved out and supervised the crowd. It was an odd feeling, standing out in such a huge crowd. They were mostly good-natured, but there were some who had a fair bit to drink and were a bit lairy.

I took my place inside the ground, and as I was standing there, I saw one of my friends (John) from my teacher training days, who was also a West Ham fan. He didn't recognise me, so I waited until all his mates were around him (for maximum embarrassment), walked up behind him and, in my best booming police voice, said: "Excuse me Sir, may I have a word!?" I put my hand on his shoulder and he almost jumped out of his skin, and when he turned around, it took a few moments for him to recognise me in my new apparel. His mates thought it was hilarious. It took him a few minutes to see the funny side. Eventually, he did. I could have gotten into trouble for that. Fortunately, I was lucky, I didn't. It was funny though!

The match went off OK, and we won. It was hard not to celebrate when we scored which, to be fair, doesn't happen very often.

We escorted the away fans to the Tube station, where they had to wait for the home fans to clear the platform. This took a while, during which a group of mouthy, drunk Brummies had found a mounted female officer, who was very patiently listening to their rather poor attempts at humour. She bore it stoically (I was glad I wasn't such a target), all until one particularly loud and drunk guy made a point of trying his arm at humour. The horse, who'd been waiting around for a while, had started to produce saliva which turned into white foam around its mouth. Our 'comedian' shouted, "Here luv, your horse is frothing at the mouth." Big laugh.

She turned to him and said: "Two hours between my legs, and so would you, mate!"

I think we had a clear winner in that contest, and all his mates turned on him, ribbing him mercilessly over being "owned" by a policewoman. Us blokes are bad sometimes, but a friendly warning: do not piss off a female police officer; they take no prisoners!

Over the next few months, I ploughed on: arrests, process, coroner's court. Honestly, it was a struggle. You learn quickly, or you'll get an earful. A small Scottish guy returned to the relief. He'd been on long-term secondment to another unit. He was short (5'8"), skinny, with wiry, brown, untidy hair. His uniform was scruffy, and he had a very strong Glaswegian accent that a number of people had trouble with.

When I grew up, a close family friend had a similar accent, so I could understand him. We were paired up on a number of occasions, and they joked that I was his interpreter, which he hated. He spent the entire shift biting my ear off about any slight infraction. But the worst thing was, unlike Burke, he was trying to improve me, and more often than not he was right. His knowledge of the law, and the rules of the street, were second to none. Honestly, my heart sank every time I'd be paired with him, because he'd let nothing go. I learnt a lot but, my God, was it a steep learning curve with plenty of ear bashing.

At that stage, as much as I was enjoying it, it had taken a huge toll on me. Physically, I didn't get as much chance to train or watch my diet as I had before. Even Sooz commented on it, in her usual sweet way.

I had to reassess, and tried to stop eating so much quick, convenient junk food, and get down to the gym more often. I slowly got back into shape.

On a busy late turn, I was out with The Law. We'd become good friends. This day we'd taken a call to assist CID with a stop that was in danger of getting out of hand. We were singing the theme from the then new *Cops*, where the film crew drove along with real cops in America.

I'd sing: "Bad boys, bad boys, whatcha gonna do?" The Law would sing the next bit: "Whatcha gonna do when they come for you?" All while on a blue-light call. As I said, we enjoyed our work.

When we got there, we found Big John (from CID) struggling with an equally large Black man, and Patience was trying to calm down a large, mixed-race woman (6'3"), who was hugely muscular. I think she was among the biggest women I'd ever seen. She was dressed in ripped jeans, torn T-shirt, and had badly braided dreadlocks. Her face (being kind) was a mess of old scars and more recent bruising, and slightly swollen.

We both jumped out. I ran to Patience (she looked the most outmatched) to help her. Now Patience was a fit lady; she worked out regularly, and was fairly strong. I was a lot stronger, and this woman mountain would have given me a real run for my money. John was about evenly matched with the other guy.

I went over, and could see Patience was being ... patient. So I matched her level of engagement. It became clear quickly the lady's name was Grace Lefevre. If ever a name did not fit a person.

Patience said: "Grace, Grace, listen, we just need you to come in with us to have a chat. You don't want someone executing a warrant on your place first thing in the morning, do you? C'mon, lets' do this in a civil way."

Grace said, in a deep, almost guttural, voice (clearly under the influence of mind-altering chemicals): "I don't wan go no police station. I wan go home, lil' police girlie."

I thought, *we've got to make this personal, so she reacts to us as people*. I said, "Hi Grace, is it? I'm Richard. Why not come with us, and we can have a sit down, and a drink and a chat? How's that sound?"

Patience picked up on that, saying: "Grace, Richard is right. I'm Patience. You know me. We can have a sit down and a chat. What do you say?"

Grace swayed a bit, as I could see a little of the adrenaline wearing off. She looked at me and said: "You're not trying to trick me are you, Richard?"

I replied: "No Grace, honest, just sit down for a minute. You look a little unsteady on your feet. We don't want you falling over."

Patience chimed in, as we gently guided Grace to a small wall: "C'mon Grace, no one's trying to trick you."

Slowly, slowly, we managed to calm her down. The man John and The Law were dealing with saw that Grace was safe and had calmed down. He followed suit, and complied, and after about fifteen minutes, we started to get them calm enough to transport them back to the nick.

This took a while, and the doctor was called due to their drug dependence. I had a chance to chat to Patience while we did the mountains of paperwork required for the stop and arrest.

Patience said: "Good work with Grace. She's a big girl, and she's very, very unpredictable. Thanks. I was getting a bit worried there. If you'd gone in all guns blazing, it would have turned into a real punch-up, and given I'm the smallest, I'd have probably got hurt."

As John walked past me, he patted my shoulder: "Thanks for the help, lads. We got them in without anyone getting hurt. That's a win in my book."

I was pleased to hear that. I had faced criticism a number of times over my low-key approach, which is more risky than the more formal, more confrontational approach.

I replied to Patience: "You're welcome. We're all here to help each other. What's the deal with Grace? She seems quite a character."

Patience grinned: "That's certainly one way to describe her. Honestly, it's a really sad story. Her mom was an alcoholic heroin addict prostitute, her father was a heroin addict pimp. They both regularly beat her, then when she was 13 her mother forced her into prostitution, and a year later, her dad got her hooked on heroin. She then started drinking. She'd been in and out of prison all her life (apparently, she was in her mid-twenties, but she looked a lot older, due to the drink and drugs).

"She became a heroin dealer a couple of years ago to support her habit, and last year, another drug dealer had started selling drugs on her patch from a minicab (which was a good front for selling drugs). She's dragged him out of the car, beaten him senseless, stolen his stash of drugs, his money, and driven off in his car, leaving him unconscious on the street. She was destined for an early grave at the current rate. If the drugs and booze didn't kill her, other drug dealers would."

Honestly, by this stage, a year in, I'd heard terrible stories of how people had grown up, but this was one of the worst. People have to take responsibility for what they do but, dear God, if anyone had an excuse for poor behaviour, that was it.

I found myself thinking about her story a number of times over the next few days. I thought, *what would I have done in similar circumstances? Would I have had the courage to pull away from crime? Could I have turned myself around from that start?*

Honestly, I don't think I could. So, "there but by the grace of God go I", as the saying goes. A sobering thought!

About a week later, we were finishing up a particularly busy set of early turns, and we were exhausted. A relief were taking over, and they were really down on numbers, with only twelve paraded (out of twenty-four on a normal relief). I looked at the custody sergeant and the gaoler who was my replacement. The sergeant was an old man, just a few months from retiring. He had a bad back, a dodgy knee. The gaoler was a 4'11", slim, Asian probationer lady who was working out her notice. The first sudden death she went to, she'd flat out refused to go in. She just couldn't handle the smell, or the sight of death. So, she had a couple of weeks left. I didn't fancy their chances much if there was trouble in custody that day.

Then, as I turned to walk out, I met Alf as he walked in, and said: "'Ere, there's that big scary Black woman in the front office. Grace, I think her name is. She's wanted on warrant, and has just surrendered herself. She's as high as a kite, and if you ask me, she's just about to kick off."

He looked at the gaoler, and she started towards the door. I thought, *there's no one else in the station*. CID and the rest of the relief are out on calls. If Grace kicks off, people are going to get hurt. Really hurt. Even though I was shattered, and I just wanted to go home to sleep, I remembered something my Aunt Vicki said (a lovely, wise lady, whom I adored). She said, there'll be a moment that defines you. It'll be a moment when you have to step forward, and be kind, even when it hurts, go beyond yourself, show kindness, show you genuinely care, and show your sensitivity.

Sometimes there are moments when you have to make choices, and you recognise their significance. This was one such. I said to the elderly sergeant: "Sergeant, given you're so short of numbers, and I dealt with Grace recently, maybe she'd respond well to me. I'm prepared to stay on and help, if you want?"

I could see the relief on his face: "Thank you, 272. I'm not going to turn down a helping hand today. Welcome aboard."

I walked through to the front office, and I could see Grace was off her head, twitchy (what they call "clucking" after the action of a chicken, in her movements).

I took her through, and I could see the start of recognition of who I was. I tried to get her to book in at custody, and she started putting her arms out and getting 'fighty'. I got her to sit down. The sergeant and the gaoler looked on, concerned. The gaoler kept putting a hand on her ASP. I signalled "no" with a hand gesture.

I sat and talked to Grace for two hours. It was touch and go. I am by nature calm and patient (when I want to be), and I've never worked so hard. So many times I thought I'd lost her, but I don't know how, I always managed to get her calm again. I spoke to dozens of police officers about what I did, and most of them (male, female, Black, white) say I did the wrong thing. You shouldn't pander to criminals, I should have just fought her, and dealt with it that way. Was I treating her differently because of her race and sex? I don't think so. It was just the whole situation was unique.

Anyway, after two solid hours of talking, the drugs had worn off, and we managed between us to get her booked in, and into the cell voluntarily.

I walked out, the sergeant thanked me, but said: "Really sorry mate; the overtime wasn't approved prior to you starting so they won't pay you for the two hours."

I shrugged: "Honestly Sarge, I'm not fussed. You needed help. I didn't want anyone to get hurt, but that was hard, hard work."

He nodded, and patted me on the shoulder. "Fine police work. Not by the book, but I and the gaoler appreciate not getting our heads kicked in. Thanks son."

I made it home, and slept the sleep of the dead.

The next day was another early, so when I finished (around 14:00 hours), I got a message from the front office. I had a visitor. I went down and spoke with Alf. He said: "'Ello son. You've got a girlfriend. That crazy, big Black woman's been waiting for you for an hour. She won't tell me nothing. Do you need backup?"

I thought for a minute: "No, I'll speak to her."

I went into the station office, and she said: "Richard, I want to speak to you alone." She looked pointedly at Alf. I knew I was taking a risk, but when didn't I?

I took her through to one of the front interview rooms. I said: "Hi Grace, how are you doing? Thanks for being patient. What can I do for you?"

She said: "Thank you, Richard Armstrong, for what you did for me yesterday. You spoke to me and treated me not like a big, scary, Black woman, but like a human being. That's the first time any policeman has done that. You didn't see the colour of my skin; you just helped me. Thank you so much!"

I could see her beginning to tear up. I was really shocked at someone so formidable being so vulnerable. I handed her a box of tissues, she took one and put the box down.

I replied: "Grace, we're all just human beings. Under the skin we're just the same. You know, we are all capable of good and bad. Inside you there is a spark of humanity. I saw it, and let you see it. You can turn your life around; there's rehab, and programmes you can go on. You can do it, Grace."

She looked at me again, and slowly and quietly said: "You and I both know that I won't. I'll die on the streets, but thank you. Just once, before I die, I'll know one person had faith in me. That's not what I'm here for. I want to give you something, for what you've done for me. I'll give you information on a really nasty armed robber. But only you, all right. It's not for those others. I want to help you."

I was shocked. People in the drugs trade just don't do that. I thought quickly. I couldn't just take information like that; I needed another person who was informant-handling trained. I knew the person. I asked Grace to wait there, and I'd be back in a couple of minutes.

I ran upstairs to the CID office, and John was there. I ran over, and hastily explained the situation. He looked on incredulously, saying "What, you got Grace Lefevre to roll over on an armed blagger (robber)? What, really? Bloody hell, I never thought I'd hear that."

I explained she wanted me to get the credit. He agreed. We went downstairs, and it took a while, and John had to promise her that I'd get credit for it. She told me, and he just wrote it down, and questions could only be asked through me.

As Grace was going, she said: "Thank you Richard Armstrong. Goodbye."

I was taken aback by this. I never saw her again. She died a year later of a drugs overdose after coming out of prison. I was saddened by that, but not surprised. For all her faults, she did retain a spark of humanity. I wonder how many of us could say the same in her shoes?

I went upstairs and spoke to John, who was on the phone. After a while, he put it down, and said: "The Sweeney are going to get a warrant to knock the place tomorrow morning. We'll see how good that intel was. Good work all the same."

A couple of days later, I had a call to see the inspector. He called me in, I sat down and he pulled out a piece of paper, and said: "This is a commendation from the flying squad (Sweeney Todd, the most famous specialist unit in the Met, they catch armed robbers). They say you gave them intelligence that's led to the arrest of their number one most-wanted armed robber. Your intel was spot on. They found his gun, with his fingerprints and DNA on it. In twenty years of policing, I've never seen one of these. Son, they're very picky on who they recruit, and they have their eye on your career. Well done!"

I found out later, he'd got seven and a half years inside!

Chapter 7
GREIFMEISTER

A few months later, we were sitting in the parade room, waiting for late turn, and as the guv'nor and our sergeants were walking in, the radio went: "Units free to deal. Reports of a man running amok in Leyton Street market, armed with a machete."

We didn't need to hear any more. We jumped up and the guv'nor just waved his hand towards to the door, and he was on the radio saying: "We've cleared the parade room. Wait for call signs en route. Can you show me attending, PT1."

This was a very rare occurrence, just the way it was said, in the present tense, an ongoing call, with the heightened state of readiness with the tension indicator. It might have indicated people were being attacked right then, and you don't take chances with those situations.

I was in the second car out of the yard, with Robbie, The Law and Pete (the best thief-takers) first. We raced along the Kenton Road, and I put out our call sign and shoulder numbers. As we arrived on scene, I could see people milling around, and the market superintendent flapping about. We jogged up to where he was. He just pointed across the market square to where a man was lying on the floor, with a man and a woman kneeling beside him. I just saw The Law disappearing off through the crowd, and caught his radio call saying he'd got a lead and was chasing the suspect. Good going!

There's a split in policing. There are those who would run past an injured victim on the floor to chase down the fleeing suspect, and there are those who'd check on the victim before chasing after the suspect. The Law was most definitely the former.

I slowed to take in the scene. There were stalls set out in a rough square (which I was crossing). The injured man was lying next to one of the stalls. Behind it were a number of shops, including a butcher. There were people standing in gaggles, talking, and a trail of blood leading off to the right.

Robbie made a beeline for the man on the ground. I went over and could see the man had a very, very serious upper arm injury. The woman had taken a pile of tea towels from the stall next to the man, and had wrapped it around his wound. It appeared, by the unnatural way the humerus was articulating, that the arm was almost entirely severed. The man was making muling noises. I quickly understood he was probably deaf, as he was not able to form words.

With the suspect being chased, and the victim being tended to, I looked around, and the market supervisor walked over to me. I think he wanted something to do.

I said: "Sir, the ambulance will be along shortly. Would you mind going to stand on the PAVEMENT, and direct it in here please?"

He looked at me and nodded.

I then got on the radio: "PT, 272."

They replied: "Go ahead 272."

"I'm on scene, Leyton Street market. Currently we have one casualty with a serious upper arm injury, possible partially severed. Can I just confirm the LAS are en route, and are aware of the situation regarding number and severity of the casualty?"

Sooz replied: "I can confirm the LAS are en route. I'll patch you through to the crew so you can update them."

A slight pause, and a there was a lot of background noise of a siren. I said: "LAS vehicle en route to Leyton Street market, this is PT272. I am on scene, and can give you an update, when you're ready."

Slight pause, then: "PT272, this is the LAS crew en route. Paramedic Des Philips here. What have you got for us?"

"Currently one casualty, male, approximately 40 years old. He has a partial severance at the midpoint of his left humerus. He has a laceration to the back of the head. We have an off-duty nurse and a police officer holding the wounds closed with improvised bandages. Over."

Des said: "Received that, 272. Just clarify, is he conscious (at this point the man screamed)? I take that as a yes. Anything further you can tell us? ETA four minutes."

I thought for a second, and noticed the guv'nor and a number of other units had arrived. I replied, "I believe the victim may be deaf. It appears the wounds were cleanly made, possibly by a sharp-bladed weapon."

Des ended the call. I walked to the centre of the square, looked around and began directing the new arrivals to preserve and secure the physical evidence (blood trail, weapon, etc.). The guv'nor walked over, and I said: "Do you want to take over, Sir?"

He shook his head: "You're doing a fine job marshalling the troops. What do you want me to do?"

This is good leadership, I thought, *he has faith in his team*. I was proud he trusted me. I looked around and saw a group of what looked like possible witnesses.

I said: "Sir, would you mind speaking to those people over there, and seeing if they are potential witnesses?"

He nodded approvingly: "Public relations, good choice Richard. Right up my alley."

He walked over to them, minding where he stepped, and said in his best Mainwaring way: "Good afternoon, I'm Inspector Manning. Thank you for sticking around. May I enquire if any of you witnessed the events, and if you did if you'd be prepared to do your civil duty, and aid the police in the course of their investigation?"

Man, he was good at the public speaking bit. There were a number of people who stepped forward and provided their accounts, and details. Good job, Sir!

The LAS appeared and were directed in by the somewhat excitable superintendent. One jogged over to me and I pointed at the injured man, while the other one got out the stretcher. Just like the LFB (London Fire Brigade), the LAS crews were never happier than when they could get every bit of kit off their wagons.

The man was put on the stretcher, and I was volunteered to go in the ambulance with him. But we didn't have his name, or next of kin so that we could inform them, and get him to hospital. My sign language was virtually non-existent, and we'd have struggled anyway, because he could only use one hand.

But I came up with a plan, and as he was being loaded and stabilised in the ambulance, I wrote out the alphabet on a piece of paper. I went over to him and said, very slowly and deliberately: "I need to know who to contact to get them to hospital."

It took a couple of attempts, but eventually we got there. I held up the alphabet and said, "What is the first letter of your name?" I pointed at A, no response, B, C, D, at which point he nodded. We were getting somewhere. I wrote down D. I took a chance and wrote DAVID on the paper. He nodded. Right, David. Doing this, I managed quite quickly to get his name, next of kin and address. I held up my thumb and nodded. He managed a weak smile, and nodded back. I then put the radio call out to get someone to his parents and take them to the hospital.

By the time we got there (forty-five minutes from the initial call), his family were on their way in a police car. The Law and Pete had caught the guy, still covered in the victim's blood, and his reply to caution was: "I wish I'd given up smoking so I could have finished the bastard."

The weapon (a meat cleaver) had been recovered, and the man and his arm survived, and we had at least a dozen witnesses who were prepared to give statements. I told you the guv'nor was good with the public.

C relief handed a completed case, with all the bases covered, to CID within an hour! Without blowing our own trumpet, that was a fine piece of team police work! No egos; we all just mucked in. If there was an exemplary job, it was that one.

When the story as to why it had happened surfaced, it split the team as to its justification. Apparently, our 'victim' had been in court and let off due to lack of evidence of sexually molesting the attacker's 14-year-old daughter. Some said that, if true, our attacker had some justification. Others said that we had to go with the courts, and people shouldn't take the law into their own hands. I wonder which camp you fall into, and if you can work out which one I favour? Things are often far more complex than simple good or evil. Nuance is everything.

A couple of weeks later, I was working a later turn with Mel, and we'd answered a call about a possible intruder at an address on the Kenton Road. We'd split up, and she'd parked the car a couple of streets away, so as not to tip them off. I had gone around the front, while she went around the back. It turned out to be a false alarm, and she'd said she'd go and collect the car, and I should wait around the front.

It was late afternoon, and there was a slight breeze rustling the trees which lined the road. I noticed a heavily pregnant young woman making her way along the wide, uneven pavement towards me. She smiled when she saw me, and I noticed as she got closer, she was very young, probably 19 or 20 years old. She was wearing cheap, stretchy jeans, and what looked like a man's old check shirt. Her hair was light brown, long and windswept, and slightly unkempt.

She walked over to me and, smiling, said: "Hello, do you know where I can get some food?"

Of all the things I expected her to say, it wasn't that.

I said: "Actually, you've just walked past a market that has a couple of cafes and a little supermarket. Are you all right? Do you need any help?"

She smiled: "Oh, I came out one of the side roads. I didn't see it. Is it far?"

"About half a mile down the road. Are you all right? Do you need a lift?"

It's not strictly within the rules to work as a taxi service but, given the circumstances, it wouldn't be unreasonable.

"No, I'm fine. Trouble is, I don't have any money, and I am hungry."

My mind was racing through the possible scenarios: drugs, people trafficking, abuse, domestic violence.

I said: "Look, there are plenty of people who can help you. Let me get in touch with them for you? Do you have a home nearby?"

She shook her head: "No I'm fine. I just need some money for food."

Alarm bells were going off at this point. Why was a heavily pregnant young woman walking the streets asking for money? I spent the next ten minutes trying everything I knew to persuade her to tell me who she was, where she lived, to accept help, to let us take her to a place of safety (police station), and anything else I could think of. To give her a lift, anything.

By this time, Mel had joined me, and we both tried to convince her (we were nicknamed "The Charm offensive" due to our low-key, friendly approach). I even found an excuse to get something from the car to let Mel talk to her, woman to woman. Still no joy. The woman absolutely refused to let us help her. Then, sensing she wasn't getting any money, the woman began walking off towards the market. She was an adult, she had not committed a crime, so we had no power to stop or detain her.

Being pregnant is not a mental illness, so we had no power under that provision to detain her. And the idea of trying to physically force a heavily pregnant woman into a police car for her own good wasn't something either of us would entertain.

As we watched her walk off, I looked at Mel and, in desperation, said: "There must be something we can do? We can't just let her walk off like that?"

Mel looked at me and said, "She's an adult. There's nothing we can do for her if she doesn't want to be helped."

I couldn't leave it at that. I ran after the woman, took out my wallet, and gave her the contents (£50), saying: "Please, let us help you, please."

She smiled, took the money and said, "Thank you. No, I don't want help, but thank you."

She carried on walking. I returned to Mel, who looked at me and said, "She's probably going to use that on drugs, and might kill her unborn baby."

"We don't know that. I just made sure she had enough money so she had a choice whether to buy food or not."

Mel shook her head: "Do you know how many rules you just broke? I won't say anything, but that was as stupid as it was kind. You're too soft for this job, Richard. Let's go."

When we'd sat down in the panda car, Mel looked across at me, thought for a moment, and said: "You are a naive fool sometimes! For all your intelligence, you are not very worldly-wise. Let me tell you something. You know I went away on that SOIT course (sexual offences investigation techniques) a while back?"

I nodded. She continued: "Well, the first rape case I dealt with was when a woman in her late thirties went out on the town with a group of her friends. She'd been having trouble in her marriage, and wanted to get away for a bit. They had a few drinks before they went out, and when they got to the bar, she saw a young (22-year-old), handsome man. She made a beeline for him, and started chatting him up. According to the witnesses, she was all over him like a rash.

"Long story short, they ended up going back to her friends' old terraced house, and going to her room, where they had sex. Thing was, the walls in this place were paper-thin, and her friends were kept up half the night by the noise. Apparently, she was very vocal about what she wanted, and how to do it. The next morning, she woke up, realised that she's just cheated on her husband, and all her friends knew about it. So she went to the bathroom, and called 999. Half the relief turned out to this rape case. We did everything by the book: he was arrested, I took the woman away, evidence was gathered, and the witnesses' statements were taken.

"Problem was, all the witness statements clearly stated that she was the one taking the lead in the sex, all the way through. Totally contradicting the woman. In fact, her friends were so disgusted with her, they all but disowned her.

"All the while, she was playing the victim. At the same time, the young man was in the cell, crying his eyes out, thinking his life was over. That he'd lose his job, his family and friends would disown him, for doing nothing wrong.

"Eventually, the woman broke down, and admitted she'd lied. Only after she realised she'd have to have an intimate exam, and go to court.

"Even then, I supported her, and asked her if she was sure, and why she'd asked to drop the case.

"She had cheated on her husband, and then wanted to be treated as a victim. Talk about having your cake and eating it! She gave no thought for the effect it would have on the poor young bloke!

"You see, Richard, women lie! Sometimes about the most horrible things, with no thought of the consequences for others. They'll lie about anything to get their own way, and will use the fact they're women to get away with it.

"But here's the truth: we all lie! All of us! No one is above scrutiny, ever. And spineless, selfish women like her make it ten times harder for the rest of us. You can't walk around with the opinion of women that they float around on little clouds, and are perfect little angels! They are just as flawed, and likely to lie, as men. Get used to it! Or women will pull the wool over your eyes for the rest of your life!"

With that ringing in my ears, the radio crackled into life: "Units free to deal, we had an attempted suicide."

The address was just around the corner. Even though we were in a panda, I looked at Mel, and she was already starting the battered, crappy old Fiesta. I took this as a "yes".

I said, "PT, this PT82, we're just around the corner, show as responding."

Sergeant Rob Smedley also responded, saying, "PT, can you show PT22 also in attendance, we're virtually on scene."

Sooz acknowledged both vehicles. The address rang a bell, but honestly you go to so many addresses, it's hard to keep track. We arrived about five minutes later, and I put us on scene, second to Sergeant Smedley, whom I had not worked with much. We made our way up to the first-floor flat, past the discarded needles, used condoms and other assorted human detritus. As we walked along the landing, we met Sergeant Smedley walking out to get a better radio reception to call PT.

I said, "Hi Sarge, what's the situation?"

"A young lass, Roxanne Templeton, has made a half-arsed attempt to kill herself with cheap booze and tablets. Her mom found her. She should be all right, just needs a trip to the hospital to check her out."

I recognised the name, then remembered the shoplifter I got into a drug rehab programme months ago. *What went wrong?*

"Sarge, I know this girl (not saying why in a hallway where the neighbours were no doubt listening). I have established a rapport with her. Do you want me to deal?"

The sergeant looked up, "Yeah, that sounds like a good idea. Mel can drop the panda back at the nick and jump in with me until you get free."

I looked at Mel, and she said cheekily "Oh, I see, you're ditching the PLONK (a derogatory term used against female police officers back in the 60s and 70s standing for Practically Little or No Knowledge) at the first opportunity."

She winked and flounced off. Don't believe anyone who says there was never any sexism against female officers, but they were making things worse by lowering the standards for women compared with men. And, newsflash, being sexist towards men does not somehow make up for the past; it merely poisons the future!

I walked in and saw a worried-looking woman in her late forties. She was about 5'6", medium build, wearing a Lidl's uniform, with a cheap raincoat over the top of it. I looked past her to see Liz, one of the police officers I hadn't had worked with yet, tending to Roxanne, who was lying on the sofa.

The sergeant said, "Mrs Templeton, this is PC Armstrong. He knows Roxanne, so we thought it was best if he take over when the ambulance comes. He'll be the one escorting you both to hospital."

She turned her tear-streaked face towards me: "Are you that nice policeman who was kind to her, and got her onto the drugs rehab course?"

I nodded: "Yes, Mrs Templeton, I am. Please call me Richard. I'm here to help and support both of you."

At that, she put her arms around me and started crying. I did my best to comfort her. I heard the LAS siren pull up outside. I moved her over to one of the armchairs in the run-down living room, with water stains on the poorly painted walls, that matched the threadbare carpet, and the heavily worn and mismatched sofa and chairs.

I knelt down and explained I needed to speak with Roxanne, and take a statement from her.

I looked up and, by serendipitous coincidence, Mel was there with a couple of MG11 statement forms and a big grin.

I said: "Thanks. For a PLONK, you're quite useful."

She resisted the urge to make a snarky comeback remark, given the situation, but gave me the I'll-remember-that-remark-buster look. No doubt, I'd be on the receiving end of some comment or remark later. I knew I was in for trouble. Something to look forward to!

I walked over, and Liz said, "Roxanne, I'll leave you in the hands of Richard here. I think you know him."

She nodded in thanks as she got up and walked off to direct the LAS crew in. I was freeing her up to do the more exciting work. This was called 'griefy' work. Not being rude to anyone, but it wasn't nicking villains, but dealing with the complicated, emotional stuff that could lead to difficulties.

I looked at Roxanne. She was pale, dishevelled, she'd been sick, and there was a bowl on the floor in front of her. Having said that, she did seem reasonably 'with it'. I said in a gentle tone, "Hello Roxanne. How are you feeling (what a silly question, or, in slang, an SQ)?"

She looked at me then, despite herself, tried to smile: "Richard, oh I'm so sorry I let you down. I'm so, so useless."

She started to cry. Well, that wasn't the reaction I wanted. I was trying to comfort, not make it worse. I gently put my hand on her arm, and said, "Don't worry about letting anyone down, just relax, and don't worry. You're all right now."

I talked to her, and got her back to a better state of mind by the time the LAS arrived with the stretcher. They spoke to her mom, and checked the empty bottle of cheap vodka and packet of anti-depressant tablets we'd seized and bagged up.

I stepped back and let the LAS crew deal with Roxanne, and a short while later the three of us (me, Roxanne and her mom) were all in the back of the ambulance. Roxanne was sitting up on the stretcher, and was beginning to be more 'with it'.

I managed to get some of the details down for my crime report. Technically, suicide is illegal, but it would be pretty harsh for the CPS to prosecute someone for attempting it.

We arrived at the hospital, where I waited with her mom while Roxanne had her stomach pumped. Not a pleasant experience! But they thought she'd be fine in a couple of days, but they'd keep her in for observations.

I waited, chatting with her mom, until Roxanne was put on a ward. The doctor told me she was not at risk, and I didn't need to stay. By then, Roxanne's aunt (her mom's sister) had arrived. I said my goodbyes, and told them I'd return the next day to take a statement from Roxanne, having already taken her mom's while we were waiting. After the emotional start, I think Roxanne appreciated having a familiar face.

I thought about this call when I got home that night. Why did she try to kill herself? She had been on a rehab course and, by the sounds of it, had got clean. I didn't get it, and that bothered me. I thought I'd helped her turn a corner, and improve things.

The following day, I went to the hospital to take the statement. This was being handled by CID, but they were tied up, and had asked me to take the statement, as I knew her.

I made my way to the ward and sat down next to Roxanne's bed, with a clipboard and the MG11 form. She looked a lot better that day, but still had bags under her eyes and seemed a little edgy. Not surprising, given the circumstances.

She seemed pleased to see me and, after I'd finished her statement, we chatted for a bit.

I said, "Roxanne, I have to ask you why did you do it?"

She bowed her head and said, "I came out of rehab drug-free, and I was so determined to stay clean. I came home, and I was doing really well. I had applied for a college course, and to work in a local shop while I waited. Then the drug dealers started hassling me, trying to get me back on the gear (heroin). It wasn't too bad at first; I just kept saying no. But they wouldn't give up, following me, throwing things at my window at night to wake me up. Craving is worse at night. I ignored all of it. But then they got nasty, threatening me, then my mom. They wouldn't let up."

She paused, and I said, "Who are they? We'll get them to stop. We can help."

She looked at me: "No, that would be a death sentence. They'd kill me and my mom. I just can't tell you. Everyone hates a 'grass'. I couldn't live there any more."

I thought quickly: "Don't you have any friends or relatives you can stay with, away from here?"

She shook her head: "Everyone I know lives in London, and they'd find me. Even if they didn't, they said that if I did leave, they'd get my mom. There's no way out of this."

I wasn't done yet. I tried for the next ten minutes to convince her to tell me who those people were. A dead end, all the way. She was simply more scared of the gangs than they were of the police.

I thought, *I'll change of topic, then go back to it. Get her talking, maybe she'll tell me then.*

I said "OK, one thing I don't understand. How did you get started with heroin?"

She looked at me with sad, world-weary eyes, and said, "I was 18, and I met a gorgeous man at a party, and he chatted me up. He was about 25. I'm nothing special, and he liked me. I felt so special; all the other girls were jealous, and he was so kind, and lovely to me.

"We met up a few times, and we'd have a drink. Then, when I was a bit drunk, he'd get me to try cannabis. Then the next time, when I was drunk and stoned, he gave me something new to smoke. Oh it was the most amazing thing I've ever tried. I've always felt awkward and nervous, like I never really fitted in. I was so relaxed, and connected with people, with the earth. Everything was great, I felt so at peace. The best feeling of my life. I was hooked from the first moment.

"He gave me some more, then he said he didn't have any more but could buy some for me, if I gave him money. I gave him all my money. I had a bit saved for a holiday. I used that, I borrowed, I took anything I could to sell at the pawn shop. I just had to have more, and more. Every day I didn't have it got worse and worse. I ran out of people I could borrow from."

She stopped and took a deep breath, and continued really quietly, so only I could hear. "I'm ashamed. I stole from my mom, my friends. I took their stuff and sold it. I lied and lied and lied. I eventually stole from the shops. I got caught. I got a caution. I tried to stop, but just before I got caught for the last time, I was walking down the street and I saw a really dishy young man walk past. I'm a young woman – I should be thinking how hunky he was, looking at his shoulders, and hips, and face. I should be thinking about what it'd be like to be held in his arms, to be kissed by him, to make love to him. I should be thinking of romance and love. But you know what I thought about?"

She collected herself, and I handed her a tissue as she shed a tear. "I thought, *what would I have to do to get enough money out of him to get some heroin*? *Would I have to charm him, deceive, manipulate him, steal from him, or even sleep with him*? I just couldn't do that, so I went up to the shop and stole those things that you arrested me for. Then, when I found out I could get on a course to get off the drugs, I had real hope. The course was so hard, but I stuck with it, and was so proud of myself to get off it. Then this. I lost all hope, and could see no way out."

I fought so hard to hold back my tears. I was in a hospital in full view of the public. I managed it, but only just. It was terrible. *There must be something we can do.* If she wouldn't tell me, I'd see Alan. He'd know. We could do something. I tried again to get her to give me names. Again, flat refusals.

I once again tried a different tack. I said, "What pushes people to need more of this stuff? I don't understand?"

She looked at me with a level gaze and said, "I'll explain it, but you might not truly understand. When you don't have it, your body goes into withdrawal. It's like the worst period pains ever, all over your body, all the time. Your muscles cramp, you twitch, and you can't think of anything but heroin. Your brain burns. It's absolute hell. There's no escape."

Well, I thought, *that explains why people go to extremes to get the money for this stuff.*

I finished the statement, and I had to go outside the hospital to check the radio calls, as we tended not to have our radios on in hospital.

"Thank you, Roxanne. Please let us help you with these people. Take care of yourself."

She smiled, and touched my arm, saying, "Thank you. You're really kind, but there's nothing you can do to help me. Take care of yourself."

I walked away, fully intent on trying to find a way to help her. Unfortunately, when I left the hospital, we were running around like blue-arsed flies, and it wasn't long until I was up to my neck in calls.

A few days later, during a paperwork day, I went to speak to Alan. I explained the situation. He gave me that look a parent gives a child, when they say something that's sweet but naive. He said, "Richard, it does you credit that you're trying, and don't get me wrong, I'll do my best to help, but you're flogging a dead horse, old chap!"

It wasn't what I wanted to hear; Alan was able to fix things, had the intelligence (literally and figuratively), so must have known how to help.

I said, "Alan, why can't we help her? We're the police. We should be able to arrest these drug-dealing thugs for harassment and threats to kill."

Alan shook his head, "You need evidence. That comes in the form of statements. If people aren't prepared to give those statements, there's nothing we can do. And they won't give statements because they're scared."

I shook my head. I knew what he was saying was logical, and true. I just didn't want to believe it. I was just about to say something else, but had a call on the radio to go back to the canteen, as I was needed. I thanked Alan and walked back, having had a little bit more of my faith in the system chipped away.

It turned out that D relief were down to the bone in terms of staff, and a bomb had been found on the Kenton Road, and they needed us to go out and answer some of the backlogged calls. Unfortunately, there weren't enough cars for all of us, so Pete and me would be walking again.

I checked my notebook to put in the date. It was almost a year since I joined. What a year; the most manic of my life. We put on our tall hats and walked out of the station, turned right, and headed up to Futures Park to cover the beat there.

It was a warm hazy day and, as we approached the park, we began to see groups of youths walking with intent towards where we were heading. It didn't look good. We crossed the road, speeding up to try to dissuade them from having a fight. We made it to the centre of the park and, with horror, I realised our presence was not going to stop the fight. A shout went up and two gangs – totalling about fifty, all bearing weapons in the form of knives, machetes, baseball bats, pieces of wood, anything they could get their hands on – were charging at each other, with us roughly in the centre.

I immediately hit the emergency button on my radio and, as I drew and shouldered my ASP, said quickly, "Urgent assistance, urgent assistance, Futures Park, fifty-plus fighting with weapons. We're in the middle of it!"

At this point I saw a youth of about 18 run up to me with a baseball bat and, while screaming obscenities, move into range to hit me on the head with his bat. He had more enthusiasm than skill, and I ducked and moved under his blow, delivering a textbook strike to the muscle on the side of his thigh with all the force I could muster. To my slight surprise, it elicited the required response, and he fell to the ground screaming in pain. Thankfully, I hadn't broken his leg, just given him a real limp for a few weeks (not one of those fake NY gangster ones).

I looked around and saw Pete facing off against three of the youths, armed with mixtures of a knife, a machete and a lump of wood. The one with the wood was trying to move to the rear of him to catch him unawares. *Not so fast, pal*, I thought. I remembered the shout the youth had tried on me. Two can play that game. So I charged him, baton raised, bellowing at the top of my lungs, like an enraged grampus (as my Aunt Anne would have said). I must say, it seemed to do the trick; he looked terrified, and ran off. I stopped next to Pete, we exchanged nods, and we started advancing on the two youths. They seemed less inclined to take both of us on.

We managed to keep them at bay with a few strikes and plenty of variations of, "Get back, police!" But we could see it wouldn't be long until one of them would get their brave heads on and have a go. Trust me, at that point, it definitely clears your head, and I was, as the actors say, "In the moment."

Then the cavalry arrived, in the form of two carriers of TSG (no doubt on their way home from trashing our canteen again). I have to give it to them – their timing was impeccable, and they cleared the park in double-quick time. There were youths running off in all directions, and it was chaos. We were left alone in the middle of the park as a dozen or so burly types were wrestling the youths to the ground and putting them in cuffs. We went to assist, and were very appreciative of their help.

I think we'd made their day, and we filled not only Earlham's cells, but Park Street's too. At the end of the shift, we'd written statements and done CRIMINT reports. It had been an engrossing day, to say the least.

When I got home, Victoria had called. When I spoke with her, she was upset; apparently her and Julia were splitting up. It turned out Victoria had been having an affair with Nina. I was asked to help Victoria move her stuff from Julia's flat. That wasn't going to be a good idea, but it was Victoria, and I wasn't going to say no. So next day I got off early, drove to Suffolk and helped Victoria move out. Julia took real offence at that and disowned me, so that was the end of that relationship. That was not a nice experience, barely six months after the happiest day ever. Two of the people there were splitting up, and one of them didn't want to see me again.

A couple of days after that, Nina called and asked to meet after work in central London, which I did. She said she wanted to remain friends. I replied, "Nina, it's none of my business what people get up to in terms of relationships, short of violence or abuse. I'm not here to judge anyone. After the help you gave me, with the street duties fiasco, I am hugely grateful."

She smiled: "Thanks. I might have been a bit hard on you through that. But I'm glad it worked out. There's another thing: while I was seeing Victoria, I was also seeing Inspector Charles Thompson, who's at your nick. Cindy, my girlfriend, mustn't find out, or I'll have to move out."

My head was reeling. It was going to get so messy, so quickly. I nodded, and the "I'm not here to judge" was being tested to the limit.

I vowed to keep my head down until it was all over. I thought I'd change the subject, and said, "How's it going at work?"

Nina nodded: "It's going really well. I'm 'acting up' (this is where a sergeant temporarily takes on the role of an inspector) in a couple of days. Actually. It's the first time I'll have done that. This is all tied into the accelerated promotion thing."

I looked at her, puzzled. "Firstly, you'll be fine. Secondly, is that because you're a graduate?"

"No," she replied. "It's because I'm female. There's a whole tranche of us who are being pushed through to have more women in the top jobs. We get priority over the men in terms of promotion and opportunities."

I looked at her: "Is that legal, to promote people based on their sex?"

She said in a flat tone, "No, technically they can't, but they've found a loophole that allows them. I know it's bullshit, but I'm just going to ride this train until I get to where I want to go as head of a CID unit and then I'll stop. All this is so that they can have the next head of the Met be a woman. It's kind of on merit. It'll be the best female candidate, not the best candidate. It's not healthy, and definitely patronising. It shows they think that a woman won't make it on their own. So, for the sake of show, they'll help the process along. Their argument would be that they think women are being held back by the men, which is definitely sexist, to think I'd let anyone, male or female, hold me back."

I thought, *well it's not just at Hendon – this stupid, parasitic ideology has spread throughout the management of the police.*

She could see what I was thinking, and said, "Look, I know how dumb it is. Here's why: say you and I are competing for a job, and there's a positive discrimination policy favouring me. If a man loses out to a woman, he'll never know if it was down to ability or sex. The team won't know and, worst of all, she won't know. That devalues what she achieves, and breeds distrust, and resentment."

She wasn't finished, "The counter argument is that women have to compete in a deeply unfair system already due to male sexism. To be fair, they have a point sometimes. The real problem is that the rules and law say that you can't do that. So if we make the system biased to 'compensate' for that perceived sexism, which may or not be in play, we make it blatantly in favour of women. So no one can be sure if women achieved anything based on their ability. It's stupid!"

I looked at her, trying to get my head around it. They were making it sexist, to compensate for a system they thought was sexist, turning it from a system which states it expects people to be treated equally, but might fail due to individuals, into a system that doesn't even pretend to be fair.

I said, "Well, I think the only way to make things fairer is to set the rules to treat people equally, and monitor compliance."

She nodded: "Exactly. You can only have equality of opportunity, or equality of outcome, not both. I opt for equality of opportunity because people know where they stand, and you're most likely to get the best candidate."

We finished our coffee, and I resolved, A) to keep my head down and, B) to text her in a couple of days to wish her luck.

Tuesday was the first of a set of nights, and a couple of hours before I started, I sent a text to Nina, saying, "Good luck mate, you'll do great, because you are a star!" I received a reply back saying, "Oh God, I'm really nervous." My reply was, "Don't worry, what's the worst that could happen?" She replied, "Thanks, but don't tempt fate!"

As with most people, I have a number of different groups of friends I keep in touch with. There's my Essex teaching friends, my group of old friends from school, the football crowd, and the university crowd of gay friends (including Victoria). Occasionally, we'd meet up in various pubs or clubs. That was always a lot of fun. If you've never been out to a gay pub or club, the atmosphere is different. Honestly, I always found it to be less pressure. I'm not into the guys, and the women aren't into me.

I'd been contacted by Jason, one of that friends group, as they were going to meet up in a nightclub which was having a "gay" night, before. He wanted to know if the token 'straight' wanted a night out on the tiles. I had to decline, because I was working. Also, Victoria wasn't going, which was always a good reason for me to go. She was keeping a low profile after the Julia and Nina situation.

As I was driving in for the second of the nights, I felt my phone buzzing in my pocket. Probably Nina telling me about her shift. But it kept going off, and going off. *Nothing I can do about it*, I thought. *I'll wait until I get to work and check them then. Whoever it is will have to wait.*

I parked the 'hairdresser' car and walked in. I was tired of thinking about the situation between Victoria, Nina, Julia, and that inspector. *How are we going to sort that mess out?*

I made it up to the locker room. It was quiet, as I was nice and early. I set out my stuff and started to get changed. Then I checked my phone: twelve texts and twenty-two missed calls. *What the hell?* I looked down the list of calls, and it was all my gay friends: Stevie, Phil, Jason, Victoria, Cindy, Stu. I listened to the first message (from Jason), "Oh God, oh God, oh God, are you all right Richy, I can't get in touch with everyone. Oh no, oh please God. They blew up the night club. I hope you're OK ..."

At that point I heard crying and police sirens in the background.

I stopped, stunned. These were my friends, people I had known for ten years. I loved them. *At least Jason's OK, but what about the others? Who blew it up?* Then a thought hit me: Nina's nick covered that area. Nina's first day as an acting inspector, and all hell breaks loose. What was the last thing I said to her? "Don't worry, what's the worst that could happen?" Oh God, I tempted fate. It's my fault.

I checked the other messages, there was one from Phil "Are you all right? Are you all right? I was just down the street when it blew up. I can't get in touch with anyone. Oh go no, no, no! Why, why, why!? I hope you're all right. Call me, call me please. Oh God I hope everyone's OK ...". The sound of crying finished the call. I listened back to call after call after call like that. I read the messages, the same. I was so scared for my friends. I started shaking, and crying. I felt like someone had kicked me in the guts. *Why has someone done this? What kind of monster does this, targets people they've never met?*

I started making calls: "Jason, Jason, is that you mate? It's me, Richard. I'm OK, what about you?"

Reply: "Oh, thank God, thank God, no one can get in touch with you, I was so worried."

"What about everyone else? What about Phil, Stevie, Cindy or Stu?"

"I know Phil and Stevie are OK, they sent me messages ... but Cindy and Stu ... (crying in the background)."

"Jason, Jason, sweetheart, just keep trying. Chances are the mobile networks will be so busy calls can't get through. They'll be OK, hang in there."

Jason replied in between sobs, "You're right, I hope you're right. Wait, got to go; I've got another call. Keep in touch. Let me know if you hear anything."

I sat on the bench in the locker room and hugged myself, trying to calm myself down. I thought, *this is what it means to be more than you are. What defines you is not what you do when it's easy; it's what you do when it's hard.*

I took a deep breath and straightened up. Without thinking I found I had my great-grandad's whistle in my hand. Just think of the number of times he must have gone to work not knowing about his friends in the two world wars. If they can do it, so can I.

I washed my face in the sink, collected my stuff. 21:20 hours. If I wanted food, I'd better hurry. A quick sandwich and a coffee in the canteen, I'd have time for that. With more determination than I felt, I walked down to the canteen, bought a sandwich and sat down. Honestly, I didn't feel like eating, and my mind kept on going back to my friends. But if I didn't eat, the 02:00 hours crash would be even harder. But the sandwich (cheese salad) was even more tasteless and bland.

Lost in my thoughts, I didn't notice Alf walk in, and queue up at the counter. He started speaking to the whole canteen, in his usual foghorn of a voice, and I looked up, glad for the distraction from my dark thoughts.

He said, "Did you hear about them bombing the queer bar. Well at least they were targeting the right people. Maybe it'll stop a few more of those lot, to stop what they're doing. It ain't natural. I reckon Hitler had the right idea, bombing the East End. Look at the filth you see walking about on the streets. Trouble was, he was fifty years too early. Am I right!?"

There was silence: no one acknowledged or challenged it. Silence!

I didn't believe what I'd just heard. I dropped the food on the plate, and felt numb. All the times I'd defended the Met to my friends, who said how homophobic it was, and I'd said that didn't go on any more.

My world changed at that moment. Stopping the killing of people based on race, sex, sexuality, religion was precisely why I'd joined the police. But there I was in a police station, listening to someone say it was OK to target people based on their sexuality, while our fellow police officers were climbing through rubble, tending to the sick and dying. While the very people we were sworn to protect were fighting for their lives, or being treated in hospital with life-altering injuries, all for the crime of falling in love with people of the same sex.

My God! I'm in the wrong job. I don't want to be here, I can't be any part of this! I looked around to see if there had been any reaction. Nothing! Not one of the half a dozen officers in there had said or done a thing! Was I the only one who thought how bad it was. He hadn't been joking. He'd been serious, as if it were self-evident.

Then the wave of emotion hit me, that I'd been holding in check. I turned and ran from the canteen and up to the locker room, and cried, sitting there stunned, numb. I felt nothing. My whole world view had been turned upside down. The people I thought were the good guys didn't care.

I heard a noise in the corridor, and it was Robbie. He looked in, "Mate, what's up?"

I had to think. The decision I made then was huge. Did I break the unspoken rule, that you don't talk? Because everyone outside the rank and file police don't care, the senior management don't care, the public don't care, the media don't care. The only people you can rely on are your mates. Us versus the world. If you have a problem, you sort it out yourself, keep it inside the team.

Robbie could see I was struggling with something. He sat down next to me, "C'mon. Off the record, what's this about?"

OK, off the record, I just don't know what to do. I need a calmer, more objective head to help me.

Taking a deep breath, I explained the whole situation. I showed him the text messages, played the voice messages and told him what Alf had said.

He sat back and let out a long breath, "God man, that's ... what a mess. I am so sorry. When we get on duty, I'll do a quick check on the names of the casualties, and let you know, so at least you can tell your mates, either good or bad. Damn, this is a mess. Alf was so out of order, that bloody idiot. He's not a bad man, but ..."

I interrupted, barely able to hold in my growing anger. "Not a bad man? NOT A BAD MAN? He said it was OK to kill people because they were gay, while they're still being pulled out of the rubble. He said that in a police station, where the very people who are supposed to be preventing it are sitting, and no one, no one, says anything. FUCKING HELL, this is SO, SO, SO WRONG! This is what I joined to stop. To protect people, everyone. No one is more or less important than anyone else!"

I stopped and stared off into the distance. I wanted to quit there and then, just walk away from that dreadful organisation.

Robbie put his hand on my shoulder, bringing me back to reality. "I know mate, I know, but right now, tonight, there are people who need us. For all our faults, for all the ways in which we're broken as an organisation – useless, cowardly management, crap food, no money for anything – people still need us. And we can and do make a difference. I've seen the way you work; you help people. Don't walk away."

I stopped and thought. *He's right. For all I feel right now, he's right. But what to do tonight?* I needed to get out and work, to get out there and remind myself of the good I could do.

I nodded: "Thanks Robbie. You're right. You're so right! I need to get out and work, to concentrate on what I can do that's good and positive."

"What do you want to do about Alf then?"

I thought, and my anger started to fade. I looked at Robbie, "Right now, I don't know. I can't let this slide."

"I can understand that. It's up to you. I can have an unofficial word with him, and explain to him how out of line he was and how much he hurt you. Trust me, he won't do it again."

At that moment, I just wanted to go out and work. "OK Robbie. Right now, I think that'd be for the best. Let's get going. I want to get out on the streets and work."

Robbie nodded, and we went down and I started the shift. It was a busy one. Robbie, as good as his word, was in the control room, and private called me. Stu was on the casualty list with a nasty hand injury and other minor injuries. But he'd survive, and no one else was hurt.

Much later on, I had a text message from Nina saying, "You bastard!" I did tempt fate, I suppose.

I threw myself into my work, and tried to forget what had happened, simply as a way of coping. Keep moving, never stop.

A couple of nights after the bombing, it was a year since I'd started. My God, what a year! Would I have joined if I knew then what I know now? Irrelevant question. Could I carry on for another year, never mind the next twenty, until I reached retirement age? I managed to speak to Nina; it had actually brought us together a bit, and she eventually forgave me. Especially when I said, "Look mate, I don't know what you're complaining about; you'll get a medal for this. Trouble will be when they hand out the guest invites, and ask you if there's anyone special. You'd have to invite half of London."

I shan't write her reply, but it was spicy!

On the second to last night, Robbie took me to one side and told me Alf was really sorry he'd upset me. He didn't know I was gay? Oh, for the love of God! Only gay people should get upset when someone says gay people are OK to be blown up? Really?! I thanked Robbie and started the shift.

The first job was reports of a stabbing at a petrol station on Park Street's ground. They couldn't deal, but could we? I answered the call and Andy drove us over there.

I put us on scene, and as I jumped out of the car with the first aid kit in hand, I could see a couple of people inside the petrol station's little shop. I jogged over there and, as I entered, I saw the petrol cashier kneeling down next to a young man covered in blood. I heard the bell ring to indicate a car had pulled in, looked up and saw on the forecourt a car pulling in to get petrol. Really!? There's a police car with its lights on, and you still thinks it's a good idea to get petrol? Some people just don't care!

I went over to the young man, as Andy walked over to the cashier, who stood up and walked behind the till and engaged the petrol pump for the customer. Really? You're going to sell petrol with a man in a serious condition on the floor?

I looked down and recognised him: Tariq. He looked pale and really ill. He was lapsing in and out of consciousness. I felt around his torso, finding a wound. There were two stab wounds in his back. That wasn't good. It seemed like internal bleeding, and there's very little you can do for that in terms of first aid. I could only patch him up as best I could and hope the ambulance got there in time to get him into surgery and get the bleeding stopped.

As I was patching him up, I talked to him. "Tariq? Can you hear me, Tariq?"

He looked up at me for a moment, and with a flicker of recognition, he tried to say something. His lips moved, but instead of words, only a spray of blood. Possibly a punctured lung. I had no time to think about it, just tried to help him while we waited for the ambulance.

Andy was getting the VHS security tape, and getting the story from the cashier, who was still working, dispensing petrol and taking the money through the hatch next to him. One of the customers even asked him to get a drink for him. Really, it is true, no one cares!

When I heard the story later from Andy, there had been a queue for the till. Tariq had walked to the front and pushed in. The bloke behind him had taken offence, pulled out a knife and stabbed Tariq in the back a couple of times, then calmly turned around and walked out of the petrol station. Man, that is cold!

The ambulance arrived, and I went with him to the hospital, while Andy followed in the car. I needed to stay with him for continuity of evidence, if he died, which was very likely according to the way the ambulance crew were dealing with him. I called up the station and asked for his next of kin details from the custody record, then asked for them to send someone round to inform them, and relay them to hospital. Andy was redirected to do that. So it would just be me at the hospital.

They rushed him into ICU, where they started cutting off his clothes while I stood around trying not get in anyone's way. The ICU is a small, square, windowless internal room with cubicles separated from one another by curtains. It was shabby, but clean. There were bits of equipment all over the place. There were a number of casualties being treated, with blood and discarded, bloody tissue on the floor. There were about half a dozen doctors and nurses all wearing pinnies and gloves rushing around. It seemed like semi-organised bedlam. Nothing new there! I felt like I was a fly in the ointment, constantly trying to get out of the way. I wanted to go and stand outside, but I was required to stay within sight of Tariq. I also needed to collect any evidence.

I noticed a man who looked totally out of place. He was a tall, slim man in his mid-fifties, dressed immaculately in a three-piece suit with a dicky bow tie. He walked over to me and, in a cut-glass English accent, said, "Good evening officer. Can I help you?"

At this point, I wasn't fazed by much, and replied, "Good evening, Doctor. I'm with this (indicating Tariq) gentleman. I need his clothes and 10CCs of pre-transfusion blood."

He nodded, smiled and corrected me: "It's Mr, not Doctor. I'm the consultant surgeon. I'll be operating on him. Nurse Beck, would you be a dear and bag the gentleman's clothes and collect 10CC of his blood."

Turning back to me, he said, "They'll be ready for you after the operation, all bagged up. That reminds me, I'd best get scrubbed up for our friend here. I'll do my best with him, but I'm not hopeful. See you shortly, young man." At that he calmly walked out of the room. I thought, *wow, that's real poise; hell is breaking loose around you and he's calmness personified.*

Tariq was taken down to the operating theatre. I was provided with the evidence, and a large plastic bag to carry them.

A while later, the same surgeon walked out, this time in scrubs, saying, "I did my best, but I'm afraid we lost him. He had two knife wounds that nicked the heart and punctured both lungs. The blood loss was too severe. Have the family been informed?"

"I'm sorry to hear that. Yes, an officer was sent around to his next of kin's address while he was coming in the ambulance. I'll wait here for them."

"We'll move him into a side room, and a member of staff will come down and liaise with you to inform the family. Thank you for your help officer. We can't save them all."

I waited around and, a few minutes later, a young nurse (5'5", medium build, long, dyed-blonde hair, with roots showing, tied back) walked up: "Hi there. When the family arrive, please show them into this room (indicating a room to my left), and I'll get the doctor to inform them, then they can see him. OK?"

It was a clear instruction, not particularly friendly in tone, being very flat and emotionless.

"Thank you. Should I knock on the door when they arrive?"

She nodded and walked off. I thought, *this is going to be tough for the doctor and the family.*

A minute or so later, I heard a number of raised voices approaching, and round the corner came four people (two large Asian men in their twenties, and an older man and woman). They took one look at me and almost ran towards me. I had to suppress my instinct to back off, as my newly acquired sixth sense of danger was going into overdrive.

The two younger men stepped right up to me, forcing me to step back against the wall. They started shouting and were quickly joined by the other two. They shouted, "Where's Tariq? What have you done with him? Where is he? Where's my brother?"

I said, "Look, please, we need to go into this room here and wait for the doctor to talk to you?"

No dice! The two brothers grab me and pinned me against the wall.

The woman shouted, "Where is my son? Where is he? Is he all right?"

One of the brothers drew back his fist and shouted in my face, "Tell us where he is. Answer my mom! Is he all right? If you don't tell me now, I'll smash your face in."

I looked at him straight in the eye; he wasn't bluffing. Could I fight back? Yes, but with four of them, I'd really struggle, and do I really want to fight a grieving family? There was only one way out of it, and it wasn't good. I could see the fist move back, so it was either do something then or have my nose broken and head smashed against the wall.

"I'm really sorry, but Tariq died. He's dead. I'm really, really sorry."

The brothers released their grips, let me go and started to weep and shout. At that point the nurse I'd spoken to earlier walked out and ushered the family into the room. She then came outside and, in a really sharp and nasty tone, said quietly, "You fucking idiot! Why the hell didn't you wait as you were told. God you police are thick and insensitive. All you're good for is beating people up. I'll deal with it from here. At least one of us should be professional and do our jobs properly. Get out of my sight you waste of space."

I thought about catching up to her and explaining, in words of one syllable, where she was wrong. But I'd learnt. I let it slide. *If she wants to be an ignorant bitch, let her!*

I walked down the corridor to see Andy walking towards me. He said, "Have you seen the victim's family? As soon as they found out where he was, they took off."

"Yeah, they found me. I'll update Control when I get outside. He died on the operating table."

"That would have upset the family. AMEP (area murder squad) are downstairs; we'll no doubt meet them on the way out. Did you get the usual samples?" I nodded.

A short while later, when we bumped into the AMEP team, I updated them.

It wasn't until I finished another manic night shift, and was lying in bed trying to go to sleep, that I began to think of Tariq. Why had he not listened? Why didn't I get through to him? Could I have done more? Why can't we save them? Why must they continue the cycle of death? It was such a waste. Outside of the bravado, he was OK. I suddenly felt really sad about the futility of what I did.

That night, I eventually got to sleep, but all too soon the alarm was going off, and I was on my way in to start another night duty. I hoped this one would be better. The banter was the same as always, but honestly, I just wasn't into it as much as I was usually. I felt a little detached, and then came the call for volunteers to do the checks on the horses at the police stables (around the back of the station). The horses were looked after for sixteen hours of the day but, at night, were left comfortable in their stables. Night duty were often asked to check on them. Without thinking, I put up my hand to volunteer. Mel was the only other one. That was sorted: the "charm offensive" would check on the horses. Mel and I walked out and got in her panda car. We tended not to get too many of the highest priority calls in the panda. That suited me that night, and a chance to say hello to the gee-gees always cheered me up.

As we were driving to the first call, I looked at Mel: "I didn't know you liked horses."

She glanced at me and replied: "I was just thinking the same thing. What got you into them?"

"I grew up in the countryside, and my godmother used to have a stables, and race horses. I was about two when they first sat me on a pony. I didn't ride it, but they took a picture of me, grinning from ear to ear. I rode horses off and on, whenever I got the chance. I love horses. What about you?"

She smiled: "I grew up in the country and my uncle and aunt had a farm and stables. I'd ride their horses as often as they'd let me, then I took riding lessons. They're lovely creatures. The ones here in the stables are such sweeties, huge but very gentle. You'll love them."

I smiled and for the first time in a while could feel myself relax. We continued for the first half of the shift, doing some of the less crazy calls, until it was time to check on the stables. We let ourselves in through the side gate.

There were six stalls, with four horses in them. All but one were either lying down asleep or standing asleep. Only one, a huge grey, looked up at us when we came in. I walked around and checked on the sleeping horses.

They were all fine. Mel was saying hello to the grey. "This is Titan. He's my favourite. Don't tell the others. He's such a cutey. He loves mints. Have you got any?"

I dug around in my pockets and found some extra strong ones, placed one on the flat of my hand and held it out to him. He slowly moved to investigate who this new person was, then very gently took the mint from my hand. I don't know if you've ever fed a horse by hand, but it's an odd feeling as you feel their breath from their nose tickle your hand. He chomped on it, and he harrumphed and crunched it down more quickly. He'd clearly not been expecting a strong mint, but seemed to like it, as he moved his head over to see if I had another. I did. I took the opportunity to stroke the side of his head and lean so I could scratch behind his ear. He loved it, as his ear twitched.

Mel said, "He likes you; you've made a friend."

"He likes my extra strong mints, more likely. Are we really supposed to be feeding them?"

Mel shrugged, "Not officially, but I asked one of the riders once, and they said it wouldn't do any harm as long it was only one or two."

There's something majestic about a big horse when they stand right next to you. There's a type of trust you have with an animal that is several times larger and stronger than you, but is also so calm and gentle. Horses always help me calm down. I forgot all the struggles and trials I'd had over the last week. All too soon it was over, and we said goodbye to Titan, and his friends.

I said to Mel, "I'll definitely volunteer to do this again. They are such beautiful beasts."

She smiled, "Yes, they are. It's really nice to work with someone who loves horses as much as I do."

She grinned, and off we went to the next call. It was an attempted suicide. When I took the address over the radio, I groaned. Not Roxanne, not again? We had been insanely busy for the last hour, and we were late to arrive, behind the ambulance, which was unusual. That's not having a dig at the LAS, but there are far more police cars than ambulances so, nine times out of ten, we arrived first.

As we pulled up, Roxanne was being taken off on a stretcher, and her mom was nervously following. This time there appeared to be far more urgency than before.

Mel said she'd follow in the panda, as I should go in the ambulance. I boarded, and this time Roxanne was unconscious. There was an evidence bag with empty pill and vodka bottles in it. It wasn't looking good.

I spoke to her mom, who looked at me with empty, hollow eyes. She took hold of my arm and said in a flat tone, "I didn't get home in time. I was late, and I think Roxanne had taken the tablets earlier. Why did you take so long to get here? If only I hadn't done the overtime at the shop, if only I'd been home earlier. She'll be OK, won't she? The hospitals are really good, they'll save her."

I did my best to comfort her, without telling her Roxanne would survive. I didn't know. I asked her if she had her sister's phone number so we could get her to come to the hospital. She provided it and I got Control to call her.

Roxanne was rushed into the ICU. Mel stayed with Roxanne's mom, while I (for continuity of evidence) stayed with Roxanne. The staff were working on her and one of them said, "Get the crash cart, now!"

Quickly, a cart with paddles was moved over, and they closed the curtains. It didn't look good.

About twenty minutes later, one of the ICU team came over. "Are you with the young lady over here?" He pointed at Roxanne.

"Yes, I am. She's Roxanne Templeton."

The ICU member of staff was a young man who looked no older than my old A level students. He looked tired, with hollow cheeks and a pasty face. He said, "I called it 01:23 hours. Are you in contact with her next of kin?"

"Yes, her mom is waiting in reception with one of my colleagues."

"OK, I'll get a room free and do the notification. Does she have anyone to support her?"

"Her sister has already been called, and is on her way."

"Good. They'll tidy her up, while I'm talking to the mom. I'll take her through. You'd better inform the coroner. We'll keep her here until they pick her up. OK?"

I nodded and thanked him. As I walked to reception, I thought how matter-of-fact it all was. We were just about to destroy this woman's world, and it was just routine. I'm not blaming the doctor. They were really busy, it was the middle of the night, Lord knows when this poor lad had last slept, and he'd just lost a patient.

I went through, and the doctor appeared, and took her mom off to give the death message. Fortunately, her sister had just arrived, so she'd have support. But her mom knew, as soon as she saw my face. It was heartbreaking. Trust me, there's a certain look only a mother gives you when you tell them their child is dead. That absolute emptiness in their stare. If you see it, you won't ever forget it. That's not to say fathers don't suffer too, I know they do, but still, that look, I will never forget.

We spent the rest of the night dealing with that call. When we finally dropped off Roxanne's mom and aunt at her aunt's house, her mom took my arm and said, "Thank you for helping my little Roxie. You were kind to her, and I know she appreciated it. You're a good man."

As we went back to the nick, neither of us two chatterboxes felt like talking. I just felt numb and exhausted. There was nothing left in me at that moment, rather like that young doctor earlier. I made my way home, and fell into bed, only stirring when the alarm went off, and back to work for another night.

When I got in, I found I was rostered with Sergeant Darling. I hadn't worked with him on the cars, and I was looking forward to someone new. We had a busy first half to the night, and popped over to Ham Lane to have a refs break and a bagel. We parked up in a side street, and I started to feel really tired. The sergeant said, "Richard, I've been wanting to speak to you. You don't seem your normal self. What's up?"

I could feel my self-control starting to go. It was around the worst time, between 02:00 hours and 03:00 hours, when you drop, and I could feel all the things that had happened to me over the last few weeks piling on top of me. This was just the release. I couldn't hold it in any more.

"Sarge, I've been really struggling with some of the calls I've been dealing with."

I explained about Tariq, about Roxanne, but I kept from mentioning the bombing of the bar. We talked for a few minutes, and the sergeant said, "Look Richard, you can't save them all, mate. We're police officers, not God. People have free will, and if they choose to destroy themselves, there's nothing we can do. And beating ourselves up about it won't change anything."

"You're right. It's just Roxanne, the system just couldn't save her. It let her down, we let her down, I let her down!" I could feel tears beginning to come. I was so tired, I just couldn't stop them.

He looked at me: "There's something else, isn't there? I know there is. I can't help if you won't tell me."

That was it; I just couldn't stop myself. It was a decision that would damage Robbie's career, break up a team, and be the start of the end of my career, if I'd only known it.

I, like a foolish kid, blurted it all out about the club bombing, the frantic phone calls and text messages, and me speaking to Robbie. As soon as I said it, I knew I'd made a mistake. I wanted so much to take it back, but I couldn't. That is a decision I think about every day. Some days I think it was right, sometimes that it was wrong.

I had just set into motion a series of events I now had no control over. The sergeant was very kind, and truly horrified at what I told him. He said: "Don't worry, Richard, this will be dealt with properly. The guy Alf was talking about, and 'targeting the right people', he also went after Black people in Brixton, and Asians in Brick Lane. So he essentially said that Black people, Asian people and gay people were subhuman, and it didn't matter if they died. That, Richard, is not even slightly OK. You were absolutely right to tell me. Robbie should have reported it. It won't go well for him because of this. You are courageous to report this, and the Met will do its best to protect you. You will no doubt be a target for some of the idiots' backlash."

Even in my dog-tired and battered state, my heart sank. *Oh God, what have I just done?* I'd unleashed the anti-racist attack dogs on Alf and Robbie. *Why am I so STUPID!* I tried to stop him from reporting it, but he wasn't having any of it. I honestly just wanted to dig a hole and crawl into it.

I finished the rest of the shift, the last one of the set of nights. The following day was an early, and I was booked into to be gaoler at Earlham. Just before lunch, I was called up to the superintendent's office, where Sergeant Darling was sitting. He explained what I had told him the night before. The superintendent asked me if this was correct. What could I do? Lie to him in front of my sergeant? Really!?

I quietly nodded, and confirmed what he'd said. Complaints were called in. Alf was sacked. Robbie was disciplined. Inspector Manning was being moved to a different team.

I'd be getting a new reporting sergeant, and the relief would be getting a new inspector. It was Inspector Charles Thompson, the married man whom Nina had an affair with. *Oh great. Talk about frying pan to the fire!*

I had just dropped a nuclear bomb on my team. God, what had I done!? I checked my calendar: exactly one year since I started.

Suffice to say, when word spread, it garnered different reactions from people. Some agreed with me, some disagreed and didn't like the way I'd gone about it. Others just plain hated my guts. We had correspondence trays, with our names on them. From then on, I regularly had cigarettes or 'fag' butts put in, i.e. saying I was a 'fag'. Nice! When I went for my officer safety reassessment course, one of the female instructors tried to fail me. Fortunately, my relief sussed what was going on, and stood up for me, and had the chief assessor reassess me. Lo and behold, I passed.

I had numerous abusive comments from other members of staff that I ignored. Fortunately, my team, although divided in their response, did support me, for the most part. One of the most vocal of my critics was Jamie Codsworth, the loud Yorkshireman who had given me the nickname. He was the one who started calling me the "Griefmeister", i.e. the master of grief or trouble. This stuck. Oh well, I'd heard worse. He really had a problem with me. He was ex-military and thought I'd betrayed the team. The worst thing was, part of me agreed with him. I had bitten the hand that fed me.

I just did the best I could. I put my head down and worked, and worked, and worked, to the point that, when I'd been on the team a year,

Manning called me in and said: "I have to say, despite your recent difficulties, you've worked as hard as anyone on the team. Do you know who has done more arrests than anyone on this borough? You. Do you know who's second only to The Law in terms of tickets? You. You have worked really hard, Richard. Well done."

A number of people on the team commented on it. Despite everything, I was earning some respect, and after it had quietened down, a number of people from around the nick said they respected what I'd done.

I had reason to go to see Alan, so went to his office. He gave me an odd look when I walked in, and said, "Oh, the troublemaker returns. You stir up trouble wherever you go, don't you?"

I replied wearily, "Guilty as charged m'lord."

He looked at me seriously and said, "You made a right pig's ear of the way you dealt with that, didn't you!?" I nodded, and he continued, "A lot of good people were caught up in what happened who didn't deserve it. However, you did stand up for the gay community. I for one appreciate it. How's your friend, by the way?"

I was a bit surprised. Not too many people were 'out' in the police. I think the only reason he hadn't mentioned it before was that, to him, it wasn't relevant. When it was, he'd mentioned it. Fair enough!

I replied, "Stu is recovering. He's had a few operations on his hand and it looks like he's through the worst of it. Thank you. Honestly, I was petrified for my friends, because I knew a few of them were going to meet up there. If I could turn back the clock and redo things, I'd still do it, but differently."

Alan said, "That's a fair assessment. Nina told me about the text that tempted fate. Really, Richard, 'what's the worst that could happen?' What were you thinking?" I agreed, and we laughed and chatted.

In the last briefing before we had a few days off, the inspector said in parade, "Right folks, I don't know if you've seen, but there was a rail crash. We've been asked to do security for the memorial on the paperwork day when we get back. So, remember to bring your hi-vis jackets, and we parade at 08:00 hours sharp. Don't be late. Otherwise, it's double doughnuts."

There were a few boos and cheers. The reference to doughnuts was that, if you were late, it was tradition that you'd have to buy the whole relief (twenty-five, including the civvy staff) doughnuts, out of your own pocket. Now this wasn't too expensive, but it was the stick you got from members of the public when you (in uniform) had to buy twenty-five doughnuts. That was the real punishment. Believe it or not, this practice is still common today.

After the shift, we had a few days off, then back to the aide at the rail crash. Thankfully, everyone was on time and we jumped into a small coach. I made sure I had all the kit I needed. No chance to pop back to the nick, as we were travelling halfway across London. There was plenty of banter in the coach on the way there. I think it was to distract us from what was likely to be a long and emotionally charged day, with all the grieving families, and the media crawling all over the place.

Eventually we arrived, and debussed into the supermarket's car park. This had been the first help the poor survivors had, when they climbed up the steep bank from the wrecked trains. They had been given first aid in the car park, right next to the embankment. That was where the memorial service was going to be held.

The atmosphere was really odd. The shop was still open, so you had people getting their weekly shopping, pushing their trolleys around. Then you had the police, some in navy search overalls on body recovery (I didn't envy them), various family members and friends, and of course the media.

We set out and went to various positions to provide an outer security cordon around the site of the memorial and the recovery site, to stop the media getting too close and filming the body recovery efforts, or getting in the search team's way.

I was tasked with getting down as near to the track as I could on a walled path. I was given strict instructions to stop journalists from climbing the stone wall to be able to take footage of the recovery operation with zoom lenses, as they might be able to film the body parts recovery. I started hearing mobile phones ringing. It was carried on the wind, and you could just make it out. Odd!

I stood there, alone, for a while, then a male and female film crew arrived. There was a 30-something, well-dressed female presenter, and the male cameraman of about the same age. The man was struggling down with a large camera and tripod, and a small folding ladder.

As they set up, the man, who was taller, could see over the wall, whereas the woman couldn't. I anticipated the radio call (we were being watched on CCTV), and walked over to the two journalists.

I said, "Hello folks." They both turned to look at me, the man with a friendly smile, the woman with a scowl. But before I could speak, my radio crackled and a message from control came through: "PT272, from Bronze (senior management), stop that film crew from filming. They were told they couldn't film there. Move them on."

They had clearly heard the message, and I replied, "Bronze from PT272, received, and will comply."

I shrugged. "I'm really sorry, folks, that was a direct order from the senior officer who's in charge of the whole operation. I'm going to have to ask you to leave."

The man nodded sympathetically and started to pick up his kit. The woman said, "This is ridiculous. I have a right to film here. You are being really stupid! I'm going to complain about you. I demand your number."

I looked on impassively, "My number is PT272. I'm afraid there's nothing I can do. You heard I've had a direct order to move you on."

She came up close, and made a big show of writing down my shoulder number. At that point, a small boy of about eight or nine walked down, holding hands with a man. The boy broke away and ran down to the film crew, and tried jumping up and down to see over the high wall. The film cameraman put down his stuff, put the ladder up against the wall, and helped the lad look over. It was OK; he couldn't see anything really nasty without a long lens. Technically, I should have stopped them, but thought better of it. Who knew if the kid had lost family in the crash?

The man went down and collected the boy, who hugged the cameraman, and the two walked off. When the two were out of earshot, I said to the film crew, "That was a lovely thing to do."

The cameraman nodded, but the woman said, "Well WE'RE not all monsters. We CARE about people. We don't slavishly follow orders. We try to do good. We don't go around beating people up, and we're not the racist ones."

She turned and stormed off. I stood impassively, and the cameraman gave me a sympathetic smile and shrugged. He then silently mouthed the words, "Thank you." I nodded in acknowledgement back.

Wow, this day was going to be fun! A short while later, we had the call to go up and provide security for the service for the families. This was a service with a number of ministers from different faiths to say their piece. I thought, *that's a good idea, all coming together in times of grief.*

As I took my place, with my back to the car park, people were still doing their shopping, and pushing their trolleys a few feet away behind me. No one stopped and I could distinctly hear people saying, while the service was on, "'Ere luv, have you remembered the peas?" "No. I thought you'd got some last week when you went to the shops." "Oh, you are stupid! Go back and get some."

Then we had a message on our turned-down radios. "To all units, we've had a bomb threat phoned in, saying they're going to blow up the memorial service. We believe it to be a hoax, so the service will go ahead."

I thought, *what kind of sick person does that?* Sometimes words fail me. Then, to top it off, the same journalist lady who had been rude to me before had her phone ring loudly during the middle of the service, when one of the ministers was speaking. She then answered it, and spoke loudly to whoever was on the other end. All the while, the families were crying and hugging each other due to the moving words of the service.

At the conclusion of the service, a number of irate family members were speaking to the female journalist, and let's just say they weren't best impressed. She turned to one of my colleagues for protection, and was escorted out of harm's way. I wondered if that day could get any more messed up.

As I made my way back to my post on the walled pathway, an older couple stopped me and were clearly one of the grieving families. The woman said, "Thank you, for the respect you showed. What do the people in the blue jumpsuits do?"

I looked, at one of the men she was referring to and said, "They're the search teams."

I deliberately didn't say they were the body part recovery teams. I thought that would have been grossly insensitive. The woman looked at me blankly for a moment, and the man with her gently touched her arm and said, "They're trying to find the people, and any evidence from the crash."

"What, like survivors?"

He sadly shook his head. "After a week, there'll be no survivors."

She looked down, and then the penny dropped. She walked over to one of the search team and said, "Thank you so much. My little girl died in there. You're doing such a difficult job. God bless you."

She hugged him, with tears rolling down her cheeks. I had to stop myself from crying. The man went over, and gently turned her around and she continued crying on his shoulder. He then looked at the search team member and mouthed, "Thank you."

The search team member nodded and mouthed, "You're welcome."

I gently put my hand on her arm. She looked up at me, and I gave them both a sympathetic look, and walked off with the search team guy. He was about my age, and looked tired, and had black marks on his blue suit.

When we were out of earshot, I said, "I take my hat off to you, mate. That can't be an easy job."

He nodded a weary nod, and let out a breath, saying, "Thanks, you're not wrong. We keep finding mobile phones, and they keep going off, so we line them up on one of the rails. We don't want to turn them off, because it might give people false hope, if they get a different tone. But honestly, mate, yesterday when I got home, my wife's phone went off with the same ringtone as one of the phones on the track, and it sent shivers down my spine. Every time I hear one of the ringtones, it'll bring me right back here."

I put my hand on his shoulder and said quietly, "I honestly don't know how you can do it. You have more courage than I do. But you're doing such a great thing for the families. God bless you!"

He stopped and looked at me, "Thank you. God bless you too."

I don't know why I said that. I don't normally mention God but, in times of real stress and anguish, people do rely on their faiths. I just didn't realise how much it meant to me.

I was lost in my thoughts, and stood on my lonely post, with no one around, just watching the slow, methodical searching of the twisted, mangled remains of what had been trains and passengers. It's funny what thoughts come into your head sometimes, and a line from Shakespeare popped into my mind: "from his mother's womb untimely ripped".

Sometimes you feel a connection with the past. People have been dealing with death in all its forms for thousands of years.

Then my radio buzzed. It was a private call. I looked around to make sure no one could eavesdrop, and pushed the receive button. A familiar voice met my ears: "Hello Richard. It's Paige here. How are you doing, hun?" Of all the times, when I needed her most, when I was really struggling and having a truly crap day (not as bad as the families), she was there like my little guardian angel.

"Hello Shorey. It's so great to hear from you. You said we'd meet up again. I didn't expect it to be like this. How are you doing?"

"It's Mrs Collins now. Brian made an honest woman out of me. I saw your name on the list, and made an effort to call you. How have you been?"

"I'm so glad you did contact me. Street duties was tough, but I'm OK. What about you? Congratulations, by the way. You do realise half the male members of the Met are in mourning now that you're spoken for."

She giggled, and it was just like we were back in Hendon, in a different life.

"It's good to hear your voice again, Richard. I'm doing fine, thanks. There's a lot you're not telling me. I have my spies, and I knew it would be hard for you. But I'm glad you stuck with it. We had a great time at

Hendon. Listen, I've got to go, but remember what I said: whatever happens, don't give up. You're a good man, Richard, even if you are a bloody fool at times. Take care and goodbye, hun."

I almost started crying, but held it back: "Thank you, Paige. You're an absolute bloody star! Good luck, and goodbye."

That was the last time I spoke with her, and I kind of knew our paths wouldn't cross again. Her words from Hendon came back to me: make new friends, and move on. Well, at least something good had come of that day.

We finished our duties at the scene and drove back to Park Street in the rattly old police carrier. The usual banter was subdued. I think we were tired and, honestly, what we'd been part of had taken its toll on us. As we were travelling through London, it was standard practice to tune one of the radios to pick up the local borough's frequency, to stop us from blundering into an active operation, or driving past a call, as this tends to annoy the public, i.e. they call police, are told there are no cars in the area, and then we trundle past.

So, as we went through Sloane Square in Westville, a call came out: "Units free to deal, we have reports of a vagrant in Sloane Square, near the fountain. He's apparently causing a disturbance."

I looked at the skipper: "Do you want me to deal, Sarge?"

The skipper nodded and we slowed down, and he called out on the radio: "Bravo Sierra, this is PS43, from the PT relief serial. We're in Sloane Square now. Do you want us to deal?"

After a slight pause: "PS43, yeah, that would be great thanks. We're down to the bare bones tonight."

The skipper replied: "Can you put us on scene? We're pulling up now. We'll keep you updated."

I made my way over to the fountain. It had cooled down since I'd got into the van, and I could feel a slight shiver through my uniform. Sure enough, there was a man sitting with his feet in the fountain. As I got closer, I noticed he had old clothes on, and was apparently washing his feet. I suddenly had the feeling I was being watched, and instinctively looked up and noticed that a number of flats overlooked where we were. I guessed one of those might be where the call had originated.

I said: "Hello Sir. Are you all right?"

He turned around, and I could see he was a slim man, in his forties, with unkempt black hair, and thick stubble on his face. He smiled at me, and with a world-weary look, said: "Sorry officer, I was just washing my feet. I'll be gone in a minute. I waited 'til there was no one about; I didn't want to upset anyone."

Something about the way he spoke, and the way he held himself, seemed familiar. I replied: "Don't worry, Sir, we just had a call to someone causing trouble. You're the only one here, but I don't see you causing trouble. Is everything all right? Do you live around here?"

It was a polite question. By then, it was fairly plain, from the dirty backpack next to the fountain, that this man was likely to be homeless. In the army, they are taught to keep themselves clean. I had seen ex-soldiers washing their feet before. Then it came to me – backpack, military. This guy was likely to be an ex-squaddie.

As he slowly turned to move his feet out of the water and start drying his feet off, he said: "Thank you officer. I will be out of your hair just as soon as I can get my kit together and ship out. I haven't been causing any trouble. There's no one about."

I took a chance: "Do you mind if I ask if you served in Her Majesty's armed forces, Sir?" I used the formal form of the question, as most servicemen I'd met had more respect for Her Majesty than any other form of authority.

He stopped, and smiled a genuine smile for the first time, and said: "Yes, I did, officer. Ten years, man and boy. Am I in any trouble? I am homeless. When I left the army, I struggled to adjust to civvy street. I don't want no trouble, officer."

"No Sir, you're not in any trouble, but do you want to dry your feet off, and come over with me to the van to warm up for a minute, and we can have a chat to see if we can help you. It's cold, and only likely to get colder."

I stood patiently, and smiled at him. He looked up at me for a moment, as if to check my motives, then dried his feet, put on his boots, collected his belongings, and we walked over to the van.

We opened the side door, and I ushered him in to sit down. The others looked at me quizzically for a moment. But, very soon, as we talked to the gent, they twigged. The ex-servicemen got it straight away. Even though we were all tired, and just wanted to get home, they could see this guy needed help.

The old war stories started coming out, and it became clear that this guy was ex-army, had seen combat, and had suffered PTSD, and had insufficient support when he'd really needed it.

I suddenly thought of the law we could arrest him under: The Vagrancy Act 1824, brought in after the Napoleonic wars to 'deal with' the large number of ex-army men who had suffered injuries (physical, and mental) and been thrown out on the streets. Then the great and the good, instead of helping them, had passed laws to have them arrested. Out of sight, out of mind. I looked around at the expensive flats, and thought: *almost 175 years later, and very little has changed.*

We were going to help this guy, if I had any say in the matter. I called up Bravo Sierra on the radio, and asked if they could check if there were any hostels that had any vacancies that night, and if they could call the special police–army helpline.

A short while later, they got back to me, saying, yes, there was a hostel just around the corner, and patched me through to the helpline.

I explained the situation to the officer I spoke to, and let them know where the man would be that night and the following morning. He said he'd see what he could do to help.

I then went back to speak to the man, and was glad to see he was eating the spare sandwiches we had, and seemed to have lifted his spirits somewhat. I explained to him what I'd done, and asked the skipper if we could drop him off on the way home. He agreed.

The man looked shocked, and soon enough we were outside the hostel. I went in, explained the situation, and the staff said he could stay, once I'd assured them he was OK.

I went back out to the van, and noticed the ex-military lads had had a whip-round and were quietly handing him a bit of cash.

As he got out of the van (pockets stuffed with the spare bags of crisps and cans of coke), he stopped and looked at me, almost teary-eyed, and said: "Thank you. I just don't know what to say. The lads and you, the banter, it was like I was back in the regiment. I don't know what to say. When I saw you over by the fountain, I thought I'd be spending a night in the cells. Thank you!"

He stuck out a cold and grubby hand. I shook it warmly and said: "If no one else says it, thank you for your service, Sir. I can't do much to help you, and it's not much. Please take care, and look after yourself."

He slowly made his way into the hostel. As we drove off, I thought that, despite all the improvements and progress we've made, still people slip through the cracks. I had tried to join the army as a young man. If I had, might I have been in his shoes? What's the saying? "There, but for the grace of God, go I."

The rest of the weary trip was uneventful. I did think, *what would it be like to police up here in Westville? That would be a totally different experience.*

As the end of 1999 was rapidly approaching, preparations began for the millennium, including extra anti-terrorist patrols, and going through alternate, old paperwork systems if the dreaded Y2K bug wiped out the computers. We had the 'Doomsday' speech, which explained that if the food in the shops dried up, you've got about three days to sort it out or they'll be rioting. Never get between an angry parent and food for their hungry kids! Then, even with all the police resources, we'd be losing control of the streets within a few weeks, and then the army could only control people for a few months. So, essentially, we were months away from absolute anarchy, if there was no food in the shops due to the Y2K computer bug. None of us believed it, but hey ho!

The IRA had still been busy, even after the 1997 Good Friday Agreement. They were still putting in false bomb threats, and timing how long we took to get there, to work out where to put a bomb for the most effect. The idea that they were only going after economic targets is bullshit. I'm sorry, but if you bring a homemade bomb into a city of ten million people, you're an evil terrorist in my book! I'm telling you, as a science teacher, making something go bang isn't too difficult. Making it go bang where and when you want is a lot more difficult.

We were kept busy running around checking suspect packages on our patch, usually more than a dozen a day.

I remember the first time I walked up to a suspect package was near a Tube station, and it was an abandoned shopping bag someone had called in. I turned my radio to 'safe' mode, in case it set the bomb off, took a deep breath and walked to what someone thought was a bomb. Instinct was telling me to be walking in the other direction very fast. Duty was forcing me forwards. I approached the bag. The top was closed up, so I'd have to pull the top apart to see its contents. I slowly pulled the two parts apart, and looked inside. It was someone's discarded rubbish of old coke cans, wrappers, old shopping bags. Phew! Not that I really knew much about bombs. We'd had an hour-long lecture showing slides of "This is a bomb", "This isn't a bomb."

I worked on the 'bomb car', with 'special equipment'. The bomb car was a regular response car that, if it was free, went to suspect packages, and the special equipment was two colours of police tape: red for the inner cordon, and blue for the outer. Ah, the Met and its extra cheapness!

Suffice to say, by the time you checked your 100th suspect package, you were a bit blasé about it.

But we were all called to an intelligence brief by SB (special branch – the anti-terrorist branch). This consisted of a lecture given by an older man (fifties, medium build, balding, 5'8" – hardly James Bond) with a strong London accent, who said: "Good morning, ladies and gents. During the millennium festivities the great and the good, i.e. Her Majesty the Queen, and some politicians (a few chuckles, including me) will be having a knees up in the plastic pimple, also known as the dome."

More chuckles. I was glad it wasn't going to be a boring and dry presentation. He continued, "So, it's a huge target for every lunatic and wannabe Marxist revolutionary. Those we can deal with. Unfortunately, the IRA are seemingly prepared to ignore the Good Friday Agreement, to blow people up in London, for the millennium. They plan to set up a number of mortars in builders' yards and other premises that overlook the dome from our side of the Thames. They need a clear view of their target.

The Thames affords them that view, so they are busting a gut to do this, as killing Her Majesty the Queen is the thing they want to achieve most in the world because, somewhere in their twisted, tiny minds, killing the most beloved monarch of tens of millions of people, who's sat on the throne for more than forty years, will bring them independence, and not the hatred and condemnation of half the world."

He waited until that sank in. If they killed Her Majesty the Queen, the backlash against them wouldn't be worth thinking of.

He continued: "Fear not: that's what we and you are going to stop. We've got twenty-four-hour helicopter support, ARVs, plain-clothed, armed SB. And a certain regiment from Herefordshire (SAS) are hiding in the shadows, and EXPO (army bomb disposal), the RAF for air cover and, if needed, army snipers on standby. But the most amazing thing: the top brass have even given us an unlimited overtime budget."

There was broad laughter at this point. Even SB understood the Met and its extra cheapness.

He waited until we'd calmed down, and said: "What we are going to do is have a number of traffic cars going to all the premises that overlook the dome. They'll be staffed by one Rat. Oh, sorry, did I say that out loud? I meant traffic officer, a local officer. That's volunteers on overtime, and armed backup if needed. They'll be doing this twenty-four hours a day for the weeks up to the millennium. So if you're up for any of that, protecting Her Majesty the Queen, and some politician or other, and most importantly help us, let us know, and we'll put you on a rota, whenever your shifts allow. Thanks folks."

I didn't need to be asked twice. Protecting Her Majesty from terrorists – where do I sign up! I put my name forward, and duly did a couple of shifts, in a nice, comfy, dual-zone climate-controlled car, with a helicopter above, and armed backup. It was great fun going from builders' yard to builders' yard checking, and checking, and checking.

The relief Christmas party had arrived. It was at a hired hall, and promised to be an entertaining night. Everyone was going to be there, and it meant I'd get a chance to chat to some people I didn't often work with. Two of them were Angus (a short Scottish guy), who I dreaded working with because he was hyper-critical and ended up shouting (it's a Glaswegian thing) at me for eight hours telling me how I'd messed up, and Freddie, a tall ex-squaddie, who was loud and obnoxious and openly boasted about cheating on his pregnant wife. This, contrary to popular belief, did not endear him to the vast majority of us blokes, who thought he was a scumbag for doing so. Some of us had a word and told him what he did in his personal life was up to him, but we didn't appreciate him boasting about it. During the party, it became clear that someone had let Freddie's wife know about his infidelity. Not cool all around. I concentrated on dancing and getting drunk. Late in the evening, I wandered outside to clear my head, only to see Angus lying on the ground with Freddie holding his knuckles and standing over him. I reversed course and had a quiet word with Campbell, who collected Jamie, and we all went outside, where Angus and Freddie were.

It became clear that Freddie thought Angus was the one who'd told his wife. A few days later, I found out questions were going to be asked about this, as Angus had suffered a broken jaw and would be off work for a while.

Pre-empting the questions, and having learnt from the nightclub bomb incident, I got Angus's telephone number and phoned him. He answered the phone, but couldn't talk easily because of the injury. I said "Hello Angus. I hope you don't you mind me calling you. Silly question, how are you feeling?"

He said, through clenched teeth, "How the fuck do you think I'm feeling?"

I replied, "OK, I'll cut to the chase. You and I don't get along, and you give me a hard time. But you're a colleague, and say for instance, someone on the relief had hurt you, I think that'd be out of order. Regardless of the shit I'd get, I know the difference between right and wrong. And I'd stand up for you. Now I've heard there's going to be questions asked. What are your thoughts?"

There was a pause, then, "Nothing happened. I slipped over and cracked my jaw on the step. Freddie was helping me up."

"OK, Angus mate, if you're sure. But understand, no matter what happens with this, I have your back 100 per cent. No one is above the law! Regardless of any backlash that comes my way. OK, it is your choice, and I respect whatever decision you make."

There was a pause, then, "Really, thank you Richard. It means a lot. Thank you! But I fell over, OK!"

"OK mate, if that's what happened."

When Robbie asked me about the incident, I didn't lie. I just said I hadn't seen anything other than Angus on the ground, which was true.

As we got closer to the new millennium, the backup plans were fully in place, in case the computers went down. Every system had its old paperwork system dusted off, and rolled out. If the radios went down, we'd use notes, and drive back and forward to the station. We had storm lanterns, in case the power went out. At the end of the 20th century, we were readying systems that hadn't been used in decades. But it proved we could do it, no matter what. We could still police, and protect people.

We were on nights over the millennium, but the other shifts would be available to assist. Old police stations were opened up. It was, as they say, all hands to the pumps, unless of course you were senior officers, then not so much. We looked hard, and no one could find their names on the shift pattern. It did make me laugh. When the Met was really being tested, the senior management were at home, because they're not really needed the rest of the time.

One of our sergeants, (Sean) Deacon, was doing the postings, and he pulled me to one side, and said he'd posted me in custody on the millennium as gaoler, saying he knew I worked hard, and it was going to get crazy in there. He wanted someone with him who'd stay calm. I'd not worked with him much, but he seemed cool, so I took it at face value. Did I think it was possible that he didn't want me on the streets? Maybe.

The night before New Year's Eve, I remember standing on the river bank, looking at the Millennium Dome across the Thames. It had lights shining on it, different colours for each night of the week. It cost hundreds of millions of pounds to build, that we paid. It now cost millions of pounds to provide security for and, at the start of the new millennium, a Labour leader, the party of the working class, would be having a huge party in a building that cost a fortune to build, with all his mates and all his favourite bands playing. Within sight across the Thames was one of the most deprived boroughs in Britain, where people had to live eight or nine to a two-bedroom flat, where there were daily gang fights and schoolkids were getting hooked on heroin at school, where there were needles and used condoms on the streets where kids played. I voted for this guy, but I was done with him. I'm no socialist, but my God, couldn't he have found a better, more symbolic way to bring in the new millennium, by showing his solidarity with the very people his party were set up to help? Why did we need the dome? Weren't there enough historic buildings in London already?

I thought that at least I knew where I stood with the Tories, who never pretended to be anything other than the party of privilege. At least they were bloody honest about not giving a shit, not lying about it like Blair!

Wow, I thought, *this police culture indoctrination is really working!*

The following day came – the last day of the 20th century. Either the computers were going to crash and spread chaos and panic, or everything would be OK.

I arrived early to the parade, and we went through the postings. Inspector Manning waited until the end of the briefing until he held up a memo, and read part of it out: "The Superintendent of Earlham states that all officers must wear their hi-vis jackets at all times."

There were groans; everyone hated those things. The inspector said, "Of course, if there are no senior officers to see, who will tell them? I don't see them on the rota. They're all home enjoying it with their families."

There were a few laughs at this point. As my old mom used to say, "The heart don't grieve over what the eye don't see."

The inspector added one last thing, "The federation have had the request for a bonus payment for working over the millennium turned down. No surprise there though, however, they did say you'd all get a medal."

There were a few ironic cheers. The Law said under his breath, "Don't hold your breath for that medal. The tight-arsed gits in charge aren't going to give those out to the rank and file. Oh, they'll make sure they get them. The rest of us, not so much." He was right: twenty years later, I'm still waiting!

I made my way to the custody suite, and settled in for a busy night. We had one of the regulars in, and when I went down to check on him during changeover, he said "Here mate, you're a nice guy. Any chance of getting out of the cell to phone my mom around midnight?"

It is technically their right to make one call (to a solicitor), and most of the time custody sergeants were amenable, but that night might be a problem. He was a short (5'8"), skinny, heroin-addicted thief who looked about 40, but was actually 25.

I said, "Honest, Michael, I can't say. Firstly, who knows how busy we'll be? And it's down to the custody officer, not me. But I don't think it's unreasonable, and I'll wait for the best time to ask him. But do me a favour, be a model prisoner, and I promise I'll do my best."

"Thanks mate. I really appreciate it!"

The night went by so quickly. We had drunk after drunk come in. I was so busy dealing with them and the constant welfare checks. We had to close custody because we ran out of cells. I spoke to the sergeant, and he agreed in principle to Michael's request.

So, what was I doing at the start of the new millennium? Cleaning up vomit and dealing with lots of drunk people. The threatened visit by senior management thankfully didn't occur. We managed to get Michael out about half an hour after midnight. He was very grateful.

The morning came, and we'd made it. The computers hadn't all broken. Around 5:30 a.m. the sergeant opened the DNA fridge. "Here's the non-alcoholic (?) champagne I've been hiding. I'm afraid it's polystyrene cups." He poured it out, and said, "To our health, wealth and happiness, gentlemen and ladies. God bless the Queen."

Well, that's the police for you. Another day in paradise, and I thought I'd find out in May if I'd passed and achieved my goal of becoming a fully-fledged, proper policeman. Essentially, four months – the countdown was on.

Chapter 8
AREA CAR

About a month into the new year, I had the opportunity to work on the area car. This was the designated pursuit vehicle, and was the most prestigious job on a relief. The drivers were trained to a higher level than the response drivers (and, oh boy, did they tell you about it).

The car we used was a Vauxhall Vectra. This was not a good car in general, but a particularly bad choice for a police car. It had an automatic gearbox that wasn't particularly robust. We'd regularly go over speed humps at speed and the gearbox had a nasty habit of jumping out of gear. So it required the passenger to hold the gear lever in place so it didn't drop out of gear. There were a number of the radio push buttons that had fallen out and therefore had the tinfoil and Blu Tack trick. The Met and its extra cheapness. They'd clearly just looked at the car's technical specs and the cheap price (because no one was buying them, because they were shit), and thought, great!

The way it worked on the area car was that you'd have the driver and operator (who operated the radio), and the plain-clothes observer in the back. This allowed the plain-clothes observer to be dropped off, and observe crime undetected. It essentially allowed for flexibility. My chance came when the observer and the operator had both got prisoners so, to allow the area car to operate, it required an operator.

I'd been freed up, so I jumped in with Jamie, my Yorkshire friend. This was going to be interesting. Neither were particularly keen on each other, after the comments he'd made about the nightclub incident. But we were professional enough to focus on the work, even if there wasn't the usual friendly chat between jobs.

We started on an early turn and the atmosphere was frosty from the start, and the radio was quiet, so we slowly drove around in the gentle rain of the early morning. As we were driving around an industrial area near the docks, we drove past one of our targets to keep an eye on. They were a couple of bonded warehouses that store high-value cargoes, before they can be assessed for import or export tax.

That area should have been quiet, as it was a dead end, but as we pulled round there were two cars parked up, directly outside the first warehouse entrance. As we slowly drove past them, the four occupants of the cars eyed us with as much suspicion as we eyed them. Jamie did not need to tell me to take down their registration numbers, and as soon as we were past them, I was on the radio, doing checks.

Jamie slowly (to give time for the radio checks to come back) drove to the end of the road, just out of sight, turned around and drove back. At the same moment the radio sparked into life. Sooz said: "PT3, the first vehicle is LOS (lost or stolen), the second we'll have for you shortly. Do you need another unit?"

Jamie nodded, and I replied, "Sooner rather than later, please."

Instant reply: "Show PT21 making our way."

Good, two units, odds of six to four, not two to four. As we looked, the stolen vehicle had made off, and the other was still parked up, and its two male occupants were walking off. I put the radio call out that the vehicle had made off, and we pulled up next to the two men, and got out.

Instantly, I had a really bad vibe from these guys. I think Jamie had the same feeling. I stood with my back to the wall, and Jamie stood with his back to the road, and the two men stood back to back, facing out. This meant Jamie and I could see both of them, and they could only see one of us.

The man I was talking to was a 5'10" muscular man, of about 30, with black jeans, a dark shirt and a thick, heavyweight, padded cloth jacket, and short, military-style black hair. He spoke with a strong east European accent.

As I spoke with him, he kept moving his right hand close to his right jacket pocket. It was difficult to tell if he had anything in the pocket, because of the padding.

You're taught to watch a suspect's eyes, hands and feet. Eyes tell you the target, hands tell intention, and feet tell you direction. His eyes were always flicking up at me, his hand was favouring his pocket, and his feet were pointed straight at me.

So my sixth sense was going nuts; this guy wanted to hurt me! But we were waiting for the vehicle check to come back. I said: "Hello Sir. So is there a problem with your car?"

He replied: "Me no understand. Car kaput!"

He again moved his hand close to his pocket. "Sir, can you please keep your hands where I can see them, there's a good chap."

I gently moved my weight onto my right foot, allowing me push off and move to my left to grab his hand if he went for his pocket. We were both watching each other, and both knew the game. Then the radio said,

"PT3, are you free to speak?" (that meant they had something to tell us they didn't want suspects to hear)

Clearly this guy understood English perfectly, as he realised he was about to be nicked, and I realised he was going to fight at the same moment. I moved to my left, so I wasn't in front of him, and grabbed his right wrist with my right hand, moving to be at right angles to him. I kept his wrist clamped, stopping him from getting his hand into his pocket, while at the same time, from the side, kicked his right leg from under him. He lost his balance, and went down quickly, and all the while I had control of his right wrist. As he went down, I clamped his wrist with both hands, and wrenched it around and up, forcing him face down to the ground. I cuffed his right wrist while maintaining pressure on his arm. This didn't take place without plenty of shouting, and I found out he certainly did have a quite extensive knowledge of English swear words.

I put my knee into his back, and eventually managed to force him to give me his left hand. I then had him fully in cuffs.

At the same moment, Jamie had taken his guy down as well. He had good instincts (ex-army) and hadn't hesitated.

I said to the suspect, as I rolled him onto his left side so I could retrieve what he'd been trying to get: "Right mate, let's see what kind of knife you've got?" As I reached into his pocket, a chill went down my back: it wasn't a knife, but a small automatic pistol. I pulled it out and looked at it. I tried to read its name: Tokarov.

I said clearly, as I held up the pistol, "Jamie, firearm." Jamie's eyes shot round to look at me, and focused on the pistol. He nodded, and checked his prisoner over as well.

Since I had my hands full, Jamie got on the radio. "PT, we'll need an ARV here. All units be aware, firearms recovered."

Sooz replied in her usual calming, unflappable voice, "Any units who see the outstanding LOS vehicle, wait for the ARV to initiate a hard stop. Are you both OK?"

Jamie, replied: "Yes Sooz, we're both fine, but we could do with those units running to our location."

Very quickly we were up to our necks in backup, and an ARV arrived and took charge of the pistol. I later found out it was loaded, cocked, and with a round chambered. It was test-fired, and found to be functional.

The two men refused to talk, but after their fingerprints were put through the PNC, it was found they were wanted in Poland for shooting and killing a policeman with a similar pistol. We didn't deal with it, but by the time we'd done all the paperwork, it was the end of a memorable first shift on the area car.

The following day we were back on early turn, and the first part of the shift had been a little less hectic, until it got to about midday, and we got a call about a mounted officer needing assistance with a prisoner he'd detained.

We took the job, because it needed a speedy response. We arrived and found the mounted officer still on horseback, leaning off his horse, holding on to a large (6'3"), white, muscular man in his late twenties. He had a white T-shirt and jeans on, was covered in cheap tattoos, and clearly a bit worse for wear.

OK, I thought, *the mounted lad has come across this guy, and he's drunk. I can deal with this.* I jogged up to the lad on horseback, and took hold of the drunk, tattooed guy, saying to the lad on horseback, "Hiya. Do you need me to nick this guy, and take him off your hands?"

"Yes, he's drunken dis' (drunk and disorderly, basically pissed and lairy). As I went past him, he got out of that black, crappy Beemer and started swearing at me."

At this point the man said, "Oye, you cunt, who's calling my motor crappy? It's better than a fucking horse, you arsehole."

Despite myself, I had to suppress a grin. I thought, *he's pissed and swearing. He's coming in.* I arrested and cautioned him for being drunk and disorderly. Between the two of us, Jamie and I managed to get the cuffs on. He wasn't really fighting us, but just being awkward. I managed to get a call in for the van. I didn't want to be in the back of a car fighting him if I had any choice in the matter.

The man on the horse said to Jamie, just before riding back to the stables, "Here, the prisoner came out of that crappy, old black Beemer. I think there's a woman in it. You might want to have a word with her."

Jamie nodded, and once again our tattooed friend piped up, "Oye, you cowboy, who are you to call my car fucking crappy, you cunt. And you big guy (Jamie), leave my fucking girlfriend alone or I'll take these fucking cuffs off and shove them up your arse!"

I must give it to this guy; he certainly had a way with words. He made almost as many friends as I did. Jamie didn't bother acknowledging the threat. Honestly, you hear threats and baseless accusations of racism shouted at you so often that you hardly notice them after a while.

He walked over to the car and chatted to the girlfriend, then got on the radio and asked for another unit. *Ah,* I thought, *not just a drunken dis'. Curiouser and curiouser, said Alice.*

Then the call came out from Sooz: "Units in the Earlham area, please be on the lookout for a suspect fleeing a racially aggravated affray and criminal damage.

"The suspect is male IC1 (see, Burke, even PT say it that way!), approximately 6'3", wearing a white T-shirt, blue jeans, with tattoos, last seen in the company of a female. They drove off in a black BMW vehicle."

I looked at my tattooed friend, and he said, "It wasn't me, mate."

Mmm, let me think about that. "PT, 272, I think we've located your suspect. We have him detained on another matter."

The tattooed man said, "Oh no, I thought I got away with that."

I thought, *Mmm, clearly this guy is either extremely pissed, or extremely thick.*

Sooz replied, "That was quick, 272. I'll let the other unit know to come and see me when you get back to the ranch for all the details."

The tattooed man's girlfriend had signs of injury on her face, but refused to talk to us or cooperate. And, although he was clearly drunk when we found him and had driven, there was no evidence saying he was drunk while he drove the car. So, although I'm certain he did drink and drive, we couldn't prove it.

We transported the man back to custody and booked him in. It turned out he was called Ryan Johnson and had a long criminal history. His family were also well known to police. When I did a name check, it showed he was currently on a driving ban for, guess what? You guessed it: drink-driving. We hadn't seen him drive, and at that point I had no direct evidence of him driving, so couldn't do anything.

I put on a CRIS and we bailed him until we had all the evidence from the other incident. Jamie said, "Don't worry about it, kid. It's a high-profile racial job; the CSU will take it."

We booked off and went home.

The next day, I was horrified to find it had been assigned to me! A probationer on relief! I had to do shift work, I had the most basic level of investigation skills, and routinely these cases were given to the specialist units to deal with, as they had the time and resources to deal with them. I mentioned it to the sergeants, and they raised it with the CSU, who confirmed they wanted me to deal with it. *Oh, here goes nothing.*

I reviewed the crime report. Ryan had arrived outside a Jewish temple in Burnside Square, had an argument with his girlfriend, walked into the grounds and urinated against the wall of the temple while the worshippers were leaving. When one of the male Jewish worshippers had asked him politely to stop, as it was their temple, Ryan had said, "Fuck off you Yiddish cunt. Fuck off back to your own country! I'll fuckin' piss anywhere I want in my own country. Fuck off back home!"

He then ran back to his car, retrieved a wheel brace from the boot and chased the Jewish man down the street and beat him repeatedly, while the victim tried to get into his friend's car. Ryan then kicked the door of the car, denting it as he drove off, all while shouting a tirade of racist abuse.

The man's injuries included extreme bruising to his upper arm. His arm was literally black and blue from shoulder to elbow. He was very lucky it wasn't broken. A description of Ryan's car was recorded in the victim's statement, but there was no mention of him seeing Ryan drive the car anywhere. So, unless he confessed in interview, I had no evidence of him drink-driving on a ban. I looked, and thought: *first thing I need to do is contact the victim, and update him. Then collect as much evidence as I can, and speak with someone to give me guidance as to where to go next.* So I went up to see John in CID, and explained what I had been given.

He said, "Do what! Let's have a look at the CRIS to see what we're dealing with." He then read through the report and said: "Bloody hell, mate, you've got the shitty end of the stick with this one. You shouldn't be dealing with this!"

He then looked closer at the screen and said: "You see that little code in the top corner? That means it's being monitored by the racial oversight unit. Everything you do is being watched in real time at New Scotland Yard. You do one thing they don't like, and they'll be down on you like three tons of horse shit! You poor bastard. I'm sorry, I don't have the authority to change it either. Other than a little bit of unofficial advice, I can't help. Have you spoken to your reporting skipper?"

I explained I had. So I went to see Sergeant Deacon as my sergeant was off that day. I asked him what I should do, and he told me I should speak to the victim, interview the suspect, then set up an ID parade for him and charge him – all while being on shift work. So, in between calls, I managed to call the victim, and the other witness/victim (the man whose car had been damaged), and update them. I went around and collected the photographic evidence, doctor's report, photos of the injuries to the man's arm and repair estimate for the man's car door.

Then I had to take time off from my relief to interview Ryan. Once I had all the evidence, I arranged more time off from the relief to do the interview, with the assistance of one of the other lads, who just sat in.

It was a full no-comment interview. This meant, Ryan would answer: "No comment" to every question. Standard procedure if you have decent evidence. Given he'd not said anything, I needed to ID him, so I researched how to do an ID parade, booked the time off and booked the ID suite in north London. I also wanted to arrange for a traffic car to be nearby, in case he drove to the ID suite, because he was still on a driving ban. I even printed off a copy of the court document. I needed the authorisation of the superintendent to legally do the ID parade, and arrest him if he drove to the ID suite. The trouble for me was that I had my final training day before the end of my probation the day before. So, Sergeant Deacon said he'd get the superintendent's authorisation while I was on the training course.

I turned up on the day of the ID parade, checked, and Sergeant Deacon hadn't got the superintendent's authorisation for the ID parade. So, I had a high-profile case being monitored by the top brass, and either I went to the superintendent and get his authorisation first thing that morning, then try to explain to him why it wasn't done before without dropping myself and Sergeant Deacon in it, or I cancelled the ID parade and got flak from the yard. That would delay the case and I'd have to rearrange the witnesses/victims. Nightmare!

OK, I'd have to hope the superintendent was available, and that I could navigate a way around all the pitfalls. I phoned his secretary, and she said he could make time for me, given the circumstances, in fifteen minutes. *Here we go!* I collected all the relevant paperwork. *God, I hope I haven't forgotten something obvious!*

I walked up to his office, took a deep breath, and knocked. I heard "Come in." I walked in to a reasonably sized office, with book shelves lined with books. The walls had clearly been recently painted, there was a nice, new, clean carpet, windows overlooking the street, a large real-wood desk with a large, high-backed, leather swivel chair, and a couple of comfy-looking leather chairs in front. How the other half live! Sat in the seat behind the desk was a uniformed officer wearing his formal tunic, with his medals on display, one of which looked suspiciously new, almost like it was maybe the millennium service medal (Mmm, still waiting for mine, twenty years later – just saying). He was about 50, with suspiciously jet-black hair which was slightly too long, with a slim face. Sitting in one of the other two chairs was a female in the ubiquitous M&S skirt and jacket. She was in her early forties, with collar-length dark brown hair, of slim build, and sitting very correctly with legs crossed, casting an appraising eye over me as I entered.

I walked in, stopped, saluted and said, "Good morning, Sir, Ma'am. I'm sorry to bother you, but I'm PC Armstrong, from C relief. I am respectfully requesting your authorisation for an ID parade this afternoon at St Agatha's."

There it was, out there. What was he going to do – stab me in the back, pat me on the back or kick me up the arse? With senior management, you were never sure. He left me standing there while he exchanged glances with the lady.

He then said, "This ID parade, who's it for? And what's the crime? Also, why didn't you come to me before now?"

All of which were reasonable questions. *Here I go, trying to navigate around dropping my sergeant in it, and not getting myself on a disciplinary.* "Sir, it's a racially aggravated ABH and criminal damage. The suspect is Ryan Johnson, and I apologise, Sir, but I was on the last of my probationary training courses and there was a miscommunication between myself and my sergeant as to getting authorisation. I can only apologise for that." That's the best I could do, without flat out lying.

He once again looked at the lady, and then looked back at me. "What were the circumstances of this incident, and is it being monitored by NSY?"

I explained the full circumstances of the case, and confirmed it was being monitored. He leant forward on his chair, "Let me get this straight. You as a probationer are being expected to investigate a high-profile, racially aggravated ABH and criminal damage that include the desecration of a Jewish temple, while you're on relief? How has this happened? Don't you think you're too inexperienced for this case? By the way, where's the other officers to help you with the ID parade and the case papers?"

I thought, *thank God, he's not ripping my head off.*

I said "Honestly Sir, I do feel out of my depth, and when the case was first assigned to me, I brought it up with my sergeant, and he contacted the CSU who confirmed that I should be dealing with it. I don't have anyone with me to help me, as I'm in on a rest day, and they couldn't authorise any more overtime for anyone to assist."

He nodded his head, and looking at the lady, said, "This is Detective Inspector Wade. She's the head of the CSU (racial crimes unit) for this borough. I'm sure she'll have something to say about this."

My heart dropped. *Oh God, really, you couldn't make this up.* She fixed me with a hard stare, "I too am concerned such an inexperienced probationer was expected to deal with this while on relief. I have asked for more resources as the unit is overstretched, and this is possibly why it was bounced back to the relief."

Oh God, I'd clearly just pissed off the boss of the CSU, the unit I'd be attached to within weeks.

He said: "Here's what we do. Firstly, do you have the authorisation for the ID parade I need to sign (I handed it over)? That seems all in order. Now can you supply any support for this officer today (looking at DI Wade)?"

She shook her head: "I'm afraid my officers are all tied up with cases. However, I'll contact CID to have one of their officers help him with the case papers, which must be completed and submitted today, so we can get it to court."

She stopped, looked down at the paperwork she had on her lap, and said: "Armstrong? How do I know that name? Ah, yes, you're joining us on attachment in a few weeks' time. Hopefully we can sort it out that you pick it up and run it through court, so you can see the whole process."

I thought, *smooth, turning something that looks bad for you into a positive; I can see how you've climbed the ranks.*

"Thank you, Ma'am."

The superintendent sat back in his chair, "Well, that's settled then. I'll be taking a personal interest in this case, and you PC Armstrong. It took real initiative to come and sort this out. Good man! You're dismissed."

With that, I walked out of the office, and quietly closed the door. *Well, you certainly know how to put the cat among the pigeons don't you!* Then I thought about how long the day was going to be, and how much I wasn't looking forward to getting up at 04:30 hours for early turn.

No point in being grumpy about what I can't change. I walked into the control room and let them know I would have to drive over to St Agatha's ID suite, as I was going off our patch. I'd arranged for CID to pick me and the witnesses up, in separate cars, to be transported to the ID suite.

The victims didn't drive their car there, as it might put them at risk of being identified as belonging to them. There were car parking facilities for the police and witnesses, and we arrived early and were kept separate, even down to having different doors on opposite sides of the building. The CID officer would drop us off and go back to collect us a couple of hours later. It was a new, single-floored building, and it was well appointed. Everything was new, clean and functioning.

There were different ID suites around London which catered for different races, because they had to provide other people who looked similar to the him: same race, height, build, hairstyle, etc. They actually had a list of people who did this regularly, as the police paid them. That would be a talking point at a party, "What do you for a living?" "I stand in police line-ups."

The building had an extensive network of cameras, which included the car park. I had spoken to the officers at the ID suite prior to arriving, letting them know the suspect may ignore the law and drive to the suite while still on his driving ban. I had a copy of his disqualification with me. I'd also let the traffic division know they might get an easy arrest for disqual if they were around at about the time our suspect was leaving. I had my radio set to their frequency to let them know what type of car it was.

The allotted time arrived. Ryan's solicitor arrived and waited around, nervously. A quarter of an hour late, a car shot in, and parked in the "Police only" car park.

They (Ryan had brought a friend) ignored the signs, tried the door, and needed a member of staff to redirect him to the correct door on the other side of the building. He'd been given very clear instructions prior to his visit about which way to enter. I didn't see the witness or suspect until after the ID parade had been done, so there could be no accusation of the police telling the witness who to pick.

When it was over, he'd been positively identified. Good news! I went to speak with Ryan and his solicitor to tell them what was going to happen next. I walked into the small waiting room where they were. His solicitor was a tall, thin man in an M&S suit, with short white hair, and in his late fifties.

"Hello Mr Johnson (I nodded at the solicitor). Sir, you were positively identified by both victims, and you'll be charged for the offences. I need you to come back to Earlham straight after we're finished here. Do you have transport?"

Ryan said: "Yeah, I got the car."

I looked at his solicitor, pulling out the copy of the disqualification notice that clearly showed his ban would run for another two months. I handed it to the solicitor and said: "But Ryan, you know you're not legal to drive. Your ban doesn't run out for another two months."

The solicitor drew in a breath, and Ryan said: "Err, well, I didn't drive. My mate here did."

I said, "Good. You know if you do drive, and get caught, you'll most likely get into a lot more trouble."

Ryan grinned, and his solicitor said, "Officer, I feel you're making a lot of assumptions here."

I replied: "Not at all. The car in which your client was transported here in drove into a 'Police only' car park and he has a previous conviction for driving while disqualified."

He replied: "Well, let me assure you he wouldn't do that today. We'll see you at Earlham custody."

He walked out, followed by a smirking Ryan, and friend. I opened the door for them, and noticed a crappy black BMW, and quickly memorised the number plate (the same one he drove before). Ryan made a big deal of getting in the passenger side, they drove out and down the road, and then swapped seats. I called the traffic unit, and asked them to take him to Earlham. They were more than happy to oblige.

A few hours later, I was standing in Earlham custody, where Ryan was being charged for racially aggravated ABH, criminal damage, driving while disqualified, not having an MOT, tax or insurance.

Some people never, never learn! He was bailed to a PDH (Plea Direction Hearing – a pre-trial hearing to determine if there's a case to answer) in a month's time to Westminster Crown Court, and to Earlham Magistrates' Court the following week for the traffic matters. As we'd been waiting for Ryan to arrive, I'd spoken to his solicitor, who upon hearing his client had been arrested for disqualified driving, had only just refrained from rolling his eyes. I said to him quietly, out of anyone's earshot, "I gave him every opportunity not to be arrested for it. Not much more I could do."

The solicitor had been very tight-lipped, but eventually said, "I know, you were very fair. That's what makes it worse."

After Ryan and his solicitor had left, I took all the documents and went upstairs to find the CID officer who was going to help me. Guess who? John was once again sprawled over his usual seat. Upon seeing me he said, "'Ello Richard. How you doing, mate? Are you the poor probbie I've got to help write a set of case papers? You're living up to your nickname, the Griefmeister. Trouble seems to follow you around, man."

I couldn't disagree with that. "Thanks Sarge. I'm glad it's you who's going to help me."

He said in mock annoyance, "Oh, I see. You didn't think I was working hard enough, and thought you'd make me do some more?"

He grinned, I smiled back, and said, "Actually, it was your winning smile, and cheery disposition I was going for. Besides, I reckon you're an example of the Pareto distribution principle."

He looked at me, and laughed, saying, "Why, bless your heart. Sarcasm is the lowest form of wit. What was that? Pray something or other? Are you taking the piss?"

I spoke quickly to assuage any misunderstandings, saying, "No, it was a compliment. The Pareto distribution principle says that 20 per cent of the work force does 80 per cent of the work. I was saying you were part of the 20 per cent."

He put his head back and laughed, slapping me on the shoulder, saying, "I'll have to remember that. It's so true. I reckon you're a part of that too. Highest arrest record, over 220 bodies in the bin (arrests in the cells) in a year. Good effort! I'll have a look over the papers and CRIS. When was the last time you had a bite to eat?"

"Breakfast this morning."

He shook his head, "Mate, it's about 17:00 hours. Go get yourself something from the canteen, and bring it up here." I logged on to my

CRIS account and handed John the paperwork I had and, as I started to walk out, said, "Oh, do you want anything, skipper?"

"Gawd bless you, sunshine. Oh yeah, a couple of cans of coke, two meaty sandwiches, a pastie if they have one and a couple of bags of crisps, Bacon flavour. Thanks mate. I'm fading away here."

Fading away? Really? I had to borrow a plastic bag from the ever-so-friendly canteen staff. Honestly, I never held it against the canteen staff that the food in the Met was diabolical. They were working with what they had.

I staggered back to John, and he had a break, and set out the plan of attack. He'd divided up the work. Andy had been right: this guy knew his stuff. We set about this task with gusto. Even then it wasn't until after 23:00 hours that I got away from the place. It cost me a fortune in food from the canteen to keep John fed. That's CID for you; they never pay for anything! But I had thanked him. I'd have been there all night doing those papers on my own.

The following day, I spoke with Sergeant Deacon, and explained things. He apologised profusely – he'd totally forgotten, it had been manic. I told him not to worry, everyone makes mistakes. I then explained I'd done my best to keep his name out of the situation. He was appreciative, and I think I was slowly learning how things worked.

For the next few weeks, I continued to work hard, until my attachment to the CSU for a couple of weeks. This was based down in the little station in Newham, next to the ATU, where I'd been six months before. It felt like a lifetime.

It was plain clothes, so I had to carry all my usual kit, ASP, cuffs, spray, and wear my bullet-proof corset, and had nothing to carry it on. A normal belt won't handle that, so I ended up sticking it in the pockets of my 'plain clothes', which was virtually a uniform. You had either high-tech

Magnums or trainers, non-ripped jeans, a T-shirt or baggy sweatshirt, and a dark fleece. Partner that with a shortish haircut, and the bulk of a corset, and every villain in London could spot you from about half a mile away. So much for plain clothes.

I thought I'd cover both bases. I wore my best M&S pure wool suit with white, pure cotton shirt, and tie, with a large kit bag of all my gear, plus the plain-clothes uniform.

I arrived at 8 a.m. I wasn't due in until 09:00 hours, but "it's better to be an hour early than a minute late". I punched in the code for the door: 1066. Original! There was a set of stairs which went up to an open-plan office on the first floor.

I walked in and looked around. It was a relatively new building. There was plenty of good ventilation and the huge windows allowed in good natural light. The carpet was clean, the desks looked new and the chairs comfortable. It was reasonably tidy. My God, had I gone to another universe?

No one was around, so I helped myself to a drink from the water cooler, and sat on the comfy, low chairs in what looked like a reception area. I waited, and waited. Eventually, at 08:55 hours, the door opened, and in walked a man and a woman, both smartly dressed in M&S suits. They looked a little surprised, and the man, who was mid-forties, slim, 5'8", with slightly too long dark brown hair, said: "Oh hello there. You must be our attachment. 272, isn't it? Nice to meet you. I'm Mark Pelton, DC actually. This (indicating the lady) is Natasha. Welcome aboard."

The lady smiled. She was in her mid-thirties, of medium build, with shoulder-length, light brown wavy hair hanging loose. She had a nice smile. She held out her hand, which I shook. She said: "Nice to meet you. What would you like us to call you? I'm a DS, but please call me Nat."

Despite myself, I was taken a back. This was something new. I think Nat could see that, and said: "Don't worry, we won't bite. I know it's different here away from the craziness that's relief work. We only work Monday to Friday, nine to five. It's very civilised."

I snapped out of it: "Thank you. This isn't what I was expecting. I'm Richard Armstrong. What do you want me to do? I've brought all my kit (indicating my kit bag)."

Nat smiled, "You won't be needing most of that. I carry my radio, minus the PSM, my ASP and cuffs. That's pretty much it. We tend to keep in touch via mobile phones. Just put your bag over in that office, and Mark will sort out the coffee. How do you like yours?"

I picked up my kit bag, took out the kit Nat had suggested and, looking at Mark, said, "Black no sugar, please."

Nat beckoned me over, "You can use that desk (one by the window); no one's using that at the moment. Come and take a seat next to me, and I'll show you what we do first thing every morning."

I pulled a chair up, and Mark brought me a coffee. I said, "Thanks Mark. I have got a job I'm supposed to deal with. It's the PDH for Ryan Johnson, the guy I nicked for racially aggravated ABH and criminal damage."

Mark replied, "I know that job. Oh, you're the probbie who got saddled with that. The PDH is a piece of piss: turn up, make sure the paperwork's there, and CPS do all the work. Nothing ever goes wrong. You can do that on your own; it'll be good experience."

Oh no. If ever I'd heard anyone tempt fate, there it was. I inwardly winced.

Nat had got into the network (the computers were new, and you could still read all the letters on the keyboard), and she showed me a list of CRIS reports. Pointing at them, she said, "That's handy, six jobs, and three of us. Two each. Don't worry, we'll help you through them."

As we went through how they worked the jobs – contacting the victims, checking all the details, interviewing any suspects in custody, charging, and doing case papers – I had a chance to talk to my two new colleagues.

I asked: "It must be really nice working in such a new, spacious office?"

Mark replied: "It's one of the perks. The Met have thrown money at these units. There's a fair bit of scrutiny, but otherwise, it's a lot nicer working environment than either uniform or CID."

"How do they decide what jobs are sent to you to deal with?"

Mark and Nat shared a look, as if I'd asked a particularly thorny question. Nat replied: "We deal with crimes that involve an element of hatred. Domestic violence, racial hatred, hatred towards people based on religion or sexuality. So any crime that has any one of those features."

She still hadn't answered my question, so I pressed, "OK, but what criteria are used to decide what does or does not involve hate?"

Nat said: "It's down to the perception of the victim, or in the case of race, it's the perception of anyone."

I thought, *wait, what?* "So there are different criteria for each type of 'hate crime'?"

She shook her head: "No, just race, that's anyone. With hate against gay people, it's just the victim or officer."

"But there must be some objective test, right? Otherwise, anyone could say any crime where the victim and suspect were of different races was racially motivated, and have all the resources of the CSU thrown at it, as opposed to me dealing with it on relief."

Mark replied, "That's about the size of it. It's the only crime I've ever heard about that is purely based on the perception of anyone, and not on a set of objective facts."

Nat said, "I'll put it this way: if you were a victim, and you didn't think a crime was racist, and I the police officer didn't think it was racist, but Mark here, who was walking by with no knowledge of the crime whatsoever, shouts out that it's racist, it's recorded as racist, and we deal with it."

I struggled to get my head around that. It was contrary to everything I'd been taught with every other crime.

"That's not the case with other forms of hate crime, though. It's just race. Why?"

Nat said slowly, "It was very recently changed after the Macpherson report, and the media attention, and political pressure."

"What, so they've changed the reporting criteria for one type of crime, due to political pressure? Really? They change the way the police operate due to some moronic politician, or idiots in the BBC or *Guardian*, not on the principle of law? That's dreadful. Does that mean they think a person getting beaten up or killed because of their race is worse than because of their sexuality? Let's face it, both sets of criteria are nuts, because they have no objective standard, but why isn't this front page news, or on the TV?"

Mark nodded and said, "Who do you think was pushing this? Not that the media care. They just want to sell papers, or increase their viewers. And bashing the police, and calling us racists, is flavour of the month."

I just sat there for a moment, and was at a loss for words. *So, the politicians only care about gaining or maintaining power, the media just care about selling more papers, or having more viewers. The senior management in the police only care about their careers, and looking good in front of the media. Who cares about the people?* This was really depressing – all the people I trusted, I found out I couldn't trust.

We got back to the work of investigating and charging prisoners. It was a lovely working environment. The other staff were great, and they were very busy, but not in the same way the reliefs were.

During the second week, I had to go to Westminster Crown Court to do the PDH for Ryan Johnson. I wore my suit, had my ASP, and cuffs, and my radio, and all the papers I needed. I arrived early to court, and as I walked into the foyer, I saw Ryan walking around, looking lost. He walked over, "Hello. Where do I go?"

I bit back a snarky comment and, looking at my notes, said, "Court three, at 10:00 hours." I looked around and saw a sign for court three up on the first floor on the right. I pointed up and said, "Ryan, it's up on the balcony, you see the one right at the end?" He followed my gaze, and nodded. As he walked off, he said, "Thanks mate."

I checked in at reception, and was directed to the 'Police room'. It's a small room tucked out of the way on the first floor. I was told I'd need to check in with the CPS lawyer in their room, which was just down the corridor.

I made my way to the police room and sat down. At that time, I was alone. A young, nervous-looking junior clerk walked in (he looked hardly old enough to shave) and said, "Err, sorry to bother you, Sir. Are you Armstrong from Earlham CSU?"

Well, he was almost right. "Yes, I am. How can I help?"

He handed me a brown, interval mail A4 envelope with a number of crossed-out names. The only one that wasn't crossed out was mine.

I thanked him, and opened it up. It was a crime report from the previous day, which was of witness intimidation. Ryan Johnson had gone to scare the two victims on the night before the PDH trial.

I thought, *how stupid is this guy? Really!? OK, where do I go from here? What do I have to do? CPS, that's who I need to talk to, get some legal advice.* I walked down to the CPS room, knocked on the door, and walked in.

There were a number of lawyers sitting around, reading sets of case papers.

I said, "Good morning. I'm looking for the lawyer who's running the Ryan Johnson case that's in court three at 10 a.m. I'm the officer in the case, PC Armstrong."

They all looked up, and a middle-aged lady stepped forward: "Good morning. Sylvia Thatcher. I'm taking that case. How can I help you?"

I explained the situation. She just stared at me, eventually saying, "Well, that complicates things. I'll have to tell the defence lawyer. I'm not too sure after that."

I replied, "Firstly, if you do that, we won't see Ryan again, and I know what to do. After the PDH, I'll arrest him outside of the court."

"You can't do that."

"Yes I can. He's committed an arrestable offence, and I'm a police officer. I'll arrest him."

She shook her head. I began to think about what I'd have to do. I was going to arrest a man a lot bigger, younger and stronger than me, with no backup, and with precious little equipment, while in a suit. Oh well, what could possibly go wrong?

I then spoke with the lawyer again about the court procedure. Once I was happy with what I had to do, I thanked her.

I phoned the office and explained the situation to Mark, who agreed that I needed to arrest Ryan, and said he'd do his best to get me backup. I looked at my watch: 09:45 hours. Very little time.

I made my way to the court and sat down where I'd been told to. The court proceedings started, and the judge set out charges, and asked if the defendant (Ryan) was present.

The defence lawyer stood up and said, "M'lord, I believe my client may have been delayed."

I thought, *you lying bastard. You told him about the extra charges, and he's done a runner. You're just giving him time to get away!*

The judge said, "I suggest you try and locate your client, and we'll reconvene in half an hour."

At that, we left the court. I was on the phone to the office, and let them know to start the ball rolling to be on the lookout for Ryan near his family home.

We reconvened, and the judge said to the defence lawyer, "Have you managed to locate your errant client?"

The defence lawyer replied, "I'm sorry, m'lord, I have not."

The judge, seemingly having lost patience, said, "If the officer in the case, PC Armstrong, is in the courtroom, please make yourself known."

Here goes nothing. I stood up: "I'm PC Armstrong, the officer in the case, m'lord."

He looked over at me, and with a slightly mischievous smile, said, "Officer, would you mind organising a taxi for Mr Johnson. You know, the white taxis with the blue lights on top, and if you find him, bring him straight here. I'll sort out the paperwork, so you can go and do that right now. Off you go, there's a good chap."

"Yes, m'lord." I turned, bowed to the court and jogged out of the court room. Now that was the sort of judge I could respect. He spoke my kind of language: "Go off and nick the geezer, and bring him straight here! I approve!"

I made another phone call to update them and jumped in a taxi (not the ones that have blue lights this time) back to the office. Once back, we organised my uniformed colleagues to visit his home. Funnily enough, he wasn't present, and his family hadn't seen him in days! Mmm, really!?

A warrant was issued for his arrest and, as I far as I know, he's still on the run. I finished my attachment at the CSU and went back on relief.

I had found my time on the unit interesting. I wanted to stay on relief, and at some point I wouldn't have minded going back.

This left a few things I needed to do before I was (hopefully) confirmed as a PC, including the end of my probation. It was still possible it might be extended or I might be let go. No one had said anything.

Firstly, I had a shield training course to go on in a couple of weeks, I had my panda driving assessment, and then I'd be on the area car for a full five-week rotation. I wondered who I'd be paired with: Campbell, Trish, Paul from the control room, all of whom I got on with? Hopefully not Jamie – the two of us didn't get on since the club bombing incident. To be truthful, we tolerated each other. But working every day with each other for five weeks would bring things to the boil. Everyone knew this. They wouldn't do that, would they?

A couple of weeks later, as I was preparing to do my shield (riot) training. I had confirmation that it would be Jamie. Why? Precisely because we didn't get along. To force us to work through any disagreements, for the sake of the team.

I turned up at the shield training unit, and spent my time running around with shields, and running around, and running! I wasn't in anywhere like as good a shape as I had been a year before, and it was HARD work. You wear what is euphemistically called a 'baby grow'. This is an all-in-one boiler suit, which is slightly prickly, and can get very hot, along with your body armour and riot helmet.

The baby grows are fire-resistant, and have a special coating which causes burning petrol to slide off when you stamp your feet. The down side is that you get sweaty, and smelly.

No problem, just wash them or take them to be dry-cleaned. NO! That removes the special coating, and the burning petrol will stick, and eventually damage or even burn through the material. Not good. You can get them cleaned through the police, but it's not a quick or easy process. Result? Most people's baby grows smell. Nice!

We had a good laugh doing the training. The instructors made sure that, although it was tough, it was also fun. You go down what's called gasoline alley, where you have real petrol bombs thrown at you, and most people experience being set alight at least once. Then you do the stomp. First time it happened to me, I saw the petrol bomb arc in and smash at my feet, spraying my legs with burning petrol. It's a surreal moment to see your legs on fire. You know, logically, the baby grows will protect you. But, shit, you're on fire. The first instinct is to breathe in, and you're treated to hot gases rising up from the flames. Not pleasant. Then, remembering your training, and hearing the shouts of your mates, you stomp your feet while walking backwards, and the burning petrol slides off your suit. Phew! It's an act of faith the first time it happens.

Then you practise using the three types of shields: the small round ones which are often carried in the cars, the medium-sized ones that come up to your nipple line, and the huge tower shields that lock together.

One of the exercises is to form a locked shield wall and move backwards and forwards while having wooden bricks and petrol bombs lobbed at you by very enthusiastic 'rioters'.

I thought, *this is fun, I'm unlikely to ever have to use it.* You think I'd have learnt not to tempt fate.

When I'd finished my training, I had even more kit (this was kept in a huge, heavy kit bag) I had to try to store in my already bulging locker.

Then it was off to work with Jamie, for five weeks. Normally you change who you work with pretty much every day. This was going to be different: you didn't volunteer for every call, but waited until there was something worthwhile, or a pursuit.

We started on a late turn and, after briefing, Jamie and I made our way out to the battered Vectra. We put our bags in the boot and got ourselves settled in the far more comfortable area car. I set out all the stuff I needed – Maglite, a couple of chocky bars, a drink.

Jamie looked at me, "Let's get things sorted from the start. If we're going to be working together (he held up the car keys), I'm the keys. In other words, anything to do with the car is down to me! You are the pen; you do all the writing, and paperwork. You get out first, and I'll back you up. Clear so far?"

I nodded. It was nothing I didn't know.

He continued, "You use the radios, but nothing, I repeat nothing, else! You don't touch the lights sirens, windows, heater, nothing! If a radio call comes in, you check with me before you take it. I decide what we do or do not take. Clear?"

I nodded.

"Bottom line, I'm in charge during this shift, and in this car! Do you understand?"

I nodded, "Yes, Jamie, I get it."

"I really hope you do!"

We drove out of the yard, and Jamie made his way along to one of the housing estates, near to where there was a small parade of shops, with a notorious alleyway cut-through.

He said, "We're going to check this alleyway. I've checked the CRIS and there's been a lot of robberies around there. You never know, we might get lucky."

As we approached, we saw three youths hanging around, watching the alleyway. As soon as they saw us, they took off running. The tallest lad ran off down the alleyway. Jamie said, "Chase that one. I'll go around the block and cut him off from the other end."

The car slowed, I jumped out and was off down the alleyway, as the car rocketed off around the block. It was a long and twisty alleyway.

I sprinted flat out, and eventually caught sight of the lad, who had slowed. As soon as he saw me, off he was again. Eventually, we came out onto the road. There was Jamie waiting for him. He parked the car at an angle across the pavement, making sure the lad could only go in one direction. He slowed, trying to see an escape route. My presence behind him made up his mind and he tried to jump over the bonnet of the car. Jamie and I both grabbed him, and he quickly gave up, realising he wasn't going to win that one. Smart!

I held him, and had a chance to look at him. He was tall (6'3), slim build, about 18 years, and of mixed race, with collar-length black hair. He was wearing trainers, a dark blue tracksuit and hoodie.

As I looked at him, I noticed he had something in his hand, and it looked like he was trying to drop it. I grabbed his wrist: "Hold on, what have you got in your hand?"

He tried to pull away, but I wouldn't let him go. He said: "'Ere, get off, I ain't got nothing." I managed to force his hand up so I could see it, and eventually managed to get him to open his hand. Inside was a large lump of cannabis resin. I looked at him and said, "What's that?"

"What's what?"

"That thing in your hand?"

"I ain't got nothing in my hand. What you talking about?"

I gave Jamie a quick look, took the resin out of his hand, and arrested and cautioned him for the drugs. While we were searching him he said, "This is out of order. I ain't done nothing wrong. You had no reason to stop me."

Jamie said, "This is an area that's had a number of robberies over the last couple of weeks, by a small gang of young men wearing tracksuits and hoodies. You all ran off when you saw us, and then you've got drugs in your hand when we do stop you. That's plenty of reason."

I had to agree. I searched him; he had nothing else on him. We called a van, and he was taken back to the nick.

As we were driving back, Jamie said, "You know, he's definitely one of the little gang of robbers, but I don't think we can get him on that. It's a pity he didn't have his knife on him. He must have ditched it. At least we got him on the drugs."

Eventually we got him to provide his correct details, and went through to see Sooz for a name check. When it came through, she said, "Oh, he's been released on licence from a youth offenders' institute three weeks ago. That means you'll have to do some research as to what he did. There's a reference on here to check."

After a bit of checking, it appeared at the age of 15 he was convicted of manslaughter. He ran a man over in an armed robbery. He was the getaway driver. So I had to put it before the courts to decide whether he went back to prison.

I relayed the details to Jamie, who wasn't impressed. I went down to his cell, to book him out for interview.

He said, "Before the interview, can I have a cigarette?"

I thought about this. It is a way to gain a little trust, and might have encouraged him to talk to us. I said, "I'll see what the custody sergeant says. If he says yes, then yes."

He made no reply. I'd had an odd feeling about this lad since the first moment I'd met him. He was very hard to read. There was a coldness about him, a stillness on the surface. It's hard to describe. Honestly, I wanted to know how a 15-year-old could kill someone. I know that doesn't sound professional, but I really want to understand things and people. I may not like them, but I want to understand them. This guy, I couldn't read at all.

I spoke with the sergeant. He agreed, so I got him out to the tiny exercise yard, and lit him a cigarette. I waited until he'd taken his first drag and said, "How are you doing?" Odd question, but I thought I'd try a different tack.

He looked at me, and almost through and past me. "Oh, I'm fine."

I then tried a number of other approaches. Every time, it was a monosyllabic answer. No emotion, just answer the question, without answering the intent of the question.

Eventually I ran out of questions, and his cigarette had all but run out too. He stopped and said, "You want to know why, don't you?"

I nodded.

"I wanted to know what it felt like to kill someone."

I was stunned. I'm pretty sure a lot of 15-year-olds want to know that, but they don't do anything to find out, because they understand that to end someone's life is wrong. This lad was different.

I said simply, "What was it like?"

For the first time, I saw him light up. His energy levels went up, he was animated and had an intensity that was frightening.

He looked straight at me and said, "It was the best feeling of my life; better than drugs, drink, sex, anything. I had the power of life and death over another human being. He lived if I let him, he died if I wanted it. I could hear him die under the car, and it was the best feeling. I think about it every day, reliving those memories. I will do it again!"

A shiver ran down my back. It's hard to describe. If you've ever been really close to an animal that can kill you, it paces, stares, bides its time, and all the time has an intention about it. That was it: he was a killer, had enjoyed it, and would do it again.

Good God, none of that could go on record, because he'd just deny it. But without him telling me, we'd have never known. I took him to the interview room. It was "no comment" all the way through. We prepared the case papers for his court.

I told Jamie about what this lad had said. I think it was the only time I saw him even slightly lost for words.

He moved closer, and said in a low voice, "Listen Richard, people say there's no evil in the world. They're wrong. There is; it's in that cell. He'll kill without remorse. Why? Because he enjoys it, and doesn't have any empathy. He feels nothing for others. Only for himself. He's pure evil. If we let him out, he'll kill again. And we are letting him out, and so he will kill. Simple as that! That's why we need the death penalty. It's the only way to guarantee that he won't kill again and again."

He turned and walked off. Until that point, I'd never understood why people were so pro death penalty. I understood then. I still don't agree, but I understand. Wherever he was, there was no coming back, no hope of redemption.

The case went to trial the next day, and we presented all the evidence, and the documentation that he was out on licence. He was found guilty, but the magistrate gave him a conditional discharge.

Jamie and I walked out of the court and, out of earshot, I said, "What the hell? Con dis? That means if he does it again we might fine him £50. What about the fact he was out on licence? That's utterly stupid!"

"You're right, it is. What can we do about it? They've put a man back on the street who's killed a man and has started committing crime within weeks of release. What's the licence mean? Nothing! We both know he'll kill again. Welcome to the real world, mate. You had the views of a comfortable, middle-class teacher. Nice, well-thought-out, civilised views. I take no pleasure in seeing you lose those. You have to understand that when reality slaps you in the face and shows you your views are wrong, you can either ignore them or change your mind. You didn't understand when you first arrived. I think you're beginning to."

I thought, *how many more things will I find out the hard way?* About eighteen months later, I saw the youth's face on the news. He and a gang of his friends had beaten a man to death with a hammer. His friends had grassed on him, as they were so horrified that he'd hit the man over 100 times in the face with the hammer. They had to identify him using DNA, as he had no face or mouth or teeth left. Apparently, what did it for his friends was the way he looked as he did it. They said they'd never forget that look. I genuinely pitied them, but not as much as the man they attacked.

Things began to thaw a little between me and Jamie, and on a night duty we started talking.

"Jamie, do you mind if I ask you something?"

He replied without taking his eyes off the road, "Shoot!"

"I heard you were in the services. What did you do?"

Again without taking his eyes off the road, "I was in army bomb disposal; EXPO for short."

I thought for a moment, "Where did you serve?"

"UK, Germany, Northern Ireland, and the Gulf."

"I've got to ask: why EXPO?"

"Someone's got to do it, and it was interesting work."

That's very matter-of-fact for such a job.

"Wasn't it a dangerous job?" How naive I was.

He replied, and from his tone I realised what a silly question it was. "Being in the army in Northern Ireland and the Gulf was all dangerous. People were trying to kill you all the time. Not much more dangerous than this job in a lot of ways."

As we were saying this, we were driving slowly around the back streets, on the lookout for people up to no good.

"Sorry if it's a dumb question, but did you actually walk up to the bombs and defuse them?"

He shrugged, "Yeah, I did, from suspect packages in N.I. to arms caches in the Gulf to old WW2 bombs in Germany and the UK."

"Why do it, though?"

"Because someone has to, and it's better it kills me than a member of the public. We wear uniforms because we're prepared to risk our lives to protect the public. Anyone who wears a uniform and isn't, shouldn't wear it."

I nodded and was about to reply when we saw a Jack the Ripper tour going around the streets. This is where a tour guide walks around at night (for extra scariness) showing people where Jack did his killings. They're popular with tourists. We had our windows down, as it wasn't a cold night, and you hear things far more easily. And as we were slowly approaching (negotiating a speed bump), the tour guide looked up at us, and said loudly, "And the police are still looking for Jack."

As we pulled alongside the group, I loudly asked the tour guide, "Sir, have you seen Jack? Where did he go?"

Playing along, the tour guide replied in an urgent tone, "Yes officer, I think he went that (pointing down the road) way. If you hurry, you'll catch him."

Without being asked, Jamie stuck the blue lights on and accelerated to the end of the road, much to the amusement of the tour group. We then turned the lights off, did a quick circuit of the block, and slowly went past the tour group again. They were laughing and cheering. The tour guide smiled, nodded and we exchanged a thumbs-up.

I looked across at Jamie and he was grinning. Was that the frost thawing? Don't get me wrong, we did still disagree, and I still didn't do everything he wanted straight away. But I think he eased up a bit, and so did I.

A few nights later, we were driving along the Kenton Road. Everyone else was tied up with other calls, and it was raining hard. I mean chucking it down, and it had been all day. When the radio went, it was Suzie: "Units free to deal, we have reports of a man with a crossbow threatening his neighbours on the Britain estate."

Without hesitation, I replied: "Can you show PT3 making our way? We're five minutes from there."

"Thanks PT3. An ARV is en route. PT1 says please can you wait for them before tackling the suspect?"

I transmitted an acknowledgement, then Suzie gave us all the details. It appeared it was a housing block, with flats. There was a ground floor, a first floor, where our victims were, and a second floor where our suspect was. Apparently, our suspect had been playing *The Dark Side of the Moon* by Pink Floyd (a classic album) all night at full blast, over and over again. When our victims had had enough, they started banging on their ceiling to get him to stop. The music did stop then, ten minutes later, they heard a tapping on their window. They opened the curtains, only to see our suspect had abseiled down and was pointing a crossbow at them. They were disconcerted, closed the curtains and promptly called the police.

We arrived and secured the perimeter, to keep people back and stop this guy if he made a run for it. The guv'nor and Sergeant Darling arrived and covered the front and we covered the rear, which consisted of a very soggy stretch of grass surrounded by trees and bushes around the edge.

Jamie casually walked over to where he had a good view of the flats, under the cover of the trees. He leant back against the tree, rolled a cigarette, and lit it, saying: "Richard, come over here mate. Didn't anyone ever tell you a good policeman never runs or gets wet? Just wait 'til the shooty-shooty-bang-bang boys get here, and it all kicks off."

I followed his lead, and we stood and chatted for a while until the ARV arrived, at which point we heard them give a countdown to do a door entry. Then all hell broke loose. There was a loud crash (the door going in), then shouts and lots of swearing, then a loud crash and thud.

At this, Jamie casually finished his fag: "Now let's go and do some police work."

I looked over and saw a crumpled figure on the grass and saw the top window had been broken. This guy had jumped out of the window. As we approached he groaned and began to stir. I moved in quickly and cuffed this tall white man in his late thirties, who miraculously did not seem seriously injured; it must have been the soft ground he landed on, as much as luck.

As I picked up our suspect, and did a quick check to make sure he didn't have any bones poking out while saying "Hello." Jamie was on the radio saying we'd got the suspect.

We escorted our prisoner around the side of the block of flats when an urgent message came out from the ARV: "Turn the gas off. There's a gas leak. We need to evacuate the building. Call the LFB."

Jamie gave a little sigh, walked over to external utility box on the wall, pulled out a bundle of keys, selected one, opened the door and pulled down a lever. We continued to the front of the building, where we saw the guv'nor talking with one of the ARV crew. He walked over and said: "Guv, we've got your suspect, and I've turned the gas off to the building. Do you want to meet up with us at Park Street nick, as Earlham is full?"

The inspector smiled a knowing smile: "That sounds like a fine idea, Jamie. Good work, by the way."

At that we walked our prisoner to the car and took him to Park Street. When we got there, we booked him in, at which point he ran into the cell, stripped naked, hid under the blankets and begged us to keep him safe. Not the usual reaction to being put in a police cell.

When the full story came out, it turned out he was ex-army and had suffered serious PTSD, hadn't been properly cared for and lost the plot. Apparently, when the ARV crew had forced entry, he'd been warned because he'd installed a hidden security camera above his door. He'd hung a lit flare from the ceiling, broken a gas pipe (in the hope of causing an explosion) and jumped out the window. As you do! From a scientific point of view, it was unlikely to have worked; you need a very precise ratio of fuel to oxygen to create an explosion.

I admired Jamie's cool. He had thought out the possible outcomes, anticipated what was likely to happen and made sure he was in the right place at the right time. That was classy!

Towards the end of my stint on the area car, on a late turn, we got a call to a suspect package outside Earlham Magistrates' Court and, as we pulled up, I saw a large blue plastic carrier bag left against the glass of the front door. I jumped out, turned my radio to safe mode and walked up to the package, like I'd done dozens of times before. The top was folded over, and I smelt the slightest hint of petrol. That was new. It was the first time

I'd smelt that. I gingerly opened the bag and saw inside a small Tupperware box and a plastic petrol can. I could tell it was full. It was exactly what the slides of "This is a petrol bomb" looked like. My blood ran cold. *Oh shit, I don't want to be burned alive!*

Immediately I went into police mode. I turned to Jamie and loudly but calmly said, "Get everyone back. It looks like a real one."

Without hesitating, he started getting everyone back. As soon as he was far enough away, he put in the radio call.

With the pavement clear, I thought about the people inside. I walked towards the sliding door, which opened just before I approached, and a portly man in his late forties walked out. He had a bald top and front of his head, was 5'10", wearing cheap jeans, a thick jumper and padded dark blue cloth jacket. Before I could stop him, he made a beeline for the plastic bag, saying, "'Ere, leave my bag alone!"

I didn't have time to think, believing he was either about to accidentally or deliberately set the bomb off. I tackled him to the ground, and struggled to handcuff him. Jamie ran over and, between the two of us, we managed to subdue him.

Eventually, we had him sitting in handcuffs in the back of the car with a cordon around the front of the courthouse. He kept saying, "It's my bleedin' lunch and petrol for me car, you fuckin' lunatics!"

Jamie listened to what the man had to say. He walked over, put his hand into the bag and took out the box, held it up to the light, put it back in the bag, picked the bag up and walked to the car.

The closure was cancelled, and he stuck his head into the back seat of the car where the man was sitting. "Sir, what possessed you to leave a can of petrol in a bag outside of a courthouse?"

The man, rather offended by the question, said, "I had to go to court for a speeding ticket, and my car ran out of petrol, so I went round to my brother's to get the spare fuel he keeps in his garage to get me home. The Tupperware box are my sandwiches. Well the stupid security weren't going to let me into the court with the petrol can. And I wasn't going to walk all the way to my brother's, cos I'd be late, so I just left it outside. And you lot jumped on me. You're out of order!"

Jamie, more calmly than I was expecting said, "You didn't think that bringing a container full of petrol to a courthouse might not be a good idea?"

The man replied, "Look, mate, my brother's house is in the other direction. I thought it'd save me time to bring it with me. And I wasn't going to do nothing with it. I'm not some lunatic. I just don't understand why your mate jumped me? You're all just overreacting."

I was annoyed by this. "Mate, I just found something that I thought was a bomb right outside a courthouse, and you come out and claim its yours and try to grab it. I thought you were trying to blow us both up. So, yeah, I did grab you to stop you. Honestly, mate, I think what you just did was one of the most stupid things I've ever seen! You're lucky we don't nick you under the anti-terrorist legislation!" I was genuinely angry at the guy.

Jamie said calmly, "He's right. We could nick for what you've just done. I used to be in army bomb disposal, and that is very close to what a petrol bomb looks like. My colleague was quite right in stopping you getting to it. If it were a bomb, he'd have saved lives. Now we'll do some checks on you, and verify your story. You need to sit and think about what you've just done."

He went off and did some checks in court and on the radio. Eventually, he came back. "You're lucky, it all checks out. I'll take the cuffs off, and you're free to go. mate. Don't do that again, eh?"

We let the man go, and as he walked off, he was still complaining that he'd been unfairly treated.

As we drove off, Jamie said, "Good work. That was the correct response. Some people really don't have the sense they're born with."

I was a little surprised; Jamie rarely gave out compliments. This was high praise. I replied, "Thanks mate, I appreciate that. I just did what my gut told me to do. I honestly can't believe anyone could be that stupid!" He nodded, and I continued, "Is that what a bomb looks like? Did I miss something? That's exactly what the slides of a bomb looked like."

"Pretty much, but they have wires, and often you see batteries as well. But for the training you've had, that was a correct call. You didn't panic, you thought of the public first, you didn't run off, and you tackled the guy you thought was going to detonate it. All correct actions. That was what I expect from a policeman. Now let's see if the lovely Sooz has anything for us."

As if by magic, the radio went. "Any units to deal, we have reports of a fight, forty-plus fighting with weapons. West side of the Kenton Road opposite the flyover."

Jamie stuck the lights on and, taking the hint, I replied "PT3 running."

Sooz said, "Any units to back up PT3?"

Silence, then, "PT, can you show PT1 and PS43 running to back them up. We're running from PT."

That was the guv'nor turning out to back us up, because we were so short of numbers. But initially it was just the two of us against over fifty.

As we approached the scene, we started to see youths walking away. It looked like we'd missed the fight.

Suddenly, Jamie spotted something, "See that tall one, he's got a bloody axe!"

With that, he stopped the car and charged towards him. I looked down, and he'd left the door open, his radio in the car and the keys in the ignition. So I got out, ran round, took the keys out, pushed the central locking button, hit the emergency button and shouted, "272 and 404 on scene and chasing suspect with an axe."

I sprinted flat out. I'd lost Jamie in the crowd of young men, who were all turning around. Eventually I spotted Jamie, and at that moment, as he jumped a railing, his ASP fell out of its belt pouch and rolled across the pavement. I split my focus, as I ran between the ASP and Jamie. He was chasing a suspect through a crowd of potentially hostile young men, with no radio, no CS (he didn't carry it) and no ASP. He had his good looks and charm to protect him. Not wishing to be unkind, but I feared that might not be enough.

As I approached, one of the youths bent down and picked up the ASP. I waited until I was close and bellowed, in my best teacher mode, "Oye, you! Give that to me now boy!"

He looked up, shocked, and instinctively held it out to me, and I snatched it as I ran, remembering to say, "Good boy, thank you."

As I ran on, I vaulted the railing and soon saw Jamie ahead. He was walking back towards me. As I got close enough, I could see he was out of breath (to be honest, so was I). He shook his head, "The little bastard got away."

He looked at me, then felt for his ASP and said, "Is that mine? I didn't realise I'd lost it. Oh shit, I left the keys in the car, and doors unlocked, and where's my radio."

I handed back his ASP, his keys and said, "Don't worry, your radio's locked in the car, and actually I'd better let PT know that the chase is off."

He looked relieved. "Thanks mate, good work. I just saw red. We can't have kids walking around with bloody axes, it just isn't right!"

"It's fine, Jamie, I agree. We didn't know if he had just committed GBH or even murder."

He nodded, I called off the chase, and we walked back to the car. I took no satisfaction at his momentary rush of blood to the head. It was instinctive, and brave. He was trying to put himself between the public and the bad people. We don't always get things right.

A few days later, we turned up for a night shift. Most nights, we were inheriting about thirty outstanding calls that late duty couldn't handle. This time, we had fifty. This meant we'd be running around on blues and twos from call to call for at least the first half of the shift.

As Jamie and I were pulling out of the station, we had a call, "Units to deal, there's a fight at a new Comedy Club in Earlham." Jamie stuck the lights on, and this was my cue to accept the call.

"PT3, show us running from PT."

"Received PT3. Be aware, just updated, the man has a weapon."

That wasn't too rare. I thought, *when we stop, I'd better get the shield from the boot. That helps with knives.*

By that point, I was carrying a lot less kit on my belt. I had ditched the PSM part of my radio and was using it like a walkie talkie, as this was the common practice on C relief. The thought was that it helped in being as light as possible, to aid in moving quickly.

As we pulled up right outside the doors to the club, I stepped out and brought the radio up to my face to put us on scene. At that moment, the doors to the club opened and a man with a broken bottle in his hand charged straight out at me, screaming. I was trapped: I had the open car door to my right, the car behind me and a radio in my right hand. I had no time to think. I couldn't back off, and if I stood still he'd no doubt slash me with the bottle. So I did the only thing I could: I stepped forward, to put off his timing. As he drew has right arm back to slash me, I blocked his swing with my left arm, and brought the butt of the radio down squarely on the middle of his forehead, stunning him. His momentum brought him crashing into me, and the two of us struggled for a moment until the effect of the radio caused him to slump down. I thought, *Oh God, I've killed him! Are radio strikes Home Office-approved? I haven't been on that course.*

I heard Jamie walking around, and between the two of us we picked up the guy and sat him in the back of the police car. He was groggy, drunk, but otherwise OK. *Thank God for that,* I thought. Jamie gave me a funny look; I wasn't sure what he was thinking. A minute or so later the security from the club came out and informed us he'd been causing trouble, and before he could be ejected he'd smashed a bottle and glassed one of the other customers, and had been running around inside. Security had tried to apprehend him, but had to back off when he'd threatened them with the broken bottle.

We arrested him and called CID down. We spent a bit of time collecting security footage, and witness names and addresses. The LAS arrived and the victim was taken away. They had a quick look at our suspect and said, "He's got a large rectangular mark on his forehead and is drunk and a little groggy. What happened to him?"

I said, "Well, he bottled someone in the club, ran security a merry dance inside, and ran out of the club straight into me. The only thing in my hand was my radio, so I hit him in the head with it."

The LAS man smirked. "Really? Are you trained to do that?"

"It was either that or be slashed with the bottle. And no, I'm not trained to do that. It was just instinct."

He could barely suppress a smile. He patted me on the arm, "You do what you have to, to survive. I can't wait to see the security footage of that though."

I looked up and, sure enough, there were two security cameras covering us. *Oh no!*

We got the suspect back to the nick and Sergeant Smedley was in custody. I walked in holding my now fully awake, if still slightly pissed, suspect. He was a man in his mid-thirties, 6'2", muscular build, jeans and T-shirt and leather jacket.

The sergeant said, "'Ello 272. What have you got for me today?"

"Hello Sarge. We received a call that a man armed with a weapon was causing a disturbance at the new Comedy Club in Earlham. Upon arrival, the suspect here ran out of the building straight at me brandishing a broken bottle, and I subdued him. It became apparent that he'd slashed another male in the club and threatened security with the broken bottle. At 22:10 hours I arrested him for assault and affray."

The sergeant nodded and typed something into the custody computer. He looked up, "Has he any injuries?"

I took a deep breath, as I noticed that my C relief colleagues present were listening in. *Oh great*, I thought. "He has a bruise to the forehead suffered while I was subduing him, Sergeant."

The sergeant nodded. "272, how did he suffer this bruising?"

My heart sank. *Here we go.* "As the man ran at me with a broken bottle, I had the car behind me, so I couldn't back off. The only thing I had in my hand was my radio, so I delivered a strike with the base of the radio to the centre of the man's forehead, which allowed me to subdue him."

The sergeant nodded, with a deadpan expression. "Did anyone witness the arrest?"

Jamie stepped forward. "I did, Sarge, and there's also CCTV footage. PC Armstrong's actions were purely in self-defence, and entirely justified in my opinion."

Phew! I thought. *Thanks Jamie.*

The sergeant turned to the man, "You've heard what the officer's said. Is there anything you want to say?"

I tensed. Was I going to be in trouble?

The man said, "Yeah, that's about what happened. When I came out the club I saw red. Sorry mate, I didn't realise you were the filth."

I could feel the relief run through me. *Thank God for that! Someone who actually takes responsibility. Rare!*

The sergeant said, "Do you need to go to hospital or see the doctor?"

The man shook his head. "I'm all right, mate, don't worry."

The sergeant said, "Just for the sake of thoroughness, I think we'll get the doc to see you."

We put the suspect in the cell and handed over the job to John and Patience in CID. It wasn't until the next shift that I started to get a few comments like, "Watch out, he's got his radio out."

Apparently, word had got around, and some had even seen the CCTV footage of how the mild-mannered, left-wing teacher had "radioed" a suspect.

Well, there was nothing I could do. The man hadn't made a complaint. Even in the interview, he'd said that he was OK with it, that it was fair enough. When his solicitor had tried to make something out of it, he'd stopped him. To him, it was fair enough; he wasn't going to complain. There is apparently a code of conduct for at least some of the villains.

After that, Jamie and I got on a lot better. We'd both backed each other up, without criticism, and looked out for one another.

On the last night duty of the five-week stint with Jamie, we responded to a disturbance at an Indian (most were, in fact, Bangladeshi) restaurant. Where it was located was a radio blackspot, so we couldn't make or receive any calls. I had to put us on scene well before we got there. Name checks were out of the window.

The restaurant was about half-full, and there were two members of staff arguing with a 6'4" giant of a man. He had muscles, tattoos, a dark-collared shirt, dark jeans with a dark jacket. He had clearly been drinking, and was swaying slightly, and his words were slurred. They all stopped and looked at as we walked in.

I said, "Good evening, folks. Can we help?"

The two members of staff, who were significantly smaller than customer, looked relieved at our arrival.

Jamie said, "Richard, you go and have a chat with the staff, and I'll have a chat with this gentleman."

Thank you for that one, mate. I went over and, out of earshot, said, "Hello there, gentlemen. What's the problem?"

One of the men said, "I'm so glad you're here. I'm the manager, and this man is a bit drunk. He was OK with us. His friends left, and he's refusing to pay. He's a lot bigger than us."

"Fair enough. How do you want us deal with him? Has he been abusive towards you? Do you want him arrested?"

"No Sir, we don't want any trouble. He owes us £65; that's all we want."

I looked at him straight on, and lowered my voice. "Are you sure? Look, if he's been out of line, we can arrest him. He's clearly drunk."

The man shook his head. "No Sir. We just want him to pay, and that's all. Don't worry."

"OK, if that's what you want. Either way, we'll make sure he's gone before we go."

I walked over to where Jamie was. "They only want the money he owes them: £65. They don't want to take it further."

He nodded, and turned to the man, "Sir, these gentlemen, just want you to pay for the meal. It's £65, and you can go home. You had the meal; it's not unreasonable to ask for payment, is it?"

After a bit of to and fro, he eventually paid. We would normally have done a name check, but there was no reception (a problem that would be highlighted in a few years' time). The Met and its extra cheapness!

The restaurant were happy, and the man started staggering off down the road (not bad enough to arrest him). As we sat, watching him from our car, I said, "He's not done yet, is he?"

Jamie shook his head, "Oh no, he's not. Five, four, three, two, one."

At that moment, the man turned around and walked up to my open window. He leant in, and with beery breath, said, "You're both a bunch of cunts!"

He turned around and staggered down the road. I looked at Jamie, "A bunch of cunts? Not one cunt? We're a bunch of cunts? I wonder what the proper collective noun is for a 'bunch' of cunts?"

Jamie said, while slowly following the man in the car with the blue lights on, "That's obvious: a *Guardian* journalist of cunts."

We both laughed, and I said, "Shouldn't I get out and nick him?"

Jamie held up his hand. "Wait, he's still got fight in him."

At that, the man turned around and raised his fists towards us. Then, thinking better of it, he turned to try to run off, lost his balance and fell over.

I looked at Jamie. "Now?"

He again raised his hand. "Not yet."

The man half-stood from the ground and fell over again. Jamie stopped the car, "Now!"

We walked over, and he was lying, snoring, on the ground. I went up the road, to get reception, and requested the van. When we got him back to the nick, we searched him and got his ID. We did a name check, and our man was wanted on warrant for a number of offences, including GBH. We contacted the CID units dealing with those cases while he slept off his hangover in the cells. Sometimes, criminals are their own worst enemies. All he had to do was keep walking, but no! His instinct took over. He had to have the last word, but it didn't quite work out for him that way.

The end of the five weeks was up, and at the end of the shift I walked over to Jamie and stuck out my hand. "Jamie, you and I have had our ups and downs, but thank you. I really enjoyed working with you and I've learnt a lot."

Jamie stopped, turned and looked at me. "You're wrong!" I thought, *Oh no, here we go. I can't do anything right!*" But he continued, "There were no downs. I disagreed with you for the way you dealt with the reporting Alf thing. But I think he was so out of order for what he said. But during the last five weeks, you've worked really hard. You did really well. I think you're a fine officer, and not only would I have no issues working with you, but if I hear anyone bad-mouthing you, I'll set them straight."

With that, he shook my hand with a grip like a vice, and walked off.

I stood there, stunned. I'd done it: my harshest critic on relief thought I was a good officer. At that point I didn't need to be confirmed at the end of my probation. I gained the approval of my hardest peers. I felt a weight lift from my shoulders, I still had a week until I (hopefully) completed my probation. But I was a policeman. I'd made it, after two years of ups and downs. I'd achieved it, and done it the hard way.

Question was, would the management confirm me as a PC?

A couple of days later, I got a notification of shield-trained aid, which means riot gear, for possible trouble. Apparently, there were a series of demonstrations organised, I honestly can't remember for what. I was no stranger to demonstrations. I'd attended at least a dozen: CND, animal rights, education cuts. I absolutely believed in the right to peaceful protest. I'd seen a bit of trouble, the bad-faith protestors and the police overreacting. Never from the other side, though. What was it going to be like?

We were picked up in the carrier, which was a high-top Ford Transit with a pull-down metal grille for the front window, and a cage at the back for the shields (a selection of full shields and the smaller round ones).

I looked around, and we were all in reasonable spirits. I was with The Law, Pete, Campbell, Sergeant Smedley, and a number of other officers from Earlham. We made our way to the briefing at another station, closer to central London. I felt a gentle dig in the ribs, looked over, and it was Sergeant Smedley. He said, "This your first protest as a level-two?" (level two was riot-trained and equipped).

I nodded and replied, slightly cheekily, "Well, first protest from this side of the line, Sarge."

There were a few oohs and arrs, and catcalls. The sergeant grinned, and said over the horrendous racket of the carrier, "I've a feeling this'll be a lively one. Stick close to your mates, and you'll be fine. Don't get separated."

I nodded and gave him the thumbs-up as we went over a particularly bumpy piece of road.

We arrived at the station. There were loads of police officers and dozens of carriers. We went into the huge canteen and had some food. We were told it might be the last food we'd have for a while. The carriers did have a box of sandwiches and drinks in them. But heaven knows when we'd be finished that night.

Then the briefing. We were all moved into what looked like an old warehouse, where there was a small platform, and a senior officer stood up and said, "Ladies and gents. It looks like it could really kick off today. It's technically an anti-capitalist rally, but we have solid evidence that it's been infiltrated by rent-a-mob elements who are just looking for a fight. Remember, they'll try and wind you up; it's what they try and do. Wind you up, start something and, when you react, they film that, and that's what's on the news. Because you know how unbiased the TV and papers are."

There was a loud chorus of boos and jeers. He continued, "Remember it has been known for the so-called journalists to either be in league with some of these extremists, or pay them to start something in front of them so they can be there to film it. So don't give them any excuse. The intelligence is that these extremist groups have set up a training camp for a few hundred of the rent-a-mob types, to show them how to attack police and get away with it. The type of things to do and say. And, more sinister this time, the word is that they are going to isolate an officer, kill them and, as they put it, 'do a Blakelock' (referring to PC Keith Blakelock who was killed and almost decapitated in the Marsh Farm riots)."

He let this settle in. There was a murmur of concern throughout the ranks. It wasn't good! He continued, "We'll keep the level ones in the front line as long as we can to de-escalate the situation as much as we can. It looks like the two places to worry about are Parliament Square and Trafalgar Square. We have eyes in the sky, and we'll try to use CCTV to spot any breakaway groups who start smashing things up. Remember folks: stick together, don't let anyone get isolated. Remember the cameras, be professional, don't let those media vultures have anything to feed on. You know how they twist things. Take care."

Well that wasn't something I wanted to hear. Off we went to the carriers. We heard we'd be sitting in a side street near Hyde Park, where the posh hotels were, and we'd be called on to go in if needed.

So we drove over and sat up, all kitted up in our baby grows, trying to get 'comfortable' for a long wait. The radio in those sort of situations can get very busy, with hundreds of officers involved. So, only the sergeants and above used them, unless it was an emergency. There were a number of frequencies in use. We listened in, and it was all going OK at the start. Without the radio, we could hear the drums and noise of the protestors from afar. We waited and waited. Eventually, it started to change, and we heard they'd seen fully masked-up groups of rent-a-mob types infiltrating the ranks of the more peaceful protestors.

Then we heard reports of stones and bottles being thrown at the police in normal uniform. The sergeant said, "They're outside Downing Street calling Blair a 'cunt'."

I really couldn't fault them on that assessment. We were all laughing, until he said, "Yeah they're sending in level-twos, as they're trying force their way in, and throwing missiles."

That quietened us down. Then there were reports coming from Parliament Square: they were shouting abuse at the politicians in the Houses of Parliament. Once again, a few wry comments about the politicians. Then they went after the Churchill statue, and ripped up the grass in the square. One of the more printable comments was: "Churchill? Really? He fought the Nazis. Are these people in favour of the Nazis?"

There was also a large gathering in Parliament Square. That was fine; they could be contained in there.

Then we got the call that a few breakaway groups had started smashing up shops and looting them. This was where they drew the line, and we were readied.

The sergeant shouted, "Right gang, gear up, small shields."

This meant mobility, snatch squads, moving fast. But it meant we were more vulnerable. I stepped out of the van and stretched my stiff muscles, pulled my helmet on, pulled the chinstrap tight, and waited until The Law handed me a shield. Arm through the big metal hoop, and grip the worn plastic grip on the opposite side. This was clearly built to a budget, and had seen plenty of service. The Met and its extra cheapness. The body armour was beginning to rub, and I felt really hot and itchy in the baby grow. We waited for directions. We started hearing reports some of the non-riot-dressed police were getting pelted and attacked. They were told to stay, and repeated requests for units to back them up were ignored. They seemed to care more about 'de-escalating' things than the safety of the officers with no protection. Better ten police get hurt than one rioter – easier to sell to the media. Cowardly senior officers!

We were stood down. Put away the shields, back in the van, and wait. It was a game of hurry up and wait. We didn't have long to wait this time.

"Gear up," was the cry. We closed the van, and off we jogged, the skipper at the front, single file this time. I was in the middle. Just look after the guys in front and behind. The uniforms weren't designed with speed or comfort in mind, and the very limited view of the world you have is made worse by the fact your hearing is reduced in the helmets. It's an altered reality, and with all the chanting and whistles and drums, you are all but deaf to what's happening around you. You rely on direct forward sight as the helmet removes most of your peripheral vision. The world shot by as a blur, just concentrating on the person in front, being shouted and screamed at (most of which you can't make out), bumped and shoved. It's both real and surreal, with the sights and sounds surreal, but the missiles and fists very real.

I've been in plenty of large crowds, but never as a target. I still have nightmares about it now. The feeling of being surrounded and trapped and constricted. Then we were forming up a line across a street. I had no idea which street. There were masses of people, mostly just standing at a distance either watching or hurling abuse. Then I got a nudge. I looked across, at what I could only just recognise as The Law. He had racked his ASP. I nodded and did the same. I held it at ready, resting on my shoulder. There were a couple of people dressed in costumes; one looked like a fairy with silver wings (it wasn't his colour), and the other had what looked like BDSM gear. Nice! What's that got to do with anti-capitalism?

They were dancing and shouting and screaming very close. A number of the very brave types in full face masks were walking up and pointing and shouting. If they got within touching distance, they were shoved back.

Isolated from the world through the sensory deprivation, it's a deeply personal experience, which is odd when you're surrounded by thousands of people. Then we were moving forward to push the 'protestors' back.

That was going to be the interesting bit. We stepped a few paces forward, stopped, a few more, then just kept going. That was where the discipline of learning to march, and trusting your mates paid off. Some of the 'braver' protestors would stop and try to grab us, our ASPs, our shields, helmets, anything. So the tactic was to shove with the shield, bend your knees and shove up, getting them off balance and, once off balance, shove them again. At that point, from the front, we started receiving incoming missiles. They were using the regular, non-violent protestors as a shield, so we couldn't identify them.

It was bottles, bits of concrete and half bricks. You could see the ones directly in front of you, but it was harder to catch the ones that came in at an angle. You relied on your mates to deflect them. It did mean that some of the people directly in front of us backed off, as they didn't want to be victims of 'friendly fire'.

I saw something off to my right (wrong side for my shield), and felt a hard blow to the right side of my helmet, and almost lost my balance. My head was ringing; I couldn't hear much. My mouth was salty, so I raised my visor and spat down, and carried on. Once we'd got to the end of the street, we stopped and waited.

We were at a road junction with a large, wide street. My sense of direction was gone. My head and neck hurt, my back ached, and I was feeling really tired. For a long while after that it varied between people coming up and trying to push through our line in gangs, and people standing back and a few lobbed missiles to bat away. Trust me, when a piece of concrete or brick bounces off your shield, you know about it.

I could feel my arm getting fatigued. The whole experience was draining. Time just dragged on. We heard something happening behind us, and we could see some film crews filming. They only arrive where there's trouble. Coincidence, I guess. There was a group of about fifty or sixty, against our twenty. They charged at us. We formed up and readied our batons, and as soon as they were in striking distance, down came our batons. There were screams and shouts and then the ones at the front were trying to back up into the ones behind them, as they didn't want to be near the batons. All the while we were shouting: "Get back, get back." They eventually backed up, and left space in front of us, and another few serials formed up ahead of us, and we were stood down from the front.

The cycle continued for what seemed like hours. Then we were moving off through the side streets through straggling groups of protestors. As we were jogging along at arm's-length distance, a shorter man (5'9"), stocky, all dressed in black, with a face mask, jumped in between me and The Law from the left. I just lowered my shield and put my shoulder behind it, and used my momentum to hit him. He was stocky, but bounced off and back, screaming some abuse that was lost in the rest of the noise. He tried the same trick behind me with similar results. Eventually we arrived at one of the top entrances to Trafalgar Square, and stretched out before us were thousands of people, all shouting and screaming abuse. I have never seen so many people. Of the chants you could make out were: “Kill the Bill, Kill the Bill!” Nice! It may sound odd, but I’ve never felt so much hate from so many people. We stood there, with people coming up to us screaming and shouting, dancing and mocking us as close as they dared. Then we were moving again.

This carried on for the rest of the day: move, abuse, missiles, pushing, shoving. We all picked up bashes and bruises. We heard our colleagues calling for aid, of people getting hurt.

Finally, we were ordered back to the van, and we were on ready, and then dismissed. Trust me, if their goal was to have a more equitable society, then I’m with you. But I’m not sure chucking bricks at the police and smashing up shops will achieve it.

It wasn’t until I took off my helmet that I noticed a large dent (about an inch deep) and gouge down the right side. The Law nudged me and said, “I saw that come in. Campbell deflected it, and it took the real sting out of it. If he hadn’t, it would have really hurt.”

I looked across at Campbell: “Campbell (he looked up), thanks mate. (I held up the helmet) I owe you one.”

He smiled, “You’re welcome, mate. I know you’d have done the same. Good battle scar, that one. A lucky helmet.”

Then off we went back to the nick, battered and bruised, but still in one piece. The news that night was the shocker; it bore absolutely no resemblance to what really happened. The TV news were showing very little of the rioters hurting the police, but every bit of bad police footage they could. The papers the next day were even worse. I understood the dislike of *The Guardian* now. All of them – what a lying bunch of shitbags. I couldn't square it. I knew a number of journalists, and they were lovely, kind, decent people who believed in balance and proportion. Yet their colleagues seemed to have an agenda!

So, back to the nick, and only a few days left. As the song went, would I stay or would I go?

I didn't have long to find out if I was going to be confirmed or let go. I was gaoler on earlies the next day with Sergeant Deacon, and he told me the inspector wanted to see me at refs in his office.

I thought, *here we go! Almost there. What's the worst that can happen now?* Even to think that is to court disaster.

I said: "Sergeant, do you want a coffee?"

"Yeah, thanks Richard. My Fulham FC mug is in my bag. I think I'll have to take a tray of the mugs over at refs when Sergeant Darling is covering for me."

"Do you want me to do that?"

"No, you're fine. You've got the boss to see."

I duly got him his coffee in his Fulham mug. We'd had a social a few weeks before, and I'd met his wife (a lovely lady who trained dogs for TV and film work). She said he was mad on Fulham, and had followed them since he was a boy. She got on really well with Sooz, and had a great sense of humour. The sergeant had really got lucky; she was a really understanding lady. I thought about my love life, or lack thereof. I still couldn't get over Victoria, and didn't think I ever would.

It was a really quiet morning, and at refs, as I walked out to see the boss, I saw Sergeant Deacon collecting the mugs on a tray to take them to the canteen in the accommodation block, to put them through the dishwasher. As I walked down the shabby corridor, past the parade room, which I'd nervously waited outside, I walked past the control room and saw Sooz turn and cross her fingers for me. Did she know everything? Probably!

I thought of the day back in May. I found my hand was holding the whistle my mom had given me. I wasn't really sure what was going to happen. So much had happened since the first day with Paige. I was a different person. Sergeant Johnson had been right – I had known nothing. I was a civilian, knew nothing of policing. Even all the family and friends I'd grown up with hadn't prepared me for it.

I'd learnt to tune out the uninformed and ignorant pontifications of my friends, who gave their opinions on matters to do with the police. They thought they knew. I know they had good intentions, but they just didn't get it. The range of things you have to do, the no-win situations you have, the way the media and politicians lied and misrepresented us, the senior management prepared to use us as tools to get to the next rank, or to push their ideology.

The bravery, professionalism and downright humanity of the vast majority of the rank and file officers went way beyond anything civilians would or could ever understand. And to have the approval of my peers meant more to me than a piece of paper, or all the medals or plaudits of senior management or anyone else.

A thank you from a person you've helped, or a pat on the back or nod approval of a trusted colleague, are what really counted.

I wondered if my grandad, great-grandad or dad were looking down seeing me, and if they were proud?

I was snapped out of these thoughts by the screech of tyres, an almighty bang, silence, then a lot of shouting from the back yard. Then the alarms going off. I ran to the control room and looked in. Sooz said: "Back yard!"

I didn't need to be told twice. I ran down the corridor I'd just walked down and out into the back yard. I could see Sergeant Deacon struggling with two young white guys, both about 18. I went to help, but my sixth sense for danger (I'd finally developed it) kicked in, and I turned around to see a BMW had smashed into the barrier, and three six-feet-plus Black guys were climbing over the car to get into the yard, shouting as they did so. The station was under attack. Not on my watch! I'd never sworn at a suspect or member of the public before then.

I stood up to my full 6'¼" (never forget the ¼"), shoulders back, chest out, drew my ASP, and I was so tempted to say, in my best Tolkien, accent, "None shall pass!" I settled for shouting, "The first one of you motherfuckers to step foot in my police station gets this stick wrapped around the side of your head!"

Not quite textbook, but it certainly had the desired effect. They stopped in their tracks. I stood stock-still and stared them down until everyone and their dog (literally) arrived. If I thought you got a quick response when you called for urgent assistance, that was nothing to when you say the police station is under attack.

It wasn't long until we were stood in custody with four PCs standing, watching the prisoners (the three Black lads on one bench, the two white lads on the other), all handcuffed. Sergeant Deacon stood there glaring at both groups. He was cut and bruised, and his shirt was ripped and tea-stained from the half-empty mugs. His favourite Fulham mug had been one of the many casualties when he'd dropped the tray to deal with the two white lads.

He said in a hard-edged voice, "Which one of you 'gentlemen' is going to explain to me why you found it necessary to turn my police station into a fucking war zone!?"

A number of moments passed, with the sergeant glaring with real intensity at the two groups. Finally, one of the two white lads put his hand up (which, comically, caused his other hand to rise, due to handcuffs): "Please Sir ..."

The sergeant glared at him, "It's Sergeant, not Sir! Go on."

"Sorry Sergeant. I nicked that man's (pointing at one of the Black lads, with his handcuffs on, which doesn't look cool) BMW. I found his address in Canning Town (I thought, *what, you nicked a car from someone in Canning Town? Bloody hell, mate, you must be braver than you look*) and we thought it'd be a laugh to do burnouts in it outside his house. You know, to take the piss, but he ran out and got into his mate's car, and chased us. We got scared, and drove to the safest place we know: the police station. Sorry mate (looking at the Black guy)."

Well, I'd heard it all now. *You nick someone's car, taunt them, then run to the police station when they react!?*

The sergeant turned to the Black guys: "Is this true?"

One of the Black lads said: "Yeah, that's about right."

The sergeant said: "Officers, de-arrest our three friends, and someone arrest those two over there."

Out of instinct, I made to walk over to nick them. The sergeant stopped me with a stare, and The Law gladly obliged. He looked at the three guys and said, "No hard feelings. You have to understand that we didn't know what was going on. Breaking into a police station isn't something we deal with very often."

One of the guys said, "It's all right. I realise what it must have looked like. You wouldn't have known who we were. At least they've been caught, even if my car is totalled."

The sergeant said, "Richard and Greg, would you like to take our three friends here through to the interview rooms, and go to the canteen to get them some tea. We appear to be out of mugs." He held up the shattered Fulham mug.

He added: "Richard, you'd better go and see the boss. You're late. Don't worry, I'll call him and tell him why. Oh, by the way, do you have your Metvest on?"

"Yes Sarge. Why?"

"Good, but you'll only need the back panel. Remember, when you speak to senior management and they pat you on the back, they're only finding a good spot to stab you in the back!"

I thought, *oh God, I am late! I'm never late!*

I took the three gents through to the front interview room and, putting out my hand, said, "No hard feelings, gentlemen. You scared me half to death, climbing into a police station. Most people can't wait to get out."

They smiled and shook my hand, "No, you're all right mate. You were proper scary back there!"

I waited for Mel to get them teas, and said quietly, "Gents, remember when it comes to writing your statements about the drive from Canning Town, you're talking to police. It might make it difficult for them if you tell them you ran red lights, or did anything really crazy."

I raised my eyebrows, hoping they'd get the hint. One of them did and whispered to the others. He nodded and said, "Thank you, officer."

I smiled, "One bit of unofficial advice. Firstly, I don't blame you in the slightest for chasing those car thieves; I'd have probably done the same.

But just think, if you'd hurt anyone while you were, how you'd have felt. Is a death on your conscience more important than a car?"

One of the lads said, "You're right. Thanks mate."

I think I made my point. Not bad from a reformed XR3i Essex boy racer.

I walked to the Superintendent's office (I noticed he hadn't come out to help when the station was 'under attack'), knocked and waited. Almost immediately I heard a "Come in". I should have been more nervous but, honestly, at that stage, I'd faced down far worse than that guy.

He smiled, "Please come in, Richard. Do you mind if I call you Richard (I nodded)? Sit down. You're late, but the good sergeant explained the circumstances. Quite a bit of excitement. Straight down to business; I'm very busy today."

I sat down and said, "Sorry Sir, I've forgotten I should have saluted."

"Oh, don't worry about that today. But don't forget it in the future."

OK, noted!

He pulled out a number of papers from a personnel folder. "I've been looking through your record. It got off to a decent start at Hendon, no problems there, bit of a dip on street duties (no shit, Sherlock!), and another with that nightclub bombing thing. But solid all the way through otherwise. Excellent work ethic, great figures on arrests and process. Best on the division, and a glowing recommendation from your time on the area car (Thanks James). What's this? A commendation from the flying squad, and the assistant coroner (wow, she'd sent in a letter to personnel, thanks!). And another from the area drugs squad. Despite all the problems you've had, I can see no reason why I shouldn't confirm you as a substantive PC. Well done, you've done it. You're a full PC. Two years later, you made it."

He paused, closed the file and looked at me, almost for the first time. "So how do you feel?"

I paused and, trying to decide how honest to be with him, said, "Honestly Sir, I don't know right now. It's been such a roller coaster. I often ask myself, if I knew back then what I know now, would I have joined? But I'm a different person now. It's not just a job, it's far more than that: it's an identity. I joined because it had been in my family, and I grew up listening to police stories. It was always brave and heroic, that we were the good guys, helping people. Driving around in fast cars and arresting villains. It's not like that. Well, it is sometimes, but it's a lot more than that. I'm proud of having achieved my dream. But the price you pay to do this job is very high. The highs are higher than any other jobs, but the lows are lower."

There, I'd been pretty honest. He looked genuinely at a loss for words. I guess most people just tell him what he wants to hear. Not me: ask me a question, and I'll usually be honest, even if it does hurt.

After a few moments he said, "Is this something you'll stay in? Is policing for you long term?"

It was my turn to be taken off guard. Wow, it was a real conversation with senior management. "Yes, I'll stay with it as long as I am fit to continue. I love this job, for what I can do to help people, for the impact I can make, even though it's only a drop in the ocean. I love the acceptance of my colleagues, the teamwork. Without sounding corny, Sir, I guess you've worked out, with all due respect, Sir, that I try to be honest. It is an honour to serve Her Majesty the Queen, and her subjects. To have the privilege to put one's self between the public and the bad guys, to protect their rights, to uphold the principles of Sir Robert Peel, and to honour the memory to my grandad and great-grandad, is hugely important to me."

I sat back in the chair slightly. I was almost done. The adrenaline from earlier was wearing off.

"That's commendable. You've clearly thought long and hard about this. What do you see next in your career?"

I replied without hesitation, "First, Sir, I want to get my response driver course done, and spend at least three years on relief. Then I'll decide where to go next. I want to have five years under my belt, so I've seen and dealt with most things, as a good grounding."

"Very wise. With your academic background, maybe either look to become a sergeant, then at least inspector, or maybe CID or the CSU. You did well there. I'll let you think about it. Now I really have to get on. Well done, Police Constable Armstrong."

He stood and offered me his hand. I stood, shook his hand, and saluted him this time. For one of the few times in my career, I respected the man as well as the uniform. He'd listened, and we'd had a real conversation.

As I walked out of the office, it was like a weight being lifted from my shoulders. *Let's have some fun.* I walked down and told Sooz that I'd passed. She gave me a huge hug, which wasn't the worst thing in the world. Then I told of my plan, and she loved it, so we plotted and schemed. We had a few rest days to enact my fiendish plan.

Chapter 9
LIVING THE DREAM

On the first paperwork day back, I was sitting alone in the back canteen 'reading' *The Guardian*, until Sergeant Deacon arrived. He looked around, "Where is everyone? They're all late. I don't think I can eat all those doughnuts."

I grinned, then in came The Law, saying, "Sorry I'm late Sarge. I heard your favourite football mug got broken. I couldn't remember which London team it was; I hope this is right." He handed him a West Ham (C'mon the Hammers) mug.

The sergeant looked at it, "Thanks for the thought, but I support Fulham. I thought everyone knew that. But thanks for the thought."

He put it on the table. A couple of minutes later, in walked Mel. "Sorry I'm late Sarge," and handed him an Arsenal mug. "I went to that new place up in Canary Wharf that sells football memorabilia. I couldn't remember which club it was."

He turned the mug over in his hand, and put it down on the table. "Thanks Mel. I support Fulham, but thanks for the thought."

A few minutes later, in walked Jamie. same thing, with a Tottenham mug. Then Campbell, with a Crystal Palace mug, then Pete with a QPR mug, then Sergeant Darling with a Leyton Orient mug, Robbie with a Millwall mug, and Sergeant Smedley with a Charlton Athletic mug. By this time, the table was half-filled with football mugs, none of which was his club. The good sergeant was getting more and more frustrated. He was trying to be polite, but it was a strain.

Finally, in walked the inspector. Sergeant Deacon looked up in the hope the inspector had remembered what club he supported. The inspector walked over, "I bought you a replacement mug for the one you had smashed. Here it is." He proudly handed him a Chelsea mug (Chelsea and Fulham are bitter rivals).

There was a lot of laughter at this, and Sergeant Deacon had joined in, but I could see he was secretly disappointed he hadn't got his team's mug.

He looked around, and eventually settled on me. "Armstrong! You're behind this, you rotten bastard!"

More laughter, and he started to lighten up. "I have to say that you got me good and proper. I'll donate these to replace the ones in custody that were broken. I'll just have to get a Fulham one, when I get home!" I tried very hard not to smirk. I thought, *this isn't over yet, my friend.*

We settled down, and Jamie looked across, "Richard, you still reading *The Guardian*? OK, I'll bite, what's in it today?"

I looked over the top of the paper. "I don't read this rag. I have no idea."

I dropped *The Guardian* to reveal *The Job*, the Met Police's newspaper.

This received plenty of laughter and some applause. When it finished, Campbell said, "What, you've been winding us up for over a year? That's some long-term planning. You're a serious practical joker. Who taught you that?"

I grinned, "That was my dad, and I was brought up on stories of my grandad and great-grandad. They were both job, and there were some epic pranks played back in those days."

We sat and had a real laugh, going through some pranks we'd heard about. The one they seemed to find most funny was when my dad was training to be merchant seaman. There was a square, with four narrow entrances between the buildings. The senior instructor's office looked out onto the square. The senior instructor went away for the weekend and, when he returned, he looked out onto the square below, where my dad had placed sandbags at each corner, and used the fire hose to fill to a depth of a couple of inches. Floating in the middle of the square was a child's plastic inflatable dinghy with the Red Ensign proudly flying in it.

The following day, we started nights, and I was doing my basic driving assessment with Robbie. It was one of the last things he'd do before he moved on (oops), and the new inspector would be starting soon too.

I sat in the parade room in civvies (high-tech Magnums, jeans, sweatshirt, bullet-proof corset, and black fleece). Eventually, in walked Sergeant Deacon, holding a new Fulham mug. He waited until everyone was quiet, then said, "PC Armstrong, when I got home last night, my good lady wife said, 'I bought you this mug to replace the one you lost and, by the way, the relief says hello!' That has to be one of the classiest wind-ups I've seen in a long time. We'll have to keep an eye on you!"

I'd kept the last bit secret, and only Sooz had been in on it. She was friends with Mrs Deacon, and she had thought it was a great joke. So the rest of the team had a good laugh.

The sergeant then said more seriously, "That was classy. You were never cruel, and I ended up with not only a replacement for my mug, but replacements for custody too. Who bought those mugs?"

I replied, "I did. I went to the football memorabilia shop, and asked for one for every team in London. It was a thank you."

Once we'd settled down, I walked out with Robbie to what we called the GP car, short for general purpose. It was typically a dark blue, bog-standard Fiesta shared with CID, to be used when we didn't want a marked police car. We were going to try to catch a burglar who was preying on companies in a local business park. But, that day, CID had 54'd (taken out of service) the GP car, so we had to use a hire car until it was repaired. The hire company didn't have any of their basic cars, so gave us an upgrade to a top-of-the-range Renault Clio. It had all the bells and whistles, and a larger, 1.7L engine. Nice!

I settled myself in the DRIVER'S seat. Man, that was strange, being in the right seat for a change. I looked at Robbie and he said: "Let's go."

I set off at a gentle pace, and headed for the business park, and we started to chat, for the first time in months, and the slightly awkward atmosphere lifted. I said: "Look, I'll just say it. I'm really sorry I handled that incident so badly. I wish I could take it back and do it again. You were nothing but kind to me, and because I handled things badly, you were punished for that. I'm really sorry."

He was about to answer when a silver Ferrari shot past like a bat out of hell. We looked at each other, and he reached for the radio: "What are you waiting for? Go get 'em, Tiger!"

I replied with a grin from ear to ear, "Do you know how long I've waited for someone say that!"

"Shut up and drive!" We were going for the cliches that night.

Channelling my best Essex boy racer, I floored it. My God, that thing took off. I was rattling it through the gears, and very quickly the Ferrari came back into view, as we approached the mini-roundabout, where he turned right, south along the road, and accelerated off. I slammed it down through the gears and shot around the roundabout, leaving skid marks on the road, with Robbie clinging on for grim death, and doing his best to keep up the commentary.

I floored it once again, and I could feel the torque steer as the tyres desperately hunted for grip, even through the power steering. I was having fun! It was so much faster than my Ka, my XR3i, and most of the other cars I'd driven. I hammered the engine, to keep up with the Ferrari, but all too soon he made a left turn into one of the expensive housing estates that overlook the Thames. I threw the car around the corner, and fought it to get around the next corner, leaving plenty of rubber on the road. There was very little finesse. I stood on the brakes, as I could see the car turn down a side road, and we slid to a stop just behind the him as he drove down a ramp to stop at the roller door into an underground car park.

I could hear the wail of police sirens approaching. I hadn't lost him, or crashed the motor. In my mind, that was job done! Maybe the boy racer instinct wasn't dead yet!

We both pulled out our warrant cards, to ID ourselves. As I approached the driver, who had got out of the car, Robbie was on the radio cancelling the other units.

The man was Black, about three inches taller than me, and about 30 kg heavier. He was very wide at the shoulders, and narrow at the hip. He looked like he was in his mid-thirties, and was well dressed in expensive black trousers and a black silk shirt. He approached in a relaxed fashion.

I said: "Hello Sir. You were in a bit of a hurry back on Marsh Lane. Do you have any ID on you, please?"

He smiled in a disarming way: "Oh, I didn't think I was going too fast. If I was, I'm so sorry, officer."

Not to be put off by this charmer, I said: "It's a 30 limit along that road; I had to do over 90 to keep up. Now, Sir, could I please have your ID?"

He shrugged: "I'm sure you're mistaken, officer. I don't appear to have my driving licence on me. Will a bank card do?"

"That's good as a start, Sir. What's your name and date of birth, please?"

The man handed over his bank card. It was in the name of Mr S Flowers. I looked and said: "What's your name and date of birth please, Sir?"

Robbie had walked over to the car, and was looking carefully at the number plate. This guy was very smooth, but slippery. Maybe Robbie had the same instinct.

He said: "Stephen Flowers, officer. My date of birth is the 25th of June 1965."

That kind of fitted in with how old he looked. I did a name check, and he was not known, not wanted. I then handed him back his card, and because Robbie was showing interest in the car, I did a vehicle check. As I was waiting for the result to come back (a little slow this time), Robbie had moved to the VIN number in the base of the windscreen.

He said: "Richard, can you get me the Maglite from the car?"

At that point, Robbie should have been looking at the prisoner. Basic street craft; someone always has eyes on the suspect. If you send your partner to go and get something, you keep an eye on them. That night, he didn't do it, and as I turned to get the torch, my sixth sense went mad, and

I turned to see Robbie engrossed in the VIN plate, and the suspect running off.

I turned and ran around the back of our car, hitting the emergency button on the radio, calling out: "Suspect running." Before I was chasing after him around a corner, over a wall, through a hedged area. All that time, bits of the kit I had in my pockets fell out, so I ended up with just me and the radio. Finally, we made it around the houses to the front of the original building where he'd stopped the car. As I came around the corner at speed, to my horror I found a meaty arm waiting for me at chest height. Bang, flat on my back, wind knocked out of me, radio dropped.

Looking up at the sky, and the side of a building, I felt an excruciating pain in my left ribs, and again. It was like a vice on my lung. I flinched and couldn't shout out because I couldn't breathe. Then I felt myself being lifted off the floor with another blow. By now I had recovered enough to protect my ribs with my left arm. I looked up and the man I'd been chasing had totally changed: he was snarling, and cursing me. He was so intent on just stamping and kicking me. Then he switched to my head, and he kicked me in the left side of my head so hard I lost hearing in my left ear. I looked back up directly at him. At that moment I realised either I got up and fought this guy, or he was going to kill me. He had that absolute hatred and intensity about him; he so wanted to kick me to death.

They say your life flashes before your eyes in moments like those. For me all I saw was my mom and brother standing at my graveside, with a senior officer spouting some well-meaning crap about how I upheld the finest traditions of the Met, while my friends cried.

I have always felt protective towards my little brother, and the last thing my dad said to me before he died was look after my mom and brother. I was not going to let this bastard do that to the people I love most in the world. I was going home at the end of the day, and I didn't care what I had to do! As they say, I saw red; if it was a fight to the death, so be it! I didn't get up as a policeman: I got up as someone who was fighting for his life. For the first time in my life I absolutely let go with all the anger and hatred I had in me, everything.

I waited until he kicked me in the head again. I put both arms around my head, and used the force of the blow to cause me to roll away from him. I then sprang up, stepped forward and caught him totally off guard with a left jab to the nose. I felt a satisfying crunch as I broke it and then, with the best-timed punch I've ever thrown, delivered a right cross that made a cracking sound (it broke his jaw, I later found out).

Then, like a rank amateur, I did the one thing you're told not to do in martial arts: stop and admire your handiwork. He took the opportunity to recover, then we were off, trading blows. He tried to grab me, and I caught him a peachy shot in the ribs. He slammed me with a right hook when I got too careless. He hit like a truck! I went down, got back up, threw a left hook, which he blocked. All the while I could hear, in snatches, sirens and cheering?!

He caught me a good shot in the face and broke my nose, not too badly though. At that point I was past caring. I just stood there throwing punch after punch, dodging his attempts to grapple. I was not giving up! Then he caught me another shot in the left ribs. I felt screams of agony and, despite myself, went to the floor. But the sirens and now flashing blue lights were so close he did something I didn't expect: he turned and ran. I threw everything I had into it, got up and charged after him, bellowing like a wounded bear, and jumped onto his back. Gone was any pretence at Home Office-approved take-downs. He shrugged me off, and I fell hard on my ribs in a flower bed, and he ran off, along the walkway.

I tried to jump up, but man I was in pain. But up I got. Honestly, I just wanted to catch him. I thought of nothing else, and I sprinted after him. Eventually I got to the corner of a building where there was an alleyway leading off, as the main path continued along the waterfront.

I must have said out loud what I was thinking: "Where's he gone?"

I heard a woman's voice from above, "He went down the side of the building, darling."

I thanked her and, without another thought, ran down the alleyway, only to see a small black car speed off. I could just make out that the man was in the passenger seat, looking back at me.

I thought, *right, radio!* I checked my pockets and realised that it, with all my other kit, was outside the entrance to the flats. I walked back up to the corner where the voice had come from. Puzzled, I looked up, and there was an open window, and an old lady was standing looking down, with a phone in her hand. She held up her hand to silence me, and said into the phone, "Oh, yes, oh, yes, you know you want it. Give it to me, big boy!"

Of all the things I expected to hear, that wasn't at the top of the list.

She hit mute on the phone, and said: "You look rough, officer. You lost him? Sorry about that."

"Don't worry. Thanks for the help. What are you doing?"

She held up her hand and said into the phone, "That's it, big fella, oh yes, oh yes, don't stop."

She said: "I'm doing the sex line bit for punters. And before you ask, no I won't give you a statement. Sorry."

I nodded despite the pain and said: "I guess you don't want to tell anyone that you're doing this?"

"God no! Hubby thinks I'm at the bingo."

I almost died when I tried to laugh. I could see she was busy with the call, so I waved, and she waved back. I walked back to the front entrance, where Robbie and Campbell were waiting. I heard voices from above, and looked up; on one of the balconies that overlooked where I'd been fighting was what looked like a party.

As I looked up, one of the female partygoers, with an Aussie accent, said: "That was a great fuckin' fight, mate. Are you going to do another take? The cameras are really well hidden."

Another voice, male this time: "When's this episode of *The Bill* coming out? That fight was so realistic."

I thought, *can tonight get any more surreal!*

I shouted, "In September, mate. Do you want an autograph?"

"Yeah, sure. Come up and have a drink." Someone hadn't heard of sarcasm.

As I approached my two colleagues, I could see they'd collected all my missing kit. Robbie said: "Are you all right, Richard? You look terrible. Do you need an ambulance, or to go hospital?"

I shook my head (it hurt), "No, I'm fine Sarge. I'm sorry I lost him."

Campbell said: "That's some good war wounds there, son! I approve! Pity you lost him, but ten out of ten for effort!"

I tried to smile (that hurt), "Thanks Campbell, but the other guy will need hospital treatment; I'm pretty sure I broke his nose, jaw and probably some ribs."

Campbell raised his eyebrows and replied softly, "It looks like he did something similar to you. Let me look at your hands."

I showed him my hands, which were scuffed and battered, but not broken. He continued, "You've not broken your knuckles. What level of training do you have?"

I shrugged, "A black belt in karate at university, but that was years ago. I'm pretty rusty."

He nodded, and looked pointedly at Robbie: "By the way, Sergeant, you MUST get this man on a response driving course ASAP. It was easy to follow the trail of skid marks and tortured brakes. I'll vouch for him. He needs to harness that, because you won't stop him. Well done, Richard, you're learning." With that, he walked off.

I looked at Robbie and he said: "Well that's about as high praise as you can get. I'd better get you on a driving course. I'll send the email tonight, and you can do the paperwork when you get back. By the way, you passed the panda course."

I tried to smile and laugh, but it hurt too much.

I said, "What about this job?"

"We got the reg of the car the woman who picked up your man was driving. We're waiting to hear back from the management of the building. The Ferrari's nicked, and rung. That's what I was looking for with the VIN number; it had a scratch on it. Ferrari don't put in VIN plates with scratches. The PNC had an advisory on that VRM, as it was on two cars. That's what the delay was."

He walked up and said earnestly, "Richard, I am so sorry I screwed up and didn't think about the suspect. That was a rookie mistake."

I nodded and said gently, "Don't worry, Sergeant. We all make mistakes, and this at least will give me a tale to tell."

He smiled, and put his hand on my arm (I flinched): "That makes us even. One screw-up that hurts each."

I stuck out my hand, which he gladly shook. He said: "Best get back to the cars. There's a recovery truck for the Ferrari on its way."

I made it around to the cars, and it wasn't long until a recovery vehicle arrived. It was a flatbed, with a hydraulic arm to pick up cars.

I moved the Clio, and he manoeuvred the recovery vehicle and stretched out the hydraulic arm over the car. He then carefully attached straps to each of the wheels and attempted to lift the Ferrari up. Trouble was, it was just too far under the overhang of the entrance to the underground car park and, as he lifted it, one of the hydraulic pipes caught the overhang and split, dumping hydraulic fluid over the soft top of the Ferrari. It also made the grab arm useless. He cursed, and tried to drive the recovery vehicle away, only to find the brakes bound on, because it had lost the hydraulic fluid needed to unlock them. So, we needed two recovery vehicles: one for the Ferrari, and another for the first recovery vehicle. Great, it was the night of mistakes!

Eventually, the second recovery vehicle arrived, and the Ferrari and the first recovery vehicle were taken away, one to the police pound, the second to the garage.

Then we got the OK from the building's management to go in, and with the car's details and a description of the occupants, the flat number had been identified. Time to 'do' the door. We got the code for the main entrance door and went up to the first floor with the 'enforcer' – a door ram with a weight inside that's really good at breaking down doors.

I was still in pain, so we waited until Campbell and Mel arrived, then went in. Campbell did the solid wooden door in one hit, and Robbie and I were given the honour of going in first. It was a lovely, clean, not-so-tidy flat that overlooked the river. I thought, *I wish I could afford something like this.*

First thing we began to notice was the number of weapons lying about the place. There were baseball bats, swords, knives, martial arts weapons. No wonder that guy had hit so hard! We looked into the bedroom – water bed. I make no judgement. Then into the living room, and there was a woman's bag on the table, and a small desk with a computer on it in the corner. The computer was still running.

I looked in the desk drawers first. Bingo! There were about a dozen different passports, of different people, mortgage and loan applications in the names of the passports, chequebooks in different names. They were all the forms of ID needed to commit fraud. If you think this is a victimless crime, consider this: you're burgled, your passport and a number of personal documents are stolen, you make all the appropriate reports. Three months later, you have the bailiffs at your door – they've come to seize property due to non-payment of a loan or mortgage, demanding with menaces. Trust me, those people are not easily persuaded. It might take months to sort out, leaving you out of pocket and in fear of how many more they've taken out in your name, using you as a reference or guarantor.

On top of that, there were details of a council flat they'd claimed in Hackney, and benefits due to their low income.

I checked the computer, and there was a number of cars they were looking to buy and put up for sale, including the Ferrari.

I joined Robbie in the main part of the lounge, while Mel and Campbell searched the bedroom. We were going through doing all the relevant paperwork, and I searched the woman's bag. It had a spare set of keys for the Ferrari (nice, that ties her to the car), and a purse with a couple of bank and credit cards all in different names. Nice! Then, two driving licences in slightly different names and dates of birth, with the same pictures on them. One was a provisional licence, the other a full licence. Naughty, naughty! Someone was playing the system. The DVLA wouldn't be impressed with that, nor the Rats.

At that point I heard a woman's voice behind me. Robbie and I looked around and the woman from the driving licence pictures was standing in the living room (she was about 5'8", slim, mixed race, shoulder-length, slightly unkempt black hair, was wearing black trousers, a dark blue blouse and light-coloured cloth jacket). She looked at me: "What are you doing in my flat? Why is the door smashed in? And give me back my bag!"

I held up my warrant card and said: "Hello, I'm PC Armstrong from Earlham. We're searching this flat because it belongs to someone we're investigating. Who are you?"

I wasn't going to put off by her bravado; it's an often-used tactic for criminals to go on the offensive to try to misdirect the police.

She said: "You don't have the right to break into people's homes and rummage through their stuff. And I told you to give me back my bag. Get your hands off it."

I said: "Are you sure this is your bag?"

I held it up towards her. She took a few steps forward to grab it: "Yes, it's my bag. Now give it to me and get out. I'll be suing you for the door, now get out!"

I grabbed her firmly by the wrist and arrested her for theft of a motor vehicle, as she was in possession of keys for a stolen car. By saying it was her bag, she'd just given me the grounds I needed to arrest her. Thank you!

She squirmed and tried to pull away. I just put the cuffs on her, and she said, "Get those cuffs off me, you racist pig. You're only arresting me because I'm Black. I can't have cuffs on me; I've got a metal plate in my wrist (when the doctor checked later, she didn't, and was lying to have the cuffs removed so she could run off). You're only picking on me because you're a misogynist bully."

I did say that everyone lied, particularly to the police, but with this 'lady', I was beginning to think she was incapable of telling the truth.

Mel came in and searched her. She had another set of car keys, and house keys, and another purse with different bank cards.

I took her down to another police car waiting outside. It was The Law and Pete, and I asked them to transport her back to the nick. As soon as she saw the two lads, she changed from being rude and snarky with me, and said to The Law, "Oh, please, you seem like a nice man. The cuffs are so tight, they're hurting my wrist. I had surgery on it. Would you be so kind as to loosen it just a little bit, please?"

She emphasised the please, and I noticed she leant forward as she said it, causing her blouse to part at the top, exposing her breasts. Wow, there were no depths to which this woman wasn't prepared to sink.

The Law took one look and, while smiling, said: "Don't worry, it's only a short trip to the nick. Once we're nice and secure inside, we can take them off then. Pete, jump in the back and supervise our prisoner here, there's a good fellow."

As she was helped into the back of the car, The Law rolled his eyes at me, clearly knowing her game, as if to say, "Thanks for this griefy prisoner, Griefmeister." *My pleasure*, I thought, *I aim to please.*

Eventually, we concluded the search, and called CID. When Patience arrived, her eyes lit up at the veritable Aladdin's cave of stolen IDs and cases of deception.

I said: "Congratulations on your wedding. You do realise half the men in the Met are in mourning now."

She laughed: "Richard, you look a mess. Did this woman's boyfriend do that?"

I nodded (that hurt), "Yeah, I think he's in a similar state too. Will you be interviewing her? She's a slippery one, and she said I was a sexist, racist pig."

She walked over, touched me gently on the arm and said quietly, "Let the little bitch try that on me. With all this ammunition (looking at the paperwork), I'm going to enjoy this."

The way she said it, I almost, almost, felt sorry for the woman.

We went back to the nick, booked in all the property, and as I walked into custody, Sergeant Smedley took one look at me and said: "Richard, the doctor's in his room. He was called by your griefy prisoner, something about her wrist. But before he sees her, you WILL let him give you the once-over."

I shrugged (ouch) and said: "Look Sarge, I'm all right, just a few scrapes and bruises. I'll sleep it off."

The sergeant leant over the desk and said in a stern voice, "PC Armstrong, that's a lawful order! See the bloody doctor before you keel over!"

I reluctantly walked over and knocked on the door. Honestly, I hate doctors (not as people, but I equate doctors with bad news and death).

The door opened and the doctor (a tall, slim man in his fifties) took one look at me and said: "Dear God, boy, you look like you lost a fight with a lorry. Come in and let me look at you."

"I feel fine and, for the record, I didn't lose the fight. He ran away, not me!"

The doctor stopped and gave me an old-fashioned look, saying in his best stern fatherly tone, "Son, there's a fine line between bravery and stupidity, and honestly, I'm not sure which side of the line you're on. Now sit down, shut up and let me examine you."

He wanted to send me to the hospital, I wanted to go home. It eventually took the governor and two sergeants ordering me to go. After an X-ray, it turned out that, yes, I did have three broken ribs, and a broken nose. I was ordered to take sick leave, which I hated. I returned a couple of weeks later and volunteered to do station office work, gaoler, anything.

It wasn't until then I realised how much I needed 'The job'. I found myself reliving past events, and kept having nightmares.

On my return I found out the response driving course had been approved, and a formal complaint regarding the last case had been lodged, on the grounds we'd stolen money during the search. Funnily enough, it was exactly the same amount as the deposit the couple had lost on the flat. Apparently, if you rent a flat in a false name, and run a deception ring from it, it invalidates your rental agreement. Who knew?

The complaint was clearly based on lies, as it had been done just before the interview, and was a well-used tactic to put off interviewers (nice try with Patience!). Then the 'lady' had failed to appear on bail. She'd gone on the run, and still the complaint was investigated. Mel's transfer to Wales (where her family were) had been cancelled, due to the outstanding complaint. After it was resolved, she'd have to reapply! Now I was getting angry with this pair.

We did a bit of digging and found the real owner of the Ferrari, and asked him in for interview and to ID the car. He arrived at the front counter at Earlham, and I was still looking a bit worse for wear. He was a 5'8" Asian man, slim build in his mid-thirties, wearing a navy suit and shirt. We identified ourselves and sat down in the interview to take the statement.

He started off by saying, "Thank you so much for getting my car back. I really didn't think I'd see it again. Apparently it's the only Ferrari that's ever been successfully 'rung' and been recovered. It made the front page of the Ferrari owners' magazine. Did the guy who stole it do that to you?"

I nodded (it had stopped hurting now) and said: "That's interesting about the Ferrari. Yes, he did do this, but it won't take long before I'm back on full duty. I'm really sorry I didn't manage to nick him. I did my best though. How did he get hold of the car?"

"I can see you tried really hard. By the sounds of it, it was the same guy who assaulted me. I'd put the car on a website, and he'd called. I took him out for a test drive. It all seemed legit, and he asked if he could drive it, and as we swapped seats. He tried to drive off, I tried to stop him, but he was too strong. I ended up on the ground after he hit me. But he drove straight at me. I had to jump out of the way."

"That really doesn't surprise me. The car is all in one piece. Unfortunately, the recovery contractor's vehicle dumped hydraulic fluid over the soft top. I'd get a garage to check it, and if there's any damage due to that, contact us, and either the Met (good luck trying to get money out of the Met) or the contractor will compensate you. Also, I have some property found in the car. We'd like you to take a look, just in case they left anything that might incriminate them."

I put a clear plastic property bag filled with the contents of the Ferrari on the table.

The man replied: "Oh no. I'll get the soft top checked. Thanks for the heads-up. (Looking at the contents of the property bag) That disposable camera isn't mine. The rest of it is, I think."

This was good news, and we got it developed. We discovered it had a number of photos of the pair of them posing in and out of the stolen Ferrari, and a number of other stolen vehicles. Good luck at interview trying to say you knew nothing of the stolen car now!

Eventually, the Ferrari was returned to the happy owner. The complaint investigation of theft was thrown out, because it was lies. About a month later, when I was back on full duties, I spoke to Patience when the woman was eventually caught again.

I said: "Patience, how's that Ferrari case going? I heard that woman was brought in?"

Patience replied with a slight smile, "I interviewed her again, once we'd got all the evidence. I spoke with the banks. They froze all the accounts, and mortgages and loans. I spoke with Hackney council, and they're investigating the pair for fraudulently claiming a council flat and benefits. The management company of the flats is going after them for the door, and had chucked them out. I spoke with the DVLA, and had the full fake licence flagged. It appears she had a number of licences in aliases, all of which have been linked and flagged at the DVLA and on PNC. She only really has a now-expired provisional licence, when she eventually comes back out of prison. She's only going to be in a few months. She was really loyal to her fella – she blamed everything on him. You'll need to give her back her real licence and have a chat to her about her driving. That's traffic, I don't deal with that. Basically, we've destroyed her thieving life, and put her in gaol. Suffice to say, she never, ever told me the truth. Honestly, I don't know if she's even in prison under her real name. Her fingerprints linked her to four other aliases."

She looked at me, and continued: "I'm pretty sure we identified the guy who assaulted you from fingerprints. He was released from a three-year stretch inside about six months back. And, get this: there was a note on it to contact HM Prisons liaison. Apparently he'd spent a lot of time in the gym, and had been overheard saying a number of times he wouldn't let himself be taken back to prison, and blaming a white policeman for arresting him, saying he'd kill the first white policeman he got his hands on. I guess that was you. You're lucky; it sounds like he tried to kill you."

I said: "He did definitely give me that impression."

I shook my head, and thought, *note to self: never piss off Patience*. She was so thorough, and utterly ruthless. Man, I loved this lady!

I thanked her, and went back to relief duties, waiting for my driving course.

During the time I took off for my injuries, I didn't go to see my mother, and didn't mention I'd been hurt. I didn't want to upset her, but my idiot northern relatives stuck their noses in and were quite rude telling me to go and see her, and that I didn't care about her. Why didn't I tell them the reason? Because I didn't trust them not to tell her. Some of my family I got on with (mother, brother, his in-laws, and the odd aunt), some not so much.

Honestly, now I was settled, my mother wanted to return "home" to the north-east. I knew why she wanted to go but, selfishly, it did mean I'd have no family within 150 miles. And, if I wanted to see her, it was a 700-mile round trip. That's a tough gig.

Still waiting for my driving course, Robbie and the inspector moved on to other divisions, largely due to fallout from the club bombing incident (I still regret my handling of that). They had a really good send-off. The inspector had been right about C relief working and partying the hardest.

I was still occasionally getting fag butts put in my tray, and the odd comment, or received treatment from those outside my relief. This meant I had a new reporting sergeant (line manager): Sergeant Sutcliffe. He was a tall (6'2"), thin man from Sunderland (a rough city, just south of Newcastle – could I never get away from there?). He wasn't a friendly or well-mannered man, and blunt to the point of rudeness, with all the charm of a chainsaw. It's best to say we tolerated each other. I think he (like Burke) had a real problem with me having been a teacher, and my handling of the club bombing incident. I now didn't have the backup of Inspector Manning.

He started picking faults with my uniform (ignoring other people's), and I started to have flashbacks to Burke's treatment of me. He didn't like the fact The Law, myself and Pete shared a lift in, although it wasn't really his business. We reluctantly stopped sharing a car.

Living alone, this cut off another bit of my social connection. It was tough enough trying to keep friendships going when you weren't available when others were. And I became unreliable because of the nature of the job. With my mother making plans to leave, I could feel a sense of isolation creeping in. I threw myself more and more into my work, investing more and more of my energy into that.

One night duty I was out with The Law in the van, and we had just left the nick when we received an urgent assistance call from two officers from the previous shift, who were finishing up a job.

This was our highest priority call, not just because they were our colleagues, but because often people will call and it's a false call. Police only call for "urgent assistance" in the most dire of circumstances.

We pulled up outside the address, which was in the middle of a row of terraced houses, and saw the police Astra parked outside. I charged in, backed up by The Law. The front door was open, and I could hear sounds of a fight at the back of the building. I ran down the corridor, into a bare room, with no furniture, an abandoned chair leg lying on the floor, and two female police officers sprawled at the feet of a man (5'10", muscular build, short black hair, wearing jeans and a black T-shirt). I could see straight away he was in a karate ready stance. From the tension of the form he was holding, he was good. I mean really good, although I didn't recognise the style.

I moved forward in similar stance, and got myself between him and my fallen comrades, allowing them to back off, and then The Law moved around to my side. This gave him two people to deal with, coming from two angles. Knowing the way The Law operated (being a musician, albeit a guitarist, his timing was predictable), in my head I said "3, 2, 1, go" and we both sprang at the guy. We didn't use our ASPs because the ceilings were low, and there were five people in a small room, meaning the danger of hitting your mates was high, similar to CS spray. He managed to partially block my grab, but less so with The Law. This gave me a moment of grace, and I clamped his left arm, or so I thought. He simply shrugged, and I was holding nothing, other than an elbow to the upper arm.

This did give the female officers a chance to get up and join the fray. I spun around and attempted a leg sweep; he simply stepped over it, even though he was wrestling with The Law, and delivered a glancing stamp to my calf. The female officers then crowded in just as he finally shrugged off The Law. At this, the first female officer went flying due to a kick in the abdomen from this guy. The other one tried to grab him, but he quickly twisted her leading wrist up in a lock, and elicited a cry of pain. I thought, *this is enough*. While he was distracted, I grabbed him in a neck hold, as tight as I could. His movement was so fast and smooth, it took my breath away, as he let go of the officer's wrist, and bent down and threw me over his shoulder, to land hard on the floor. Even though I was used to being thrown, as I went over, my legs struck the ceiling and left me off balance. But this left him bent over, as I still had hold of his shirt. The Law and the freed female officer used their weight to drag him face down on the ground. We eventually, after several minutes of extremely intense struggle, had him face down with two of us sitting on him, and his hands cuffed to the rear.

Man alive, that was tough. I looked up and could see the two female officers were 5'6" and 5'4", and slim. Their combined weight was probably less than this guy, and he was a very, very good martial artist. It took four of us, two of whom were his size or bigger, and who had a decent level of martial arts training (The Law had done karate). And, as much as TV and films try to tell you otherwise, nine times out of ten the big guy beats the little guy (or gal) in a fight. Can a well-trained smaller person beat a bigger person? Of course, but it's not the norm. And, let's be honest, the police, at least in terms of fighting, aren't well trained.

In most struggles between villains and police, it's grab hold, drag them to the ground due to weight of numbers and stick the cuffs on. Nothing more complicated than that.

Why? Well, if you deploy your ASP, all you can do with it is hit people, which either injures them or pisses them off, and the CS spray is like chucking a bag of smarties in the air, because everyone gets hit with some.

Anyway, we had this bloke on the ground, and our female colleagues made the call to call off the cavalry.

I spoke to the taller of the two ladies, "Hi, I'm the Griefmeister, and this is The Law. We've got the van outside. What are we doing with this guy?"

She grinned despite the obvious pain she was in: "I think we need to go and get checked out by the doctor (often at the nick), and then we're supposed to be off shift. This guy is a bit Dagenham East (four stops from Barking, as in, they're Barking MAD), and we were called by his friends because he was acting up, off his meds. That's why there's no furniture – he's smashed it all up."

She moved in close and said quietly, "He has a long history of mental illness after his brother died. He was a European karate champion (that figures), and has been in and out of hospital. He needs a mental health evaluation at the hospital. Would you mind taking him? It should literally just be a drop-off there, where he'll be put in their secure room."

I said: "No problem. Would you mind giving us a hand doing a full cell relocation job?"

She nodded grimly. I looked at her partner, who also nodded.

Having got the back of the van and cage doors open, we started the cell relocation procedure. This involved the smaller female officer walking forward to the van, guiding her colleague, who was walking backwards holding the prisoner's head down, while The Law and I had our arms through his cuffed hands, forcing him to bend forward at the waist. This may sound harsh but, done correctly, it allows even the most formidable prisoner to be moved without any injuries to anyone.

Even though he was still very strong, and kept trying to turn his head and trip us up, we eventually managed to get him in the van and locked in the cage.

We thanked the ladies, who had called ahead so the Newham severe mental health team were ready with the secure room.

As we settled down for the drive to the hospital, the man, 'Dave', started screaming and shouting. He looked at me and screamed, "You're the Antichrist. You're the bringer of evil, the bringer of the end of times. As long as you live on this earth we're doomed. You're the Antichrist!"

Honestly, I felt this was a bit harsh. I might not be the nicest of guys, but the Antichrist? Really?

I said: "C'mon mate, calm yourself down. You'll be fine."

He shouted "I'm not going to the hospital. They'll take my brains out with a spoon. They'll rip my thoughts out of my head. They can see into my mind. They'll take my brains out again."

Now I'm no fan of doctors or hospitals but, again, that's a little harsh.

He then started banging his head against the inside of the cage. I mean really, really headbutting it. The thump was sickening. But what could we do? If we opened the cage, he'd be extremely difficult to control. So we just stuck the lights on, and tried to get there fast. All the while he continued his rant, adding, "Those doctors, they'll take my brains out. I'll stop them. I won't let them. I'll fight them."

I kept an eye on him, although anything I said to him seemed to make him more angry, so I kept quiet. As we pulled up, and his head lolled, it appeared he'd knocked himself unconscious. I noticed something fall out of his mouth. I went to the edge of the cage and saw it was half a razor blade. He was carrying half a razor blade under his tongue, all the time, in case he needed it. That's a level of paranoia I'd never seen.

We pulled up directly outside the emergency entrance, and I jumped out to let the staff know what was happening, and I said to the young doctor (late twenties, in a white coat, about 5'10", slim, with straggly ginger hair), "Hi doc. This guy we're bringing in, he was extremely violent. It took four of us to arrest him. He was a karate champion and is one of the most violent prisoners I've dealt with. He called me the Antichrist, and made specific threats against you doctors, saying you'd take his brains out with a spoon, and he had concealed under his tongue a razor blade. He continually banged his head against the inside of the cage, knocking himself semi-conscious. We have him cuffed in the cage. Where do you want us to take him?"

The doctor looked at me, nonplussed: "Listen officer, this is my hospital, I'm in charge of clinical matters. I'll make an unbiased assessment based on my own observations. Bring him in and put him in the secure room to the left, and take the handcuffs off him."

I said: "I respect you're in charge doctor, but he is very violent and has made threats to doctors. So, respectfully, we'll keep the cuffs on until we get him in the secure room. Please doctor, be careful with this guy; he's really dangerous."

With that, I turned and went back to the van. I relayed to The Law what was said. He let out a long breath and said quietly, "We'll play by the doc's rules, but one of us will get hurt protecting him!"

We went to the back of the van, opened the cage and dragged his semi-conscious form out of the van and into the hospital. We both could feel him slowly coming around. He started to tense up and to find his feet. All the while the doctor was scowling at us disapprovingly.

We then got him into the secure room, and the doctor closed the door. We stood either side of 'Dave', holding his arms, and I could feel he was faking how out of it he was. He was getting ready. Oh shit! I thought, *the doctor isn't going to listen, and we're going to get hurt.*

The doctor walked towards us: "Officer, he seems perfectly calm now. The poor chap is semi-conscious, no doubt at your handling of him. I demand that you remove those cuffs."

I couldn't stop myself: "Doctor, with all due respect, he's going to go for you if we do that. Please let us keep the cuffs on until you're out of the room?"

"Absolutely not. You will remove those cuffs now!"

The Law gave me a look and said: "OK doc. So are you taking responsibility for this man?"

"Of course. Let him go."

I started to undo the cuffs, while The Law held on to him. As soon as I'd taken off the second cuff, 'Dave' brought his elbow round and absolutely belted The Law in the temple, and he went down. He struck out at me, but I was already moving and his strike glanced off my shoulder. I was moving forward, as was he, straight at the doctor shouting, "I'm going to fucking kill you, servant of the Devil!"

The doctor, stepped back, stunned. I threw myself on the guy, and managed to drag him to the ground, but he was so much stronger and faster than me. He easily pinned me and, once I looked up, he said: "You're really crap at fighting. I'm going to kill you." He drew back his hand into what I knew was a knuckle strike, which I was pretty sure was going into my throat.

I just said the first thing that popped into my head, "I may be crap at fighting, but I'm fucking amazing at running away. So you're not going to kill me."

He actually stopped and, seeing I was defiant, he looked at me and replied, "You're funny! So I won't kill you." He moved his face to within an inch of mine and said quietly, with a determination I'll never forget: "I'll kill someone else instead!"

The pause had allowed a somewhat groggy The Law to get up and fly at 'Dave'. Between the two of us, we got him pinned down again. Then The Law, with calm but steely professionalism, said to the doctor, "Do you think it would be a good idea to leave our friend here to calm down, before you do an evaluation?"

The doctor didn't answer. He just left the room and stood by the open door. The Law did a silent countdown, and we both let him go and sprinted out of the room. We made it out, and the door was shut and locked.

We both leant against the door, and let out deep breaths, and I dropped my head to recover. When I looked again, the doctor was talking to The Law. I walked out of the hospital, sat in the van and awaited The Law. He arrived back a couple of minutes later. He got in and started up the van.

I said: "Thanks mate, you saved my neck back there. Are you all right? He didn't half clock you one?"

The Law grinned his usual infectious (babe magnet) grin: "No worries mate. That doc didn't listen, did he? He still didn't quite get it even after that. What the hell did you say to that guy? I honestly thought I was going to watch him kill you with a throat strike."

I told him and, despite ourselves, we laughed. As we were driving out of the hospital past some female nurses, he gave his now infamous grin (I swear one of them swooned), and said, "We lived up to our nicknames: you found the grief and I, The Law, saved the day."

We did laugh at that.

The next night, I was sitting in the parade room (we'd arrived separately, due to the new sergeant's complaints), and The Law walked in and said: "You're not going to believe this, but you know that crazy bloke from last night?"

"The one we arrested or the one in a white coat?"

Still sore from the previous night, he didn't smile, but said: "They let him go. He promised them he'd take his meds and see the doc more regularly. A new doctor had come on shift, seen how compliant 'Dave' was, and let him go? Can you fucking believe it?"

I was stunned. I just sat there unable to comprehend what he'd said.

I eventually shook my head and said, only loud enough for The Law to hear, "He's going to kill someone, and we, the system, could have stopped it. This will come back to bite us!"

I looked at him and he shrugged: "We'll never know. And besides, we did everything by the book, all the paperwork. There's absolutely no comeback for us. We can't change the system. We're not God, mate! If you worry about it, it'll send you mad. We've got a shift to work. Focus on that."

I wasn't convinced, and stayed quiet. I had a bad feeling about things. The Law said: "I spoke to the skipper, and we're on PT25 tonight. We always find trouble, but A relief are so short, they'll have to do something about rebalancing the reliefs; they paraded twelve for lates. We've inherited ninety outstanding calls. That's insane!"

I said: "Sounds like trouble will find us tonight." Tempting fate again.

The new inspector arrived, and had barely made it into the room when the radio went. Sooz said: "Units to deal, we have multiple casualties at a fight with weapons at The Comedy Club in Earlham."

The inspector held up three fingers, and called out, "PT3, PT21 Liz and Edward, PT2 Jamie and Mel. Off you go. If you need more backup, call. Be careful, folks."

He smiled as our colleagues jogged out, and settled himself on the corner of the desk, opening his mouth to speak, when Sooz (on cue) interrupted him: "Units free to deal, we have a FATAC (fatal accident), junction Kenton and London (Kenton Road and the London Road). Traffic are tied up."

Sergeant Smedley asked, "I'll take that in PT23, if that's all right, Guv?" The inspector nodded, and he started to move towards the door, as did Pete, his partner.

That left four PCs, one sergeant (the other was either manning custody, or one was on another posting), and the inspector.

The inspector managed to get out, "PT25, you go out last ..."

Sooz was on the line, "Units free to deal, we have a stabbing on Old Ford, between Vicky Park and Grove Road."

The inspector said: "Show PT24 and PT1 with Ps23 dealing, thanks Sooz."

As he got ready to leave, he looked at us and said: "Looks like you're it tonight. The thin blue line, at its thinnest. I left you two until last, as you're the thief-takers. You arrested more between the two of you than did the whole of A relief. Keep this up and they'll want to poach you. Take care, boys, and do what you do best: nick villains!" With a grin, he jogged out.

I looked at The Law, and he too grinned. Was it something in the air that night? I said: "Best go and see what Sooz wants her thief-takers to do?"

He grinned: "More than A relief? That's quite a boast. It's time for The Law to ride! Yeehar!"

Grinning like schoolboys, we went to see Sooz. She had, while talking on the radio and smiling (wow!), handed me a CAD printout, and blew us a kiss (wow!).

We jogged out to the car and could both feel it: that night was going to be a busy one!

I looked at the job, a disturbance at a pub, with one man suffering a knife wound. Another day, another dollar! We jumped in the car and BLATTed (Blue lights And Two Tones) our way to the pub. As we pulled up, I put us on scene, confirmed CID and the LAS were en route, and I walked into the pub. It was a real spit and sawdust place. There was a small bar to the left, and a few tables to the right, and about half a dozen patrons. I noticed a young man leaning on the bar, and over on the white wall by the toilet, there were blood marks.

I went to speak to the barman: "Hello mate. Is there any trouble?"

"Yeah, there's a guy in the toilet who's been hurt. This lad here (indicating the man leaning on the bar) is his brother."

I looked at the lad leaning on the bar: "Here mate, what happened?"

His brother looked up at me. He was drunk and crying, and slurred at me, "Dad told him. He told him, 'If you go to the pub, I'll bottle you.' And why didn't you listen, Larry? He's in the toilet."

I looked at The Law. He had the first aid kit in his hand, and we walked to the toilet. I swung the door open, and a scene straight out of a horror film met me. It was a white-tiled (walls and floor) room. There were bloody handprints along the wall from the door all the way around to the sink, where a young man with a really nasty, jagged wound across the back of his head, almost from ear to ear, was slumped over the bowl. There were splashes of blood on the floor, and the place had that strong metallic tang you get with lots of blood.

Avoiding the blood trail as much as I could, I checked on the lad. He was moaning, so at least he was alive. I took hold of one arm and The Law the other, and we sat him down and started first aid, as best we could. This revealed a thick pool of blood in the sink over an inch deep. Nice!

After a short while, the LAS arrived, and we handed him over to them. We went back into evidence-gathering and scene-preservation mode. We got the names and addresses of anyone who'd talk to us, the suspect's name, the victim's name, then were bagging up the broken bottle as Big John and Patience arrived.

I spoke to them outside the pub. "Hi Sarge, Patience. Good to see the A team are on tonight. We've got a lovely situation to deal with. Dad and son had an argument. Dad said if you go to the pub, I'll bottle you. Son ignored dad, went to the pub. And sure enough, dad walked in and bottled his son from behind. Nasty injury. He's in the ambulance."

John said, in a cheery tone: "Why, thank you so much, gents. I'll go down for this one. You get the next one, Patience. Witnesses?"

He said the last bit with hope. I held up the bagged bottle: "The barman, and the brother. The barman 'didn't see much', and both your victim and his brother are paralytic drunk. There's a couple of people in the bar, but they didn't see much. Oh, the scene's at the bar. We found the victim in the men's toilet, and it's straight out of a slasher film; claret all over the shop."

Patience smiled at us: "Do a quick book (IRB notes), and we'll take it from here. You're the only free unit in Earlham tonight. Take care, boys."

We did as we were asked. That was one pair out of the three pairs of rubber gloves I was carrying. We cleaned up. We got back in the car and called up for another job. Sooz said: "How do you fancy another pub fight, other side of the ground?"

I replied: "You're the boss!"

"Don't you ever forget it, hun."

And off we went again, another BLATT, but we had to take the narrow side streets, as the main Elm Road was at a standstill with the FATAC.

As we were belting along one of those narrow side streets, out into our path steps a tiny woman (5'1") with a bloody knife in her hand, and she just stopped and stared at us, a marked police car with blue lights and sirens going down a narrow street where we couldn't avoid her. We slid to a stop about twenty feet from her. As I got out, I could see she was drunk from her eyes and the way she was swaying. Stone drunk, with a large kitchen knife in her hand. *Calm*, I thought. *Don't scare her.*

I got out of the car but, keeping the door between me and her, said: "Hello darling. What's occurring?" (This is not what they teach at Hendon.)

She seemed to focus, and replied: "I've stabbed Bobby. I've stabbed Bobby."

"What's your name, darling?" I was trying to get her to focus.

"I'm Trish. I'm Trish." It is far more effective to use someone's name, not just "Oye you!"

I said: "Trish, darling, would you just put the knife down for me, there's a good girl."

She looked at me blankly for a moment then, looking down at her hands, saw the knife, and very slowly bent down and put it on the floor.

"Thank you, Trish. Do you just want to come towards the car for us. Come towards us, slowly now sweetheart."

Like a small child, she slowly walked towards the car, turned and sat on the bonnet. Phew, no knife incident.

Normally men don't search women but, in extreme circumstances, they are allowed. To make sure she didn't have any more weapons on her,

I put the cuffs on the lady and arrested her. Then, putting on my second pair of rubber gloves, I patted her down and retrieved a set of keys. This lady was stinking drunk, in more ways than one. She stank of booze, and stale urine, and old sweat. I had to take a deep breath before checking her pockets.

I said: "Trish, where's Bobby?"

She looked at me, tried and failed to focus, swaying all the while. She replied: "He's in the bedroom. In the bedroom at home."

I thought, *thanks, very informative. Where's home?* "Trish, Trish, that's it, look at me. Where do you live? Where's home?" She took a moment to focus her thoughts and coordinate, then pointed up at a block of flats directly in front of us.

The Law nodded and got on the radio, saying: "PT from PT25. You'll have to cancel us from the last job, we've come across something direct. Stabbing at Maplin Towers, Maplin Street. Can we have CID attendance, and the LAS. One in custody, knife recovered, victim not yet located."

This was an unusual call. Sooz Replied cautiously, "Received PT25. Please update ASAP."

While I took 'Trish' around to sit in the back of the car, The Law collected the knife, put it in a plastic knife tube, and bagged it as evidence.

We drove up to the tower block. All the while, I was trying to get a flat number from the clearly disorientated Trish. Eventually she told us: Flat 34.

Now normally you don't take a suspect back to the scene of a crime when the victim is still present. But, given a man's life was at stake, we had no choice. So, we improvised. Not wishing to leave a clearly very intoxicated and unstable suspect locked in a police car, we did the only thing we could – took her with us. It was her flat, after all.

The three of us got in the enclosed mobile public toilet/knocking shop also known as a lift, and went to the third floor (a guess – 30s are usually on the third floor). We got out and, while I held our prisoner, The Law checked the flat numbers. He shouted to me as he made for the stairs, saying, “Bloody useless arseholes. When will the people who build these blocks learn we’re not in sodding America and learn that the ground floor starts at zero, not bloody one? Useless bastards!”

And our happy little band went down the stairs (avoiding the used condoms and needles), and eventually located Flat 34 on the SECOND FLOOR, YOU FUCKING MUPPETS! Strange how things like that annoy you when you’re trying to save someone’s life! The Law used the keys and entered the flat, and immediately took half a step back out of the door, screwed up his face and pinched his nose. We took a deep breath and went in, to a scene of utter chaos.

The first thing that hit you was the smell. I’ve been in flats where people have been dead for six weeks in the middle of summer that smelt better than that. It made your eyes sting and, if you didn’t want to vomit, you breathed through your mouth. As I looked around their small living room, the carpet was in the late seventies style, chocolate brown, with swirly patterns. It was threadbare, and your feet stuck to it. The sofa was ancient and in a badly faded and stained floral pattern. There were bits of detritus abandoned willy-nilly, half-eaten takeaways, dozens of cheap, empty bottles of spirits strewn about the place, human faeces on the floor. The worst part of it by far was the smell. It was clear that one, if not both of the inhabitants, were alcoholics who didn’t bother walking to the horrible toilet, and simply urinated on the floor or sofa. Anywhere they passed out was OK.

Trish sat on the sofa (braver than I was), and The Law called out, “He’s in here. He’s alive but only just. His intestines are coming out.”

Keeping an eye on Trish, who was now falling asleep on the sofa, I looked over into the bedroom, and sure enough Bobby was lying on the bed covered in blood with part of his intestines showing through two large cuts in his abdomen. Trust me, the one-day first aid course and the car's minimal first aid kit did not cover this eventuality! On top of all of that, the man had clearly not woken up throughout all of it, due to being so drunk!

I went back and kept an eye on Trish, and got on the radio: "PT from PT25."

"Go ahead 25."

"We're at Flat 34, I repeat 3 4. It's on the second floor. The victim has been located. Two large stab wounds in his abdomen. He's unconscious but breathing. When they get here, tell CID and the LAS to let us know so we can let them in."

"Received PT25. Be aware we're getting CID assistance from PD (Park Street)."

A few minutes later, CID arrived. It was Patience, and a young guy I didn't know (Park Street, no doubt), soon followed by the LAS, who took over on the first aid duties. Everyone had the same reaction when they went into the flat. One of the LAS crew almost gagged.

While The Law took his turn keeping an eye on Trish, I explained the circumstances to Patience. She said: "Yes, Trish and Bobby Hope (you're kidding, right!) are well known to us. They've been in and out of prison for domestic violence towards each other. They've been arrested countless times. Usually they retract the allegations within a couple of days."

I looked at her incredulously: "Let me get this straight. They knock each other about, get sent to prison, go back to the same flat and carry on drinking?"

She nodded: "The worst thing is, when they are vaguely sober, they declare their undying love for one another. Usual MO is, he beats her when he's awake, when he goes to sleep she beats him or stabs him."

I struggled to form a question: "Why don't we do something to stop it?"

"They've both been given countless opportunities to live elsewhere, but they always come back to each other. We can't force people to live the way we think they should; we're not in an authoritarian state, thank God. But the price of free will is sometimes people will keep making dreadful choices."

The new CID guy went to the hospital with Bobby, and Patience, Trish and The Law and I went to Earlham, where we booked in Trish and did the minimum amount of CRIS and IRB work we could to help Patience (this still took several hours). Then off we went again, still the only unit that was free.

As we were leaving Earlham, it was the early hours of the morning. Sooz looked at us, and said: "Another job for you, came in a while ago, a stabbing. The bloke's not happy. You look beat, gents. Take care."

Great! Another stabbing. The third we'd dealt with that night. Off we went on another BLATT. The call was the other side of the ground. As we arrived, we found it was in a block of flats with a security entry door. Neither of us had the keys for it (sometimes police are given keys to the main entrance to blocks of flats, but not in this case).

We looked for the flat, number 13 (I hate that number). We pushed the button, but no reply. We pushed it again, then out of the speaker blurted: "Don't keep pushing the fucking buzzer, you cunts! I ain't that fucking quick! Who the fuck are you, pushing my fucking buzzer in the middle of the fucking night!"

Whichever charm school this gentleman attended, I felt a refund was in order.

I said, in my best cut-glass English accent, “Good morning Sir. We’re the police you called. Would you mind awfully facilitating our entry to your abode?”

The Law grinned at that, and the man said: “What the fuck did you just say you fucking pig?”

The Law piped up, “Look mate, do you want the police or not? If you do, let us in.”

The reply was instant, “How fucking long does it take you fucking pigs to get your lazy, fat, doughnut-eating arses here? I pay your fucking wages, you useless, fat, motherfucking cunts. I could have died by the time you’d bothered coming to see me.”

At that the security door buzzed, and I pushed it open. I grinned at The Law. Someone else who’s happy to see us.

As we made our way across the little internal courtyard to the stairs to the flats, a man whose face was covered in blood leant over the balcony and shouted, “You fucking useless, fat, doughnut-eating cunts. How long do you call this? Did you stop on the way to shag the local whores, or to take bribes from the local councillors? You’re all dirty. I know you’re a bunch of racists. I watch the BBC. I know it’s true cos they said so. You hate Black people, don’t you? You fucking n****r haters. And the P**i’s – you hate the fucking lot of them. You’re all fucking racists! Hurry up, get up here now!”

I called up Sooz. “PT from PT25, on scene. Can I confirm that the LAS have been called?”

“25 from PT. He refused LAS until police had arrived. Confirm you want them called?”

The Law replied, "PT, we'll confirm in a minute when we speak to the man again. He has got a bad head wound. And is very anti." (Short for 'anti-police'.)

We made our way up the long corridor, and along to the open door to Flat 13. I looked in, and there, on the battered sofa in a shabby, disorganised flat, was the man we'd 'spoken' to earlier. He had what looked like two parallel and horizontal deep cuts across his forehead.

I said: "Hello Sir, may we come in?"

"No you fucking can't! Get out. I ain't having the filth in my bleedin' flat! That's your fucking problem you arrogant, racist (he was white, we were white, where does race come into it?), fascist scum! You think you own the fucking place, always around when you're not wanted and giving innocent motorists tickets. I call it racist, fascist tax on the poor motorists. I bet you use the money to buy extra doughnuts, you fat scum! Then, when we do call you, where are you? Two fucking hours late!"

The Law had had about enough of this: "Look mate, you called us. Sorry it took so long to get here; there were so many calls tonight. Do you want an ambulance? You should get those cuts seen to."

"Oh, I see that's how it's going to be? Of fucking course I want a fucking ambulance, you fucking idiot!"

I ignored his abuse, and called Sooz: "PT from 25. Yes, could we have the LAS attend this address – the man is conscious and breathing, with two deep cuts to the forehead."

The Law tried a different tack, "Look mate, let us at least look at your wounds."

"Oh, I see, now you're a fucking paramedic, are you? I bet you wouldn't do that if I were Black, you fucking Nazi, racist pig."

I'd had enough, but I was just too tired to argue. He clearly had plenty of problems, and his potty mouth was the least of them.

So I said: "Sir, who did this to you?"

"Oh Sherlock Holmes here thinks he can solve the crime! Do you think I'd be standing here talking to dickheads like you if I knew. I hear a knock at the door, when I open it, there's this bloke dressed in black, wearing a ski mask, and he slashes me across the head and runs off. Never seen him before."

Total bollocks, but I nodded: "OK Sir. Do you know of anyone who might have wanted to hurt you?"

"No, I get along with everyone. I ain't got no enemies, you fucking idiot. I ain't the police."

I thought, *and the word for the day, children, is irony!* "Sir, to write a crime report, I'll need your name, date of birth and address, please."

"Oh, I see, that's your game, you Nazi scum. I ain't giving you my name or address. That's how you get me, that's how you do it. I've read *1984*. You can't trick me."

I said: "Sir, you called us. What do you want us to do? To record this as a crime, I need your details. Do you want us to report this?"

"I want you to do your job. I ain't giving you my name or address."

We continued on like this until our patience ran out, and we went and waited out near the entrance for the LAS to arrive. When they did, we escorted them up to see him, and he (while still abusing us) went into the ambulance to hospital, and repeatedly refused to give us his details.

As we sat back down in the car, I said: "I don't get it. Why call us if all he wanted to do was shout abuse? He clearly knew his attacker; someone let them in through the security gate, and what's with the two parallel cuts?"

The Law shrugged: "He was a grass. It's called letter-boxing, as in someone who gives information, a letter. They stick two blades close together, which makes it hard for the cuts to heal, and leaves a permanent scar, to show he's a grass."

I said: "OK, but why the abuse?"

"He was making a show of it, to show he wasn't a grass, that he hated the police. That's why he didn't want to go to the hospital before we got there. He was using us to make a point."

By then, it had calmed down and the shift was nearly over. When we made it back Sooz said: "You know every call tonight involved blood being spilled."

The Law grimly said, "That was the night of blood!"

I thought, *that's a good title*. We made our weary way back home.

Update on Trish and Bobby: he survived, she went to prison, and who was there when she came out? Straight back into the arms of Bobby! Patience was right.

A few weeks later, and my new reporting sergeant was still making my life more and more unpleasant. Picking up every little thing I did, ignoring others and focusing on me. It wasn't in the same league as Burke, but it started to chip away at me.

I had another chance to work with Jamie on a late turn on the area car, and we picked up where we left off, and I began to relax again.

As we were driving around, I noticed Jamie wasn't quite his usual self. So I said: "Jamie, are you all right? You seem a little quiet."

Without looking, he said in flat tone, "One of my old colleagues from Hainault retired a couple of days ago. He was my mentor, and had done his thirty years, and they wouldn't let him stay on any longer. He seemed fine when I spoke with him at his retirement do, then on the way home, he drove to the woods, took a rope from his car boot, and hung himself."

I just looked at him: "Mate, I am so sorry. That's awful. Do they know why?"

He shook his head, waited a minute to think, and said, "It's 'the job'. It's more than just employment. It was his life. When the job ended, so did his reason for living."

I could sense Jamie did not want to talk about it any further. Out of respect, I wasn't going to push it. I thought, *I suppose I can understand that. He couldn't just move on. His whole life was the police. It was who he was, and when it ended, so did he. He had no identity any more.*

As we were driving past a parade of shops, we got a call: "Any units free to deal, we've got a silent alarm at William Hill bookies."

I could actually see the bookies as we passed. Jamie slammed on the anchors, and we legged it across to the door. As I was going, I called "PT3 on scene."

Jamie and I drew our ASPs and charged in, to find a small bookies with half a dozen shocked-looking punters staring at us. We calmly walked up to the counter and I said: "Is everything all right?"

I was looking around behind them, and it appeared nothing was amiss. The shocked cashier behind the counter said: "No, we're fine officer. Is there a problem?"

Jamie replied by silently mouthing the words, "Your silent alarm just went off. ARE YOU OK?"

She nodded: "Oh God, really? I moved a box out of the way under the desk; it must have hit the silent alarm. I'm so sorry."

I said: "Are you sure everything's all right?" I did a slight hand gesture pointing at her and then moving my thumb from a down to the middle to thumbs-up. So, if she was under duress, she could silently indicate it.

She showed thumbs-up: "Really, everything is fine. Thank you."

At this, a woman in a William Hill suit walked in from the back, and said to the lady at the counter, "Julia, did you know you tripped the silent alarm? I've just switched it off."

She looked at us and said: "Wow, that was quick. We really appreciate the response. I'm the manager. It's fine. Thank you."

I shrugged: "As long as you're OK. We were just passing as the call came out."

Jamie said on the radio, "PT from PT3. Cancel the alarm call. We're talking with the manager, and it's a false alarm. Cancel any other units."

Another voice came on the radio. It was Sergeant Sutcliffe: "272, return to PT immediately, and report to me in the writing room. Confirm you heard me, 272."

I could hear an edge to his voice. I shared a look of puzzlement with Jamie. Before I had a chance to say anything, the sergeant was on the radio again, "272, did you receive my last? Confirm you received it."

"I confirm I received your last, Sergeant, and will comply."

We made our way back to PT. I looked at Jamie, he shrugged and replied to my unspoken question, "Not sure what that's about. Best you go and see him; he seems to have a bee in his bonnet about something. How are you two getting on?"

I remained silent. He took the hint, "As bad as that? OK mate. Take it easy."

We made it back to the nick, and I went to speak to the sergeant, while Jamie went to speak with Sooz. I know who got the better deal.

I walked into the writing room, where Sergeant Sutcliffe was sitting at one of the computers.

"Hello Sergeant. You wanted to see me?"

In a hard-edged and raised voice, he replied, "What the hell were you doing, answering a call of an armed robbery without armed backup? You're a fucking idiot, 272. You're sloppy and unprofessional. You take unnecessary risks. I've read everything about you and I'm not impressed. If it had been up to me, I wouldn't have passed you!"

I stood stock-still, and just stared at him. I clenched my hands behind my back so he couldn't see my fists. I clasped my hands tight, so I wasn't tempted to let one fly. Give me a gobby suspect, I won't flinch. With the worst kind of criminal, I'm a total professional. But a cowardly bully who uses their rank as a shield, and I really struggle to keep my cool. Dealing with Burke had made me vow I'd never suffer another one.

He stood up, walked towards me, and started shouting in my impassive face: "I fucking spoke to you, worthless cunt. I won't take insolence from a piece of shit like you. I'm going to make your life hell. I'm the sergeant around here! You will respect me, or I'll make you respect me, you arrogant little shit! You'll step out into the yard right now. We'll sort this the old-fashioned way, with fists."

I remained absolutely impassive.

There was silence for a moment, and it was only then we both realised we weren't alone: Sergeant Deacon and Sergeant Smedley, Campbell and Jamie were staring silently at us.

Sergeant Sutcliffe said: "You saw that, his insolence. I'm going to discipline him for that. Give me your pocketbook, you little shit!"

Sergeant Smedley was the first to speak. When he did, it was in a very low but calm voice: "Richard, I think Jamie has a call for you. Off you go son. We don't want to keep the great British public waiting."

I turned to walk away. Sergeant Sutcliffe shouted, "I haven't finished with you yet," and grabbed my arm.

Sergeant Deacon said very clearly, "Let him go. He has a call to go to."

To emphasise the point, Sergeant Smedley (a real brute of a man) walked over next to us. Sergeant Sutcliffe stared at Sergeant Smedley, eventually let go and I walked off. Campbell gave me a little pat on the back as I walked past.

We spent the rest of the shift busy as ever. Jamie said nothing about it, and nor did I.

At the end of the shift, Campbell was waiting for me, and took me to one side: "I shouldn't say this, but there's a really strong core to this relief, and we self-police. A number of us seniors on the team, including the sergeants, could see what was happening, and waited until he really stepped over the mark. The other sergeants absolutely nailed him for that. He's only just qualified as a skipper, and was trying to stamp his authority. He went about it in the wrong way. We won't stand for bullying like that. Trust me, he won't give you a hard time like that again! We look after each other."

I looked on with real respect. *They really do have my back!*

I said: "Thank you, and I'll have to thank the skippers."

He shook his head, "Don't Richard, there's no need. It would make things difficult for them. Just leave it. Oh, by the way, Sergeant Smedley had told Sergeant Sutcliffe that they saved him, because if he had fought you, you'd have murdered him."

I looked surprised, and said simply, "Thanks!"

As good as their word, the sergeant, although I wouldn't say he liked me, backed right off. On the next paperwork day, we were called to the parade room, where we were going to receive a talk by one of the senior officers. Apparently, there were changes afoot.

We all filed in, and eventually, when the boisterous C relief had settled, in walked a tall, stocky man in his early fifties with short, greying hair, and plenty of metalwork on the shoulders of his tunic. We all stood and, waiting until we were quiet, he said: "Good morning ladies and gents. Please sit down. I'm Deputy Commissioner Johnson. I'm here to explain to you the new reporting rules we're rolling out across the Met. I'll explain it first, then I'm open for questions. This is pretty informal, and I genuinely want your feedback, to get a feel of how the troops at the front are thinking.

"The first point is a reporting difference for racially aggravated crime, as a response to the Macpherson report. When you report a racially aggravated hate crime, instead of it being reported as a racial crime if either the reporting officer or the victim think it is of a racial nature, it's now if anyone thinks it is. It's flagged as a racial crime, and will be sent to the CSU to be dealt with. Any questions so far?"

I stuck up my hand: "Good, a question. Go ahead."

I took in a deep breath. *Brave or stupid, here I go*, "Sir, is that change just for racially aggravated hate crime, but not for, say, homophobic crime?"

He nodded and said cautiously, "Yes, that's right. Your point is?"

"My point is, Sir, that it might appear to the gay community that it is considered by the Met that hate crimes against them are of a lesser priority when compared with a hate crime involving race. Especially in light of the recent case of the homophobic attack on the nightclub. I was just wondering why that was, Sir? Political pressure?"

There were plenty of whispered remarks, and I could see that had hit a nerve. He replied, "No, of course not! Are you suggesting, Constable, that the Met cares more about race than sexual orientation, because of political pressure?"

I looked him straight in the eye: "Yes Sir, I am! How could I not, if you change the reporting criteria for one, and not for the other, yet claim they are equally important? How am I going to be able to look my friend who was injured in the club bombing straight in the face and explain what is a relative downgrading of the importance of homophobic crime?"

At this a number of other hands went up, and he was absolutely taken to task by my colleagues, who relentlessly pushed the point. Honestly, I was proud of them for standing up for what was right. The senior management must be kept accountable by the rank and file.

He then went on to explain there was now a new category of "Incident" we had to deal with. He said: "As of now, you'll be reporting 'Hate Incidents'. These are 'Incidents' where no crime is involved, but a level of hate has been displayed. It will be recorded on CRIS as a crime/non-crime."

I put up my hand, and he patiently said: "Go ahead!"

"Excuse me, Sir. Isn't CRIS the Criminal Reporting Intelligence System? So why is it being used to report something that isn't a crime? Surely CRIMINT would be a better fit?"

"Look, we need to record these incidents so we can track them, and identify possible troublemakers for the future."

Straight away, up went a number of hands, and Sergeant Darling said: "Sir, on the CRIS system, where do we record the details of the person who has committed this 'Crime/non-crime'?"

"In the 'Suspect' section."

The sergeant replied, "So, let me get this right: we're recording people who haven't committed a crime, on a criminal reporting system, as suspects? Even though they haven't broken the law? Don't you see the problem with that?"

"Look, as much as I can understand your concerns, this is happening, and you will all do this. So, moving on, if you get a call or report that someone perceives that something is 'hateful', it will be recorded as a 'Hate Incident'."

We sat there, stunned, not really understanding what he was saying.

He continued: "Example, if an Asian or Black person says that they perceived a white person to be in any way racist towards them, then it gets investigated, and recorded. There's no discretion. They'll be 'I' calls, and you don't question their account. You accept it, and investigate, and record it. To do otherwise is a disciplinary offence. I will answer no more questions on this matter. This meeting is over!"

At the end of it, the senior officer walked out of what had probably been a routine briefing with his ears ringing. I was probably now on some troublemaker hit list somewhere. Sod it!

I got a few pats on the back after that. Then we had a sit-down with our new inspector, who explained that Park Street and Earlham were going to be merged into one division, in line with the Borough of Earlham, to allow more political accountability.

This meant our shoulder numbers would now all be PD, not PT and PD. The control rooms would alter in roles. Earlham would handle only incoming calls, which would be sent across via CAD to Park Street, where they'd be sent out. So no more listening to the sultry tones of Sooz. And although there'd still be two of each relief (one at Earlham and one at Park Street), they'd cover both areas.

When we were told this, Campbell sat back in his chair and said what we were all thinking: "Sir, so that means, we'll be covering twice the geographical area, half of which we don't know, which will take longer to get to. Park Street has a lot longer response times, so the people of Earlham will have to wait longer for a police response."

The inspector nodded and said: "Yes, that's about the size of it, but we've been told not to think of it being Earlham and Park Street, but just Earlham. There'll also be more movement between teams and nicks, to balance things out more. We'll be hit hard, because we're the best-performing relief, best response times, most number of arrests (he looked at me and The Law)."

Jamie said: "Guv, what happens to the ANPR (Automatic Number Plate Reader) in Earlham? Instead of just being able to put a call out straight away over the radio, by the time they create a CAD and ping it over and the call gets put out, the nicked motor will be halfway to Earlham. That's bollocks, Sir!"

The inspector looked around conspiratorially: "I know that, you know that, the superintendent knows that, but he's refused to budge. He'll discipline anyone who tries to get around these new rules, even if they will have a negative impact on the effectiveness of our response."

True enough, the rate of stolen cars we intercepted went down from about 95 per cent to about 35 per cent as soon as they implemented it. I think that's what the management in the Met call progress!

Mel said, ever so innocently, "Sir, but the Met didn't pay for that ANPR. I wonder if the council or the public know the system they paid for at a stroke is going to be rendered virtually useless due to the decision of a senior officer."

The inspector grinned, and a there were a few laughs. Campbell once again said what many were thinking. "Sir, with all due respect, I know it wasn't your decision, but this is utter bollocks! We on C relief have worked our arses off for years trying clear all the calls every shift. Most arrests, most process, best clear-ups, least number of complaints, everything! We've sweated blood to do our duty, and it feels like the management are punishing us! Guv, this just ain't right!"

There was a round of applause. When it eventually subsided, the inspector had a hard look about him: "I know how you feel, but this is what's happening, and don't any of you cause trouble that will make things worse, with a backlash against the rest of us. For the sake of the team I will come down hard on anyone who tries to fight this. You'll find the new letter 'D' in your trays. Put them on. This starts in four days' time at the new shift. Dismissed."

And that, as they say, was that! Nothing any of us could do. We were, as it was called, going to be "boroughised".

This was the beginning of the end of the happy band of brave, hard-working crazies that made up Earlham C relief.

The next day, I found myself on a late turn with Campbell. We hadn't worked together much, so it was a chance to have a chat.

The first call was to reports of a 'Hate Incident' and the 'Victim' was at the offices of Earlham Council main offices. We arrived, walked in, and were directed to one of the small, private offices in a swanky new building.

Campbell and I walked into the room, and we were alone with a Black man in his mid-forties, with short black hair, of medium build and tall (6'0"). He said: "Please come in officers. I'm Abidemi Wakesa, and I'd like to report a hate incident."

Campbell let me deal with it. I said: "Sir, I need to take your details, and then we can investigate the incident."

He gave us his name, address and telephone number (which he gave as the council offices).

I then said: "Sir, would you like to explain the incident you wish to report?"

"I was walking across the road, and a white man driving a car gave me a racist look."

"Where, and when was this?"

"It was at lunch time, about 1:30 p.m. I was crossing Kenton Road. The car pulled out of the Four Keys pub and drove down the road towards me."

"Did the car have to stop?"

"Yes, he had to stop, because I was walking across the road. He gave me a racist look. Are you questioning my account, officer?"

Wow! I thought. *This guy has read the guidelines, and is testing us out. Thanks!*

I replied, "Not at all, Sir! I am merely trying to get the most accurate information to allow us to investigate fully. Now did the driver do or say anything that indicated any racism?"

"No! But he did give me a racist look."

"OK, did he mouth anything, make any hand gestures? Did he rev the engine?"

"No. He just came to a stop as I walked out in front of him, and looked at me in a racist way. Officer, are you questioning my account?"

"Absolutely not, Sir! As I said, we're just collecting as much information as we can to investigate as thoroughly as we can."

He then gave us a description of the driver, and car, minus the registration number. Then, as we were leaving, he said: "So officer, where will this be recorded?"

"When we've fully investigated to see if there's any criminal offences, it will be recorded on the Criminal Reporting and Investigation System, as either a racially aggravated crime, or as a non-crime hate incident. Depending on what we find, we'll contact you to let you know once we've conducted our investigation."

This seemed to placate him, and we left. As we were walking back to the car, Campbell said quietly, "I'm so glad you dealt with that. That guy was really trying to trip you up with the new policy, wasn't he?"

"I certainly think he was! I wouldn't be surprised if we were being recorded while we were in there, collecting evidence to make a complaint if we put one foot out of place."

It took us a couple of hours to interrogate the ANPR system for cars that matched the description. We eventually found out that the man's name was Glen Hughes and noted where the car was registered, then went down to the pub he'd mentioned, the Four Keys, and spoke with the bartender. She said "Glen, a racist? Are you kidding? Absolutely no way! He popped in for a pub lunch, and soft drink. He's a regular. He's never said or done anything racist."

We checked with the other customers, and they all agreed.

We then went to the address where the car was registered and knocked on the door, and spoke with Glen. He absolutely denied any racism, he said: "Look, I remember driving down Kenton Road and this guy just stepped out in front of me. I had to stop to let him across, but I didn't say or do anything to him. Now he's complaining about me! Why?"

With no evidence, it was recorded as a crime/non-crime 'Hate Incident'.

It is up to you to decide if the perception of a person is enough for them to be able to have something investigated, and recorded as a hate incident by the police, and have that man's details recorded as a "suspect" on a criminal reporting system.

Several weeks later, as we were trying to get used to the doubling of the ground we had to know, the percentage of twenty-minute 'I' (emergency) response times we'd made had halved. That's right, before, we were there in twenty minutes 80 per cent of the time. After, it was, roughly, 40 per cent. We were getting to the public later, and were consequently facing much angrier people. Good job, senior management. All for the sake of allowing dickhead politicians to have a bigger say in how we were run!

On a night duty with The Law, we'd been informed that a whole load of heavy-duty fireworks (the big rockets) had been stolen, so to keep an eye out for them. This didn't take long. Just after the start of the shift, we heard a still-unfamiliar voice saying, "Units free to deal, there's fifty-plus youths in The High Street, outside the college. They've blocked the road with burning metal wheelie bins, and are apparently using drainpipes to fire big fireworks at cars and people. There's over a hundred calls come in about it."

A call like that had the cavalry out. It ended up with six cars and twelve officers, all armed with the small shields we carried in the cars and our ASPs. As we had been driving up, the rockets had started to be fired at us.

One would hold the plastic drainpipe (no doubt from some housing development), another would carefully slide in the huge rocket then light it. There'd be a few seconds' wait and, whoosh, it flew in an erratic course at us, sometimes bouncing off the ground, buildings, cars, shields. Then they would detonate with a huge concussion, that you could feel in your chest and bashed the ears. Then an enormous light display. We were lucky; none of us had been hurt. But there had been a few close calls.

Their trajectory was hard to anticipate and, as I ducked behind a car, a rocket whistled a foot or so over my head to detonate yards behind me. Then came a few rocks and bottles.

The inspector arrived and quickly realised that if we stayed there any longer, one of us was going to get hurt. He got out the megaphone and literally read the riot act to them. Basically: disperse, or we will disperse you. He got almost all the way through it before a rocket ricocheted off the ground and only just missed his head.

He quickly finished reading it, and gave the required time. Then, on his megaphone, he shouted what we'd all been waiting for: "Charge!"

Honestly, it was exciting when you and most of the team rise together from behind the cover of your cars, where you've had rocks, bottles and rockets fired at you, and you have only a small shield to defend yourself, to be able to charge, shouting and screaming at the people who've tried to hurt you.

I looked at The Law. His face was lit up by the light of the fireworks and he had a smile from ear to ear. So did I. We were off. The kids who'd been throwing the missiles and launching the rockets just dropped everything and ran. They did not want to face C relief in full cry! Surprise, surprise, The Law and I both ended up with prisoners. Thief-takers to the end!

When we booked them into custody, I noticed a photofit of a man wanted for the stabbing murder of a priest in a church in Wembley. The picture looked familiar, but I couldn't quite place it. I called The Law over and said: "Here mate, do you recognise him?"

He walked over to the noticeboard, and we both looked carefully, then at the same moment the penny dropped, and we both said: "'Dave', that crazy guy we took to hospital."

My heart sank. After all we'd done, it couldn't be? I tried to convince myself we were wrong. It's amazing how easy it is to convince yourself of something you don't want to believe is true. The Law said, "Here's a reference number, and a DC from AMEP. I'll go and call them. It really might be him." Off he went to make the call.

A couple of nights later, I received a call from The Law at home that changed everything! It's one of those moments you never forget. I'd just woken up (midday) and he said: "You're never going to believe it. I got a call back from AMEP about that 'Dave' guy, the crazy martial artist. It was him, and here's the kicker: he killed himself just after. They're checking now with DNA but it looks like he murdered that priest and then killed himself. He jumped off a building. Nasty business. Looks like they'll link the cases, and we'll give evidence. Probably be an enquiry. What do you think of that, mate?"

I dumbly replied, "Thanks for telling me, mate. I'm a bit tired. I'll talk to you at work. Take care."

I hung up. I loved The Law and his always-positive, always-happy approach. But, that day, it was too much. I could feel myself slowly crumbling.

I sat on the floor and alternated between weeping and shivering. I'd never felt so alone. What had we done? What had I done? We were supposed to protect people. The system was supposed to protect, but two people were dead, and we could/should have prevented it. He had told me, TOLD ME he was going to kill, and he did! The worst bit was, I knew I'd done it by the book, with every T crossed and I dotted. Yet still, they'd died. If you did everything right and people still died, how can you work in that system? What happens when you get it wrong? How could I trust any decision I'd made, if it led to the deaths of people? We were there to protect.

All the pain and guilt I felt about the deaths of Roxanne and Tariq came out. That day, something broke. I didn't really understand it then, but nothing was going to be the same again.

Over the next few weeks, the relief started slowly being broken up. First, Mel finally got her transfer home to be with her family, Sergeant Smedley got his inspector and joined the 'knuckle-draggers'. As a jokey leaving present, I presented him with a box of plasters for his knuckles. That went down well.

The inquest came and went. I will never forget the look 'Dave's' mother gave me when I gave my evidence, and had to say to her face that he'd told us he was going to kill, and we let him out to do it. That still haunts me.

The investigation pointed no blame at The Law or me, saying we'd done all that could be reasonably expected of us. Really? Then why did two men die?

I became more and more withdrawn. Eventually, Campbell spoke to me when we were alone one night in the writing room. "Richard, you're struggling, aren't you mate?"

I nodded and, barely keeping it together, told him everything about Tariq, Roxanne, 'Dave', and that I couldn't trust my own judgement any more.

You might have thought that a big, tough guy like him would have scoffed or belittled me. None of it. He waited until I finished and said: "Richard, you need a break. You've had no let-up since you joined. You need to go and speak with the inspector. He'll listen. You're too good to lose. Hang in there. Trust me, there's not a copper in this nick who hasn't gone through what you're going through. Hang in there. Let's go and speak with him. He's in the control room chatting up Sooz. Let's go."

We walked over to see the guv'nor, and we had a quiet chat. I went over the whole thing again. He sat patiently, and eventually said: "Don't worry, you're not alone. I think you need a break from this. I have an idea that might kill many birds with one stone. I'll see you tomorrow, and fill you in, see what you think. For the meantime, I'll see if you can't get a few postings as gaoler, or on pandas. Keep your head up mate, you're not alone."

I was so thankful. The support was amazing! The next day, as promised, I was gaoler, and at refs he called me into his office, and said: "Here's my plan. Now you understand, this is all unofficial and doesn't normally work this way. But I think I can swing it. You go on unpaid leave for a few months. When you come back, you'll be moved teams to A relief, Park Street. I believe you know Inspector Miller. I had a quiet word, and she was very keen to have you. Now she is desperate for response drivers. In fact, if you wanted to do a response course you'd have to leave C relief anyway. Now the way we do it is, we transfer you to A relief before you go, we do all the application for you now. Then, when you come back after Christmas, you go on the first response course in New Year, and join A relief straight after that. It means you get a break to recover a little, you get the driving course you want, and A relief gets a good response-driving PC who will help their figures. We have to lose people anyway. So, what do you say?"

I just sat there for a minute, and I didn't know what to say. They'd tried so hard to help. This was my dream. But I'd really miss all my mates where I'd grown up as a copper and as a man. I remembered what Paige had said: "Don't be such as wuss! Make new friends and move on!" Damn if she wasn't right. A few months to unwind, and then back for the next chapter!

I said: "Sir, yes!" No more words than that.

He beamed, and stuck out his hand, saying, "I know the relief will be sad to see you go, but I think you're making the right choice. After Christmas, if you still can't face coming back, you did what you set out to do. No one can take that away from you. But keep it under wraps; I need to get it past the super. It's the trick with senior management – make them think it was their idea. He'll no doubt want to see you. Remember, play nice!"

Soon enough, we started the paperwork for the transfer and driving course application. This took its time, but eventually it was done. I felt far more relaxed having something to work towards.

Finally, it all fell into place, and the trip to speak to the superintendent came and went with it all confirmed. I pretended like I didn't know, and was very grateful for his brilliant plan.

The hard part came when I finally left. A leaving do had been organised. I wonder who by, Sooz?

It was in the middle of September at The Round House bar near Covent Garden. Everyone turned up, and we had a meal and presentation. Edward even handed me a police shield with C relief PD 272 on it. It's still proudly on my wall. A few speeches went by, until it was mine. I stood up, looked around at all my friends, and said: "Thank you so much, folks, for the presentation, and this party. I really appreciate it. I started on C relief under a cloud. It would have been easy for you to see me as a lost cause. But you didn't. You treated me from day one as a brother. We've fought together, we've laughed, we've had each other's backs. Even when I screwed up you were there. Wherever I go, this will be the gold standard. This is the way it should be done. Not perfect, but the best real people can do. I am proud, PROUD to have served with you. Now get pissed and dance your arse off!" There were plenty of woops and hollers and cheering, and we drank and danced.

While we were still sober enough, I had a chance to have words with a few of the team. The first was Campbell. I walked over and clasped him forearm to forearm, and we locked eyes. He nodded, I nodded; no words were necessary. We hugged and walked away. Jamie came over next and said: "I don't mind saying, I was wrong about you. I thought you were a whiney, griefy, lefty teacher. But mate, you're alright in my book. You're solid. Good luck, mate!"

We shook hands. Then it was Angus's turn. He walked over quietly and said, when he knew no one was listening, "First time I met you I thought, 'you're a fucking idiot, Armstrong!' But I learnt to see what you were. You're a mess, but no more so than anyone else. And between you and me, you're the only one who had my back when it counted. I won't ever forget that, not ever! Take care, you fuckin' soft English cunt!" That is, believe it or not, the nicest thing he'd ever said to me.

Then it was The Law. He walked over on the arm of his gorgeous girlfriend, and introduced us. She said: "I'll just go and powder my nose, and let you boys talk."

I grinned at him, and he said: "I've still got it, mate!" We laughed, and he said: "It's the end of the two thief-takers of C relief. The Griefmeister and The Law. The villains will sleep a little safer in their beds tonight. It's been a blast, mate!"

I nodded and we hugged. I replied, "Don't do anything I wouldn't."

He laughed and said: "Which means I have free rein!"

I nodded and walked off to find the last person I needed to say goodbye to: Sooz. She was, as always, the centre of male attention, dancing like a goddess. She saw me, and we took a seat at the bar, and clinked glasses. I said: "Thank you, Sooz, you're one in a million!"

She grinned and said: "You're such a sweetie." Then she paused, looked at her glass, then back at me: "Are you gay?"

I looked puzzled, and replied: "No, why?"

"You're one of the few single men who hasn't chatted me up. Why?"

I smiled: "Honestly mate, I like you too much, and I fell in love a long time ago, and it didn't work out. It broke my heart, and I'll never get over it."

She looked at me intensely for a moment, and said quietly, "She must be very special, because you're still in love with her now. I can see."

She leant forward and squeezed my arm, and kissed me gently on the cheek: "Take care, hun, but now it's time to dance. Let's go!" She took me by the arm and we ended up dancing on the tables, until I was eventually poured into a cab and sent home. The end of one chapter, start of another.

Thanks, C relief, Earlham!

Chapter 10
ESSEX BOY RACER

I spent the next three months reconnecting with my friends, and my old life. It felt odd, like there was something missing. I found just how much I loved the police life, the atmosphere, the banter, the wordless and instant understanding of things. Honestly, it was so frustrating when you say something, and then have to explain it, then they get the wrong end of the stick. Or they try to argue with you when they have absolutely no clue what they're talking about.

You start to appreciate what you're missing. Truthfully, there was a chemical addiction to adrenaline. I found myself having to consciously slow my driving down. I did a fair bit of flying, just to get an adrenaline fix.

With no income for three months, I was spending a lot more than I had before, because I now had time to enjoy it. I burned through the money I saved up in overtime. I bought a new, handmade bass guitar and bought lavish Christmas presents. After Christmas, I looked at my bank balance, and almost had a heart attack!

It was great to have a Christmas and New Year to take time to see family and friends. But they'd moved on, and so had I.

I felt a bit like a fish out of water. The nightmares were still there, but I guessed that was normal. I had a few offers of teaching jobs, which I thought about, but I wasn't ready. I wanted to get back and do what I loved. I wanted to do that driving course.

What's it they say: absence makes the heart grow fonder? I was chomping at the bit to do the driving course. But I missed Sooz, Mel, The Law, Campbell, Pete, Jamie, all of them.

So, when January came around, I was ready. I drove to Earlham, moved the contents of my locker to my new nick, (ghastly place that it was) Park Street, then got changed into half-blues and made the trip to the driving course centre, in Hertfordshire.

I had been looking forward to it for so long. It didn't disappoint. It was a three-week course. It had been reduced to two weeks, to save money (the Met and its extra cheapness), but the results weren't good, so they changed it back.

When I arrived, I received a lot of stick for, A) coming from Essex and, B) driving a "hairdresser's" car.

The first week was looking at "Road Craft". Then they assessed your driving, tearing it to pieces. Then, over the last two weeks, they rebuilt it. There were skidpans, fast drives and loads of rules and regulations. But you put up with it, to drive! It almost made driving not fun, because they leant on you so hard.

The thing I learnt most was reading the road ahead. To act, not overreact. Most problems can be avoided way before you get anywhere near them, by focusing. You have to think about what every other car is doing. Anticipate problems. There's an old saying in flying that covers it: "A superior pilot uses their superior judgement to negate their superior skill!" Yes, you might be able to take a corner at 60 mph (and it's good that you can), but should you? Would taking it at 50 mph give you more margin to correct things if it goes wrong?

In other words, improve your ability to control the car, improve your observation and reading of the road. Then, drive at 70 per cent of what you're capable of. Then, if something unexpected does happen, you've got another 30 per cent to get you out of it.

There were eight of us on the course, and six passed. The final drive was the ultimate test. You had to drive with an instructor, navigate, read the road, drive fast, and give a commentary the whole time of potential problems, other vehicles, pedestrians, road surfaces and conditions. The flying did help, as it's generally about twice as hard as driving a car.

I passed, with a decent grade. Not bad for an Essex boy racer in a bird's car.

Then it was back to Park Street, and my first day on a new relief, at a new station, as a driver, and it was a late turn – the busiest shift we had. Baptism of fire time!

I drove up to the rear gates of Park Street, and after I'd punched in the code, the gates slowly opened, to reveal a parking nightmare – too many vehicles in a badly designed car park. I eventually found a spot (one of the benefits of a small car), parked up and made my way into the new station. I collected all the stuff I thought I'd need, and went to the parade room. I was a little later than I had intended, because every corridor looked the same, and it took me a while to find it.

I walked up to the door labelled "Parade room" and walked in. The contrast with C relief Earlham could not have been more stark! It was a clean, tidy, almost sterile white room, with neat rows of new, office-type chairs. There was a desk and chair at one end with a whiteboard and TV screen on the wall.

The police officers were very different too. They were all sat, quietly chatting, wearing the same uniform, long-sleeved shirts, jumpers. They had similar and full equipment belts. I, on the other hand, was wearing a short-sleeved shirt, no tie, my belt had an ASP, cuffs, CS spray, and radio (in the walkie talkie style), with a couple of IRBs tucked in my top pocket, my warrant card and pocketbook tucked in my back pockets, with a few bits and pieces in a battered old sports bag.

My heart sank. *I'll stick out like sore thumb, again.*

I looked around and saw some familiar faces: Roger (from street duties), Mary (Hendon), and Jack (street duties reassessment). These were the people I recognised and, as I looked around, they all smiled, and quietly acknowledged me.

There were a few others I didn't know, and they seemed engrossed in their own conversations. The whole atmosphere was subdued, with none of the energy of my old team. On the surface, more professional, like this was a job, not a calling.

Roger leant over and we shook hands. I noticed a few more officers filing in, all giving me odd looks. He said: "Good to see you, Richard. Congrats on passing the driving course. We're so short of drivers. This relief really needs people who have service. Half of this lot are probationers. You'll be driving every day."

I looked around and noticed the age of the others there. I was one of the older ones, in my mid-thirties. I thought back to C relief where, out of twenty-four, there'd been between two and four probationers at any one time. It looked like half this lot were. I'd be teaching the 'kids' how to do it!

He looked at me and said: "Where's your tie, mate, and your jumper?"

I shook my head: "I didn't know we needed it. On C relief, we just turned up in whatever. No one cared, once you'd got through probation."

Roger said: "The guv'nor expects us to parade and present our 'appointments', three IRBs, pen, pocketbook, cuffs, ASP, cap and tie. Once you're out on the streets, it's up to you."

My heart sank, and as I was getting up to go back to my locker to collect the rest of my kit, Roger stopped me as the guv'nor walked in. Everyone got up, put on their caps, holding up a pen in their right hand, and pocketbook and IRBs in their left.

I looked around, and fumbled as I tried to organise my kit. I dropped my pen, bent over to pick it up and knocked Roger, who also dropped his pocketbook. There were a few laughs, and when I eventually stood up, with my hat on askew and the pen and books in the wrong hands, I looked straight at Ma'am Miller, who was smiling in a friendly way at me: "Good to see you, Richard. Don't worry about the tie today, but I'd appreciate it if you remember for tomorrow."

She then turned to the rest of the twelve PCs and two skippers in the room and said: "I'd like everyone to meet Richard Armstrong, 272. He's our new driver from C relief. Those of you who are probationers would do well to learn from him; he has the highest arrest record for the last two years in the Borough of Earlham."

She smiled, and turned to the first skipper, who was standing next to her. He was a 6'2", thin man in his mid to late twenties with a well-cropped, stylish moustache and tiny goatee, and short brown, curly hair. He looked around and said: "You may be seated, A relief."

We all sat down, with the scraping of the chairs being the only sound (a total contrast), then he looked at me and said: "Hi Richard. Welcome to the team. I'm Sergeant Appleton, your reporting sergeant. We could really do with your skills and experience."

"Thanks Sergeant. I'll do my best. I'm looking forward to this new challenge."

He nodded and went through a series of 'hotspots', which is jargon for high-crime areas. He went through the 'prom noms' and 'dev noms' to look out for. This stands for prominent nominals (most active criminals) and developing nominals (the up-and-coming criminals).

When he'd finished, he looked back at Inspector Miller, who said: "Thank you, John. Now, Sergeant McLeod, would you like to go through the postings, please?"

A 5'10", stocky, balding man in his mid-forties with a thick black moustache stepped forward and said in a strong Scottish accent: "Right, get your pocketbooks ready."

I flipped the page open. He went through the list, and I looked around, until everyone except me had been called. My heart sank. Was I gaoler? Was I not driving on my first day? I felt real disappointment. Then he finally said: "And PD1, with 272 and Ma'am Miller."

I thought, *WHAT! My first day driving, and I'm driving the guv'nor, who's really by the book? Will I lose my driving on my first day!? Oh, crap!*

The inspector looked at me and smiled, saying: "You're my driver today, Richard. Right (everyone stood up again, this was going to take some getting used to), parade dismissed. Come with me, Richard, and I'll show you where the keys are kept."

I gave Roger a nod, and he gave me an encouraging wink. I picked up my bag and followed the guv out and along a number of faceless corridors until we were somewhere near the front desk.

There was a book and a rack of keys, along with a row of battery chargers. Under that were a series of labelled shelves with car logbooks in the form of small binders.

She took some keys off the rack and handed them to me. On the key fob, handwritten on a faded sticker, was "PD28". I looked for the corresponding, battered ring binder.

I flicked through it. No serious defects. Good. When was the last fuel put in? Early turn, no fuel, night duty, no fuel. Late turn yesterday had fuelled it up first thing. *I need to check that.*

She said: "Everything OK, Richard?" She was clearly watching me to make sure I did things by the book. Great!

"Yes, Ma'am. So far so good. We might be a low on fuel. It was last filled up at the start of lates yesterday, so we'll have to go to the petrol station at some point."

She smiled and said: "Good, I can get a sandwich. My husband normally makes me one, but he had to take our dog to the vet this morning. Don't worry, he's all right. The dog, not my husband."

I smiled politely. We walked out to the yard. I let her lead; the maze of corridors still had me confused. Outside, I checked the reg number of the car and, after a minute or so, located it. *By the book*, I thought, and did the vehicle inspection: tyres, water, windscreen wipers, etc. Then I got in and checked the fuel. Just less than an eighth of a tank. Not desperate, but we needed petrol at some stage.

I looked at my first proper police car, a well-worn Astra Mk3, a few minor scuffs, faded Met Police sign, peeling decals along the side. But, hey, it was mine, for a shift at least.

As I sat down in the driver's seat, and got comfortable (a relative term with a knackered, torn, old seat, while wearing a bullet-proof corset), I looked at guv'nor, and said: "We ready, Ma'am?"

She was about to answer when the radio interrupted, "Units to deal, reports of fifty-plus fighting with weapons in Burnside Square. A number of calls on this now."

Before I could say a word, she said: "PD, please show PD1 running to that."

I didn't need to be asked twice. I was pulling out of the car park and, as soon as I was clear, I stuck the lights on, and when we'd cleared the first junction, I added the sirens (local residents complain about the sirens), and off we went. It was one of the most nerve-racking drives. I was so, so bloody careful. If I don't say so myself, the instructors would have been proud. I courteously waved to motorists to thank them for giving way, the whole bit.

We didn't speak while I was driving. As we pulled into the square, there were indeed many people fighting with weapons. It was a large, residential square, with rows of reasonably sized properties. It had a well-maintained, fenced garden in the centre, with an ornamental flower bed around the edge. There was a large number of Asian youths fighting with each other and struggling with a number of our colleagues.

As I pulled up next to one of the entrances into the garden, the guv'nor said over the radio: "PD1 on scene." She then jumped out the barely stopped vehicle and ran into the garden, tackling one of the fighting youths. As partners, you have a responsibility to look after one another, and I thought, *oh great! My partner, the guv'nor, is going to get hurt, on my first day!*

I removed the keys, shut and locked the doors (never good to have your stuff nicked) and charged in to help, only to see the inspector fighting on the floor with one of these youths, and losing. Her head was being rammed into the peat of a flower bed. I thought, *10/10 for effort, 2/10 for effectiveness*. I charged in, grabbed the youth and hauled him off the inspector, and cuffed him, leaving him face down on the grass.

I looked over as the inspector was spitting bits of peat out and trying to straighten her hair. She stood up, and I said: "Do you want me to go down for this one, guv?" (do you want me to arrest this one?)

"Absolutely not! You get your own. This little bastard's mine!"

I grinned and made to charge off, to do as I was told, as she took charge of the prisoner. I said: "Cuffs, Guv." She looked blankly, then chucked me her handcuffs (mine were on the prisoner). She replied, "Car keys." I chucked them to her.

I then charged off and tackled another one of the fighting youths, dragging him to the ground and cuffing him.

After a few minutes, we'd got things under control. The youths were either in custody, had run off, or had melted back into the crowd of people coming out of the houses. I walked around and located one of the vans, and deposited my prisoner.

I then walked back towards the garden trying to locate the guv'nor, when I met an older Asian man (in his sixties), who looked at me, and said: "Thank you, officer. It's been a problem for us over the last few weeks. There's a gang who arrive in a number of cars. These young men come and upset the women and children. Our young men go out and defend them, and there's trouble."

"I'm glad to have helped. We've managed to arrest a number of the men involved."

"Yes, I can see that, but I fear that some are our young men, and they were only defending us."

"If that is the case, that's unfortunate, however, when we turn up, all we see are young men fighting, so we arrest everyone involved. If we want to stop this happening, Sir, we need to work together. May I suggest that if you see these young men arriving again, you get everyone indoors and call us, and take note of the registration numbers of the cars. Then, when we turn up, we can arrest them."

I noticed the old man look past me. I turned around, and there was the guv'nor listening in. I said: "Ma'am, do you want to take over?"

She shook her head: "No, you carry on. You're doing a fine job."

I then continued chatting with the old gentleman for a bit, trying to elicit his support in catching the troublemakers.

I then went back to the car, with the guv and her prisoner. We transported him back, booked in our prisoners, and spent the next four hours dealing with them.

It was about refs time, so we went to eat in the canteen, where we had a chance to chat. I said: "Ma'am ..."

She stopped me: "When we're working together, it's Chloe, OK." She then took a mouthful of the flaccid pasta.

"Thanks Chloe. I'm really looking forward to getting out and helping the probationers learn. As well, of course, as driving and nicking villains."

"Oh, yes, you were a teacher. I think they'll benefit from a little push on occasion. It's one of the downsides of having such a probationer-heavy relief."

I pushed my luck a bit: "You do realise, Chloe, you're taking a chance. My nickname was 'the Griefmeister' due to the fact I always find trouble. That's why I get so many arrests. I'm always where the trouble is."

She sat and looked at me for a moment, and I thought, *oops, too far Richard!* She said in a semi-serious tone, "Yes, I'd noticed. First call, and I'm in the middle of a fight. I don't hold with nicknames. Look, can I level with you, Richard?"

I thought, *a plain-spoken inspector. Good!*

"Ma'am, always!"

"I want you to be an example. To go out and show them how to do this job properly. I won't tolerate sloppy police work. Absolutely, catch as many villains as you can, but do it right!"

"Honestly, I always try to, but I do it the lowest-conflict way I can. I'm not one for going in all guns blazing, unless it's the only option. Talking, and persuasion, is always preferable to going hands-on. It's the smart long-term strategy, and it's the right way to go about things."

"Good, I think we're on the same page. Don't get me wrong, I believe in the spirit of the law, rather than the letter. On rare occasion. If you get my drift."

I nodded. I thought I did. She continued: "We need to get you on some courses, to keep your career moving. I was thinking SOIT (sexual offences investigation techniques)? Then I think you're absolutely sergeant, and then inspector, material? What do you say?"

That made me stop. "I'd never thought about promotion. I've been totally focused on working hard to get through my probation, and getting my driving."

As she finished her sad excuse for a pasta dish, she replied: "I definitely think that's a good fit for you. You can still be a driver as a skipper. I'd absolutely support your application. Think about it."

We finished off and we popped over to the garage, to get petrol. The rest of the late was made up with BLATTing from one call to the next. *Damn, I love this job.*

I went to bed happy that night but, as it had been off and on for the last few months, I awoke in a cold sweat, shaking, trying to piece together what those nightmares were, without success. Images shot through my mind, as I tried to get back to sleep. I still woke up the next day, feeling only half-rested, and ill at ease. I shook it off, as the aftermath of a stressful day at a new job.

Back for another late turn, and as I attended parade, I'd just remembered to put on a tie. As I settled down, I waved at Mary, Roger and Jack. I wondered with whom I'd be working that day – probably one of the fresh-faced probationers. I looked over at them.

There was Lucy. She was young (early twenties), slim, very pretty and had a certain swagger that indicated she knew it, the way a small section of women have when they expect special treatment from people.

There was Thomas. Man, this lad looked no older than my A level students. I think he was 19. He was skinny, 6'2", with a mop of curly ginger hair. I thought, *this lad is going to get no respect on the streets.*

Penny was 5'4", slim, mid-twenties, with short, mousy, light brown hair. Although she seemed inexperienced, she was the most promising of the really young crowd.

Brian was an older man, an ex-para, about 30, muscular and 5'10", with short black hair. He presented himself with a certain authority and was handsome in a kind of rugged way. I could see Lucy thought so, but she had no chance with him: like me, he saw straight through her. I wasn't too sure how he'd shape up.

There was also Stella, a 5'8", stocky lady, aged about 30, with short blond hair. Even at her stage of service, she had steamed her hat so that the sides were vertical, and constantly wore sunglasses. I honestly thought she was trying far too hard to be tough. If I could see through it, so could every villain in London.

The briefing started, and I was paired with Brian. Good. I'd get a chance to find out what this guy's deal was. At the end of the briefing, I collected the keys and logbook for the same Astra PD28 as the previous day. I checked the fuel and it was low. It looked like I was the only one to have put in fuel, again! First job, get fuel, and call up for work!

As I was getting the car prepped, I had a chance to talk to Brian. "Hi mate. I'm Richard. It's Brian, isn't it?"

He looked at me for a moment, sizing me up: "Yeah, that's right. How do you want to play it today?" Straight to the point. Good.

I looked at him square on: "I work hard. If I can, I talk to people first, and only go hands-on if there's no choice. We take whatever call comes up. You get first refusal on all the arrests. If you want me to deal with an arrest, I have no problem with that. If there's case papers to do, I'll help as much or as little as you want. We work together, and back each other up, contact and cover. Someone always has eyes on the suspect. If you see something you want to deal with, let me know. If I miss something, politely let me know. Any questions?"

He nodded, in seeming approval: "Good, that suits me. I'm here to learn, but I'll do things by the book. I've got your back." Sounded like a sensible guy, so far.

We filled up the car, and I bought a sandwich. Unusually, I'd forgotten to take one that day. We spent the first part of the shift running from job to job. Brian did pretty well, but he was a little stiff and formal with people. But not bad. We had a chance to have a quick stop for a sandwich, at which point I got a private call. It was Control (I still hadn't sussed out who was who in the control room). This was a guy.

He said: "Hi Richard, it's Lewis. We haven't met yet. I'm sorry, but we've got a griefy one for you. I guess that nickname of yours, Griefmeister, is well-founded. We have a ferry job for you. There's a young couple who had a six-month-old baby. Hubby is travelling back from a work trip and is incommunicado. Wifey took baby to see grandma in Westville. Baby became ill suddenly, she took him to the hospital, where he died. We need you to wait outside his address, and transport him to the hospital. Kicker is, she doesn't want you to tell him his baby is dead;

she wants to do that. So you've got to tell him the baby is ill, and you need to get there on the hurry up. Use your own discretion regarding blue lights."

I looked at Brian. He had the same reaction I did – a grim determination. God, it really was a shit job at times. I got back to them, and took the names and addresses.

I then said: "We're to sit outside? What if a job comes up we can't ignore?"

He replied: "Just go and deal with it. If you get tied up, we'll assign someone else."

One part of me so wanted that to be the case. It was a truly shit job. But I felt so guilty, because that would mean one of my colleagues would have to deal with it, which wasn't good.

We made our way to the address. I stopped the car directly outside the terraced house. The lights weren't on. I got out and took the lead. Brian seemed slightly relieved. I am the Greifmeister, after all, and I was the more senior.

I collected my thoughts, remembering the names, so I didn't have to look at my notes. A deep breath, and I took what they call the 'long walk' from the car to the front door, to give news that will devastate a family. I'd given death messages before, to parents about kids, and to kids about parents. I don't know which is worse. And I can still remember every one.

I stood before the front door, checked my pocketbook one more time, looked at Brian, and he nodded. Then I knocked on the door. Silence ... I knocked again ... silence. The house was in darkness, with no one home yet. I felt relieved, and guilty at feeling relieved.

As we were walking back to the car, an urgent assistance call came in, across the other side of the ground. Brian answered the call, and I drove off towards it. Once again, relief and guilt in equal measure. As we got about halfway there, a cancellation. So I turned a corner, switched off the lights, and turned around to return to the house. Was it me, or did I drive slower than I normally did getting back?

Again the house was in darkness, and we took the 'long walk' to the door. Again, no reply. Again, relief and guilt. We turned around and were making it back to the car when a man in his early thirties, with a bag over his shoulder, approached. He said: "Hi, can I help? I'm Stephen Walters. I live at the house you've just knocked at. My wife should be home by now."

My stomach dropped, and I opened my mouth to speak, and nothing came out. I swallowed and, in as an even a tone as I could, said: "Mr Walters, I'm PC Armstrong from Park Street Police Station. You're not in trouble, but please can you come and sit in our car. Thanks." I wanted to do it in his house, but that would just delay things, so in a car was the next best thing.

He looked at me, confused, and Brian took the hint, walked over to the rear door and opened it. The man dumbly followed and sat in the back. Brian walked around the other side, and got in next to him. I sat in the driver's seat, turned around, and when the doors were shut, I collected myself and said: "Mr Walters, your wife Michelle is with your son Zach. He was taken ill this afternoon. He's at the Westville Hospital. I don't know the details; I've just been told to get you there, as quickly as I can. I'm really sorry. I know this must be a shock. Please put your seat belt on. We need to go now."

He looked at me. I will never forget that look – he knew I was lying to him! He knew his son was dead! I was lying to a grieving father, giving him false hope. I have never, never felt such a heel in my life. I hated the job at that moment. I wanted to be anywhere but there.

I don't blame the mother. I can't imagine the pain she must have been in. She wanted to be the one to tell him, but it meant our job was truly horrible.

He just sat there, stunned for a moment, and just as I was pulling away, he started: "What's wrong with him? You must know! Tell me, is he all right? Is he going to die? He's dead, isn't he? He's dead, isn't he? You're lying to me. What sort of fucking monster lies about that!"

At that point I sped up, and once out on the street, put the lights on. I could feel myself gripping the steering wheel so tight. I thought about my training, trying to distance myself from the act of driving, shutting out the man's sobs and shouts. Brian and I kept trying to do whatever we could to calm him.

I said: "Sir, I really don't know any more. We'll get you to the hospital as soon as we can, so you can be with your family."

Despite everything we said, he was having none of it, and moved from shouting abuse to weeping, and silence. That was worse.

That was the hardest drive I've ever made, and it's a good distance from Park Street to Westville. Every minute seemed like an hour. Every car that could seemed to get in the way. Every light turned red in front of us. It seemed to go on forever. All the while, I had to work hard to remember the route. I sketched it out in my mind. Down along the embankment, up through Parliament Square, once again along past the Thames, then cut up towards Westville, around Sloane Square, then eventually to the hospital.

As I got close, I put a radio call in: "PD from PD28, approaching the Westville Hospital." The reception at that distance was very poor, but eventually I got through, and there'd be someone waiting for us at the main entrance.

As we pulled up, the man didn't say a word. As soon as the car stopped, he got out and ran towards the two officers and hospital staff waiting to take him to his wife and dead baby son. I felt sick for the man, and his family. The one remaining officer (the other had gone with the man) walked over and told us they'd deal with it from there. We handed him the bag the man left in the car.

I was shaking and sweating as I turned the car around, and let Brian get in the passenger's seat. I drove back slowly, trying to calm myself down, deep breathing, focusing on the road, and the traffic. No matter what I did, I couldn't clear it from my mind.

Neither of us talked on the way back. I don't think we had anything to say. No words could come close to what we had just dealt with, but it was nothing to that of the family.

For the rest of the shift, we just drove around and dealt with the calls, without a word about that incident. We never did say a word about it to each other, or the rest of the relief. I, for one, had no words, nor stomach for it. We just went through the motions for the rest of the night. We had a body late on, an assault. It needed to go to court the next day, so it wasn't until about 2 a.m. that we got off, having done the case papers. We had to be at court for 10 a.m., barely eight hours later, then go back on duty for another late turn at 2 p.m.

The only thing Brian said, wearily to me as we walked to ours car to drive home, was: "I can see why they call you the Greifmeister." I couldn't disagree with him.

We went to court, and the man was found guilty. Straight after court, we went back to the nick and got changed into our regular uniforms, with just enough time to have a sandwich and get ready to do another late turn.

I was tired at the parade, despite the strong cup of coffee I had in the canteen. We went through the briefing, and I was again out in the same car, again with low fuel. Was I really the only one putting petrol in? My partner that day was Penny, one of the young probationers. She was 5'4", of average build, with shoulder-length, curly brown hair. She was a bubbly, chatty lass. She constantly made me grin with her infectious good humour.

Once I'd done the vehicle check – four wheels outside, one inside, lights, siren, job done! – I said: "Penny, I'm Richard. I try to be as hands-off much as I can, talk to people first if possible. Remember, contact and cover. You can do as much in the way of the work as you like. I'll back you up, or take over if you want. Take what calls you like, and I'll be your taxi. I've got your back. Any questions?" I knew she'd have plenty, which I don't mind.

She beamed, and dove straight in. I did have a soft spot for her, in a professional capacity, of course. "Why do they call you 'the Griefmeister'?"

I kept a blank expression: "I have the reputation for being in the right or wrong place at the right or wrong time. Plenty of arrests, but plenty of the shittiest jobs. Sorry about that."

She quickly said: "Good. I need to arrest more people. I want to experience every kind of job. So bring on the worst of jobs."

My heart dropped, not because of her enthusiasm, which was great. "Please don't tempt fate."

"How do you arrest so many people?"

I started the car and thought, *I'm going to get 101 questions tonight. I hope I have the patience, as I'm tired today.* "Luck, mostly! But just keep your eyes open, never have a zoned-out moment. Keep your head on a swivel. Where's that car going? Why's that person walking about?"

About 101 questions later, we'd got some petrol, and the radio went, "Units to deal, robbery in progress, Elmbridge Road, male IC4, blue tracksuit hoodie, running south."

I hit the lights, and Penny called it in. I said: "This is your chance."

As we rounded the corner, there was a male IC4, blue tracksuit and hoodie, running along the pavement towards us. I stood on the brakes (damn, I didn't even have time to put on the siren).

At that point in the road was a railing, and a stone wall holding up a bridge, so there was nowhere for this guy to go. Penny jumped out the car, vaulted the railings and, even though this guy was bigger than her and tried to jink around her, she put her shoulder down and executed a scissor tackle my sadistic Welsh rugby coach would have been proud of, dumping him on his backside.

As the two were struggling on the floor, he was stronger, but she had the initiative. I jumped the railings and piled in. Between the two of us, we had him face down with the cuffs on in short order, and just in time for the woman who'd been robbed to arrive, panting. The van arrived a couple of minutes later. The lady was so grateful. She hugged Penny so hard I thought I'd have to nick her for attempted murder.

She nicked him, and he was put in the van. Custody at Park Street was full, so we were off to my old stomping ground, Earlham. We were taking the victim back with us, to take a statement.

I turned and said to Penny: "Was that your first robber?"

She grinned: "Yep!"

The lady looked at her: "Wow! Really, that was so brave. I can't believe you two got there so quickly."

Penny smiled: "That's him (pointing at me). He's always in the right place at the right time."

I cringed as she tempted fate like that. As I slowly drove past the front of Earlham police station, and turned into the barrier-controlled back yard, I noticed a young Asian man (18ish) walking along with a huge kitchen knife partially hidden in his back pocket. His shirt only partially hid it. I pulled across in front of him, barring his path. I said very calmly, "Ma'am, please stay in the car. Penny, please look after her, and stay in the car."

I jumped out, and in a relaxed and nonchalant manner walked up to the young man, saying: "Hello mate, how you doing?"

He looked a bit surprised and, as he was about to answer, I said: "Put your hands out like a scarecrow (and demonstrated), please." He looked confused for a moment but, as I approached, he complied. I stepped up, took hold of his right wrist with my left hand, and with my right hand reached around his back and took the knife out of his pocket.

I then tucked the knife in my back pocket, and applied the cuffs, while saying: "Mate, you're under arrest for carrying an offensive weapon." I cautioned him. This was all done without hesitation. Basic rule: action beats reaction, especially if you confuse people.

I turned back to Penny, and indicated for her to step out of the car. She did so, and I said: "Penny, when I've taken our friend here around the other side of the car, would you direct the lady to wait in the front office, and then drive the car into the car park, and park it while I walk our friend here into custody. Thanks."

To her credit, without any hesitation, she did exactly what I asked. It wasn't long before we were both stood in custody with our prisoners – one for robbery and one for an offensive weapon. They were booked in. The robbery suspect was handed over to the robbery team, and we did a quick interview with the guy with the huge knife (Crocodile Dundee would have been proud). The guv'nor cautioned him.

Contrary to popular belief, the vast majority of knives we took from mostly young men were, in fact, kitchen knives. Successive governments of all stripes have put in laws banning 'combat knives' etc. Honestly, they make zero difference to the knives carried on the street. The only impact is on law-abiding collectors, while the government is making a show of dealing with knife crime.

Think of it this way: if you're 16, are you going to spend £200 on a combat knife, and have to go through all the hoops to get it, or are you going to your mom's kitchen drawer to take one? Those who say to just ban all kitchen knives are missing the point. They'll find something else, and if they'll ignore one law, what makes you think they'll follow another? We already have plenty of laws to deal with knives. It's often the same politicians who balk at the implementation because, if you want to stop knife crime, you need to stop and search the young men who carry them. But that's politically unpopular, because the lovely media scream 'racism'.

The choice is, put up with being called a racist for stop and search, or bury more young men. Take your pick! And, by the way, in the poorer parts of London, an awful lot of those young men buried will be Black or Asian.

After we'd dealt with that, we stopped off at Earlham to have a quick sandwich. Penny was bubbly, as always. She said: "Wow, that was so much fun! Can we do the same thing again. I want more bodies!"

I thought, *oh no!* I tried to smile: "Penny, don't tempt fate. You might get more than you bargained for."

Undeterred, she said: "That was so cool, turning the corner, and seeing the robber, right there, and then you getting that guy with the knife."

I nodded. That had been lucky.

Just as we finished, Penny got her wish. The radio went: "Do we have a unit to deal? A welfare check."

Penny didn't hesitate: "PD, PD28, we've just finished refs, we're free to deal."

Control gave her the address, and we walked out to the car. Penny was so chuffed I'd let her drive the car, albeit a few yards.

As I pulled up to the address, we discovered it was a first-floor flat on an old and poorly maintained block, in a rough estate. I looked up and thought, *I have a bad feeling about this.*

We made our way up to the door, and Penny put us on scene. A welfare check means that we have to check on the welfare of someone who hasn't been seen for a while. Why do the police do it? Because we have the power of entry, and it could be a crime scene.

After we'd tried knocking a few times, I got down on my knees and carefully lifted the letter box and sniffed. There it was: putrefaction. I thought, *Penny, you got your wish for a body. Just after a meal, too – I hope you have a strong stomach, mate!*

I looked at her, got out the Vicks, and said quietly (so any eavesdropping neighbours couldn't hear), "Penny, prepare yourself, this might be a bad one. Breathe through your mouth. If you need to step outside for a moment, there's no shame. I use Vicks on my upper lip, to reduce the smell. Are you OK?"

Still with her trademark enthusiasm, she said: "I'm fine. I've got a strong stomach. Can I kick the door in?"

I'll give her credit, she wasn't easily put off. I put in the call, to record the breaking of the door, and stood back. She started enthusiastically kicking the door. It took a while, but eventually the door gave way. Then a strong smell hit us. I was ready, but even with that, it was bad.

She said: "OK, that's not too bad."

I thought, *I wonder if she means that, or if it's bravado? We'll see.*

We went into the small, run-down, untidy flat. Along the hall, into the living room, and there were the remains of what had once been a man. The fire was on. His bloated remains were deeply discoloured, and the carpet was wet and sticky with the putrefied liquid from his body.

The smell was indescribable. I focused on breathing through my mouth, and gave my abdominal muscles a real workout while stopping myself from retching.

We had to turn the body. I looked at her, she nodded, and we both bent down. One had his head, one his feet, and we slowly turned the body. The squelching sounds and sudden burst of smell had me really fighting my instincts to throw up, then run away. The entire time, it was a battle of willpower to remain and do my job. Penny seemed to be hardly affected.

Good, no signs of injury. Then we stepped outside to get some fresh air. I could still smell the foul stench, even on the balcony. I let Penny make the call to control, for the doctor, and coroner. We eventually had to go back in to collect his ID, next of kin details, any valuables, bag them for the coroner, and make the death notifications.

The doctor came and drily said, "With that stench, I could record the death in the car park." He did his job, though even he struggled. Then the coroners came, and even they had to step out once, and were coughing.

We spent the rest of the shift completing the paperwork, and being given a wide berth by everyone.

At the end of the shift, I said to Penny, "Who's your reporting skipper?"

She looked at me, slightly concerned, and said: "Edward Johns. Why? Have I done something wrong?"

"No, quite the contrary; I'm going to say how well you've done. You were utterly fearless tackling that robber, and then you didn't hesitate with that sudden death. Really well done today mate, good effort!"

A beam a mile wide cracked on her face, and her eyes lit up. "Thank you, Richard. That was great fun, but I do see why they call you the Griefmeister. Never a dull moment." I thought grimly, *ain't that the truth, sister!*

I showered, then put my uniform in for the special dry cleaning service the Met offer for especially smelly items.

I made my weary way home. My sleep was filled with nightmares again. *This is becoming a habit*, I thought. *It's probably normal. It's a stage I'll get through.*

About a week later, I was on a Sunday early turn with Penny, and for once it was quiet. We were driving along north of the Elm Road, near the ETNA (Earlwell Tunnel Northern Approach), when the radio went. "Units be aware, there's an LOS vehicle that was lost on Newell's ground. It might be coming your way. It's a silver Subaru Impreza."

Penny made a note of the VRM. She said: "I hope it comes our way. What am I saying? Of course it will."

I took that as a challenge, and started making my way towards Fish Island. I said: "I lived in Earlham when I was a student; I've got a hunch where it might pop out."

We crossed the flyover to Fish Island, and started combing the streets. Sure enough, out from a side street, right in front of us, a silver Subaru Impreza. Penny looked at me and said: "My first pursuit! Sweet!"

I stuck the blues and twos on, and floored it! To say the two vehicles were mismatched wasn't to fully understand the gulf that existed between them. The Astra was a 1.4L 60BHP, front-wheel drive family car, and the Subaru was a 2.5L 165BHP four-wheeled drive (derived from a rally car).

My advantages were: I knew the roads like the back of my hand, I was chasing (always easier), I was recently trained, and I'm from Essex!

Whoever was driving that car knew what they were doing! But, by the looks of it, they didn't know the area. I was having to thrash the living daylights out of the car to keep then in sight! We went around corners, down alleyways, in what was an unguided trip around Fish Island. Fortunately for us, there was nowhere they could really get a head of steam up, as it would have been game over if they did.

Penny did a great job on the radio. Then our luck ran out, and the driver managed to find the main roundabout, and the way out of the maze of backstreets. We both approached at well over 80 mph (30 limit) and, with horror, I saw the Subaru sliding all over the place on the diesel dropped at this huge open roundabout used by the lorries. I desperately tried to scrub off as much speed as I could. Just as we entered, I knew I was in trouble, and as I tried to negotiate the turn, we started to spin. I turned away from the skid, while keeping my eyes glued on the bandit car. Then, as the back came round, I span the wheel, and turned into the spin. This caused the car to do a full 360, and carry on, just!

While still broadcasting on the main set, Penny said: "Oh SHIT!" Then regained composure: "Apologies MP!" and continued with the pursuit.

When the bandit car had a bit of straight road, it left me for dust, and at a right-hand bend in the road, I noticed the driver – it was a woman! It's unusual for women to nick cars, and even rarer for them to be involved in high-speed pursuits.

As we approached the junction with the ETNA, I could see the area car sitting waiting for it at the other side of the junction.

Excellent! I'd bought them enough time to box them in. Then the bandit car turned down the off ramp of the ETNA, driving head-on at traffic going through the Earlwell Tunnel under the Thames. No way was I following her. I pulled over, and Penny called off the pursuit.

That was insane! My blood ran cold. If there was a crash, it would go down as a police accident, and I'd be responsible. Fortunately, it was quiet enough that she'd managed to zigzag through the oncoming traffic, with a closing speed of over 100 mph.

The car was recovered a couple of hours later in south London. We never did find out who was driving.

I turned to Penny, and she said: "You lost her. You lost a pursuit to a woman!"

I took the bait: "No, I called off the chase, with a lunatic! Only a crazy person drives through a tunnel against the traffic! Besides, what's it matter if it was a woman? I thought you were a feminist?"

She genuinely looked annoyed, and punched me in the arm saying: "How dare you! I've never been so insulted in all my life! I don't hate men, I kind of want to find one to marry. Not you. No disrespect. I expect to be held to the same standards as the men. I don't want special treatment from those patronising idiots who think I can't do it without their help!"

"That's because you don't need their help! By the way, why not me?"

She replied, without hesitation: "You're too old!" We both had a chuckle at that.

When we'd finished our shift and made it back to the nick, we both got stick. Me for losing a chase, and her for swearing on the main set!

On the next set of nights, once again I was paired with Penny, and we were assigned to guard a flat on the first floor of a rather run-down estate near the Elm Road. The story was that a man had not been seen for a while, we'd been called, broken down his door, and he was found dead. Trouble was, he'd been brutally beaten to death with a spade, and was in a bit of a mess. They'd checked on his neighbours, one of whom couldn't be found. They did checks on this gentleman, and found that he was Julian Austin, a large Black man who was the first person convicted and sent to prison for stalking a young nurse. He'd spied on her, followed her, and generally made her life hell. His behaviour had been escalating, and if he hadn't been stopped, it was thought he might have done worse.

So, they put two and two together, and had police waiting outside his door for when he returned, to arrest him on suspicion of murder. As we stood outside his door, I looked over the balcony and, to my horror, recognised the rear of the nurses' accommodation block.

I turned to Penny: "What kind of idiot gives an ex-prisoner a flat overlooking nurses' accommodation when he was released for stalking a nurse? I really don't get how people can be so short-sighted?"

She shrugged: "There's no accounting for stupid, as my gran says. By the way, given your reputation, this Austin guy will turn up on our watch, won't he?"

My stomach dropped. Penny, and the tempting fate bit, again.

Around 1 a.m., we heard a car pull into the car park and, a couple of minutes later, who should we see walking towards us along the narrow balcony? You guessed it: Julian Austin. He was a big guy. I mean a really big guy! As tall as me, and about twice as wide. It was not only muscle, but fat too. He strode with real purpose straight towards us. I noticed his gaze wasn't on me, but on Penny, and then he looked over the edge of the balcony. I had a sudden image of what he was thinking: he hated women, and he wanted to throw Penny off the balcony, and if he was twice my size, he was four times hers.

I had intended letting Penny have the arrest, but at that point I decided I'd better do it. So I stepped forward to meet him, pulling myself up to my full height (6'¼", never forget the ¼), stepped forward, and said: "Mr Julian Austin, I am arresting you on suspicion of murder."

With that, I took a very firm grip of his arm, and put on the cuffs, giving him no time to react (action beats reaction, most of the time). Then, between the two of us, we had him under control. I'll never forget, he looked at me, and smiled. It was chilling. You've just been nicked for murder, and you smile. That's not a normal reaction.

Penny called it up, and he was transported back to the nick, where AMEP took over. When we got back in the car, Penny said: "Bit disappointed you didn't let me nick him, Richard."

"Yeah, I know mate, but first I've never nicked anyone for murder, and second, he hates women, and third, did you see the way he looked at you? He wanted to throw you over the balcony."

She shrugged: "Yeah, I know, I saw that too. And yes, he could have done that. I wouldn't have been able to stop him. I hate to say it, but you did the right thing. But is it all right to say it sucks?"

"I would expect nothing else."

When eventually we got the rest of the story, it turned out when they searched his car, they found mud and a spade with human blood on it. Trouble was, it wasn't the victim's blood, or his. So when he smiled, was it because I'd arrested him for the wrong murder? Had he murdered someone else? I never did find out the full story on that.

Over the next few weeks, I spent time with a number of my younger colleagues. I had been working with Brian again, and we'd just finished refs, after bringing in a prisoner for shoplifting, when we got a call to return to custody, urgently. I looked at Brian, and said what we were both thinking: "Why is it, you always end up with the griefy jobs?" I shrugged, and made my way to the custody suite.

When we got there, the custody sergeant quickly informed us that our prisoner had self-harmed, and we were needed to take him to the hospital to get stitched up. Apparently, he'd broken up the plastic knife and fork he'd been given to eat his food, and proceeded to force the sharp broken bits under is skin, all the way up his arm.

I looked at the skipper incredulously: "You're joking right, Sarge?"

He shook his head: "I only wish I were, son. Best you two get the van ready, and the gaoler will help you get him in the back."

A short while later, with the prisoner safely searched and handcuffed in the back of the van, on the way to A & E, Brian looked at me, saying: "Does this happen often? I mean, not just to you, I mean in general?"

"Not as far as I'm aware. It's the first time."

He nodded, and with weary resignation, said: "How do we play this? What if he refuses treatment? Where do we stand legally? I must say it doesn't sit well with me, holding someone down to have medical treatment against their will. What about you?"

I shook my head: "Legally, he's in our custody, and he's clearly mentally ill, and hurting himself. I think we're covered in that respect. But, yeah, I am with you on the moral side of things. If you think back to who did force people to have medical procedures against their will, it's not great company to be in, is it?"

Brian nodded, and we continued our way to somewhere, and to do something neither of us wanted to be involved in. A short while later, we were shown into a treatment room by a doctor, and we had to bodily lift our scrawny little prisoner onto the treatment table.

The young female doctor looked on, unfazed, and said to the man: "Sir, do you consent to me treating you?"

"No! Leave me alone. I just want to die!"

She nodded, made a note on her clipboard, and said: "Under the Mental Health Act, and for your own good, I will remove these shards of plastic, and treat the injuries. Officers, please hold him steady."

This was all said in a matter-of-fact way. No emotion, no justification, just cold. Honestly, when I thought about what we were doing, I felt sick. He tried to wriggle as the doctor injected him with a local anaesthetic. It was more of a token gesture, as he knew he was no match for the two of us, but that made me feel worse. I began to notice how hot and stuffy it was in the room. I started sweating. I found I had to look away as the pieces of plastic were slowly removed from his arm, and then methodically the arm was stitched up. It is a feeling of self-loathing. I know, logically, it was justified, but I'll never forget that feeling of holding another human being down, forcing them to have a medical treatment. Not just for him, but if the state could justify this to him, what else could they justify doing to the rest of us, if it suited them?

The other thing that sent a chill down my spine was the cold, emotionless way in which the doctor had approached the whole thing. Totally impassive. I knew I'd never look at a doctor the same way, and a little bit of my trust in them disappeared forever. I knew I'd never fully trust them again. Every time I see a doctor, even now, I still have a dread inside me.

When the treatment had been concluded, we drove our prisoner back in the van to the nick. Brian and I once again didn't speak; I could see it had had a similar effect on him. God, I hated the job sometimes!

Once again there were riots in the centre of London. Park Street was designated a processing centre, so we took our prisoners to Earlham, while a number of the probationers were taken off from regular duties to help.

From the sound of it they were very busy. I spoke to Jack after he'd dealt with the rioters, and he said: "Richard, you know, just when you think you've seen it all!"

"Yeah, I was in the thick of it last year. What were they doing this year?"

He shook his head: "They'd covered their faces, so we were doing ID from their clothes. So the procedure was that if they'd been flagged as having been involved in throwing missiles, or fighting us, then we'd seize their clothes as evidence. You know what they did?"

"I shudder to think."

"They shit and pissed themselves, so that we'd have to deal with it as we took their clothes. Can you believe that? They had badges saying they hoped the Queen Mom died. I mean, how sick are these people?"

"I believe in the right to protest peacefully, but they lose any support from me as soon as the first brick goes flying! There are some seriously sick people out there, mate."

I checked the date and it was three years in the job. It seemed like a different person to the one standing outside the gates of Hendon. Maybe it was, maybe it wasn't – I couldn't make my mind up.

The shifts came and went. Arrest after arrest, the manic late turns with far too many calls and far too few troops. There was even the rumour they were going down to single crewing. To say this didn't go down well with the troops was an understatement.

I had a meeting with the inspector. I stood outside her office door and wondered if it was something I'd done? Was there a complaint? I couldn't quite work it out. *Oh well, only one way to find out.*

I knocked. "Come in." I walked in, and she asked me to sit down.

"Good morning, Ma'am."

She smiled: "I wanted to have a chat with you. How do you think you're doing with the new responsibility of being a driver, and new team?"

I began to get a little nervous. "Fine, as far I know, Ma'am. Is everything OK?"

"Oh yes, as far as I'm concerned, it's really good. The arrest record of this relief has gone from the bottom, to the middle. You're in the top quarter in terms of arrests, and the probationers' arrests have gone up by 50 per cent since you joined. Well done!"

I sat there, stunned for a moment. *Really?* I was confused, and said quietly: "Well, that's good, Ma'am."

"I want you to consider applying for a SOIT course, and putting in for your skipper's exam. I want you to be our relief's designated training sergeant. I know Sergeant Hetfield will be retiring next year, and I'm due to do a promotion board then too. There'll be plenty of opportunities for you then. If you're interested?"

I could feel myself pull back from this. I thought, *I've only just got my feet wet in the driving thing.*

She could see my hesitation: "Look, I'll level with you. I know Sergeant Appleton is applying for a promotion to inspector, and I'll recommend him to do so. Then I'm looking to you and Mary to become the backbone of the relief in terms of sergeants. I think you'd make a really strong team. She's great with the admin and personnel management, and you're great at the training and momentum of the team. What do you say?"

What? It was a lot to think about, if I was being honest, I was feeling a bit overwhelmed as it was. It was a lot of pressure I wasn't sure I was ready for. But she did have faith in me. It felt like boom or bust. Firstly, I was told I was useless, now I was being pushed too fast. How to tell her, though?

I took a moment, and slowly said: "OK, Ma'am. I am blown away by your confidence in me, I really appreciate it. But I'll have to have time to think about it. I will start the process for the SOIT course, and look into what I need to study for the sergeant's exam, if that's all right. And by the way, if I may be so bold, I think you're right about Mary: she'd make a great sergeant."

She smiled a knowing smile: "Funny, she said the same about you. Anyway, I'll get Sergeant Appleton to help you with the course application, and skipper's exams."

At that I was dismissed, and walked out with my head spinning. Finally, I thought about what she'd said, and the way she'd said it about Mary. Was I missing something? I guessed she just wanted to set up the basis of a new team before she left. That was logical, leaving things better than she found them. Maybe she needed to show team development for her promotion board?

I carried on working. Call after call. And then, following a meeting with Sergeant Appleton, I had to complete the long and complicated form for the SOIT course, and start studying for my first set of two sergeant's exams, followed by a board. The first exam was in a couple of months and if I passed that, the second was in another few months, with the board around the end of the year.

I was kept very busy. My nightmares continued, and I found the slow toll on my health taking effect. I went out to see my friends less, and there were fewer trips to the gym. My relationship with Victoria and my other friends suffered. I was becoming more distant. I did occasionally bump into my friends around my hometown when I was off, including members of my old football team, their wives and kids. It seemed strange to see people I grew up with having kids of their own! I was now an uncle. That seemed very strange, and I was so chuffed for my brother and sister-in-law. There was a sadness, as I knew deep down that path wasn't for me, and that I'd never be a dad.

The day eventually came to find out about the SOIT course, when I was approached by a female inspector, whom I didn't know. She looked at me, checked my shoulder number, and said: "PC Armstrong?"

"Yes, Ma'am." *Was I in trouble?* She said: "You didn't get that SOIT course. Sorry about that."

She went to walk off. I was shocked, and just stood there. She stopped: "Look, I shouldn't tell you this, but yours was a very good application, and it's not down to you personally, but they wanted a woman for this post. She was on the accelerated promotion scheme to have more women in top jobs. Better luck next time."

With that, she walked off. I thought, *what the fuck! This moronic ideology is infesting every aspect of the police.*

I carried on for another couple of months, and remember standing outside the sergeant's exam room. I knew I'd done all the preparations I could. It wasn't going to be easy, but I was reasonably confident. In the end it was tough, but not dreadful. I heard a short while later I'd passed. Well, that was a relief. One part done, one exam, and a board, to go. Honestly, at that stage, I wasn't entirely sure I'd even take it. The strain of constantly being the number one on a team with, shall we say, varying abilities in terms of the probationers? Constantly having to think two steps ahead of them, to say nothing of the villains?

One example: I was out with Thomas, a tall, skinny lad, no older than one of the A level students, with wild ginger hair. He wasn't an unpleasant lad, but he was utterly clueless at times. He'd arrested this guy for assault. Common assault is non-arrestable, unless it's under certain specific conditions. ABH is arrestable. So, if you do arrest someone for a relatively minor assault, you arrest them on suspicion of ABH, and then wait for the hospital report, and you can drop the charge to common assault if necessary. This is basic stuff you're taught at Hendon.

So there we were, with his prisoner, in custody, and the sergeant behind the desk says, "Officer, on what offence did you arrest this man?"

Thomas replied, "Common assault."

The custody officer raised his eyebrows, and I coughed loudly and said: "And suspicion of ABH."

Thomas looked at me with surprise. I stared intently, and he said: "I meant on suspicion of ABH, Sergeant."

The sergeant said: "OK, right. Sus ABH."

When he'd finished, he said: "PC Armstrong, can I speak with you?"

I walked over to where we couldn't be overheard, and he said: "Please can you make sure your probationer knows what he's arrested someone for, before they are brought in?"

I bit my tongue: "Yes, Sergeant, it won't happen again."

When I had a moment to talk to Thomas, I said: "Mate, didn't you know that you couldn't arrest for common assault, under sec 24 (of PACE 1984)?"

He looked at me with big, round, fearful eyes: "No, I ... I didn't think. I'm sorry."

By that stage, I was tired and a bit grumpy, but still managed to say, "OK, right Thomas. It's all right this time. But please, next time, if you're not sure about something, ask. I don't mind questions, even if you feel silly. That's OK; it's how you learn."

He nodded, and looked close to tears.

A few days later, we were on an operation to help out the revenue officers on the London buses. I didn't envy their jobs. They got even less respect from the public, and less backup from their management (if that were possible). Working with them also served as a way to gather intel. There'd been an increase in robberies (ten to fifteen a day, just in Park Street), and there'd been a pattern. The victims had been travelling on buses, and their attackers had followed them off, waited until they were somewhere quiet, and groups of two to four lads all dressed in tracksuits and hoodies had attacked. So the plan was, if someone had committed the offence of travelling without a ticket, we'd do a name check. If they were also young, male, and in groups of two to four wearing tracksuits and hoodies, it's turn out your pockets time, boys.

I was paired with Lucy, and we were in plain clothes, trying to stay low-profile, so as not to alert the gangs. Fat chance – they could spot us a mile off. She was up to her regular tricks, flirting with anything with a pulse and a penis. Honestly, it was embarrassing, the way she walked, fluttered her eyes, the make-up. All saying: look at me, I'm so pretty! Not cool, or professional. I ground my teeth and made the best of it. We'd started off as three pairs, but the other two had got prisoners (drugs and a knife), but Lucy had been so slow, she hadn't got a prisoner. I'd overheard her say to Penny that she didn't want to get a prisoner, as she wanted to get off on time (it was a day shift), to get ready for her "hot date" with some hunk she'd chatted up, never mind the boyfriend she was living with. This was the newest in a long line of boyfriends. The last one she'd strung along while he and his dad redecorated her flat, ready for him to move in. The day after he'd finished (which was her birthday), she ditched him. Nice!

We'd ended up that day at the bus stop on the Earlham one-way system, which at that point was nine lanes wide. There was only one revenue officer left, a 5'4", slim guy in his fifties, who was nice enough.

I said: "This is the last bus of the day." I looked at Lucy and said: "This'll be your last chance to nick someone."

She made a face, and her phone rang. She held up her hand and answered it. What the hell? Who doesn't have their phone on silent, and who answers it, when they're working? She opened the car door, and I could hear her having an argument with her current boyfriend, who'd apparently found out about her date with another guy.

I looked at the revenue officer, and he rolled his eyes: "Just like my daughter; always on that bloody phone."

I nodded and said, as the bus pulled up, "Last one of the day."

We got on and checked. One man on board. Bingo, no ticket. Really? One passenger and he hasn't paid!

We got him off the bus, and I had a really bad feeling about this guy. All the alarm bells were going off. I tried to attract her attention, but she had her back to me. I looked at the guy. He was Black, 6'3", muscular, thirties, dressed in dark trousers and shirt. As we went through getting his ID, he was very cagey about showing us anything with his name on it. Eventually, he found something in his wallet, and appeared to drop something. As the revenue officer looked down, the man gave him a huge shove, into me. The revenue officer lost his balance and fell at my feet, and by the time I looked up, he'd jumped over the railings, and was sprinting across nine lanes of live traffic. Really?! I charged after him, hitting the emergency button, shouting: "Suspect running, Earlham roundabout."

I made ground on him. He was slowing the traffic as we ran across the road. Finally, two lanes from the possible escape route of the Tube station, a van seeing him hit the brakes, but too late, and he ran into the side of it, bouncing back towards me. He moved to run around it, and I went to grab him, realised I still had my radio in my right hand, so grabbed his collar with my left hand. He moved to go around the back of the van, but I held on. My arm was now straight out. I then felt an almighty impact in my back.

Lucy had finally made an appearance, and tripped over just as she got to me, and had barrelled into my back. I fell, with my arm straight out above my head. I had both hands full so couldn't stop myself. I fell on top of the guy I was chasing, and with Lucy on top. There was a sharp pain in my lower back, which burned, and an incredibly sharp pain in my shoulder as it bent back behind me. I cried out in pain, and my hand and arm went numb.

The three of us started to struggle, and were quickly joined by the revenue officer. Between the three of us, we managed to subdue and cuff our prisoner. It turned out he was an illegal immigrant, who'd beaten up an immigration officer and escaped a couple of years before, and had been on the run since, using various aliases, but his fingerprints were on the system.

As we were waiting for the van, I found my arm was really painful, and I was feeling cold. The revenue officer said quietly to me: "You don't look well. See a doc when you can, son."

Lucy had made it clear I would be dealing with "my" prisoner, as she needed time to sort herself out as she had to "save the day" when I let my prisoner go.

Park Street was full, so it was off to Earlham, and as I took the prisoner in to be booked in, the doctor (who had just finished looking after a prisoner) took one look at me and said to the custody sergeant, "When this officer is ready, order him to come into my office, please."

The custody officer nodded and, looking at me, said, "You heard what the doctor said. As soon as this gent is booked in, the doctor's office, and no arguments!"

I was shaking at this point and felt sick, so I did as I was told. After the doctor examined me, he told me I'd dislocated my left shoulder, but fortunately it looked like it had gone straight back in. Also, I'd probably suffered disc damage on my lower back. He ordered me to have an X-ray. I was promptly put in a car and taken to hospital. I did make sure Lucy had support from one of the skippers, so she could deal with the prisoner. She was not happy!

I learnt at the hospital that, yes, I had dislocated it. It was back in place, but I did have rotator cuff damage, and disc damage to my lower spine (this has got worse over the years, and now prevents me from driving). None of the injuries were too severe and, with a couple of days' rest, I should be fine. I turned up for work the next day, and was promptly sent home to rest.

The end of the summer rolled by, and the nights started drawing in. In the second week of September we were finishing off a set of nights. They'd been long and busy, rarely getting off on time. My sleep was still disturbed, and I'd been struggling to keep my eyes open at times. I woke up in the afternoon, and while lying in bed, I thought I'd text Sean, a mate of mine, to see if he wanted to see a film on one of the four days off I'd have. I sent the text, and within a minute, he was calling back. *Good,* I thought, *there's obviously something he wants to see.*

"Hi Sean, how are you doing mate? I'm off in a day's time; what film do you want to catch?"

"Richard, haven't you seen the news? You're going nowhere for a while."

"Mate, I'm on nights, I've just woken up."

"Turn on the news, now!"

I reached for the remote, clicked the ON button, and it came into focus just as a plane struck one of the twin towers in New York. I just lay there watching, stunned, mouth gaping.

What the hell was I seeing? Clearly, it was a film. I changed channels – same image. I flicked back just to make sure. Sean said quietly: "You're going to be busy for a while, my friend. I think you need to get up and start preparing. When you're free from work. Call me, and we can go out then. Take care, buddy."

I wasn't on duty for hours, but I thought I might need all my uniform. I took all my shirts and stuck them in a quick wash cycle. I got out kit that I needed, and started to prepare to be away from home for a while. I got my largest backpack, put in a sleeping bag and loads of spare underwear. I checked the fridge, and used or threw out anything perishable. I thought of all the things I'd need to take care of if I couldn't get home.

A few hours later, I was ironing my shirts when the phone rang. I almost knocked over the iron in my rush to answer it.

"Hi Richard. Adrian Appleton. I take it you've seen the news? All police leave cancelled. So we all need to prepare for an extended time on duty."

"Thanks Sarge. Yeah, I'm ironing all my shirts, and I'll bring in all my spare uniform. I've got a sleeping bag, and plenty of changes of clothes. I'm chucking out anything that'll go off."

"Oh, yeah, you live alone, don't you? That sounds all in order. Good thinking. I don't want to think where this'll go, mate. Sounds like they're opening up the old accommodation block at Earlham. Still very much up in the air as to what's happening next. There's a briefing at nine, so you'll need to be in at least an hour early. I'm getting in for around eight. Anything you need to know?"

"No, I can't think of anything at the moment. I reckon I'll get in about 20:00 hours. I'll see you in the canteen just after that."

"OK, mate, take care."

I put the phone down, and just got straight back to ironing. I spent the next few hours cleaning my boots, taking a new spare pair I had, collecting all the spare batteries for my Maglites that I could find. I remembered an old mechanical alarm clock I had.

I fussed around the house until it got to 18:30 hours, then took all my stuff to the car and shoehorned it in. I'd cleaned and tidied the house, and left my "Goodbye" letters on the sofa, in clear view, in case the worst was to happen. If a young PC had to go through my stuff if I didn't make it home, I wanted to make it as easy for them as possible.

The drive in was an odd feeling, almost surreal, and as I drove past City Airport, I couldn't help but notice how the runway lined up directly with the Canary Wharf towers. Was this their next target? On the way in, as I was so early, I stopped, and bought loads of chocolate bars, crisps, and drinks.

I made it in, and thought about taking all my spare kit to my locker, then remembered what Adrian had said about Earlham accommodation, and left most of it in the car.

I went into the canteen and had some food, where I met up with Adrian, and found out where the briefing was. We chatted about the situation, and what was going to happen.

I arrived early to the briefing, and sat down. There was a buzz of expectation. We were in the briefing room, and the inspector explained that we'd be doing our normal shifts, but there'd be extra shifts as well. Some for everyone, some for shield-trained. We'd be getting a briefing from Special Branch.

At that point, in walked Alan. I remembered he'd transferred to Special Branch, and was based at NSY.

Once we'd all settled, he gave us a briefing I'll never forget. He stood, patiently waited until we were all silent and, in a very calm and even tone, said: "Good evening, ladies and gentlemen. Today in New York extremists attacked the twin towers, the Pentagon, and we believe attempted to hit another target. These terrorists used passenger aeroplanes as weapons, by means of hijack, leaving thousands dead. New York was today; we believe London is next."

He paused to allow us to take it in. He continued: "So what we are doing is having a huge police reserve in London. You will do your normal shifts, then you'll go on aid around London. What does that mean? When there's an attack on London, you'll be on hand to do whatever you can to deal with it. Some days you'll be required to work between twelve and sixteen hours. Therefore, Earlham's old accommodation will be reopened, for the times you won't have time to get home. The stores will be opened up to hand out clean shirts and spare uniform. We will arrange for a cleaning and ironing service, through your sergeants and inspector. We don't know how long this will going on for. Any questions?"

We all just sat in silence for a moment. London was next, and we were the first responders. Shit! That was stark! I thought, *OK, that's what we get paid for, let's do this.*

Over the next few days we worked hard on our regular shifts (there were a number of well-meaning, but paranoid, false alarms), and then either gear up in our public order kit and sit in the side streets waiting for the call which thankfully never came, or were a visible presence to help reassure the public.

We were working so many hours that days and nights blended into each other. There was much talk of the DPG (Diplomatic Protection Group) or, as they were more commonly called, Doors, Porches and Gutters (after where they spent most of their time, on static guard), being repurposed to provide armed support. Every firearm-trained officer was needed to bolster the capital's defence.

According to rumour, the commissioner on the day after the attack asked one of his aides: "What plans have we got to arm every police officer in London?"

"None Sir."

"Well, best we bloody make some."

They asked Glock how quickly they could provide enough G17s to equip the Met. Reply: "Tomorrow, 09:00 hours."

A good start. How about training the 30,000 police officers, of which, almost none were trained? The current training facilities were for maybe a dozen officers at a time, and it was a two-week course. If you do the maths, dividing 30,000 by twelve, then multiply it by two weeks, that's an awfully long time. So they looked at getting the army involved and shortening the course to one day. ONE DAY! If you want a really bad outcome, equipping people with one day's firearms experience with a pistol, and expecting them to police the streets of London, seems like a good way to get lots of people killed in a very quick time!

The Met had spent the last few years stripping police officers from the centre of London, forcibly moving them from jobs they were happy with and experienced at, to stations further away from home they had no experience in. It was called Tenure. Then, after 9/11, they reversed the policy, forcing officers back into the centre of town, where terrorists were more likely to attack.

After completing a tough late turn, our relief were tasked with guarding the memorial garden to those who had lost their lives in the attacks. It was in the garden in the centre of Grosvenor Square, outside the American Embassy. We were bussed up there, and it was absolutely chucking it down. So we took turns patrolling the garden. Apparently, they were concerned about a possible attack on the US Embassy, and possible vandalism of the memorial. Yes, some people are that sick.

One of the US Embassy staff made an appearance, and thanked us personally for our support. Honestly, I, like most of my colleagues, was moved by this. I just felt so sorry for all those poor people, and wanted to do whatever I could to help and support them. In that spirit, we lined up to sign one of the books of remembrance. As I was queueing to do this, there was a board with names of those they had confirmed had died.

I looked down the list of newly released names. Then my eyes stopped at a name. It was one I recognised. It can't be them!? Then I looked at her age – same as mine. Then the nationality – British. And then the town – same as mine. (I won't record the name, out of respect for her family)

My God, no! The town where I grew up was a commuter town which supplied a lot of people for the financial sector of the City of London, which had strong ties with NY. A lot of the companies which had offices in the twin towers also had offices in London.

I thought about the last time I saw her, a few weeks before the attack. I bumped into her and her husband, and two small children. I thought of how he'd have to tell those two that Mommy wasn't coming home. How he and they'd struggle coming to terms with that.

The lady and her husband had been in the same class at school. In fact, they were childhood sweethearts. They had been inseparable ever since. We'd known each other for more than twenty years. I'd played football with him and copied from her in maths. How was my friend going to deal with this, and raise their kids as a single dad?

My heart broke, and I don't know if it was how tired I was, but I barely held back the tears. I signed the book of condolence and volunteered to patrol the garden. As I walked around, I found a quiet spot where no one could see, pushed back my helmet and wept. I let the rain wash away my tears. When I'd stopped, I wiped my face and went back in the dry. I never did tell anyone. We had a job to do, and I didn't want to upset anyone else.

At that moment, I felt something break inside, like the straw that broke the camel's back.

After a few more weeks, things calmed down, and we stopped with the insanely long shifts. We had a few days off. Until then, I'd been working on autopilot: no time to think, just work, eat, sleep, work, etc.

The first night I slept fine. The next, nightmares. The next, nightmares. And again. I started waking up in a cold sweat. Sometimes, I'd wake up because I could hear someone scream, but there was no one there. I eventually worked out it was me. I let this go on for a few weeks, hoping it would go away. It didn't! I was constantly tired, and found myself jumping at shadows. The constant diet of adrenaline at work – running from fight, to stabbing, to sudden death – finally took its toll.

It came to a head when I got up early for a late turn. I'd been tortured all night. Every time I closed my eyes, horrific visions of the stuff I'd seen were there. I felt the emotions of those moments. I started to dread going to sleep, as I was constantly reliving the worst moments.

I was shaking so hard, I could hardly put the keys in the ignition of my car. It took both hands to eventually get the keys in. I practised deep breathing. I thought, *I can't go on like this. I need help, but I can't stop. I'll get through this. What can I do?* I thought, *Next day off, I'll see the doctor. But I hate seeing doctors. They might stop me from working. They might put me in a mental institute.* I couldn't think that way; I had to carry on.

So the next set of rest days, I bit the bullet and managed to book a doctor's appointment. Why do doctor's receptionists make you feel like you're wasting their time every time you talk to them? As if you're a malingering wastrel?

The day came, and I made way down to the surgery I'd being going to since I was a kid. I looked around the tiny waiting room that was no larger than a living room. My hands were sweaty, and I could feel myself shaking. What was wrong with me? I'd face down people armed with knives or guns, but I was scared of a bloody doctor's appointment. All I wanted to do was run away at that point and, the longer I waited, the stronger the feeling became. I'd worked so damned hard to get into the police, pass out at Hendon, complete my street duties, get through my probation, earn the respect of my colleagues, and get my driving course. It was all I'd ever wanted and more than I could have expected. I just couldn't countenance losing it. It was who I was, the person I was meant to be. I had purpose, meaning in my life for seemingly the first time. Everything was there, ready for me, and as I was reaching out to grasp it, it was crumbling to dust in my hands. My own body was fighting me. I could fight the enemy without, but not the enemy within. What was wrong with me? Failure was not an option. *I must find a way through this. The doctor must be able to fix this.* That's what doctors did: if you were ill, they fixed you.

Roused from my thoughts, I heard my name being called, and I looked up slightly embarrassed, and went in to see the doctor. It was a small white office with a medical couch to one side, and a desk and a couple of chairs. The doctor (a man I hadn't seen before) smiled a kindly smile: "Come in. Please sit down, Mr Armstrong. What can I do for you today?"

I did as I was asked and, looking at the doctor (he was a man in his forties, wearing a suit and tie, slightly portly, with tidy, short, light brown hair), I took a breath – and my mind went blank. I couldn't find the words, and just started crying and shaking. It was a visceral reaction. I totally lost my composure for a minute, until I could fight the emotions down. I fought to slow my breathing down and regain self-control.

The doctor handed me the tissue box, and said gently and calmly: "Best you tell me what's going on."

I explained the whole situation: all the things I'd dealt with, the nightmares, the feelings of panic.

He quietly took notes, and at the end said: "I have some tablets to help you cope, and different ones to help you sleep."

I must have shown my concern, and he anticipated my question, "Don't worry, you can still do your job, and no you're not going mad. Given what you've dealt with, it's a perfectly natural reaction. But, if you can, find a less stressful role for a bit. Are there any postings you can get outside of the East End, for instance? It won't take long for you to get through this. You'll be fine."

At this, I thanked him, took my prescription and, feeling a lot more positive, went to the chemist to get my medication.

When got home, I looked at the packet of tablets the doctor gave me. SSRIs, I think he called them, and they looked familiar. Then it dawned on me – they were the same pills the doctors sometimes gave to the prisoners in the cells. Was I really that far gone? I couldn't think that way. I had to take his advice, take the pills, look for a transfer, and everything would be all right.

I thought about what he'd said, and it seemed to make perfect sense. Might there be a quieter, less frantic police station I could work from? Yes, that would solve it – a quieter place, where I could recover, with less pressure. A transfer, that's the idea. A place to heal, and then I could go back to the busy boroughs again. Good!

As luck would have it, at briefing, the inspector read out a note: "Good afternoon, ladies and gents. Before I start the briefing, I'm sure it won't interest any of you, but Westville Police Station needs people to transfer in. But I can't imagine it'd interest anyone. Who'd want to go to Sleepy Hollow? It's so quiet, they barely have anyone working there."

Bingo! I thought, *thank you God!* I'd apply there, find somewhere really quiet, get something from the doctor to help and get back to my normal self. A plan!

It was a busy shift, and it wasn't until the end that I managed to look on the map. *Damn!* That was a long commute, but it was my chance to recover, and heal.

I contacted Westville, and yes, they were interested. I spoke to Sergeant Appleton, and gave him my transfer request. He said: "What!? Why? You've just got here? You're doing so well?"

I thought, *I can't tell him. He'll try to stop me, and I need this.* So I said: "Given the current circumstances, I feel it's my duty to help out in the place of most need. They are desperate, and there's always the threat of terrorism, and the focus is now on the most likely high-profile targets."

He tried and tried to get me to change my mind, and I stuck doggedly to that line. Eventually, he agreed, and my application was passed.

Sometimes in life, you are so focused on one thing, you fail to notice the warning signs of an impending disaster. I remember attending a lecture during my flight training in America, which was about an air crash when a passenger aeroplane was on final approach to the airport. The crew became so focused on the fact the undercarriage locked down lights weren't on that they ignored the fact the ground was coming up to meet them until it was too late. That killed them and all the passengers. I was so obsessed with continuing in "The Job" that I wasn't seeing what it was doing to me. How could I give up my identity, my life? I just closed my ears to everything and everyone else, and kept on the path I thought would help. Take the pills, and transfer to a quieter nick.

In very quick time the transfer was approved (such was the Met's desperation for bodies 'up town'). When word got out that I was leaving, a social was organised for after my last day (a paperwork day, 11:00 hours to 19:00 hours).

The inspector asked me to go to her office. This is one of the conversations I will remember for the rest of my life, as I know it was one of the worst decisions I've ever made. Trust me, that comes up against some pretty stiff opposition!

She said: "Richard, I respect your right to leave, but I have to say I'm extremely disappointed. You've done so well here. You're on target to become a sergeant, to have a really good career. I understand from our previous conversations about your desire to go where you're most needed. I absolutely respect that, but why now?"

I really struggled with that. I wanted so much to explain why, I really did. She and that relief had done nothing but treat me well and support me. But how could I tell her I was living a nightmare where every time I put my head on the pillow, I was tormented and tortured? That all I could see and feel were those images playing out? This was the only way.

I said: "Thank you, Ma'am. I am so appreciative of your support, and that of the relief, but I must carry on with what I believe is best for my career."

She nodded, but tried one last time, "Look, it's not too late. You can still stay. I'll help and support you in your career. Please reconsider. We need you on the team. Is there something that's wrong?"

I've played this over and over for twenty years, and If I could go back and change it, I would. There are maybe three decisions in my life I really regret, and that I would give almost anything to be able to go back and change. This is one of them.

Even as I was saying the words, I knew it was a dreadful mistake. Why oh why did I not tell her the truth? Sometimes I truly hate myself for being so stupid. This was one of those times.

"No, everything's fine, Ma'am, and genuinely I am certain of my decision. But thank you so much for your support."

By that stage, the PTSD had started to really take hold, and cloud my judgement, and the only person who couldn't see it was me.

She nodded, and with deep sadness wished me good luck. WHY AM I SUCH AN IDIOT!

At my goodbye drink, I went round all the people I'd gotten to know. A number of the probationers were very kind.

I sat and contemplated my non-alcoholic drink (I had to drive home), and was thinking, *why have I get myself into this mess?* I don't know if you've ever made a decision and, even as you're going through with it, you know it's a mistake? I took one last look at my shoulder numbers, 272PD. That was who I'd been, who I was. Why was I giving that up? I felt alone, adrift, with nothing anchoring to reality. Everything was falling apart, and I didn't know what to do.

I was pulled back to reality by the chair next to me scraping across the floor. I looked up, and it was Mary. I could tell she was troubled, but was putting a brave face on it.

She said: "Hi Richard. Are you excited about your new challenge?"

I smiled. Mary had always been very kind to me. "Thank you, Mary, I am. I'm not sure what to expect."

She smiled a slightly sad smile: "We'll all miss you here. I thought you were fitting in really well. I have to say how much I admire your determination. You always follow your own path. The way you stood up for yourself."

I felt myself blushing slightly. "Err, thanks Mary. I've had loads of help. I really appreciated how you warned me about Burke. That was good of you. I think you'll make a fine sergeant and inspector one day. Take care of yourself."

She smiled, and touched my arm, "Take care of yourself, Richard Armstrong." She walked away, and I thought, *That was nice. What a nice person.*

A short while later, Penny walked over, slightly drunk, and sat down next to me: "You're a fucking idiot!"

I thought, *well, she may have a point, but that's a tad harsh as a goodbye!*

"Nice to see you too, Penny. Exactly in what way am I a fucking idiot today?"

"Mary just left. She was heartbroken you're leaving."

I was puzzled, "Well, that's very kind of her. She's a nice person, and an excellent police officer."

She looked at me as if she was talking to a total imbecile, and said bluntly: "How can you be so stupid? She likes you!"

I still wasn't understanding: "Well, I like her too; she's always been very kind to me."

Failing to keep the exasperation out of her voice, she said: "No, she REALLY LIKES YOU!"

I still didn't get what she was saying, and I just stared blankly at her. She said: "How can men be so utterly clueless!? She likes you like a woman likes a man. Dear God, do I have to draw you a fucking picture?"

I was stunned, "Why?"

She rolled her eyes. "Err, because she's a woman, and you're a man. I thought you taught biology, the birds and the bees."

I said blankly, "But women don't like me; I'm not attractive. Only the crazies like me, and she's normal, and nice."

I really thought Penny was going to punch me. She gritted her teeth: "Normal and nice, that's one of the harshest things you can say about a woman. I'm just glad she's not here to hear that."

I was genuinely shocked and weakly replied, "Why didn't she say anything?"

"Oh, for the love of God! She was carrying a torch for you from the first moment she saw you at Hendon. She couldn't have made it more obvious if she'd flown a flag. Here's the thing: women like her, they want a man to notice and make the first move."

I was even more puzzled. "So she didn't tell me she liked me, I was supposed to work it out by myself, then make the first move? And she's heartbroken I didn't? If I like someone, I say so. Why can't women just do the same? Instead of all this cloak and dagger stuff."

She shook her head: "You know nothing about women, do you?"

"Guilty as charged!"

She stared at me for a moment, and eventually smiled. "Good luck at Westville!"

She walked off, and I thought, *well, I didn't see that coming!*

Chapter 11
WESTVILLE, A SLEEPY HOLLOW NIGHTMARE

I had received the parking instructions via internal email. It was an underground car park, just across the road from the nick. It said parade for late turn, a 14:00 hours start.

I had set off in plenty of time; it was a long trip. About an hour and a half after I set off, I arrived and stood outside Westville Police Station, with all my kit on my back, and in a couple of kit bags (including my public order gear).

It was late October, the nights were drawing in, and there was a cold wind whipping around the trees that lined the street outside the stone and brick building before me. The door was on the corner. This building had character – real character. I approved!

The Borough of Westville or, to give it its proper title, The Borough of Churchleigh and Westville, was a world apart from that of Earlham. We were almost within sight of the Westville Road, one of the most trendy (and expensive) places to shop in London. In the summer, anyone who's anyone is seen parading along the Westville Road.

The houses around there might not look much different from some of the nicer areas of London but they were a lot more expensive. If you wanted to see the newest, most exclusive cars, that was the place.

Yet there I was, just a little nobody, an upstart, there to police them. Did I really know what I was doing? On past evidence, absolutely not!

I had seen the doctor during my couple of days off between shifts. He'd given me a higher dose of the tablets he'd called the SSRIs, and they took away some of the worries. He'd started me off with a low dose, but thought I could do with a higher dose and gave me some more sleeping pills. I'd taken one and, although I did sleep, I didn't wake up for hours. I also woke up still feeling drained, so decided to take them sparingly. I don't know if it was the placebo effect, or the new station, but I had felt slightly better and had only one bad night out of four, which was a big improvement.

I suddenly realised I was standing on the pavement, lost in my thoughts, staring at a police station. Yet, this time, no one talked to me. I guess I really was in Sleepy Hollow. I smiled to myself, picked up my bags, and walked in.

The front office was something straight out of *Dixon of Dock Green*, with the dark wooden panelling, the high ceilings, the ancient lights hanging from the roof. In front of me was a desk and a half-panelled, half-glass-enclosed interview room

I squinted to see through the glass screen in front of me, and I saw an older lady in the dark blue uniform of a civvy. I didn't have to say a word; the lady took one look at me and said: "'Ello sweetheart. You must be our new policeman. I'll get the door for you."

I was relieved to have the door opened for me as I struggled through. I had a sudden twinge from my lower back. It was the injury I suffered when lovely Lucy had run into the back of me. Thanks!

As I struggled in, she shut the door, and I said: "Ah, thanks. I'm Richard, by the way. Sorry, I'd shake your hand but ...". I indicated I had both hands full and a bag holding my dress uniform and shirts.

She smiled: "Nice to meet you, Richard. I'm Sylvia. It's the usual Met code for the door. What's your shoulder number?"

I had to think, "FH327, if my memory serves me correctly. I take it the code's Her Majesty's coronation year?"

She smiled and looked up at the picture of Her Majesty overlooking the front desk, and directed me down some stairs and to the left. She said: "Of course, deary, what else? It's the same for the outer door into the yard. The locker room is down the corridor and to the right. Mind yourself, there's some steps."

I made a mental note: "Thank you. I'll be back to say hi when I've got changed."

I followed the directions and, when I got there, it was a large room with a number of lockers around the side and half a dozen in the centre, back to back. It was more space than I'd ever seen in a locker room. It had clearly been for a lot more people.

I put my heavy bags down, and then said out loud: "Great, which locker? And where's the keys?"

I almost jumped out of my skin when a voice from behind me said: "Ooh, hello 327. It's locker 13, over in the middle."

I turned around and saw one of the saddest excuses for a police officer I've ever had the misfortune to lay eyes upon. He was short (5'3"), medium build, but out of shape, with mouse-brown hair. His uniform hung like an old sack. Nothing looked smart. He was slightly hunched, and if you've ever seen *The New Statesman*, he sounded like Piers. For those who haven't, imagine an almost childish, high-pitched, whiny voice that sounds like the little kid who always had his lunch stolen and tried to toady up to the bullies believing, if he did so, they'd leave him alone. The one who always told stories behind your back.

All my instincts told me to watch myself around this guy. A big sign: WATCH YOUR BACK!

I said: "Oh, thanks. I didn't see you there. I'm Richard Armstrong, by the way. Sorry, I didn't catch your name?"

He said in an uppity tone, "It's Acting Sergeant Devenish to you, Constable."

I bit back a comment, and determined to complete my full sergeant's exams asap, so this odious little toad had no sway over me. I thought, *I'll dig here.* "Oh, sorry about that. Have you completed part one or part two?"

"I don't see what business this is of yours; I'm your acting sergeant, and you'll address me as such."

I thought, *oh, so he hasn't done either. Sounds to me like he's the only non-probationer and they had to have at least an acting skipper at the station. So he's been given it through default. Right, pal, let's get things straight from the beginning.*

I said, in a friendly but firm tone, as I was opening my locker door (*13, really? 13? Are you fucking kidding?*), "From my part one I passed in August, I recall that you don't have to address acting sergeants as sergeant, as they haven't reached the substantive post. And also, in the case of a disagreement between two constables, the one with their part one or two completed takes precedence. Is that not correct?"

I could see him flinch. He didn't like that, but I was not going to let this self-important little pipsqueak get the upper hand.

"But I'm acting sergeant. You're not."

I stopped and turned towards him: "Look, I don't want to get into a pissing contest on my first day. But if you really want to call the inspector down so they can decide which out of the two of us is more senior, then I'm game. I know I'm new here, but I'll not allow myself to be pushed around. So let's get it straight: I'll be respectful, but I will not call you sergeant. I will call you by your first name. I will not challenge what you say in front of the probationers, but you won't throw your weight around. Is that clear!?"

He started to say, "I'm going to ..."

I raised myself to my full 6'¼" and looked him straight in the eye, and he stopped: "I suppose that'll have to do."

He turned around and walked out. I could hear Terry's voice, "You certainly know how to make a good first impression." But I thought about it and, for once, I didn't care. I wasn't sure why – maybe the tablets? (Yes, it was the tablets.)

I finished getting changed into my uniform. I looked at my new shoulder numbers and it still didn't look right: I was FH327 on my shoulder, but still PT272 at heart. It was going to take some getting used to. I walked through to the front office, where Sylvia was waiting. She beamed: "Settling in, sweetheart? Good. Glad to see you met Neville. He left here like a scalded cat. You didn't upset him, did you?"

I shrugged: "He tried the old 'I'm an acting sergeant' routine, and expected me to call him skipper. I've clearly got more service and experience, and I'm studying for my part two. I technically outrank him, and he thinks he can lord it over me. He's got another think coming."

Sylvia laughed: "That would ruffle his feathers. Yes, he only just passed his probation two months ago and, as the only substantive PC, he got the acting sergeant's stripes. Speak to Inspector Windbourne; she'll be happy to promote you."

I shook my head: "Look, if he wants to have his little power trip, I don't care. But he's very much mistaken if he thinks he can push me around."

She smiled: "Well, which station have you come from?"

"Earlham then Park Street. I've got three and a half years in, done my shield training, and response course. And part one of the skipper's."

She raised her eyebrows: "Those are busy stations. Come here for a change of pace, have you? It'll be a culture shock around here. Sleepy Hollow is right. Oh, by the way, at the moment you're the only shield-trained officer and response driver on your relief."

Astute of her; I was most definitely going there for a change of pace. Then I thought about what she'd said, and was just about to answer when, into the front office, stomped a 5'1" stocky lady, in her fifties, with untidy, greying, shoulder-length hair, wearing the uniform of an inspector.

She punched in the door code, and walked right up to me, while waving to Sylvia: "'Ello mate. Are you our driver from Park Street?"

She smiled and stuck her hand out. I shook it: "Yes Ma'am. I'm Richard Armstrong FH327, from Park Street and Earlham. Pleased to meet you."

She indicated for me to follow her, and over her shoulder said: "Sylvia babes, I'm going to have a chat with our new driver. Be back in ten, if anyone is looking for me."

I followed her down the corridor, which had beautiful half-panelling, to a door on the left, with an old bronze plate labelled "PC's Writing Room."

I walked in and it was a medium-sized room with an old, worn carpet, and about half a dozen aged monitors around the walls. There were old swivel chairs neatly tucked under the desks.

The inspector pulled out two chairs, sat on one, and indicated I should sit on the other. She said: "Down to business. Welcome to Westville B relief. I act as inspector across the two stations, here and Churchleigh, which is a shithole. There's nominally five of you here but, most of the time, you'll parade three: one in gaol, and one vehicle, but there'll be others covering you from Churchleigh. They have around five or six. You'll be driving every shift, as there's two probationers and a basic, and, err, Neville. But, between you and me, I give him admin jobs, cos he a fucking liability on the streets. Have you met him, by the way?"

I nodded: "Yes Ma'am. He introduced himself when I arrived."

She chuckled: "Oh, I bet he did. Did he try the 'Acting Sergeant' stuff on you?"

"Yes, Neville and I had a little chat about service and part ones and twos."

She laughed: "I think you and I have a similar assessment of our Nev. Seriously, watch your back with him. The rest of the team. There's Jack. He's got three years' service here, still on a basic, pretty lazy, but he's OK in a pinch. There's the wide boy, Ryan. Nice lad, but more interested in dipping his wick than policing. But he can do the job. Then we come to Freddie. She's a lazy, lazy little toad, and she's in danger of failing her probation. If there's a corner, she cuts it. She spends more time avoiding work than doing it.

"I want you to work with both the probbies, and show them what a real East End grafter like you can do. I'm going to put Ryan with you first, then a week of nights with Freddie. She needs to get bodies in the bin. She managed two last month. Two arrests in a month!"

I raised my eyebrows and let out a sigh. She continued: "She needs to be in double figures at least. Same with Ryan. He's about 80 per cent there. She's capable, but at the moment she's 20 per cent. The really annoying thing is they're both more than capable. Ryan listens, she doesn't. She's a looker. They call her Foxy Freddie. And, truth be told, she's about as popular with girls as she is with the boys. Not that I give a crap, but I do when she cares more about the bodies she takes to bed than with the bodies she puts in the cells. She commutes from Guildford; I joke not! Fucking bunch of leftie, communist, politically correct arseholes!"

I thought, *I like this lady*. I smiled, and she looked sideways at me. I said quickly: "I'm not laughing at you, Ma'am. Just the way you said it reminds me of my relief at Earlham. I used to be one of those leftie types, but three and half years in the East End has, shall we say, given me a hard dose of reality."

She chuckled, and slapped me on the arm: "I think you and I speak the same language?"

I said: "If I were going to sum it up, I'd say work hard, do the job properly, but humanely, and realise the senior management couldn't find their own arseholes with a mirror and a copy of *Grey's Anatomy*."

That did make her laugh. She said: "Look, I don't give a flying fuck about the bullshit those fucking idiots in charge spew out. I'm about to retire, and I'm female, so if they come after me, I'll take them to the fucking cleaners. But you mate, you haven't got any cards to play. So watch your back. There's so many evil fuckers in the senior ranks who like nothing better than fucking up other's lives. Why? Because they can, and they have rank to get away with acting like cunts without anyone knocking them out, which they would if they did that in any other profession."

She looked at her watch, and said: "It's getting towards briefing time. Let's go and see who we have today?"

We walked further down the corridor, until we got to a much smaller room, with a number of old seats left abandoned around it. We sat down and waited. Eventually, at 13:45 hours, in walked three people. They looked over at me and sat down.

The inspector said: “Four of you, that’s good; one panda, and a van. This (pointing at me) is Richard Armstrong. He’s our new response driver. He’s just transferred in from Park Street. I’m going to have you partner up with him, Ryan, in FH20, and Jack and Freddie in FH82. Any questions?”

Silence. “Off you go.”

A tall (6’2”) young man, slim build with sharp blue eyes, and slightly too long hair, smiled at me and stuck out his hand: “A pleasure to meet you, Richard. I’m Ryan. Welcome to Sleepy Hollow. We’re a small but happy bunch.”

I looked at him. *Yes,* I thought, *I can see you’d get a lot of female interest, and some males too*. He did have a posh accent, and a certain charm.

“Nice to meet you too, mate. Now, let’s go and locate our chariot for the late turn?”

“Walk this way, as they say.”

As we walked out of the room, I looked at the other two. Jack was a man in his late twenties, about 5’10”, average build, slightly unkempt black hair. He smiled and nodded. Freddie was a slim, young woman in her early twenties with the closest thing I’d seen in the police to a punk haircut. It was slightly long on the top and almost shaved at the sides. She looked down her nose at me, which was difficult, as she was only 5’6”. To be fair, the inspector had been correct: she had a real cuteness about her. Not car-stopping beauty, but a certain something I couldn’t quite put my finger on.

We made our way along the corridor, where we stopped, and I collected the van keys from the hooks, and the logbook. Then, through the locker room, and past a security door into the custody area, and through a loading area out onto the street, where a number of police vehicles were kept. There was no 'yard', as such. We had to get the prisoners out, across the pavement and into custody through this loading area. *Not ideal*, I thought.

I walked around the van doing a vehicle check. The Mercedes van did look in better nick than the Ford Transits I was used to. I got in, checked the fuel – a quarter of a tank. Really!? I said: "Ryan, first question: where do you normally get fuel?"

He walked around the corner: "The petrol station's just there. Can we get a sandwich for later, please?"

"Sure. Let's get this show on the road."

We spent the next few hours driving around, doing 'S' non-urgent calls. No calls waiting. The radio was, as far as we were concerned, pretty quiet. Later on, towards the end of the shift, we did get an 'I' immediate call, to a bar about half a mile away. I looked at Ryan, but he hadn't taken the call.

"Ryan, aren't you taking that? We're pretty close."

He held up his hand, and waited. I got tired and answered it, accepting the job, and BLATTed it down the road. He looked and I said: "Yes?"

"Why did you do that? We might have to arrest someone, and get home late?"

I ground my teeth: "It's an 'I' call. We're the response vehicle, we're free, so we take it. Simple!"

"That's not the way we do it; you wait until you see if anyone else will take it first."

I said simply, as we approached the location, "That's the way I do it. I'll do the arresting if you don't want to."

I was hoping to use guilt to get him to take the arrest. No joy. He replied: "Oh, really! Thanks."

My stomach dropped. It was going to be harder work than I thought!

We arrived on scene, and could immediately see two men struggling with one another as a small group of young party types were standing watching. I jumped out, and jogged across to separate the two men. As I did, it became very clear the taller of the two men was drunk, and by far the more aggressive. I managed to pin this man against the wall, looking around for Ryan's support. Where was he? You guessed it! Taking details from witnesses, i.e. names and contact details. The only thing was that all the witnesses he was talking to had a few things in common: young, female, short skirt!

Thanks mate! While I'm nicking drunks, you're sorting out a date for Saturday night. I cleared my throat. Nothing. I did it again. Nothing. I then said loudly: "Ryan!"

He looked around, as did the young women. "Sorry to bother you, old chap, but would you mind awfully giving me a hand with this chap. He's just a tad bothersome."

The drunk guy, who was bigger than me, really started struggling. Ryan waved at me, finished what he was saying to the young ladies and came over.

I said quickly, under my breath, "Am I doing this, or do you?"

"Well, you did say you were."

I thought, *fine!* Between the two of us, we got my cuffs on him, and after giving him a quick pat down, got him into the cage in the back of the van.

I locked it up, and returned to the guy he was struggling with, as Ryan went back to the young ladies. I said to the guy, "Hello Sir. What happened?"

"Thank you, officer. I was waiting for some friends and that man started to bother my girlfriend Tara here. So I asked him to leave her alone, and he wouldn't. Eventually he began to get physical. I merely defended myself."

"Do you want to press charges?"

"No officer, that's fine."

"If you wouldn't mind holding on for a minute, I need to speak with the owner of the bar."

I went inside and spoke to the owner and bar staff. They corroborated the story from outside. I went out and took their details, letting them know the man would be spending the night in the cells.

Ryan was still chatting to the ladies. I walked back to the van and started the engine. He eventually took the hint, and we drove back to the nick. I did a quick book, and booked in the prisoner at Westville on drunk and disorderly.

As I was finishing off, Ryan went to go home, and I took him to one side. I was more disappointed than angry, but I wasn't happy! "Ryan, listen, if you don't want to nick people, that's one thing, but not backing me up, mate, is out of line!"

He looked at me, thought about saying something, then thought better: "OK, yes, I'm sorry. But did you see that brunette? She was hot!"

I bit back a comment, and more calmly than I thought, said: "When we work again, I will expect you to pull your weight, and we will take all the calls we're free for. Are we clear on that!"

He wasn't happy, but I think he could tell it wasn't a request. He nodded: "Yes, all right, I suppose I do need the arrests."

I made my weary way home, and thought just how many minutes he would have lasted on B relief before any one of them had bitten his head off.

***

The nightmares had subsided, to some degree, with my move to Westville, so now I'd only lose one night every two weeks through the waking up in the middle of the night, constantly reliving the most horrific moments, over and over again. It felt like I'd lost control of my own mind, and I tried so hard to ignore it. But it wouldn't stop. I didn't realise it was seriously affecting my judgement.

On one of the lates, there'd been a fight between some of the squaddies from Westville barracks, out on the town. We had the whole relief turn out for that. After we'd dealt with it, I was talking with the inspector, and one of the young, very fresh probationer lads came up, and nervously said to her, "Errr, excuse me, Sir."

She turned around: "Sir? Sir!? These (indicating her breasts) are 38DD. Are you fucking blind!?"

The poor lad looked mortified, and stammered. She let out a sigh and said, in a far kinder tone, "Look, I know you're new, but please acknowledge I'm a woman. So, it's Inspector, Ma'am, or Guv', not fucking Sir! All right!?"

He passed on a message, and walked off. The inspector and I exchanged grins. I did like this lady!

Finally, it came around to the set of nights where I'd been paired up with Freddie, and would have to find a way to get her to stop impersonating a police officer, and start being one. I'd thought about a number of approaches.

I stood alone in the parade room at 21:30 hours. There was supposed to be four of us: Jack and Ryan in the panda, and Freddie and I in the van.

Fifteen minutes later, in walked Jack and Ryan, at the same time as the phone went. It was the inspector: "Hi Richard. Sorry I'm not able to attend briefing today. Just take out the vehicles and let control know your call signs and shoulder numbers. By the way, is everyone present?"

I thought for a second. *Do I want to cause Freddie any more trouble than she has already? I can't outright lie, but I can obfuscate the truth just a little.*

I said: "Hello Ma'am. Jack and Ryan are ready to go. I believe Freddie is in the changing rooms."

There was a pause: "Right ... make sure you book on with control, when you're ready."

Jack and Ryan went out, and at 22.05 hours Freddie sauntered in, bag over her shoulder, and looked at me with slight contempt: "Are you ready?"

I bit back a comment, got on the radio and put us as ready to go.

I said: "The van's ready to go. There's one call we need to do and then, unless something comes up, we can do a bit of proactive work."

She rolled her eyes! *Really! You're a probationer and you roll your eyes at work!* Without comment, I picked up my bag and walked out to the van.

We took the call and it resulted in a drunk being nicked and put in the bin.

By then it was midnight, and our refs were in two hours, and the radio was dead, with no calls. I struggled to get my head around just how quiet it was.

We pulled over, and watched the cars go around Westville Square. Not a bad spot. I had done some work on the CRIMINT system, and there was an entry about cars being involved in burglaries transiting through our ground at night, doing burglaries in some of the expensive properties north of Westville and returning back to south London. I thought a good spot was on the main road leading to Westville Bridge. There might be some good stops and arrests from stopping cars along there.

There was silence in the van. I got the distinct impression from Freddie she thought I was a pain in the arse, and she wanted a quiet life of doing as little as possible.

"I thought we'd sit up on the main road leading to Westville Bridge, and do some car stops. What do you say?"

She let out a sigh: "I'm tired. I've been out with my friends all day. Can't we just pull over and sleep? I know of a quiet spot; no one will see."

I smiled (hiding my annoyance): "Look, c'mon, it'll be fun."

She replied in a grumpy voice: "I don't want fun; I want to sleep! I don't want to do any stops. No one else does any!" Patiently, I replied: "OK, if you don't want to do any stops, just call out what cars to stop, give me a reason, and back me up. I'll do all the work, and paperwork if I need to arrest them. How's that sound?"

She sighed, again, and I swear this is what she said: "Whatever!" She looked out the window. I really was back at school, I thought. We were going to work that night, and I would help her get through her probation, if I had to do it kicking and screaming!

I drove the van along to a side turning, from where we had a good view of the road, and parked up. I looked at Freddie: "What car do you want to stop, and why?"

She looked out the side window: "C'mon, I said I didn't want to do this. You choose!"

Wow, she was really going to make me work hard to help her. I said: "OK, I'll do the stop, but you will back me up."

She nodded: "All right, I suppose!"

I spent the next hour pulling car after car, for having lights out, a too-loud exhaust, and a number of other offences. I wasn't looking to hand out tickets; I wanted to find crime.

Slowly, slowly, as I did more stops, Freddie got slightly more involved, doing the vehicle checks, the name checks. Most were just words of advice from me, such as, "Please Sir/Madam, can you get that headlight changed?"

Then a breakthrough. As we were watching, she looked up: "Here Richard, that black old BMW, what about that one?"

As I started up the engine, and pulled away from the kerb, I said: "OK, why that car?"

"It came around the corner too quick, and it looks wrong."

I could have jumped with joy. Little victories! I said: "Good enough for me. Let's give it a pull."

I drove out behind it and noticed one of its brake lights was out. I put on the blue lights, and BINGO. The car made to slow down, started to pull over, then took off.

I didn't have to say a thing; Freddie was on the main set, and started a commentary. YES! I was having difficulty keeping pace as it accelerated towards the embankment, going east, then, at the last minute, turned south towards the bridge. I kind of thought it might, so I was ready, and made up some ground. I was having to really think about my positioning of the Mercedes van, as it was not a match for this old-style 7 Series BMW, although it did seem to be chucking out a lot of smoke as the engine was given a real workout.

All the while, Freddie was doing a pretty good job on the radio. As we hurtled over the bridge, she said to me: "Oh shit! I don't know south of the water!"

"No one does. In my bag there's an A-Z – use that."

She nodded, and rooted around in my bag until she produced the large A-Z. Just as we went south of the water, she said: "Got it!," and continued the commentary, holding the radio in one hand and the A-Z in the other.

I thought, *I don't know these roads either. Next time I'll set up watching cars come into Westville, not leaving it.* The car tried to take a left turn way too fast, and slid. The driver eventually caught it, but the engine was really smoking. I could see the entrance to a housing estate come into view. I said: "Prepare for a decamp."

I followed the car, and again the driver misjudged the corner, and struck a wall at the entrance to the estate. The driver – a tall, 30-something Black guy, dressed all in black – jumped out as the car slid to a halt. He was off. Freddie was out of the van first, and as I followed I could hear the sound of sirens getting nearer and nearer.

This guy was pretty quick, but Freddie was quicker, and I wasn't too far behind either. He turned down a side alleyway and down some stairs between the tower blocks where the bins were kept. Freddie took a flying leap from the top of the stairs and landed on him. Good girl, get in there! He slowed, and half-stumbled, then managed to shrug her off into some of the bags of rubbish. But it had slowed him, and now it was my turn to launch a 6'¼", 12 stone, very pissed-off copper at him. He didn't shrug that off, and I pulled him to the ground. I noticed he was trying to pull something out something of his jacket pocket with his right hand. I managed to loop my arm over the top of his and put my knee into the back of his leg, and with my left hand around his neck, drag him to the ground. But man, this guy was strong.

Freddie recovered, went around the other side, jumped on his back and worked on wrenching his left arm out. Between the two of us we managed to pull his arms out a little wider, and get his body closer to the ground. But what a struggle. He kept trying to get his hand free to get to his jacket, and had thus far resisted us getting his arms behind his back.

I managed to say: "Mate, it's over, it's over. Give in, we've got you. We don't want to hurt you. Stop struggling. I don't want to hurt you."

"Fuck off!"

OK, if that's the way. I moved my knee up towards me and placed it firmly in the area between the spine and his shoulder blade and started applying pressure, leaning with more and more weight on it. This is very painful, and he shouted a number of times: "Get off. Get off you cunt."

I calmly said: "No! Not until you relax your arms, and let us get the cuffs on. Then I'll stop."

After about a minute of me slowly increasing the pressure, until almost all my weight was on him, he eventually gave out a low moan: "Get off, get off!"

I replied as gently as I could: "I don't want to hurt you, so relax your arms."

Eventually, he relaxed his left arm enough for Freddie to get one cuff on. His right arm was still rigid. I really wanted to stop him getting that hand into his pocket.

He said: "Get off, get off. I did what you wanted."

I slowly reduced the pressure on his back: "Now relax your right arm!"

He started flexing his arm and, despite my best efforts, he got has hand moving towards his pocket. I said: "Freddie, he's going for his pocket."

She instantly applied really hard pressure on his left wrist using the cuff. He stifled a cry and twisted in pain. Freddie said: "If you don't relax your right arm, I will assume you're going for a weapon, and break your wrist! Now relax, and I'll stop!"

Wow, I thought, *she ain't messing around.*

He still tried to fight, and Freddie slowly started applying more pressure until he arched his back, bellowed, then said: "OK, OK! STOP! FUCKING STOP!"

He relaxed his arm and, between the two of us, we got the cuffs on, stacked to the rear. We immediately turned him on his side, and I locked my arm through his right shoulder, into an arm lock. It wasn't going to hurt him if he didn't resist. Freddie moved around the front and checked his pockets, and he started struggling. I applied pressure and he fought me for a bit, but eventually let up enough for Freddie to pull out a wicked kitchen knife from his right pocket. Well, I'm glad he didn't get a chance to use that!

At that point the local old bill found us and, with their help, we got him into the van and searched the car. There were bags of stolen small electricals, a wallet, purse, passport, some cash, and some items for breaking into houses: gloves, a small crowbar.

We arranged the recovery of the car, let the burglary squad know and made our way back to Westville. As we were driving there, Freddie said: "Who gets this arrest?"

"Up to you. You put up the spot, and laid hands on first; he's yours if you want him."

"Are you sure?"

"It'll be a book, and a CRIS. The CID should take it over from there. I'll help you in whatever you want me to. If you want, you might to able to talk the CID into letting you sit in on the interview."

"Really, that's cool! That was my first commentary, and the chase, and the fight. It was so much fun!"

I grinned, and thought, *HOOKED! Gotcha!* "You did really well. It is fun, isn't it!?"

We made our way back, she booked in the prisoner, and sat in on the interview. We checked the CRIS reports and one had just gone on for a burglary. The couple had woken up in the middle of the night and found they'd been burgled. They were asked to come to ID their property, which they did. It took the rest of the shift to deal with and, at the end, the couple whose property we'd recovered arrived, and I got Freddie to do the ID.

When they saw their property, they were literally overjoyed, and said: "Thank you so much! How did you catch them so quickly?"

Freddie looked a little embarrassed, and regaled them with the story. They listened, in stunned amazement, especially the bit about the fight and the knife.

The lady said to Freddie: "You're so brave. We were so scared to wake up and find someone had been in our house. But you two caught him, you got him. It makes me feel better to know you're out there protecting us." She gave Freddie a hug.

After the couple left, I looked at Freddie and could see something had changed. She could see what her actions had done. They mattered; it wasn't just a game. I smiled, and she grinned back: "That was cool, so cool. I want to do that again tomorrow. I haven't had so much fun. It was exciting, and scary. It, it, it was ..."

"It was policing! That's what happens when you keep your eyes open and you get lucky."

The next night, she was fifteen minutes early, and eager to go. As we pulled out of the yard, she said: "When we get the calls out the way, can I spot cars again?"

"Absolutely, but you will let me have at least one arrest; I have a reputation to uphold."

She grinned: "No chance, old man! Get your own!" We laughed.

For the rest of the nights we worked, we had arrest after arrest. Despite what she'd said, I did get my fair share. In seven nights, she got twice the number of arrests she had in the two previous months.

At the end, the guv'nor appeared at the parade, and said to both of us: "You two have been busy – more arrests than the rest of relief put together. Well done!"

Freddie grinned, and the guv'nor looked at me: "Richard, how did Freddie get on? Was all this down to you?"

I shook my head, aware Freddie was listening: "Honestly, Guv, I gave her a little encouragement at the start, but the rest was all her own work. She's a really, really good officer! I'd have no trouble recommending her."

Freddie looked at me and beamed. The guv'nor said to Freddie: "Well done. The burglary squad sent me this." She produced an email, and handed it to Freddie. She continued for my benefit: "It's a letter of thanks for catching a prolific and well-known burglar. He's been responsible for dozens of burglaries. That goes for you too, Richard; there's one on your file."

Freddie just stared at the email. The guv'nor walked off, and eventually Freddie looked at me, and I said: "By the way, thanks for helping me get that knife off that guy. When he went for it, your actions stopped him from getting it out and possibly stabbing me. That was some good teamwork, mate. I appreciate not being stabbed. Thanks."

I could see that affected her. She replied: "You know, when I first met you I thought you were some pervy old guy just trying to get me into bed. But you're all right. And you've made me realise how much fun this can be. It's awesome!"

"What do you mean, 'old'?"

We both laughed, and I continued more seriously. "It's the reason we put up with the shit, the crap food, long hours and useless leadership. It's why I never want to do any other job. I'm just glad you love it too."

This was the end of the shift pattern, and we had a 'paperwork' day. This meant we had a briefing from the Sex Offenders Register compliance officers. This sounds run-of-the-mill, but it was something I'll never forget. It was held at the Westville Police Station, which was a rather ugly, run-down, red-brick building. When we arrived, we were shown into a long, narrow briefing room, on the top floor. There were about a dozen of us, from both Westville and Churchleigh. I had a chance to meet the other members of the relief I hadn't yet met. They were an eclectic bunch, mostly young in service, with a few slightly more experienced officers (these, no doubt, had been transferred in recently).

The briefing began as a middle-aged, slim man in plain clothes introduced himself: "Good afternoon, ladies and gentlemen. I'm Sergeant Wilson from the Sex Offenders Register compliance unit. What you are about to hear is highly classified, and absolutely not to be spread about. If it gets out, it could remove our leverage over the people on the register, and possibly lead to us losing track of them, and them reoffending."

He looked around, to see if that had sunk in. It certainly had. Everyone was paying attention.

He continued: "In simple terms, I keep tabs on registered sex offenders in this borough, and attempt to stop them from reoffending. The number of registered sex offenders on the borough is in three figures, and I am the only dedicated officer to deal with all of them. I work with them on an individual basis, and this can include requiring them to sign in at the station on a certain day and time. It can include unannounced home visits, requiring them to inform me prior to going on holiday at home, and abroad, or changing their job. They are not permitted to move outside of the borough without letting us know in advance and providing us with their new address.

"These people are some of the nastiest individuals I've ever met. They can be sneaky, deceptive, snide, and underhand in their dealings with police.

"I will give you an example of one of the individuals I am currently monitoring. He grew up in a little town in the Republic of Ireland. When he was 15, the eight-year-old daughter of the couple next door went missing. He, like all the other neighbours, banded together, and searched the local area for her. They couldn't find her. Six weeks later, his parents began smelling a terrible odour from the loft. The father went to investigate, and found the little girl. She had been dead for weeks, and was badly decomposed. She had been stripped naked, gagged and tied to the cross-beams holding up the roof, and repeatedly raped, both anally, and vaginally. The family reported it, and very quickly the son was arrested. At the post-mortem, it couldn't be determined whether the little girl had been raped before and after her murder, or just before.

"This guy was then tried, and put in prison. Due to the fact he was still considered a child (15) he was let out when in was still in his early 20s. Obviously, he couldn't return to the town he grew up in, so he moved to London. Due to the bad relations between the Irish and British governments, no information was being exchanged between the two police services. Therefore, when he arrived in London, no one knew what he had done, and no one could check up on him. So he lied about his criminal record, and got a job in the council. He worked his way up, and eventually got a top job in that council. Then the Good Friday Agreement was struck in 1997, and the police forces of Ireland and Britain began talking, and exchanging information. Then we found out about all the criminals we'd allowed into our country.

"The Met Police contacted the council, and informed them they had a sex offender as a senior officer. Unfortunately, he had made some high-profile political friends, who then put pressure on the Met to keep it quiet. They did, and he was put on the register, and his punishment for getting a job under false pretences, was ... a caution for lying on his application form. He kept his job."

There was silence, as we took this in. I looked around, and caught the eye of a tall, slim, Asian PC. We shared a sickened look. *My God!* I really couldn't believe what I'd heard. I knew the political classes were slimy and odious, but protecting a brutal child rapist and murderer? If anyone asks why I hate the political classes, and have so little respect for them, you now know why.

The sergeant just let us sit and come to terms with that for a moment then, in a very matter-of-fact tone, carried on: "That is not even the worst case I have dealt with, so welcome to my world. You might ask, 'Why do you not go to the press?' Well, if I did, I could lose the trust of the rest of the sex offenders on the register, and have hundreds of sex offenders running around with no way of tracking them. It's honestly a deal with the Devil, so to speak. It's a no-win situation. Whatever you do, it's a really bad option."

He took questions for a while then concluded the lecture. We adjourned to what passed for a canteen. I bumped into the Asian guy I'd seen earlier, and we sat down and had a sandwich and cup of coffee. His name was James, and his father was white, his mother Asian. We started chatting. I said: "How much service have you got?"

"Five years in Campden. What about you?"

"Four years in Earlham. Have you just transferred in?"

"Yeah, but it was a compulsory move. I hear the East End is busy?"

I smiled a weary smile: "It is a late-turn ground, and it can really kick off. What's Campden like?"

"Pretty much the same. This borough is so lacking in officers with any service, it's not even funny. I turned up to a job with a skipper, and three officers, and I had the most service. Most of them are clueless."

"Yeah, it's hard work sometimes, and I spend half my time wondering what these kids are going to do."

"You and me both. Listen, next set of nights, I've been asked to go over and help Westville, as the rest of your team are either off training, or on holiday. So it looks like we'll being working together."

"Honestly mate, it'll be good to work with someone who knows what they're doing for once." He agreed.

The rest of the day was spent finishing off paperwork.

Sure enough, on the next night duty, James and I were working together. We had a blast; it was almost like old times. We took turns driving and taking calls. Around midnight, we received a call from the Continental Hotel in Churchleigh, of a man collapsed in suspicious circumstances. We made our way on blues and twos, and when we arrived to a very expensive-looking hotel, we were shown up to the posh suites where, according to the receptionist, the collapsed man's party had booked out the whole floor (how the other half live).

Upon getting out of the lift we could see the nearest suite door open, and hear agitated voices speaking in what sounded like an Arabic language (as best as I could tell). I gave a sideways look at James. I could see he was thinking the same: *this is going to be trouble!*

As we entered the suite, I noticed it was very untidy, with clothes strewn on the furniture, and floor. There were ashtrays full of old cigarette butts and a number of passports lying on the table to the left of the door. There were several seemingly highly agitated Arab men, dressed in traditional white Arabic clothing, milling around shouting at each other, and at us as we walked in. On a large, messy double bed was an Arab man dressed only in black silk boxer shorts, and he was unmoving.

James looked at me and nodded. I stood guard at the door, where I could watch his back, and control who entered or left the room. He went over to the man on the bed, and with our woefully inadequate first aid kit, attempted first aid. He was checking for vital signs and obvious signs of injury. Without turning, he called to me: "He's breathing, but unconscious. Can you update CAD, and check the ETA of the LAS, please mate."

I replied as I was getting the radio ready: "Will do."

I keyed the mike: "Foxtrot Hotel, this is Foxtrot Hotel 21."

"Go ahead 21."

"Regarding the Tower Hotel job, we're with the collapsed male. He's breathing, but unconscious. We have a number of people at the scene. Is there any chance of another unit attending, preferably FH1? Also, can you update the LAS, and ask for an ETA, please?"

"Can you show FH1 attending."

Control replied: "Thank you, FH1, will do. I'll update the LAS. Their last ETA was fifteen minutes. That was ten minutes ago."

"Thanks FH. Will update you upon their arrival."

I then attempted to talk to the Arab gentlemen, but to no avail. They just responded by loudly repeating what they'd just said. It's not just the English who think saying things more loudly will make you understand a different language.

A couple of minutes later, things started getting more confused as a number of the Arab men tried to leave the room. I stood in their way and said clearly: "No!"

I needed to find out who everyone was, so that if this guy died, I didn't just let, at best witnesses, at worst murderers, walk off. This caused a lot of shouting, and waving of hands. I thought I might have to get physical with them. That was what we'd both feared might happen. Just when I thought things couldn't get any worse, who turns up to 'help'? Our favourite fake sergeant, Neville. Great, just great!

He walked up to the door, and said in his horrible, nasal voice: "Constable, why are you stopping these people from leaving? I order you to let them go, as you're clearly causing them distress."

The clear answer came from James and myself: "No!"

Neville visibly recoiled, and when he'd recovered, said: "Did you not hear my direct order, Constable? As your superior officer, I am ordering you to let them go!"

I looked on impassively and ignored him, merely standing my ground against him, and the men in the room.

In the nick of time, out of the lift walked the inspector. She looked at pseudo-sergeant Neville, and walked past him to talk to me. He looked somewhat peeved, and said: "Ma'am, Ma'am, this officer refused my order to get out of the way and let these gentlemen out of this room. I want him stuck-on."

Without turning to look at Neville, she looked at me questioningly. I replied to her non-verbal question: "Guv, we've got a gent in here who's breathing, but not conscious, possible drugs OD, a number of unidentified males who apparently can't speak English. I've stopped them from leaving until we can properly identify them, in case this goes sideways."

She nodded and turned to Neville: "Neville, this officer probably saved you your job. Now go to reception and find me an interpreter, pronto!"

He stood for a moment, like a gasping fish, then turned and went to the lift.

She said to me when he'd gone: "Well done. That bloke is a fucking liability."

"Thanks. There was no way in hell I was going to let these guys go until we'd properly IDed them, and got some sort of idea of how our friend here had got in this state."

After a bit of searching around we found the unconscious man's passport, and an interpreter arrived, as did the LAS, who took the man to hospital, with James accompanying him (for continuity of evidence). He didn't look good; he was very pale, sweaty, and unresponsive.

The inspector was dealing with that, while I guarded the door. She walked out to me and said quietly: "What was your nickname back in Earlham?"

"The Griefmeister. Why?" I had a bad feeling about this, as they say in the best films.

She grimly replied: "Well, it's well earned; this job you've got me messed up in is what we call a career-destroyer. Our friend who went to the Churchleigh Hospital is in fact a member of a foreign royal family. If he dies, it'll be all over the front pages of the newspapers tomorrow. Just as well you two did your jobs properly. Now we need to work to cover all our arses, in case matey-boy croaks it, and the shit hits the fan, and this is our last job in the Met."

My stomach dropped. I really was a bringer of grief, it seemed. Wherever I went, trouble followed me. Marvellous! But this time I could take others down with me. I went to Westville for less pressure – fat chance of that.

We eventually established we were dealing with high-profile members of an Arab royal family, and their staff, a number of whom had diplomatic immunity. That meant, as far we were concerned, they were untouchable, which was great!

The guv'nor certainly earned her money, liaising with the yard, and the interpreter. It became clear this guy had an English driver, who might know more. When it had settled down, I was sent to reception to see if they had any idea who this driver was. Long story short: I found the driver in the underground car park, waiting in a black 7 Series BMW.

After I'd reassured him that I wasn't there to arrest him (yet), he said: "Look officer, I just drive for the guy. I don't know anything."

I thought, *this guy is scared he'll lose his job. I knew the feeling!*

"Look, I just want to find out what happened, and what he took. It might help the doctors treat him. Just tell me what happened. C'mon mate."

He shrugged: "OK, all right. Look, he may have said he wanted, errr ... female company. And I might happen to know the number of an agency that could provide that company. All legit, and above board. The women are all consenting adults, and everything. They're a classy outfit ... so I'm told. Occasionally, some of the clients want that sort of thing. It's all legal."

I thought, *OK so far. Let's have details.* "So what happened tonight?"

"Well, the client, who's actually a nice guy, he's not allowed to be with women in his country, and I felt a bit sorry for him. Then he asked me if I knew of anywhere he could get some company, and I asked what he wanted. He said he wanted two tall, slim birds. Well I called the agency I know, and these two ladies turned up a few hours later. Then the client, he says, did I want to, you know, share in the night's activities? Well, I said, 'No'. Look, I've got a girlfriend, and all of that. It just ain't my thing. So he took the two ladies back to his suite. Then a few hours later, all this happens. I don't know anything else, honest."

Honestly, I thought he was telling mostly the truth, which I was impressed by. I took his statement, and eventually got the agency telephone number from him.

I reported my findings back to the guv'nor. She wasn't surprised. She told me to go back to the nick, record it on a CRIS, and call the agency to find out from the ladies what had happened.

When I got back to the nick, I did as I was asked, and sat down to call an escort agency. As I was dialling the number, I started thinking, *what should I say? How should I approach this? I must just be up front, as I'm sure they get all sorts of crank calls.*

When the phone was answered, I heard a woman's voice: "Hello. Can I help you?"

I explained who I was, and said she could call me at Westville Police Station, and that the number was in the telephone book. A short while later, the phone rang, and she'd got through to the CAD room, had verified who I was and that it was a valid call. After some persuading (honestly, Hendon don't have lessons on this), I managed to get the two ladies to come to Westville nick to have a chat.

As I waited, I kept myself busy with the mountains of paperwork I had to do regarding the case. I also had a call from the inspector that CCTV footage from the hotel had shown two tall women (one blonde, one brunette) entering the hotel and going to the man's room a few hours before we were called, and leaving a short while before we were called. Then I had a message from Sylvia that two "ladies" had appeared at the front counter asking for me.

I made my way to the front office, and tried to ignore the quizzical look Sylvia gave me. I went to the special room set aside in reception. It had wooden panelling up to waist height, and glass from there on up, so everyone could see what was going on.

I walked in, closed the door and said: "Hello ladies. I'm PC Richard Armstrong, FH327. Would you like a drink of tea, or coffee?"

The two ladies were both tall (around 5'10"), slim, well dressed in skirts, blouses, and long jackets. One had long blonde hair, the other, long brunette hair. They were, not surprisingly, very good-looking. They both smiled, seemed very calm, and not at all nervous, as I might have expected. After a quick introduction, it was apparent the blonde's name was Victoria (she was from Australia), and the Brunette was Julia (English), and they were both well spoken. It turned out they were both graduates.

"Ladies, to explain, there's a gentleman in hospital, apparently with a drugs overdose, and it appears that you visited him a short time before he was found unconscious. Now I have no reason to suspect you of anything, and I quite honestly don't care too much what happened outside of what happened to him. Any information regarding what he may have taken could help the doctors looking after him."

I stopped and looked at Victoria and Julia. They both sat impassively looking at me. I continued: "Could you give me any information as to what happened to him, please?"

Victoria, aided by Julia, explained they had stayed with the gentleman for a few hours, and that had all gone fine. Then, as they were leaving, they noticed him prepare to snort what they thought was cocaine. That was all they had seen, and they had no idea where he'd got the drug from. After they'd done this, they asked for some coffee, as it was the early hours of the morning, and they were tired.

I stepped outside, relayed the update to the boss and made some coffee for all of us. I got the message back that our man had regained consciousness, and it seemed like he'd pull through. What a relief! I returned to the interview room, relayed the good news, and gave them the coffee. This seemed to break the ice, so to speak, and we started chatting, as I took their statements.

I said: "Victoria, what brings you to London?"

She smiled: "The bright lights, the fact us Aussies always love to see the world. I guess what you're too polite to ask is, 'What's a nice girl like me doing in a place like this?'" She had a wicked twinkle in her eye as she said it.

"I guess I am. Yes, you got me."

"Look, it's not cheap travelling around, and doing this allows me to pay off my credit card, put a deposit down on a house back home, and set myself up for an easier life when I get back. I work two to three nights a week, and it's very lucrative. Not boasting, but I probably get paid in two nights more than you do in a month."

She sat back, to let that sink in. I went to speak, and then stopped: *bloody hell! That's thousands of pounds a night. Who's the mug here!*

I then looked at Julia, and she said: "It's like Vic said. I work a regular job during the day, and work once or twice a week. For me it's more about excitement. But the money is nice. It allows me to go on wicked holidays to the Caribbean."

"What? You have work tomorrow? Oops, I mean to say today. Best you get back to bed. Oops, I didn't mean it to come out quite like that."

The two ladies laughed, and Julia said: "Yeah, yeah, that's what they all say."

With that, we finished the statements, and the ladies left. I was left wondering how many other women did the same thing? Would I ever know? They both seemed very charming, but normal as well. I guess that's what they get paid to be.

At that point the guv'nor let me know our man was recovering, and was likely to be discharged the next day. I tidied up the loose ends and handed over what I had to CID. Then the end of the night shift came, and I made my way home.

The next day, when I woke up, I saw no mention of it on the news. That was a relief. When I got in and checked for CRIS updates, it wasn't available for me to see, which was unusual. I spoke to the inspector, who just shrugged: "Just forget about it. It's all way above our pay grades."

I heard nothing more about it. That was a close call!

During one of the late turns I was working with Ryan and, to be honest, he was still a little lazy and lackadaisical, but we'd slowly worked out a way of working. We received a call to a large department store. This was a regular call, with lots of people out doing their Christmas shoplifting, like you do. Until you get caught.

So we made our way there on blues and twos in the Merc van. As we were about to arrive, weaving our way through the morass of cars, people, motorbikes and suicidal cyclists, we received a radio call: "Foxtrot Hotel 21, from Foxtrot Hotel. We've got a redirect for you. Cancel the call, and go to the rear entrance at another large store. There's an employee theft waiting there for you."

I screwed up my brow: "Foxtrot Hotel 21, received. Has this job been cancelled?"

"No, just a redirect. Please confirm you are complying."

This was unusual; that was very formal. I shrugged: "Foxtrot Hotel 21, will redirect to the larger department shop. ETA two minutes."

They acknowledged the call. A minute later, we pulled up at the rear entrance, and as I got out I said to Ryan: "Do we normally go in the rear entrance here?"

"Yeah, we're barred from entering through the front. They complain if you do, and you get a bollocking from the top brass."

I stopped and looked at him: "Is that true for all the shops around here?"

"No, just this one. They get special treatment. Why do you think we were redirected here from the first store? They employ a number of very senior ex-Met officers as 'advisers' and they pull strings for them to get special treatment. I thought you knew."

I felt a chill down my back: "So much for 'without fear or favour'. I suppose that only counts if you've not got friends in high places. This is out of order. Why doesn't someone say something?"

He shrugged: "You're dealing with powerful people, in and out of the Met. They'd just deny it, and bang goes your career. It wouldn't change anything."

The radio went: "Foxtrot Hotel 21, are you on scene yet?"

That was unusual. They hadn't been that pushy about any other job. I replied: "We're right outside now. I was just about to update you."

"Received. They've been on the phone again, over."

I acknowledged the call, and with a sense of annoyance and foreboding, entered the larger store. We were politely greeted by uniformed security officers, and were asked for names. When these were recorded, we were shown through to an underground area which had a taped interview suite, and a number of secure rooms. The young man who had shown us in, ushered us into a clean, well-equipped video suite, and showed us surveillance footage from above a till, which showed an older lady take cash out of the till, move it out of shot, then return it to the till. The man said £50 had gone missing from the till during the ladies' shift, and they had this lady detained.

He showed us into one of the secure rooms, where a female security guard was sitting with a well-dressed older lady (early sixties, at a guess). I said: "Hello there, Ma'am. I'm PC Armstrong from Westville Police Station. You need to listen to what this gentleman (indicating the young man) has to say."

The young security guard said: "I am a security guard at this store, and over the course of the last few weeks a quantity of money has gone missing from a till this female employee (indicating the lady) was working on, and we set up a hidden camera to monitor the till. Today when we reviewed the footage, we noticed a quantity of money being taken out of the till by this employee, and then part of it being returned. This clearly shows that she stole the money. I therefore detained her, and my female colleague searched her and found the money on her. We then called you."

I said: "Ma'am, you've heard what this security guard has had to say. Do you have anything in way of reply?"

She straightened herself up: "I did not steal any money. A customer asked to change some money, and I did just that. I saw the footage, and it does not show me stealing the money, because I didn't do that. Other employees also have access to that till. They searched me, and took my money, saying I had stolen it. I did not. They then interviewed me before you arrived."

I looked at the lady, then back to the security guard. The evidence was solid, but circumstantial, and if she stuck to her story, without other evidence, it might not be enough. And why were they interviewing someone? That's not usual.

I looked at Ryan, who gave a non-committal shrug, so no support there. I looked at the lady, and thought, *there's enough for reasonable suspicion, so I can arrest. But probably an NFA, and they must know this? Are they using this as grounds to sack her without comeback?*

I arrested her on suspicion of theft of £50. I didn't even consider handcuffs.

The security guard, said: "Aren't you going to cuff her?"

I half-turned as I ushered the old lady away, saying: "It's down to the officer's discretion and, given all the factors, I don't deem this lady to be a flight risk."

At this I carried on out, as Ryan collected the video tape, and signed for it as evidence. The security guard didn't hide his disgust towards me. I ignored him.

When I got outside, I politely escorted the suspect to the rear of the vehicle, and as the lady got in the back, she said: "Thank you, officer, for not putting the handcuffs on. That young man wasn't very polite to me before you got here, and laughed when he said I'd be in handcuffs."

"Not a problem. I decide who I need to handcuff, not a store detective. Are you OK?"

She smiled as she sat down, and replied that she was fine.

After the short trip back to Westville nick, I booked her in and went through the custody procedure, and put on the CRIS. I did a name check and it came back as no trace. I booked out the interview room and conducted the interview, and she stuck to her story.

I spoke with the custody sergeant and the inspector, both of whom concurred with me that there wasn't enough evidence to charge the lady and proceed with the case. Did I think she was guilty? Probably. But the evidence wasn't even close to being beyond reasonable doubt, so I closed down the case and NFAd it on the CRIS. In other words, that was the end of it as far as we were concerned. We released the lady and, by then, it was the end of the shift, so I went home.

The next day when I came on, I had a message regarding the NFAd case from one of the really high-ups at New Scotland Yard. It was someone I'd never heard of, and not part of the borough at all. It basically said they'd reviewed the case, and I should take another look, and any other cases I dealt with might be reviewed. The whole tone of it was ominous, with a 'you're being watched' vibe to it. I bumped into the inspector in the corridor, and when I told her what it was about, she led me down to her office.

"Ma'am, I don't get this. I did everything by the book. I ran it by the custody skipper, and you. There just wasn't enough evidence to charge. What's going on?"

She went over, put the portable kettle on, and some instant coffee in two mugs: "That's true if it wasn't that store, but it is. You do know they get special treatment, because of their, err ... ties with senior officers at NSY, don't you?"

I could feel a knot in my stomach, and that I wasn't going to like what I was going to hear. "Go on, Ma'am."

She sat down and, as she waited for the kettle to boil, said: "Look, I know it says 'without fear or favour', but that doesn't count when you have the rich and the powerful involved. And the boss of that store is rich and has powerful friends. Well, when I say friends, I mean bought-and-paid-for friends. Normal rules don't apply to these people, I'm afraid."

I couldn't contain myself: "With all due respect, Ma'am, that's fucking bullshit! And you know it. It's just not right!"

"I know, mate, I know. Welcome to the real world. That's not even the worst of it. He has really sharp lawyers who will tear you to ribbons in and out of court. Private security who will dig up anything they can pressure with. The worst of it is, they even have so much sway with some senior management in the Met that they can cause you grief. That's not even the worst of it; you'll like the next bit."

The kettle had boiled, and she poured two cups of strong black coffee, topped them up with cold water, handed me one and sipped the other. Once she'd settled herself in her seat, she carried on: "As the line from the song says, 'there's a law for the rich, a law for the poor, and I'm just a simple working man'. There's nothing you can do about it. Trust me, I've tried."

At that moment, I knew she was telling the truth. The first job I had was working as an outdoor clerk for a very posh solicitor near Covent Garden, and he'd told me the same thing. It wasn't until now I believed him. It was no comfort; it just made me feel sick, and ashamed.

The inspector waited for a moment, let it sink in, then said: "I'll be in touch with that senior officer, and do damage control on your behalf. But your card will be marked from now on. These people don't forget, and they have lots of friends, in all branches of the service. Watch your back, mate. I know it sucks. You just did your job, and tripped a landmine you didn't know existed."

I walked out of her office with less faith in the system than I walked in with. The job sucked sometimes.

The next few weeks went by quickly, as we approached Christmas. The nightmares slowly started coming back, first once a fortnight, then once a week, then twice a week. I went to see the doctor and he increased the dosage of the tablets. That seemed to help a little, for a while. There was nothing I could do to stop them. I loved the job, but the longer I did it, the worse the nightmares became. But I wasn't going to give up. I could definitely feel the effect of the increased dosage; it's hard to describe if you've never felt it. It feels like a comfy duvet over your brain, just a warm, comforting feeling. You know you should be feeling things, but you just don't.

Then the panic attacks started, the paralysing and irrational terror.

The first was when I was driving to Sussex to see Victoria, which I did less and less often, as she seemed less and less interested in answering my calls, or meeting up.

As I was driving along down the A12, towards the M25, I got a real sense of danger, and it built quickly. My sixth sense of danger went into overdrive, I could feel my adrenaline levels spiking, my hands began to shake, my heart rate shot up, and there was perspiration on my brow. I was back in the car driving that man to see his dead baby. It all flooded back, but with real vengeance.

I had to stop, get off the road. I was in danger. I was going to crash, I'd be trapped, the car was burning, I'd burn alive, and I could see it all coming. It was so real. Was I going mad? Was this what it was to be mad – to see yourself losing control, and being able to do nothing about it?

So I pulled the car into a layby and shook, and had difficulty breathing. I managed to get myself back under control enough to breathe. I sat there and couldn't understand what had just happened. Why had my body rebelled? I was in charge of it, not the other way around? I took deep breaths, and thought, *I can't do this, I need to get home, where I'm safe. My home is safe!*

With shaking hands, I pushed the buttons on my phone to tell Victoria I couldn't make it. She answered and wasn't impressed that I'd cancelled at the last minute. I tried to explain, but I couldn't find the words, and she put the phone down on me.

I made it home, and sat and tried to make sense of what had just happened. *If I couldn't trust my body, what would I do if I was working?* I was OK when I was working. *Keep working and going out, surrounding myself with others. That's the key.*

I saw the doctor, and he increased the dosage of pills again.

I threw myself into work, and every chance I got, I went out with my friends, to the nicest restaurants, the most expensive shows, everything. It helped for a while (not the bank balance, though). I ordered another handmade bass – that would give me something to look forward to. I started hitting my savings, but it was fine, I was working. Trouble was, I had to start borrowing money to continue, but I just didn't seem to care any more. It was just a number on a piece paper. That's what the pills do: make you not care. You know you should care, but you don't!

Christmas came, and I bought lavish presents for my friends and relatives. That made me feel better but, no matter how hard I tried, I couldn't bridge the widening gap between Victoria and myself. The more she pulled away, the harder I tried. *I must be doing something wrong. If I try harder, she'll like me again.*

At work, there were dwindling numbers in terms of the relief. I paraded on one early turn and the guv'nor turned up and said: "Well, Richard, you are the thin blue line today. You're Westville police."

Wow. Well, that was new. I took out the van, and just drove around on my own, looking for work. In all the times I'd worked as a police officer, I'd always worked with a partner. Even if I'd hated them, they were there. The dark thoughts started to creep in.

A few weeks later, on a late turn, I worked with Jack. We had a call from a local resident that a young Black male, approximately 6' tall, wearing white trainers, a dark blue tracksuit with a thin white stripe down the leg, and riding a dark blue mountain bike, was riding slowly around the street, looking into cars and fiddling with the locks.

We arrived at the address, and started slowly driving around the almost deserted residential streets. Within five minutes, we saw a young Black male, about 6', wearing a dark blue tracksuit with a white stripe, on a dark blue mountain bike. He was two streets from the initial call, and sat on his bike looking into a car as we drove up. He saw us, and looked surprised. We stopped in front of him, and Jack got out and escorted him to the kerb, while I parked the van.

I went over, and noticed Jack hadn't started asking questions; he was waiting for me to do so. I pushed that to the back of my mind and said: "Hello young man. How are you doing today?"

"Yeah, all right. Is there a problem?"

"We've had a report of someone who closely matches your description looking into cars. Where do you live?"

He said defensively, "Well it ain't me."

I continued, "Where do you live?"

"Wembley. Why, what's that got to do with anything?"

Wembley was miles away. "Do you have friends around here?"

"No, I was just out riding around."

"OK. When we arrived, you were looking into that car, and I believe you are the person who was reported to us as having looked in a number of cars. You say you live miles away. I'm going to search you under sec 1 of PACE, for items to break into cars with. I'm PC Armstrong FH327 from Westville Police Station, and you're entitled to a written record of this search for up to a year."

He looked at me, and continued to protest his innocence as I went through his pockets, and found a bundle of twenty-five car keys on various key rings all connected together. I held them up, and raised an eyebrow.

"I love cars; I collect car keys."

"How old are you?"

"16. Why?"

"Who do these car keys belong to?"

"They're mine. My mom has had lots of cars."

"You're under arrest for going equipped to steal." I cautioned him, and we put him in the back of the van and took him to Westville custody.

After we'd dealt with him, Jack said: "Richard, you were so decisive with that section 1 stop. I wouldn't have done that."

I looked at him, puzzled: "Mate, that was a textbook case for a search: a witness saying he was going around looking in cars, we saw him looking into cars, he lived miles away, and had no good reason for being there. Why would you not search him?"

He looked back at me straight on: "Well, cos he's Black, and I don't want the possibility of having a racist complaint."

I was lost for words. He cared more about being called a racist than he did about doing his job. I didn't say anything, and just walked off. I'd always suspected some officers might feel that way, but to hear it so blatantly. I was shocked, sickened. Was that really where we were going?

As the new year rolled around, I started to really struggle with the nightmares and lack of sleep. I started making mistakes. I cut my hand. I forgot paperwork. Then, one morning, I woke up from a late turn. I got dressed and thought about work, and started shaking, sweating, feeling sick. I just couldn't do it. All the horrible things I'd seen, all the nightmares came back during the day. I wasn't even safe during the day. Every time I closed my eyes I was back, in a horrific sudden death, being held against the wall in the hospital, looking into the eyes of 'Dave' the martial arts guy. I couldn't carry on.

I made an appointment, saw the doctor, and broke down in front of him again. I just wept. He genuinely looked shocked, and increased my dose of antidepressants (up from the initial 15 mg of the SSRI to 60 mg a day) and signed me off work. I went home, and called in sick. I felt a wave of relief. I could relax. No more work, no more nightmares, and for a few days I felt better, and the new dose of pills took effect.

I called Victoria – no response. I spoke to my mom. She told me she was putting her house on the market, and moving back home to

Sunderland. This set alarm bells ringing, as she'd had cancer over twenty-five years before, and had always said it was likely to come back. She said she'd wanted to go home to be with her remaining family. For me this meant she thought the cancer may be coming back, and might be getting ready for the end.

I tried to block out those thoughts, and continued to buy expensive things, further eating away at my money. I felt a small spike of excitement and contentment every time I bought something new. I knew it was stupid but, with those tablets, I didn't seem to care any more.

When the doctor's note ran out, I went to see him again. He wrote me another one, for a few more weeks. I was beginning to struggle with guilt at not doing my job, at not having the daily adrenaline hit. With Victoria distancing herself, my mother moving 350 miles away, and the job I loved receding, I felt the horrible feeling of all the things I cared about moving out of my reach, like reaching for an object that is forever an inch from your fingers.

Personnel at Churchleigh called me in to check up. I explained the situation, and they were very sympathetic, organising a week's trip to Goring House, which is convalescent home for police officers. That was helpful; they showed me ways to relax and help reduce stress.

But when I returned home, I found out mom had found a buyer, and would be moving in a couple of months. That hit me like a train. It wasn't like I spent every minute around her house, but she was there, and I knew I could go to see her if I just needed some company. I always felt relaxed when I saw her. I'm not blaming her; she was doing what she needed to do.

I tried calling Victoria, and found she simply didn't return my calls, with no reply for weeks. Then the return to work was imminent. I was called into personnel again, and explained how I was struggling, and they suggested I do my initial return to work at a station closer to my home, in Kenton. I'd be helping out setting up a prisoner processing team. It was a new idea at the time to allow relief officers more time on the street.

It sounded ideal, so I checked my uniform, and I must admit it felt very odd putting it back on. Then I drove into Kenton, a place I knew all too well.

It was spring, and I remember standing outside the seventies-style police station in Kenton I'd walked past countless times when I was a student, living just down the road. It was going to be odd. I made my way in and was shown through to the superintendent's office. I knocked on the door and heard: "Come in." I walked in and saluted. There was the usual real-wood desk, with a nice leather chair behind it, and a couple of cloth-backed office chairs facing it. There was a nice, patterned rug on the floor. The wall had the usual rows of policing books and the ubiquitous framed passing-out photo from Hendon on the wall. For a moment I was taken back to that day I passed out – the happiest day of my life. Where was I now? Then I snapped back to reality, and looked around.

The dominant feature was the huge wall-to-ceiling window, which looked out over Earlham. It was an area I knew well, but it took me a moment to get my bearings because of the new view.

I turned my attention to the two officers present. The contrast between the two could not have been more stark. The superintendent, who was seated behind the desk, was a tall, slim man in his fifties with long, sandy-coloured hair and a kindly face. He came across as relaxed and friendly.

The other was a shorter (5'8"), stocky man in his late forties with collar-length black hair with a few hints of grey coming through. His manner was entirely different. He had a hard sharpness to him, and glared at people. He was the type of person who had very little compassion or empathy. He actually made me flinch when I saw him.

The superintendent said: "Hello Richard. Please come in and sit down. I'm Senior Officer Crowther, and this is my right-hand man, Inspector Poole."

As I approached his desk, he stood up and offered me his hand. I leant forward and we shook. He continued: "Please sit down."

I did as I was asked, and said: "Thank you, Sir. I appreciate the opportunity."

He smiled: "Think nothing of it. You'll be working with Inspector Poole; he's the one who'll be setting up the CST (Custody Support Team), and I'm sure he'll appreciate your help. So, Richard, tell us a little about yourself. Personnel at Westville say you're returning to full duties. What's your background?"

I thought quickly about how much to share; they probably wanted to know what kinds of jobs they could give me. I said: "I've been in 'The Job' for about four years, and before that I was a science teacher."

The superintendent looked at the inspector, who spoke for the first time. When he did, there was an edge to his voice. It seemed like he used words as weapons. There was always a point, a bitterness. He said: "That's useful – good organisational skills. There's a team I'll need to recruit. That takes organisation; you may be useful in that."

The super turned to Poole: "I'd like to have a chat with Richard, and I'll bring him down to the office in a short while."

Poole, taking the hint, nodded and walked out, closing the door behind himself.

We spoke for a while, and I began to relax, until the topic turned to my current situation. He asked: "So Richard, you've done really well so far in your career. What's happened recently? Why are you here?"

I could feel my back stiffen, and my heart rate rise. Taking a deep breath, I said: "Well Sir, I dealt with an awful lot of tough incidents in a short period of time, and they all came on top (police slang for: it's all getting too much). I've been really struggling to come to terms with them. I've been suffering from nightmares and lacking sleep."

He nodded sympathetically: "I think we all go through times like these in our careers. It's just something that you get over. You'll work through it. Don't worry."

I tried my best to smile back, but he could see I wasn't convinced. He tried again: "Look, we'll be as supportive as we can. You'll get through this. Come on, talk me through some of the incidents."

Honestly, I think he was trying to help, but the last thing I wanted was to relive those moments again. Over the next few minutes, I tried to explain them to him. It was often broken and bitty, and I struggled to keep my emotions in check.

He said: "So explain this to me. What does it feel like? I don't understand?"

I tried to find the words to express complex emotions. I settled on, "Sir, you know when you work in the job you compartmentalise your life, and your thinking. You think and feel one way at home, another way with the regular jobs, and then another with the really nasty jobs."

He nodded, and said slowly, "I think I know what you mean. Go on."

"Well, I have put an awful lot of those nasty jobs, those horrific memories, in a box, to deal with another time, because you have to be able to focus. There and then. Then one day the box gets too full, and all these memories, and feelings, start to leak out, then it's a torrent, then flood, and for the life of me, I can't get the lid shut. I'm drowning in nightmares. They resurface when they are least welcome, and overwhelm me."

I could see he was trying to understand and be supportive, and he could see I was struggling.

"Look Richard, I don't normally do this, but here's my phone number. Call me anytime if you need to talk. I know it can get tough."

I thanked him, and noted down the number, and began to feel a little more at ease.

We went to Poole's office, and the super left us together, so he could get on with his work. Poole lost no time in explaining what he wanted to set up. It was basically a small group (initially) of about eight (expanding to twelve) officers who consisted of a couple of CID and the rest uniformed officers, who would provide cover twenty-four hours a day, with the majority during the day. These officers would take over the interviewing, charging and writing of case papers ready for court, leaving relief officers free to go out and deal with more calls. This would be more efficient, because they would become more specialised in those jobs, and we'd develop more streamlined procedures, speeding up the overall process.

Our job was to get the staff recruited, the resources gathered (computers, printers, stocks of the relevant paperwork, networks of people in the CPS), then get the whole thing rolling. This was envisaged to take a few months, which fitted the time frame of my rehabilitation.

I started with a new purpose. I worked hard, coming in from 9–5. The inspector would set me a goal and I'd do it – contact the CPS, contact different officers for the team. It looked like only some of them were volunteers.

I emailed a PC at Kenton, a PC Colin Tarrant, and he didn't get back to me for a few days. Then he was evasive and tried to find a hundred reasons why he couldn't come in to see the inspector. Eventually,

Inspector Poole checked up: "I notice that Tarrant hasn't been scheduled to meet me, so I can arrange his transfer. What is the reason?"

I thought quickly. I did not want to set Poole on him. "Sir, he's been very busy, and there's been a clash in the timetables; whenever he was free, we were busy, and the reverse was also true."

He looked at me and, in his usual blunt style, said: "I don't accept no for an answer. I'll email him direct!" With that he walked back to his office.

A couple of days later, I saw someone going into and out of Poole's office whom I recognised as PC Tarrant. A few minutes later, Poole came out and said to me, "Well, he won't be any more trouble. How dare he think he can mess me around. Listen here, Armstrong." I put down the paperwork I was working on and looked up at him. He continued: "I used to work in complaints, and I enjoyed it. I dealt with him before. I was interviewing him under caution, and he kept going 'no comment', so I stopped the interview and told him I'd discipline him if he refused to answer my questions. Obnoxious little shit. How dare he question my authority."

With that ringing in my ears, he walked off. I started to think about what he'd just said. I wasn't surprised he had been part of the complaints department, but at the fact he'd threatened an officer with censure because he was invoking the fundamental right to silence enshrined in law. Because he was a police officer! That meant he was saying we had fewer rights to a fair trial than any other member of the population. That was fundamentally wrong! Man, did I not want to get on the wrong side of this authoritarian nightmare!

For the next few weeks, I worked hard assembling the team, organising training for them at the training unit, with lectures from the CPS, to allow them to put a face to a name. I also worked hard with the admin staff who process the case papers to make sure they knew what was expected, and with a member of the CRIS unit, on how to speed up the process.

I was taking the train in and out of work, as it was the most convenient method, with parking being severely limited at Kenton. One evening after work, I went up to town, and had a meal out with some friends, so came home after the rush hour, and as I was sitting staring out of the window of the train, letting my mind wander, I heard a disturbance behind me. My sixth sense went bananas. I turned around and two young men were arguing and, before I could do anything, they started trading blows. On instinct I got up, shoved my way between the two of them, and caught a drunken blow to the head from one of them.

I stood between them and, showing my warrant card, said: "This fight is over. You (pointing at one of the youths) sit down over there, and you (the other lad) go and sit over there."

The bigger of the two started squaring up to me, and I said quietly: "Mate, you've got two choices: one, go to the cells, or two, go home. Your choice."

I think that finally got through to him, as the two of them sat down well away from each other, and I stood between the two of them until the big one got off. Thankfully, the other lad got off at the station before my own.

I thought nothing more of it, until I was chatting with one the recruits to the CST, and Poole walked past and clearly overheard. He said: "You shouldn't be getting involved off-duty. I won't get involved at all. When I hang up my uniform for the night, I cease being a police officer. I don't care what happens, I don't risk my life or career for anyone." With that, he walked off.

I thought, *wow! Really?* Clearly he had didn't care about the oath he took. You're never off-duty in terms of certain humane responsibilities, but he still made such a blanket statement about never getting involved. Man, that guy was cold. He wouldn't help someone who was in need because it might risk his career? That's appalling.

I was still struggling with the nightmares, and it seemed that every time I went to talk to the doctors, they increased the dosage. I was struggling with my weight; I'd put on almost three stone in a year. I'd always kept myself in good shape, and had stayed at between 11 and 12 stone, but I was topping 15.

The expensive spending was taking its toll. There was a realistic possibility I might not be able to pay my mortgage, and I had started borrowing on credit cards.

I ignored all of it. I don't know why, but the antidepressants just seemed to stop me worrying about it. I didn't care any more.

It came to a head when, on the day I was supposed to say goodbye to my mother as she moved out, I had a letter from the credit card company saying I'd maxed it out, and I'd missed a payment. If I didn't start paying them back, they'd take action. It suddenly hit me, and I spent the rest of the day in a panic, rushing around trying find a way out. There was none. The only way to pay off the debts was to sell the house, as I'd already borrowed against my mortgage. I'd got so used to the money from lots of overtime.

I calculated I'd walk away even, and have to look for a cheap flat to rent. It broke my heart to sell my lovely little house. I felt so embarrassed that I let it go so far. I hated myself for being so stupid, and so blind to what I'd done. I could feel my life slowly spiralling out of control, and all I could do was watch it.

I felt like I was a passenger, like there was nothing I could do, with a feeling of absolute powerlessness, rushing towards a cliff, frozen with fear, but conscious the whole way through.

I went back to work. By then I was having counselling through the police, and I spoke to them on a weekly basis. I was due to increase the number of days, and when I spoke to the counsellor, I'd agreed with them that the increase in days would be delayed. Trouble was, I didn't realise they didn't tell the personnel department.

The whole time, my mind became more and more foggy through the lack of sleep, the antidepressants, the worry about money. I started losing my grip on my life, and the harder I tried, the less traction I got.

It came to a head when I finally heard from Victoria, and she said she couldn't see me any more. She needed to move on, had things in her life she needed to deal with, and she was sorry, but that was that.

I fell to pieces, and was signed off sick for a couple of days. In desperation I phoned the superintendent at 10:00 hours on a Monday, on the number he'd given me.

"Hello Sir, Richard Armstrong here. I hope you don't mind, but you did say I could call you if I needed someone to talk to."

He replied angrily, "I'm at home on holiday!"

"I'm sorry, I didn't mean to bother you, I ..."

"Listen, Constable, I'M ON HOLIDAY. SHUT UP AND GO AWAY!"

My stomach sank, and I thought, *how have I managed to fall so low that I can't read basic hints? That he gave me the number, but never wanted me to call it? I'm so STUPID!*

The following day, at 09:00 hours, there was a knock on the door, and I struggled to focus my mind on what was happening. I opened the door. It was Poole and a female sergeant standing there, and before I could say anything, he'd walked into me, forcing me to step back, virtually pushing me out of the way, saying: "Armstrong, we're here to talk. You need to listen!"

They walked past me, and into the living room, which was far from tidy, and sat down on the two-person sofa. I didn't have a chair; it was a tiny starter house, so I was forced to stand.

Poole said: "Aren't you going to be polite, and offer us a coffee? Where are your manners? We're your superiors."

I was stunned. It was my house, my home. Who the hell did they think they were? The sergeant looked at me: "You heard the inspector. Be respectful."

I dumbly walked to my tiny kitchen. My head was reeling. *This is wrong. How can I fight this? What can I do?*

So I did the only thing I could think of, and started making coffee, to give me time to think. *The federation. I should call them.*

I made two coffees, and put them on a tray with the sugar bowl and walked through and held them out. Poole took one look at the coffee: "This is black? Where's the milk?"

"I'm sorry, I don't drink milk. I don't have any in the house."

The sergeant said snappily, "It's SIR! When you talk to the inspector and sergeant, when you address me. IS THAT CLEAR!? I WON'T GIVE YOU ANOTHER WARNING. Next time, I'll stick you on! Is that understood?"

I dumbly looked at her, and heard myself saying, "Yes, Sergeant."

Poole said, "I think you're very selfish. Only a selfish man like you wouldn't have milk in his house for guests. Just goes to show how few friends you have."

I dumbly took the tray away. I should have felt angry, but I felt nothing, just blank. I'm pretty sure it was the tablets. I was on a dose of 120 mg a day, and you start off on 15 mg a day. I returned and just stood as he went through a list of what they'd done to help me, and all the things in my career that I'd done wrong, from the street duties until that day.

He finally said: "You were supposed to be in work today. You weren't. Why not?"

I stammered, "But I spoke with the counsellor and was told I didn't need to be."

"Liar! Personnel at Churchleigh expected you in today. Why weren't you?"

I stammered again, "I'm, I'm, I'm sorry s-s-sir. I thought that the counsellors talked to the p-p-personnel department, I d-d-didn't know."

"Liar. You're a liar. You're the kind of lying, useless, lazy, scrounging excuse for a police officer I hate. I've taken over your line manager duties, and I'm making it my mission to get you out of the police. You're not fit to wear the uniform. You're a disgrace!"

Then he calmly went back to sipping his coffee, while the sergeant explained that I needed to be in tomorrow morning at 09:00 hours sharp, regardless of my health state, or they'd consider it a disciplinary offence. With that threat ringing in my ears, the two of them walked out.

I just sat on the sofa, and felt like I should cry, but no tears came. I couldn't cry. I knew I should feel sad, but I felt nothing. I fully realised those tablets had robbed me of feeling. It was like having a thick blanket over my brain, a fog that stopped you caring. I couldn't go on like that; I needed to stop them. But maybe not that day. I'd stop in a few weeks.

I arrived early the following day, and stood outside the familiar Earlham Police Station. I tried to clear my head. What was going to happen? I didn't know. I had no way to prepare. The federation were good, but nothing was set, so I couldn't bring them in.

I walked in, and found my way to Poole's office. It was 08:45 hours. I straightened myself up, took a deep breath, and knocked. Nothing. I waited. Then I heard a voice behind me. It was the sergeant from the other day.

She said: "Armstrong, come with me." Nothing more, no explanation, nothing.

I dumbly followed. We walked out to an unmarked panda. She opened the door and, without a word, got in. I got in the passenger side, and put the seat belt on. Without a word, she started to drive west towards Westville.

"Sergeant, are we going to Westville?"

She replied in a harsh voice, "Yes. Shut up Armstrong! I don't want to waste my breath on a piece of shit like you!"

I should have flinched, but I didn't, with the levels of anti-depressant, and my experiences so far. I was numb. I sat there, not past caring – deep down, there was a voice screaming at me – but almost resigned to my fate. I was a passenger at that stage.

We arrived at Churchleigh, parked the car, and walked straight up to the personnel office. After a short wait, we were ushered in, where the head of personnel was seated at a long conference table. The head of personnel, whom I'd spoken to before, and who had been very supportive, had a hard look about her. She looked at the sergeant, then at me, and said: "PC Armstrong, I've got a report here from Inspector Poole. It's most disturbing. He says your presence in Kenton is no longer required. Sergeant, would you like to explain why?"

The sergeant then went through a long list of utter rubbish, from the most minor of matters to outright lies, concluding by saying that I'd been disrespectful to them when they, out of concern for my welfare, had conducted a home visit.

The head of personnel said: "Given what I've read and heard, you'll be returned to active duty at Westville tomorrow. He believes you're lying and so, as of tomorrow, you'll be back at Westville, on restricted duties. Do you have anything to say?"

I stared straight ahead: "May we speak alone for a minute, please?"

The sergeant jumped in and, in an aggressive tone, said: "No, you'll say what you've got to say in front of me!"

I waited for the head of personnel, and she just looked at me. As I said, by then I wasn't feeling too much, so I carried on. "May I have a federation representative present, please?"

The head of personnel replied: "No, that would delay proceedings, and I'm going on holiday for two weeks. So no."

"I thought that was my right, under my terms of my employment?"

The sergeant said sharply, "You heard her. No! You have what rights we decide you have."

I took a deep breath and said: "Then I'd please like it noted that I object to this meeting, and ..."

The sergeant said: "We don't care. Just shut up. No one cares what you object to."

I ignored her: "For the record, I dispute the account of Inspector Poole, and the Sergeant here. They are not true."

The sergeant said: "One more word from you and I'll stick you on. You don't get to call superior officers liars!"

The head of personnel did not note anything down, but merely said: "This meeting is concluded." She closed her papers, walked to the door, and held it for us.

I walked out first, and the sergeant followed down the corridor, and towards the back yard. I could tell she wasn't finished. About halfway down the corridor she said: "You don't get to call me a liar, you fucking little shit. I should take you out to the yard and kick your head in."

I simply carried on walking to the door and held it open for her: "After you, Sergeant!" At that moment, I felt nothing towards her. I felt very little towards anyone. I could have fought without any empathy, without compassion or mercy. I didn't know whether I'd opened the door so she could drive off, or whether I'd agreed to fight her. Honestly, I don't think I cared. The most dangerous person is the one with nothing left to lose, and I felt I had nothing to lose. I might as well lose everything. I think she could sense it, and simply walked past me, and went to the car. As she drove off, I stood and just stared at her.

At that moment, I realised I was scared! Really scared. More scared than I had ever been, not at anyone else, but at myself. I knew what I was capable of. They say, when you look into the abyss, it looks back, and it knows its own. I had seen evil, and what scared me most was that I recognised it within myself. I was capable of true evil. I don't know if I'd have stopped in a fight with the sergeant. I might have killed her. And, the worst part is, I think I'd have enjoyed it!

That realisation stopped me in my tracks. To realise that about yourself is truly horrifying. As a child, you always imagine yourself as a hero, as the good guy. What if you weren't and found you enjoyed being the bad guy?

They'd lied and lied about another colleague to try to get me out of the job I loved. They'd kicked me when I was down, with the lowest of low blows. There's a special place in hell reserved for those two. I try not to hate people but, in their cases, I make an exception. I suddenly realised, as I thought this, *my God, how far have I fallen?* I reached for my great-grandfather's whistle – not there. I'd left it at home.

I made my way home, to find that someone was interested in the house. I arranged a viewing while I was out. It was summer, and as I made my way back to Westville, I just let my mind wander back to all the fun I'd had on C relief, and all the crazy calls with The Law. God, how I missed that right then. Just one friendly face. Then what a fool I'd been leaving Park Street, where I had it all.

I went back to work at Westville, and sat about doing paperwork and worked in the custody as a gaoler for the next few weeks.

The buyer for my house offered me the asking price. He was a first-time buyer. I started making arrangements to rent a small flat on a housing estate nearby, then looked at getting rid of my furniture. The credit card companies were still hassling me.

I started getting pressure to travel up to Newcastle to see my mother, eventually getting a nasty email from one of my uncles saying what an awful son I was, and that I didn't care about my mother. I sent a blunt email back telling him to mind his own business.

I eventually contacted the federation, and they weren't happy, but said I'd have had to make a complaint to the head of personnel about the home visit and lack of federation representation within two weeks. But she'd been on holiday for those weeks. Thanks!

They did contact occupational health and it was arranged that I'd be assessed by the chief medical officer (CMO) of the Met Police – the highest medical authority in the Met. The appointment was set for September. It was moving on apace.

I'd decided I couldn't take the antidepressants any more, so I just stopped taking them. There wouldn't be much of an effect for a couple of weeks, I thought. This is not a good idea, but at that point I didn't care.

The nightmares were still as intense and frequent. I thought, *why am I taking these pills, that have the side effects of making me stop caring, about what people say, my health, my weight? It's just not worth it.*

The day of the house sale came, and I stood in the living room of my home (for the hour it still was mine), and visualised the inspector and sergeant sitting there. Was that one of the reasons I felt so little. I walked past the spot where I sat and cried when I heard that 'Dave' had killed the priest, then walked up to the bedroom where I watched, transfixed, as the planes hit the twin towers and had killed my friend. I walked around and thought of the hope I'd had when I moved in. A job I loved, a sweet little house, the people close to me – all gone!

I knew I should have felt devastated, but I didn't, at that moment. I felt nothing. Just empty, alone, just nothing.

Selling the house got rid of all my debts, but I started again. I had enough money to keep the flat for six months, nothing else.

I went back to work and started to shut down. Any time I dealt with the public, I flinched. Something inside had broken. I couldn't be out there in uniform. I had a couple of offers from friends in different departments to go to work for them, within the police, but not on the front line.

My appointment to see the CMO at New Scotland Yard arrived, and I went up and spent an hour with him. He was a very patient and kind guy. He had reviewed my medical file and, at the end, he said, "Richard, it's clear to me that you're suffering severe post-traumatic stress disorder. I am recommending that you are found a desk job for a while until you can make a full recovery. There's absolutely no way you are fit to go back on active duty."

It was like a weight being lifted from my shoulders. I finally had it in writing, and with the option of doing a paperwork job. I thought, *I'll slowly recover, get off these damn pills, and rebuild my life. I've hit rock bottom; the only way is up.*

As I walked along the corridor, I bumped into Inspector Miller. We looked at each other and smiled. She said: "Well, of all the people I thought I'd see here, you weren't on the list. Do you have a moment? Do you want to grab a coffee? The canteen food here is actually good."

I agreed, and we went and had a coffee, and a bite to eat. The thing I was most surprised about was that the food was actually really good. Then

I thought, *of course it is – the senior officers wouldn't stand for eating crap food themselves.*

I said: "It's really good to see you Ma'am, and you're right about the food. Are you still working at Park Street?"

She shook her head, and when she'd finished a mouthful, said: "No, I moved on. Part of this accelerated promotion group to have a female-only shortlist for the head of the Met in a couple of years. Oh, and I've been promoted."

We had a good chat. I was cagey about what had happened, but at the end of the conversation, she said: "Look, it's great to catch up. I hope you're back on full duties soon. Here's my number; keep in touch."

I took her number, tucked it in my warrant card holder and made my way home.

The day for the latest case conference came, and I again found myself in the personnel office at Churchleigh.

The head of personnel said: "I've seen the CMO's report. I disagree, and there are no desk jobs open at the moment. You'll start back working on full-time duties as of tomorrow morning. If you go off sick again, we'll take you down to half-pay and start proceedings to get rid of you."

"But your own chief medical officer said I shouldn't be on the front line. Isn't that constructive dismissal, and against employment law?"

With a deadpan expression, she said: "We're not under regular employment law. So no, we can do whatever we like. So either be at work tomorrow, or we'll start proceedings to dismiss you. This meeting is over."

I walked out, crestfallen. Either go to work, against what the most senior doctor in the Met advised, or lose your job. What kind of people were they?

I went back to my new home and contacted the federation, and they confirmed what she'd said. I, basically, had no rights in that situation.

With my stopping of the tablets, I started to feel a bit more like my old self. I began to come back to my senses, and I sat and thought about what I'd have to do. I'd try. I wasn't going to just give up. I'd go in the next day and try.

The next day, I was going back on a late turn, so I'd have the morning to rest. I tried to get an early night, and prayed I could close my eyes without those nightmares appearing. I thought I'd done it, but I suddenly woke, shaking and sweating, with fear foremost in my mind. I looked at my hands, and I was shaking. I was going to do this! I went back to sleep, and woke three more times before dawn. I WAS going to do this! I got up and made myself busy, ironing all my shirts. I collected all my uniform, cleaned my boots, getting everything ready. I was hours early. I tidied and found 101 jobs to do. I was going to do this. It had been the tablets that had been holding me back. That was it, I'd be fine now. Positive thinking.

Eventually it came to the time to leave, and that is where it started. I put my stuff in the car, got in, and sat, and just stared. All my instincts were screaming at me: NO! NO! NO! I said to myself, "You're going to do this! Move!"

Slowly, I got control. It took both hands to get the keys in the ignition, as they were shaking so much. I eventually started the car and started driving. I could do it. I had to do it!

I made my way there, and arrived early, putting all my kit in the locker. I got changed and ready to go. I was going to do it. I walked to the briefing room and sat down. I heard a jingling. *What was that?* I looked down, and it was my hand shaking with the keys. Embarrassed, I quickly put the keys down, and waited. Eventually, the guv'nor came in, looked at me and said: "You look like shit, Richard. Are you sure you should be here?"

I went to speak, but my mouth was dry, and I struggled to speak. I tried again, and finally managed, in a quiet, squeaky, voice: "I'll be OK, Guv."

She looked at me: "My eyes tell me differently. Come into my office, and we'll have a chat."

I wasn't in a position to argue, so I followed her down the corridor, putting the keys in my pocket so they wouldn't jingle. She went to a small kettle on the windowsill, and made two black coffees. We shared a love of the stuff, and she handed me a cup. I quickly put it down. She said: "Don't worry, it's not too hot; I put some cold water in it."

I picked up the mug, and quickly supported it with both hands. She looked and said: "Richard mate! You're shaking. I could see it a mile off. You've got to face it. You've got to know when you've got to give it up. You're not ready. Why are you back here, when you're in this state?"

I thought about trying to bluff it out, but she wasn't the type of woman to fall for that. I sat and explained everything, all that had gone on. What had happened at Kenton, what the head of personnel had said. I hung my head, and there was silence. I knew I was done. I couldn't do it any more. She put her hand on my shoulder, and I looked up.

She slowly shook her head: "Richard mate, I know how much this means to you. It's your life! I can believe what they've done to you. That's what scares me. Nothing I can say will help, because it'd change nothing. Given time in a side posting, maybe you'd recover enough to go back. But now, you can't. It's over, mate. It's over!"

I thought for a moment: "Can I have one more ride in a police car?"

"That, I can do! Then you stay in the station, and I'll contact personnel."

We made our way out, and I handed her the keys. She handed them back, shook her head, and I got in the driving seat of a police car for the last time. I turned the ignition, hit the lights and sirens and drove around the block. My last BLATT. I turned off the siren and lights, pulled up and turned off the ignition and, as the engine died, so did my dream. I just sat. There was silence in the car. It was over.

I started to say, "Thank you."

She stopped me: "I know! Go back in the nick, and get your stuff ready."

I nodded, and walked back in.

I spent the rest of the shift tidying up and making tea and coffee. I got my stuff ready to leave at ten, and not return. I drove slowly home, and slept the first uninterrupted sleep I'd had in months.

I had a call the next day to attend a case conference at Churchleigh, the following day. I started to feel my emotions coming back, in a huge flood. The despair, self-loathing, everything was starting to come back. I found myself shaking again.

I took my warrant card and looked at it. I looked at the fresh-faced, happy 'me', and thought it felt like a different person. I don't think I recognised myself. A piece of paper fell out, and it was Miller's number. I put it to one side; I didn't feel like talking to someone in the job.

I phoned a friend, who was a solicitor I'd worked for when I was first out of school. I hadn't spoken to Charles in years but I called him and, fortunately, he picked up the phone. He said he'd call me back and, true to his word, he did. Once we'd got through the niceties, I explained my situation and asked for advice.

He said what I already knew: it was a solid case of constructive dismissal. If the Met's own CMO says you're not well enough to do a job, and you're forced to do it, that's the very definition of constructive dismissal, and it's illegal in this country. Unless you're the police, when it doesn't apply.

Finally he said: "Richard, my old friend, I wish, I really wish, I could help you. I'd love to sue the Met on your behalf. Working for them made you ill. Then, when you're too ill to work, when their own doctor says you are, they force you out. Truly disgusting!"

I thanked him for his time, and hung up. I picked up the scrap of paper that had fallen out of my warrant card. I stared at it, then put it down. I didn't want to bother her. I eventually picked it up and dialled the number, and it was the answerphone, and I struggled to think of a message. Eventually, I just left my name and number.

An hour or so later, the phone went, and it was the guv'nor, saying: "Hello Richard, lovely to hear from you. What can I do for you?"

This indicated she was busy, but had made a bit of time for me. So I was brief, and explained what the situation was.

The phone was silent for a moment, and I'll never forget what she said: "Richard, I'm really sorry mate. You're a damn good officer. I wished you'd have come to me earlier. But at this stage, there's nothing I can do. There's only two grounds you can fight this on: sex and race. And you're white, you're male, and you're fucked!"

It was my turn to sit silently. I eventually said, "Thanks Ma'am. You know, it's my biggest regret that I didn't talk to you earlier. But honestly, I've been really struggling with this. I love this job, it's all I want, but it's over."

"Yes mate, it is. Take care. I really have to go, but look after yourself. There's something rotten in this job, and I'm not sure I can do anything to fix it. But I'll bloody well try! Bye Richard."

I put the phone down, and sat and stared – no feelings, nothing, just emptiness. I don't know how long I sat there for.

I eventually went to bed, and had bouts of fitful sleep, waking up repeatedly, shaking, sweating. My mind was filled with the same images, over and over.

I got ready, and made my way up to Churchleigh. I was dressed in a suit; I didn't care any more. I'd left all my kit in my locker at Westville.

I stood outside Churchleigh Police Station. I felt numb. I knew what was about to happen, but I could do nothing to stop it.

I walked in, showed my warrant card for the last time, eventually made my way to the conference room and knocked on the door. The personnel officer opened it, and I went in and sat down.

She said: "I've read what your inspector said. I have no option (I wanted to scream, "Yes you FUCKING do, you lying sack of shit") but to leave the two options open to you. Resign, or I'll start taking actions to have you removed. What do you want to do?"

I sat for a moment, and slowly took out my warrant card. The proof of my identity. It was who I was, and what I was. As I said "I'll resign," I slid my warrant card across the desk towards her. I really didn't want to do it. Every instinct was shouting "NO!" But I knew, at that stage, I had no choice.

She said: "OK, I have the papers ready for you, you just need to sign them. We can pay you until the end of the month, and your record of service will reflect the exemplary nature of your service."

Without looking up, I took the offered pen, and signed the form. I tried to hide the tear that landed on it. Before I handed it to her, I asked: "Can I have any support, in terms of counselling?"

"No, you've left the police now. You're not our responsibility. That's what the NHS is for."

She took the pen and paper: "That concludes our meeting. Goodbye."

She got up, opened the door, and showed me out onto the street, where I stood, and then slowly walked away, back to my car.

I woke up as a police officer; I'd go to bed a civilian. I made the slow drive home. I couldn't feel anything. It hadn't hit me, and I knew it. I didn't want to be driving when it did.

I arrived home and the phone was ringing. It was my mom. I didn't tell her; I needed time to come to terms with it myself. She didn't sound well, and she wanted me to visit her. I told her I'd be up as soon as I could, that I'd been busy at work (the truth). As I hung up the phone, somewhere deep down I knew she thought her cancer was coming back. As she always said, it was a reprieve. It was, because she died a few years later.

I thought about calling Victoria. I part-dialled her number a dozen times, but didn't. I looked around the tiny, cramped flat. It was poorly decorated, and I shared it with a colony of ants I had to keep at bay with ant killer powder. I had paid up the rent for the following five months. I had £20 in my current account. My car was coming up for its first MOT. After the five months, I'd be living on the streets.

The reality of the situation struck: I had no job, no money, I was three stone overweight, I had enough food in the fridge for a couple of days. I had £20 in the bank. I was suffering from crippling PTSD. I both hated and was terrified of myself. I had no relatives for hundreds of miles. The ones I did have up north hated me, my mother had moved away to die. The woman I loved had walked away, and didn't even want to be friends. And everything I had ever wanted in terms of a job had gone. I'd failed! I'd put everything into it and I'd failed. I wasn't good enough. They'd been right all along – Burke, Poole, all of them, I was a failure! Just too stupid to see it. Fooling myself all along! Lying to myself!

I had a tiny circle of friends, who probably just pitied me (they didn't).

I felt so, so, so alone. As I sat and negative emotions crashed on top of me like a wave, I can honestly say I've never felt anything like it. I was crushed, terrified, alone. I wanted to curl into a ball and die. There was no escape.

There was nothing, nothing left in this world for me. It'd be better for everyone if I left. No one would miss me, not really.

I wept and wept. It changed nothing. By the time I could collect my thoughts, it was dark. I had no idea of time, and tried to fall asleep on the sofa, but the same images and visions of hell kept waking me up.

I couldn't do it anymore. I couldn't. I stopped thinking rationally. Random thoughts came into my head. Just grasping at anything. I got changed into my old USAF flying jacket I'd bought out in America from the shop on a military base. I thought, *I'll go flying!* I walked outside. I didn't close my door; I wasn't coming back. Who cared. Nothing mattered anymore!

It was raining. *Fuck it! What do I care. Nothing matters.* I walked. I didn't think. I just walked, and walked. I was shivering and soaked. It didn't matter; nothing mattered. I didn't matter. I walked on grass verges, on pavements. All the time in my mind were all the things that haunted my nights and now, seemingly, my days.

There's nothing that matters. Those bastards in the police, they lied. Everyone dies. What's it matter if another one dies? No one cares. I shouted out as I was walking, "No one fucking cares. Do you hear that, world? NO ONE FUCKING CARES!"

Nothing. No response. So I did it again: "Nothing fucking matters! I don't matter, you don't matter!"

I walked and walked for miles.

I started to get angry. Really angry. I was looking for something to be angry at. I then saw a bridge. It had a brick wall, about five feet high. I climbed onto it, and carefully walked along. It was wet, slippery, but it didn't matter. *Nothing matters.* I'd tried so hard to do the right things, in the right way, at the right time. It didn't matter!

I found myself on the edge of this wall overlooking a sixty-feet drop onto a railway line. I started shouting. Really shouting: "It doesn't fucking matter. Nothing matters!"

I then started to get mad at God. I shouted: "God, you fucking bastard, why have you taken away everything I love? Why? Why snatch away everything I've worked so hard for? Why? Because you're an evil bastard. You're an evil God! All you do is give us pain! Everything I worked for, everything is gone. You're a cruel, cruel bastard!"

I looked down and realised I was soaked. I thought of having to go home and live with the living nightmare of broken sleep and broken dreams, with no real rest. I had no more hope, no job, no life. Everything I'd worked so hard for was gone. All the people I loved had either walked away or were dead. *Who fucking cares!* I put my head back and thought, *life isn't worth it. All this struggle and pain, it's not worth it. I'm not worth it. Tonight, the pain ends.*

I screamed at God: "You fucking bastard. Go on. Go on. I'm soaked. Everything and everyone has gone away. I bet you can't even make it rain harder. Go on. Go on, you bastard. I dare you – try and fuck my life even worse."

I took a deep breath, and put my arms straight to the sides like an aeroplane, and for a moment I was a child again, at the top of the stairs, pretending I was a spitfire. I thought I could fly. I dreamt of two things: being a policeman and flying.

One last flight, and it'd be all over. All the pain would be gone. Release from this torment! I looked up one last time, arched my back and slowly started to move forward to fly, shouting: "Go on, God, go on. You're so fucking useless, I bet you can't even make it rain harder, can you? You're so useless."

At that point the heavens opened. The rain was torrential! It hit my face so hard, it was painful. It jolted me out of my thoughts. I caught myself, steadied myself, and started thinking: *Oh God! What am I doing? What am I doing?*

I slowly climbed down, and sat with my back to the bridge wall. It was muddy, but I didn't care. I just sat there, and stared off into the distance, with rain running down my face. No tears; I just sat, and lost track of time.

Eventually I got up, and slowly started walking, soaked, caked in mud, but alive. As I walked, I thought of what Paige had said: "Don't give up!" I almost had. I was so damn close.

I tried to clear my head, and eventually started thinking, not of what I had lost, but what I had left. That day, I had a roof over my head, food to eat, and people who cared about me. I started thinking of the people I loved, and who loved me. A short list, but a list all the same. I thought of all the people around the world who didn't have that.

I realised I was so damn lucky. I thought, *focus on today. What can I do today to make things better? Don't worry about yesterday – it's gone. Tomorrow, I don't have; focus on today.*

Because:

Everyone lies – I won't lie to myself any more.

Everyone dies – but not me, not today – maybe tomorrow.

No one cares – some people do, some of the time.

I vowed to show I cared at least once a day. I'd smile at someone, help someone, talk to someone, let at least one person know that someone cares – because it might be the only time someone does.

EPILOGUE

I write this seventeen years later.

I slowly managed to turn my life around (with many ups and downs), and have taught in schools for the last fifteen years. There's a real satisfaction in helping young people. It's a privilege.

I re-connected with my family and friends, I am so lucky!

I still struggle every day with PTSD. The nightmares vary from once a fortnight to every night for a week. But everyone has something to deal with.

Every day, I'm glad I didn't step off that bridge.

If you ever find yourself in a position like that, please, I beg you, don't do it. Step back, get help. You are not alone. It is worth it!

Do I think of suicide? Yes, every single day, but so far I've always thought, "Not today. Maybe tomorrow."

But I am NOT a victim! I chose to join the police. If I didn't know what I was letting myself in for, I should have found out! That was my responsibility.

The one thing I am very critical of is that, after I left in poor health, there was absolutely no support or help! That's unacceptable!

Do I regret joining the police, and serving the public? Not for one second! For, whatever the cost to me, it was an honour!

As much as I am still angry at the cowardly bullies in the police, and their stupid system of 'equity' and 'diversity', I've learnt to live with it, but I'll never agree with it! You should only be judged on what you do and say, not on what you are.

What I tried to do is show you the personal effect of the current policies in the Met.

'Equity' means equal outcomes, regardless of how good people are.

'Increasing diversity' means putting in place policies that treat people differently based on their sex or race. That is wrong!

If your child is sick, do you want the doctor to be chosen on the basis of their sex or race, or their ability? Then why do you accept that in police officers?

I will never forget the vast majority of brave, selfless police officers who risk their lives for us every day. Thank you!

So how do you judge me? Hero, villain, brave, cowardly, wise, foolish, strong, weak?

That's up to you.

This is my story, warts and all.

ABOUT THE AUTHOR

Originally a Yorkshireman, who now is most definitely an Essex-boy in his late 50's. I am now retired from teaching, due to a recurring back injury, and PTSD. I am so proud of the kids I had the privilege of teaching. Learning to enjoy everyday, trying to look for the positives in life, and people.

It's best summed up in a song called: "Time stand still," there's a great cover version done by the US Army band, to note the passing of Neil Peart.

I thank God everyday, that I am blessed with a great family, and friends, who without who's support I would not be here. I must admit, I'm failing miserably at adapting to this crazy new digital world, I feel like a bit of dinosaur, with a 3G phone, paying cash as much as I can. I still love music from the 60's, 70's, 80's and 90's, and do play the bass guitar, as much as I can. It was love at first play. The first time I found I could make the beautiful tone of the bass, I was hooked. The mixture of rhythm and melody, the fact that I could get people up and dancing when I played as part of a band, was one of the coolest things I have ever experienced.

www.marciampublishinghouse.com

BV - #0196 - 041223 - C0 - 229/152/43 - PB - 9781913905903 - Matt Lamination